INTRODUCTION TO APPLIED LINGUISTICS

WILLIAM GRABE
Northern Arizona University

ROBERT B. KAPLAN
University of Southern California

SANDRA J. SAVIGNON
Consulting Editor

ADDISON-WESLEY PUBLISHING COMPANY

Reading, Massachusetts • Menlo Park, California • New York
Don Mills, Ontario • Wokingham, England • Amsterdam • Sydney • Bonn
Singapore • Tokyo • Madrid • San Juan

i

Library of Congress Cataloging-in-Publication Data

Introduction to applied linguistics

   p. cm.
   ISBN 0-201-54975-1
   1. Applied linguistics.
P129.I54   1991   91-9447
418--dc20

ISBN: 0-201-54975-0

  3 4 5 6 7 8 9 10-CRS-99 98 97 96 95 94

This volume is respectfully dedicated to the memory of

PETER DEREK STREVENS

who died in Tokyo, Japan, on November 2, 1989. The purpose of this dedication is not so much to mourn that physical presence which has passed away, as to celebrate his contributions not only to this chosen profession, but also to the lives of all he knew. Those contributions will not pass away. He was a good scholar, a good teacher, a good man, and a good friend. He was working on a revision of the first chapter in this collection at the time of his death, and we have done our best to be faithful to his intention. The fact is, however, that without his first chapter, the wholeness of this volume would not have existed. What he wrote here may well have been the last thing he wrote; it can stand not as a summary of his life, but as an emblem of his contribution to our lives. We are proud to present to our colleagues his summary of the field and our synthesis, which is heavily in his debt, and we are proud to dedicate this volume to him.

December 14, 1990

William Grabe
Flagstaff, AZ

Robert B. Kaplan
Los Angeles, CA

Contents

Introduction

Robert B. Kaplan and William Grabe

University of Southern California and Northern Arizona University

The concept of applying linguistic information to the solution of real-world problems is certainly not a uniquely Anglo-American invention; language scholars have, for centuries, used linguistic information in real-world tasks, and language teachers have, for a comparable period of time, drawn upon the findings of language scholars to define both what will be taught in the language classroom and how it will be taught. The term *applied linguistics* is, however, an Anglo-American invention. As Peter Strevens testifies (in his chapter in this volume), the term came into existence in the mid-1950s, and it came into existence almost simultaneously in Britain and the United States. Soon after the term appeared, Mackey (1965) pointed out that it probably came into use because language teachers wanted to dissociate themselves from subjective literature teachers and to associate themselves with something scientific and objective (like linguistics). The use of the term as modified for academic titles (e.g., assistant professor of applied linguistics, etc.) is even more recent. But to the best of our knowledge, wide use of the terms applied linguistics/applied linguist has occurred largely in North America and in Britain; even in Australia and New Zealand where the term is now used, its use is not widespread, nor has it been long in use.

The point of this historical background is to explain why the present volume, which purports to be an exploration of the development, practice, and meaning of applied linguistics, contains contributions only from North American and British scholars. The editors wish to assure readers that this is not yet another example of cultural imperialism; this volume is not compiled on the presumption that applied linguistics is somehow the property of the English-speaking world, nor on the presumption that only British and North American scholars do applied linguistics. On the contrary, it is well know that applied linguistics is practiced in many parts of the world; indeed the Association Internationale de Linguistique Appliquée (AILA) was formed in Europe, and its first secretary general was Gerhard Nickel of the University of Stuttgart; work in applied linguistics is being conducted in Singapore and Hong Kong, in India and the Philippines, in Cameroon and Tunisia, in Israel and Eastern Europe. But, for better or worse, virtually all of the work in the field is published in English, and many of the best know practitioners reside currently in North America and Britain, or were trained in one of those two areas. This regrettable fact is reflected in the contributions to the journal *Applied Linguistics (AL)* and to the ongoing series known as the *Annual Review of Applied Linguistics (ARAL)*, and in the forthcoming *Oxford International Encyclopedia of Linguistics (OIEL)*. It is an unfortunate reality of the contemporary scholarly world that, if one wishes to be widely read, one is more or less obliged to publish in English in a journal likely to be produced in the English-speaking world. The editors in a sense regret the necessity to perpetuate this hegemony, but see no way to escape it.

Since one of the editors of this volume was the first academic in the United States to hold the title professor of applied linguistics, and since Peter Strevens was the first academic to hold the title in Great Britain, we thought it appropriate to complement Strevens' view of applied linguistics briefly with a North American perspective. Strevens relates a story about a colleague of his, engaged in a lexical project, who needed to have a precise definition for the term *dog*. Quite reasonably, he turned to a group of colleagues in biology and zoology for help. After due deliberation, they proclaimed that "a dog is a four-footed mammal recognized by another dog as being a dog." This is, obviously, akin to Groucho Marx's notion that if something quacks like a duck and walks like a duck, it must be a duck, and any other self-respecting duck would know that.

Other disciplines can be defined in terms of the dominant paradigm for that discipline at any given moment in time. In the current environment, for example, linguistics can be defined as the study of language for the purpose of building models that will account for all and only the possible structures of particular languages, identifying those elements of the underlying structure (which generate those possible structures) that are universal, and that will deal with the relationship between language and mind. Not only does the dominant paradigm help to define the discipline, but it also determines the instrumentation which, in turn, proves the rightness of the paradigm; e.g., if you do not believe that "Equi NP deletion" is a real phenomenon, there is no reason to try to account for it, or if you do not believe in the theory of temperature, there is no need to construct a thermometer to measure it. So the dominant paradigm defines the possible questions that may be asked, defines a subset of interesting questions from the larger set of possible questions, and defines the mode of answering them.

Applied linguistics is an unusual discipline; there is no question that, like the dog in the above anecdote, applied linguists around the world can nose each other out, but beyond that there is often less agreement. Some people have pointed out that the name is an oxymoron—it is not linguistics that is applied; we agree with that notion, and presently we will explain why. Some people simply do not see that there is a definitional problem; if that were true, it is unlikely that so many volumes would be presented that address this very issue (e.g., Brown 1976; Crystal 1981; Kaplan 1980b; Shuy 1984; Stern 1983; Tomic and Shuy 1987). While there is still debate as to the scope and defining criteria of applied linguistics, it is now evident that applied linguistics is evolving into a well-recognized, broadly defined discipline.

Applied linguistics, as is widely recognized, is a field the purpose of which is to solve real-world language-based problems. In order to do this, the field draws upon linguistics, but not exclusively; it draws on knowledge from a variety of other fields as well—from anthropology, educational theory, psychology, and sociology, and from the sociology of learning, the sociology of information, the sociology of knowledge, etc. George Jean Nathan, the American theater critic, once remarked that the theater is the point at which all the arts come together and are actualized; we would like to extend this metaphor and say that applied linguistics is the point at which all of the social sciences (and many of the humanities) come together and are actualized.

In order to try to define applied linguistics, two large questions need to be answered: First, what part of linguistics can be applied to the real-world language-based problems that applied linguistics presumes to mediate? Second, what kinds of problems can be solved through the mediation of applied linguistics? In a paper delivered at a recent meeting of the American Association for Applied Linguistics, Paul Angelis (1987), also trying to answer these questions, reported on a number of empirical indices. He looked at the titles of articles published in the journal *Applied Linguistics* over the first eight years of its existence, and in the *TESOL Quarterly* over the past decade, and he looked at the descriptors in the *ERIC* dictionary under the heading *Applied Linguistics*. We have tried to add to that base by including entries in the forthcoming *Oxford International Encyclopedia of Linguistics* (Bright), the titles of articles which have appeared in the *Annual Review of Applied Linguistics*, and the names of the several scientific commissions of the International Association of Applied Linguistics (AILA). These data sets show rather clearly that there are some distinct trends in applied linguistics.

First, something on the order of half of the items in these several sets are in some way or another related to language teaching and language learning (including second-language acquisition and educational language testing). It would, then, be fair to say that one of the areas in which applied linguistics has had a significant impact has been language pedagogy. While about one-half of the entries are in this area, that is not sufficient grounds to rename the field educational linguistics, though there may well be such a subfield, as Bernard Spolsky (1978b) has suggested. About five percent of the total set of items relates to what might be classified as meta–applied linguistics: that set would consist of discussions of applied linguistics itself—items like this book, or Paul Angelis's paper, which attempt to define the field, or articles that discuss the employment opportunities in the field (Kaplan 1980b; Crystal 1981).

The remaining 45 percent of the items appear to fall into four broad categories. One of those categories includes the broad area of language policy and language planning (as well as the subarea of language-in-education planning). This is not to suggest that language policy and language planning is a subset of applied linguistics; rather, the point is that a substantial part of the field of language policy and language planning is applied, or perhaps that people who consider themselves applied linguists apply themselves to language policy and language-planning issues.

A second of the categories involves the professional uses of language. In recent years, there have been detailed studies of the language used between doctors and their patients, of the language of the courtroom, and of the language of the classroom. To the extent that the point of such research is the description of particular categories of speech acts, the domain properly belongs to sociolinguists, but, to the extent that the purpose is to understand and, perhaps, modify the behavior of the holder of power in an unequal interaction, the domain properly is the concern of applied linguists (Cazden 1987; Shuy 1987a; van Naerssen and Kaplan 1987). The propensity of applied linguists also to be concerned about language pedagogy has tended to make the research from this area available to teachers. This phenomenon has largely provided the basis for special-purposes language teaching—a pedagogical variety that is not merely concerned with lists of lexical items appropriate to certain disciplinary areas, but that is also concerned with the syntactic and discourse features of disciplinary language and with the marking of language by parties in unequal interaction (Richards and Schmidt 1983; Swales 1986; Widdowson 1983; Wolfson 1989).

A third category on which attention seems to be focused is one concerned with both aberrant language behavior and language assessment to determine what sorts of language behavior may be classified as aberrant. In this category, the work of applied linguists has overlapped and interacted with the work of speech clinicians, neurolinguists, and psycholinguists. It is here that knowledge from a variety of areas has been used to solve real-world language-based problems for various groups of people who are, for any one of a number of reasons, either deprived of information or more dramatically cut off from equal opportunity to participate in their society. Among those whose problems have been addressed by applied linguists are the hard-of-hearing, the mute, individuals afflicted with various sorts of aphasias, the elderly, and a number of other groups. Again, this is not to suggest that applied linguists function as clinicians; rather, the work of applied linguists augments the work of psycholinguists and neurolinguists in making available to clinicians a variety of strategies for dealing with the immediate problems of their clients (Crystal 1984).

The fourth general category of activity on which a great deal of attention seems to have been focused is one to which it is difficult to attach a clear label. It is that category that has been concerned with the fact that the natural condition for most human beings seems to involve their exposure to and acquisition of more than one language. Included in this area are such topics as bilingualism, multilingualism, multiculturalism, and a number of other similar topics. This area is not the language planners' (or the sociolinguists') concern about linguistic change in languages-in-contact situations; rather, this is a concern largely but not exclusively of the education sector, a concern about how and why individuals learn and use more than one language (and tend generally to pick up a set of cultural assumptions along with the additional language). The applied linguist is concerned with understanding what it means to be bilingual, how bilingualism happens, where (in addition to the classroom) bilingualism may be acquired, and what bilingualism does to the community in which it exists in human, ecological, social, political, and economic terms.

This brief survey indicates areas in which applied linguists have been active; they have in these functions, as in others, intervened between theoretical models and practitioners, moving traffic in both directions, and thereby helping to bring theoretical concerns to the classroom and at the same time expanding theory by bringing from the classroom problems and issues which have not been (or have not adequately been) addressed in theory. Most recently, there has been a growing interest in discourse, both oral and written; and discourse is gradually becoming an area in which a number of previously separated concerns are beginning to coalesce. Concern with discourse weds interest in the actors, in their social roles, in the negotiation of meaning between them, and in the ways in which discourse operates linguistically. It is possible that discourse studies may constitute the core of an evolving applied linguistics. Nils Eric Enkvist, in a relatively recent paper, remarks:

> discourse linguists . . . believe that we must learn to describe textual and discoursal forces and principles if we are to understand how individual sentences work and why they look the way they do. In this sense, text and discourse linguistics are apt to surround, engulf, and absorb traditional sentence linguistics. And once this happens, terms such as "text linguistics" or "discourse linguistics" become redundant because all linguistics will always reckon with text and discourse. Such ultimate successes of text and discourse linguistics might, paradoxically, lead to their presiding over their own liquidation. (1987:27)

The paper in which this quotation occurs is, interestingly, entitled "Text linguistics for the applier." If, obviously, text linguistics surrounds, engulfs, and absorbs traditional linguistics, and if applied linguistics is at least to some degree involved in the application of linguistics in the practical world, applied linguists will have to be concerned with the applications of text linguistics. Indeed, they already are, and there are in existence a variety of applications of text linguistics to issues in language in the professions, language in the classroom, language in power relations, language for the hard-of-hearing and the otherwise impaired, language and literature, language and stylistics, and so on.

These past several comments have tried to answer the two questions posed earlier: What aspects of linguistics can be applied; that is, what information from linguistics can be brought to bear on real-world language-based problems that applied linguists presume to mediate? And what kinds of problems can be solved through the mediation of applied linguistics? It is the case that virtually all areas of linguistics contribute to applied linguistics; that is, pertinent information comes from phonology, from syntax, from semantics, from text linguistics, from sociolinguistics, and from psycholinguistics. The kinds of problems that applied linguists become involved with can largely be identified as communication problems, whether the communication is between individuals, either of equal or of unequal status, between communities of individuals, or between whole nations.

Applied linguistics recognizes that there is pressure to communicate between human beings, that human beings use language to communicate, and that communication problems develop because language is an imperfect tool, but also because language is a mechanism of territorial defense. Applied linguistics applies information from the social-scientific disciplines, including linguistics, to solve these problems; indeed, it draws upon linguistics because linguistics is the discipline that contributes information dealing specifically with language. But it is not interested in describing language itself; on the contrary, unlike linguistics, it does not regard language as an isolate to be examined away from its social environment. Half a century ago, a great American linguist, Leonard Bloomfield, took the view that the focus of concern in linguistics had to be the sentence; the contention fixed attention on syntax rather than on other features of language, and it has taken most of the intervening half-century to realize that meaning does not lie in the sentence, but in the uses to which language is put by human beings; that meaning is not inherent in the sentence, but rather is negotiated between users of language; and that meaning transcends sentences.

Because applied linguistics is concerned with the uses of language, it has been heavily identified with language teaching. In the kind of society in which we live, the education sector has been charged with the protection and transmission of 'right' language, and the education sector has also been charged with the inculcation of 'second' languages (in the numerical sense; that is, in the sense of 'additional'). Applied linguists have been involved with teachers in more or less formal educational settings. There are several reasons for this phenomenon. First, language teachers wanted to separate themselves from literature teachers and wanted to be perceived as scientists rather than as humanists. They tend to identify themselves with the science of linguistics (because it was objective, concrete, explicit) and to dissassociate themselves from the subjective, abstract, and implicit concerns of literature study and literary criticism. Second, the emergence of applied linguistics as a discipline occurred during the "Sputnik era," when the United States was concerned that the Soviets were gaining an edge in scientific achievement; that concern resulted in the heavy investment of funds by the U.S. government in education. It was predictable that in the United States the newly identified area of applied linguistics would be shaped to some extent by the availability of these funds. Third, the emergence of applied linguistics as a discipline also coincided with the great growth in English as a language of wider communication, particularly in science and technology, as those areas related to modernization in the developing world. This phenomenon caused attention to be focused on English and on the teaching of English as a foreign language for use in modernization in the developing world. Fourth, the other side of the phenomenon of English as world language is the major influx of international students into U.S. tertiary academic institutions and the concurrent need to develop assessment instruments to gauge English proficiency and to teach English as a second language to those students so that they might succeed in their academic endeavors. Finally, the influx into the United States of large immigrant groups, coming in political cohorts as the result of political events in various places—Hungary, Cuba, Vietnam, Haiti, Mexico, El Salvador, the USSR—created a different kind of need for ESL instruction; that need was expanded by the recognition of indigenous non-English speaking groups (e.g., the Hispanics) and by the recognition of nonstandard varieties of English spoken by large indigenous populations (e.g., blacks). All of these forces funneled through the educational system and served to create a bridge between applied linguistics and language teaching—a link of such power that other areas of applied linguistics tended to be overlooked and in some instances ignored even by applied linguists. But that link misrepresents the field and obscures the development of a paradigm within which applied linguistics may operate in the future.

The point is that applied linguistics is alive and well, and applied linguists are doing a great deal of interesting work. The field is a young one. One of the reasons for the difficulty in defining the field lies in the fact that its disciplinary paradigm is not yet fully fleshed out; it is, however, emerging. But even without a fully articulated paradigm, applied linguistics continues to work at solving real-world language-based problems. It continues to draw upon linguistics in that work, but not exclusively upon linguistics; it draws upon information from all the social sciences. Now that programs purporting to produce individuals qualified to do applied linguistics are coming into existence in a number of academic institutions, it may be time to take a hard look at what an applied linguist ought to know. Discussions in the field will center around this issue for a while, and, by the time there is some agreement as to what an applied linguist ought to know, there may also develop a better conceptualization of applied linguistics itself. Such a new perspective is needed. As one effort in this direction, the present volume replaces an earlier attempt by one of the editors to define the field (Kaplan 1980b). That attempt, undertaken a decade ago, is now clearly outdated (and, in the United States, out of print). Much has happened in the course of that decade. The present volume attempts to correct the faults of the earlier one. However, given the nature of science, the editors recognize that this volume, too, perhaps soon after it sees the light of day, will be out of date. We trust that our students and our colleagues will be quick to point out our errors and will be equally quick to offer a better, clearer view of this fuzzy field.

In closing, we would like to acknowledge that even this volume does not cover all of the possible manifestations of applied linguistics (e.g., document design, lexicography, pathology and rehabilitation, and translation). There are two important reason for this failure. First, given that the paradigm is not yet fully realized, it is difficult to anticipate what will eventually be subsumed within it; this problem is complicated by the independent movement of subareas toward or away from total independence. As will be noted elsewhere in this volume, language testing and second-language acquisition, once squarely part of the area, have moved powerfully toward autonomy, and discourse analysis, once fully independent, has moved under the umbrella. Second, and purely pragmatically, white it is true that a book must have pages, it is also true that a book may not have an infinite number of pages. Physical constraints limited the number of contributions that could be included in the volume, and the editors chose to exclude areas that they believed, at the time of planning, to be insufficiently developed or differentiated. The editors may have been incorrect in their judgment; if that is the case, they accept responsibility and apologize to those colleagues whose work is, as a consequence, inadequately represented. The only rationalization we are able to offer for our choices lies in the fact that this volume is, admittedly, a survey—an attempt to cover a great deal of material in somewhat compacted form, and simultaneously an attempt to offer a variety of views of the parameters of this still-developing field.

In extended introductions, the latter part of the chapter is customarily used to introduce the various contributions to the volume and provide a measure of coherence to the organization of the chapters. We have refrained from doing this for two reasons: first, we believe that the organization of chapters in the volume is somewhat transparent; second, and more important, we believe that the opening contribution to the volume, by Peter Strevens, provides an elegant rationale for the arrangement and selection in this volume.

The sudden and untimely death of Professor Strevens in the final stages of this volume's preparation has led us to dedicate this volume to his memory and to his work. His chapter introducing the volume serves not only as a framework for the volume as a whole, but also, and more importantly, as an elegant testimony to his life's work, to his dedication to the field, and to his influence on generations of applied linguists who have taken up his profession.

An Introduction to
Applied Linguistics: An Overview

Paradigms, as they mature, cause reconfigurations in their structures. Applied linguistics is no exception to this rule. Two examples may suffice to illustrate the point. In the early 1970s, language testing was included within applied linguistics; however, as more was learned about psycholinguistics, and as more sophisticated algorithms in statistics became available, language testing developed an independent paradigm and essentially separated itself from applied linguistics to become an independent structure. The field of second-language acquisition (SLA) provides the second example. It was originally a subarea of applied linguistics, contributing basically to language teaching, but as the interlanguage hypothesis emerged, SLA moved to independence from both applied linguistics and generative theory, and now contributes to both from a new vantage point. Thus, the applied linguistics that is described in this volume is rather different from the one described in *On the scope of applied linguistics* (1980). It is fair to say that applied linguistics, when it first emerged in the 1950s, was virtually synonymous with second/foreign-language teaching. In the United States, at least, it drew heavily on the structuralist notions of C.C. Fries and on the behaviorist psychology of B.F. Skinner, and it had not evolved an independent paradigm.

But in the 30 years since then, it has to a significant degree abandoned both structuralist linguistics and behaviorism. It has retained a tie with language teaching (and in that context has given rise to a number of curricular models—humanistic and naturalistic approaches, notional/functional syllabi, and communicative curricula, to name a few), but it has incorporated a number of other concerns including, for example, computer-assisted language learning (CALL), American Sign Language (ASL), SLA, testing, reading theory, discourse analysis, language (status and corpus) planning, and so on.

The affinities of early applied linguistics in the United States for the audio-lingual method led scholars to believe that there was essentially one way of teaching language to learners of all ages and conditions in all circumstances and in all places. Gradually over the years, there has been a growing recognition that different learners have different needs, that learners can be differentiated by age and by a variety of sociolinguistic features, and that circumstances are differentiated by a wide variety of features, including the relative degree of centralization of the educational system, the relative training of the teachers, the relative availability of teaching materials and support structures, the relative intensity and duration of instruction, and the relative fiscal support available. Now, rather than insisting on a single approach, applied linguists perceive a three-dimensional matrix based on learner needs, sociolinguistic variables, and educational variables; this more complex view gives rise to a very large number of cells, each of which conceivably contains a different set of features. Furthermore, there has been a powerful shift from the initial focus on teaching to a focus on learning, as recognition has emerged that language is communication, and that in the absence of real communicative need, there may be precious little motivation to learn.

Applied linguistics, at the the same time that its perspectives on teaching and learning have changed, has also expanded its concerns in ways that more appropriately match its title; for, if applied linguistics is indeed the application of language knowledge to language-based problems, then applied linguistics must, by its very nature, be involved with many more concerns than the learning and teaching of languages. However, while language testing and second-language acquisition no longer fit within a restrictive learning/teaching definition of applied linguistics, they remain important fields within an enlarged view of applied linguistics as it has emerged over the last ten years. In fact, as Strevens points out, applied linguistics has expanded its domain of inquiry considerably since the 1950s. Not only are educationally related fields now seen as applied linguistics, but other fields of language-oriented research with applications may be viewed as applied linguistics; these include speech therapy, translation, lexicography, language uses in professional contexts, literacy, etc. Strevens highlights a number of these expanded contexts for applied linguistics in the following article.

Strevens' career followed the development of applied linguistics, or perhaps more accurately, he led the field, at least in Britain, in the various stages through which it has passed. The article that follows lays out a number of trends that will be taken up and evaluated in other sections of this volume. This is not surprising, for some of the contributors have been students, colleagues, and/or friends of Professor Strevens.

The view Strevens presents here is not necessarily one espoused by all applied linguists. Probably no one could articulate a model that would enjoy such prestige. To a certain extent, the view Strevens presents is more British, though certainly, and perhaps especially over the past decade, there has been much cross-talk between applied linguists in Britain and the United States. The point, however, is that the view Strevens presents is one that has historical validity, and therefore one that properly stands at the front of this volume. Together with the position assumed by the editors in their introduction, Strevens' article opens the field for discussion and analysis.

Applied Linguistics: An Overview

Peter Strevens

*Late of Wolfson College, Cambridge University,
and the University of Illinois, Urbana*

1. INTRODUCTION

Considering that applied linguistics as a unified field of study came into being only in the late 1950s, it has blossomed and diversified in a remarkably rapid way. In order to characterize the present nature of applied linguistics, this paper will briefly trace its origins; it will then outline the principal disciplines and subject areas—in addition to linguistics—that are drawn upon by applied linguistics, as well as the domains of human activity where applied linguistics is of practical value. Finally, it will suggest that the task-related problem-solving nature of applied linguistics has led to the development of an intellectual give-and-take. The collaboration of applied linguists in language-based projects has helped to disseminate a greater awareness within the educated community of the nature of language and its role in society, and has certainly created a willingness among applied linguists to examine concepts within other disciplines and assess their relevance to applied linguistics.

2. ORIGINS OF THE CONCEPT

The term *applied linguistics* (AL) has been in use at least since the founding of the University of Edinburgh School of Applied Linguistics in 1956, and of the Center for Applied Linguistics in Washington, D.C., in 1957. In the case of Edinburgh, the impetus behind the creation of a new department with an unfamiliar title came from two different directions. From the one side came an initiative from "cultural diplomacy": the British Council for English aimed to provide specialist courses for high-level teacher trainers and senior educators from both Britain and overseas countries so that the practical teaching and learning of English in Commonwealth countries and the developing world would be substantially improved. Edinburgh University accepted that a number of language-related areas of academic study, not solely English as a foreign language (EFL) and English as a second language (ESL), would be supported by the founding of a new department of this kind under the pioneering direction of J.C. (Ian) Catford.

The Center for Applied Linguistics in Washington, D.C., owes its genesis largely to the concern of the Ford Foundation to assist in solving the problems in language education then being encountered in many countries in the developing world. They saw the need to collect and analyze data about the role and use of English and other languages, international and local, particularly in those countries that had recently obtained their independence from France or Britain, or were about to do so. As a consequence of these surveys, it was anticipated that large-scale projects would be mounted for the design and production of language-teaching materials and for the training of teachers in their use. Dr. Charles Ferguson of Stanford University was appointed the first of a series of distinguished directors of the center.

Thus, in the case of each of the academic institutions that first bore the term *applied linguistics* in its title, it was in the national interest of a major English-speaking country—Britain in 1956 and the United States in 1957—to promote the learning and teaching of English for educational development, and to unlock the considerable funds necessary in order to establish an institutional base.

Although the two directors and their colleagues came from academic posts in linguistics, they were faced with the immediate necessity of addressing practical tasks. At Edinburgh, a principal task was to articulate for the first time, in new graduate-level courses, the intellectual bases of language learning and language teaching for the benefit of senior educators working in the developing world. In Washington, a principal task was to design and carry out multiple large-scale surveys of language use in Africa; these, in turn, would be used as part of the design criteria for new programs of language teaching, including the preparation of new generations of teacher trainers. Applied linguistics was thus produced simultaneously on both sides of the Atlantic, not as an a priori concept, but as the consequence of creative minds aware of the developments then current in the discipline of linguistics, applying their talents to specific language-related tasks.

It is a central feature of applied linguistics that it is task-related, problem-oriented, project-centered, and demand-led. It is also fundamentally based in academic disciplines. This point is an important one since many people outside applied linguistics jump to the erroneous conclusion that applied linguistics is a high-flown name for advanced English-language teaching. It is, of course, true that much of the demand for specialists with applied linguistics training arises in connection with language teaching. There is, though, an increasing demand for other international, regional, and national languages also, as is evidenced by the growing number of programs offered by the "cultural diplomacy" arms of the countries concerned (emulating the achievements of the U.S. Information Agency and the British Council for English) for the teaching of, for example, French, German, Italian, Japanese, Spanish, and Portuguese.

Throughout the world a surge in English multilingualism is occurring—one so strong that more and more courses are being offered to a growing range of learners with ever more specialized learning aims and needs. In order to meet these needs, it is not just classroom teachers who are required, essential though these are, but specialists able to analyze in close and relevant detail the new learners' needs and the nature of the conditions in which the learning and teaching would take place, conditions that crucially affect the design of most-appropriate teaching courses. Applied linguistics is uniquely capable of imparting the knowledge, understanding, and conceptual skills necessary to undertake these analyses and to devise the accompanying material. But again, although it is applied linguistics, uniquely, that offers unified solutions to these higher-level conceptual problems in language teaching, it is not solely in language teaching that applied linguistics contributes. Rather, it contributes in a wide range of language-related areas.

The term *applied linguistics*, then, has a history reaching back over 30 years, starting from nearly contemporaneous beginnings in Scotland and the United States. The subsequent expansion of centers for the study and teaching of applied linguistics has been more rapid in Britain and Europe—including the establishment of 'daughter' centers such as those in Hyderabad, Singapore, and Hong Kong—than in the United States (although the latter country has helped to facilitate the teaching and learning of English in Guam, American Samoa, and the areas earlier known as the U.S. Trust Territories in the Western Pacific, as well as in a number of other countries through Binational Centers). The British have found that one-year, postexperience master's-degree courses in applied linguistics have attracted large numbers of high-quality applicants who subsequently find a wide range of jobs open to them—most of them, it is true, in higher-echelon positions in EFL/ESL.

In addition to centers for the study and teaching of applied linguistics, there have emerged a number of serious academic and professional associations, notably the International Association of Applied Linguistics (AILA), the British Association for Applied Linguistics (BAAL), the American Association for Applied Linguistics (AAAL), and similar bodies in many countries. The many thousands of members of these associations are served by a range of journals, among the most prestigious of which are *Applied Linguistics* (AL), *Annual Review of Applied Linguistics* (ARAL), *English Language Teaching Journal* (ELTJ), *International Journal of the Sociology of Language* (IJSL), *International Review of Applied Linguistics* (IRAL), *Journal of Multilingual and*

Multicultural Development (JMMD), *Language Learning, System, TESOL Quarterly* (TQ), and *World Englishes.* Many other journals also now exist, often with more restricted circulation than the journals named here.

The economic and logistical success of applied linguistics has occasionally led to contrary or even hostile reactions, in particular from some specialists in theoretical linguistics, on the one hand, and in literature on the other. Even today it is not unknown for non-applied linguists to maintain that "there is no such thing as applied linguistics," or at least to seek a return to the conditions and attitudes that prevailed before applied linguists became influential in language-teaching policy and decision making (see the contributions of Politi and of Fernando in Quirk and Widdowson 1985). Such reactions reflect complex sentiments that include some of the following: frustration with the fact that graduate-student demand, and therefore funding and resources, is typically greater for applied linguistics than for either general linguistics or English literature; an elitist belief that theoretical or purely literary studies are morally and intellectually superior to applied studies; a low opinion of the art of teaching and a lack of understanding of the possibilities of serious intellectual work relating to language teaching and learning; nostalgia for earlier times when foreign-language teaching was the handmaiden of the teaching of literature; and a view among some specialists in linguistics that practice (i.e., classroom teaching) must be determined by the results of research, which in turn is determined by theory, and that, therefore, foreign-language teaching must necessarily be dominated by linguistics.

Among this latter group, even when there is tolerance of the existence of applied linguistics, it is often conditional on applied linguistics' being narrowly interpreted as "linguistic theory applied." There is a subtle presupposition within such a formulation that the intellectual paradigm for applied linguistics—its "rules of engagement" as it were—are agreed by all concerned to be those of theoretical linguistics, and indeed of one particular school of thought in linguistics, even though the purposes of applied linguistics are (unfortunately) utilitarian. Yet the considerable and growing strength of applied linguistics is evidenced by the continuing demand for specialists trained in that field, by the continuing extension of the uses of applied linguistics into new fields, and by the growing flow of valuable contributions to research, publications, and action that applied linguists are producing.

3. DEFINITIONS, DISCIPLINES, AND APPLIED LINGUISTICS

The definition of applied linguistics rests on six fundamental propositions:

1. Applied linguistics is based in intellectual inquiry, gives rise to and makes use of research, and is discipline-related;

2. Linguistics is essential to applied linguistics, but is not the only discipline that contributes to it;

3. The choice of which disciplines are involved in particular applied-linguistic circumstances, and which parts of those disciplines, is contingent: it depends on what the circumstances are;

4. The multidisciplinary nature of applied linguistics requires that its practical operations be realized in a number of different domains of human activity;

5. Applied linguistics is typically concerned with achieving an end, with improving existing language-related operations, and with solving language-related problems;

6. Linguists are not exempt from being socially accountable, from displaying a social conscience, and therefore, when possible, they should use their knowledge and understanding in the service of humanity.[1]

These propositions are summed up in the following often-employed short working definition of applied linguistics: Applied linguistics is a multidisciplinary approach to the solution of language-related problems.

The multidisciplinary dimension of applied linguistics requires further explanation. Some aspects of at least the following disciplines may on occasion be engaged in applied-linguistic operations: linguistics, psycholinguistics, psychology (and various subdisciplines within it), semantics and semiotics, lexicography, sociolinguistics, social theory (and various subdisciplines within it), education (and various subdisciplines within it), mathematics, computing, statistics, logic, philosophy, rhetoric, discourse analysis, philosophy of science, neurology, anatomy, physiology, speech communication, language pathology, literature and literary criticism, translation and interpretation, toponymy, artificial intelligence, information transfer and storage, jurisprudence and public administration, etc. It is important to add that this list, as well as being incomplete, is open-ended. The disciplines quoted are those known to the author to have been drawn upon (or contributed to) for applied-linguistic purposes in the past and present. New demands in the future may make new domains of human activity relevant and may require the assistance of yet other disciplines.

4. DOMAINS OF APPLIED LINGUISTICS

The relation between disciplines and domains in applied linguistics is rather parallel to the relation in, for example, engineering between, on one hand, the disciplines of mathematics, physics, chemistry, and so forth, and on the other hand, the engineer's aims in given practical circumstances. Thus, civil engineering draws upon geology, meteorology, "big-number" applied mathematics, etc; marine engineering makes use of hydrodynamics, metallurgy, the chemistry of thermoplastics, marine architecture, and so forth. Applied linguistics creates a similar dynamic; depending on the purposes of the application, the disciplines relevant to those purposes will differ.

In an important paper delivered at the 1987 International Conference of AILA (from the French title: Association Internationale de Linguistique Appliquée), the director of the Center for Applied Linguistics identified in his "Overview of Applied Linguistics," "four exemplary foci which . . . characterize important strands of our work." These were: innovative language education; language-education policy; newer technologies and language teaching; and the expanding role of the linguist in nontraditional settings, notably in law, business, and the sciences (Tucker 1987, quoting Kaplan 1987:vii–x). A more detailed analysis of the domains of applied linguistics—though far from exhaustive—would provide examples such as the following.

4.1. Language Teaching

It will be clear from what has been said already that, although the learning and teaching of languages is a domain in which applied linguistics has from its beginnings made an important contribution, applied linguistics is not be be equated with foreign-language teaching (FLT). It is possible to be an excellent language teacher while knowing nothing of linguistics or applied linguistics. (Though other things being equal, a language teacher would probably be a better language teacher if s/he did have such knowledge.) Nor does every applied linguist know much about language teaching, though most do. If, however, the question is how to harness intellectual effort to bring about improvements in the learning of foreign languages, then an applied-linguistics approach would see as relevant aspects of a number of disciplines concerned with language: linguistics, psychology, education, etc. Today, applied linguistics can be seen as supplying the intellectual bases for advances in language teaching in numerous contexts and in a number of countries. It is important not to interpret this as a claim that applied linguistics is the only source of advancement in language teaching; far from it. In methodology, especially, many advances come directly from experienced teachers with no knowledge of applied linguistics. What is unique is that applied linguistics is synoptic, systematic, and principled. It is synoptic in the sense that it keeps in view the whole range of concepts and practicalities in language teaching; systematic in its manner of operation; and principled in being firmly based in theory.

4.2. Language Policy and Planning

In recent decades, it has become recognized by national governments and international agencies that demographic changes, especially large-scale population movements, refugee flows, the attainment of political independence, racial and ethnic upheavals, and similar events possess a crucial dimension in which politics and administration become entwined with linguistic, social, and psychological effects. Applied linguistics has often been a source for the illumination of the complex social, political, economic, linguistic, and cultural tensions involved in such situations; a focus for interdisciplinary collaboration; and a contributor to ideas for avoiding the worst consequences of traumatic linguistic and cultural conflicts.

The issues embraced by language planning do not relate solely to the national and local languages of the countries directly concerned. It is important to note in this regard that language-planning efforts are increasingly economically driven; thus, the recently authorized Australian National Language Plan in part encourages improvement in the teaching of the languages of Australia's trading partners, and the currently evolving national policy in New Zealand is likely to follow suit. Japan's 1984 policy calling for drastic growth in the intake of international students into Japanese tertiary education can be seen as an attempt to disseminate Japanese throughout Asia as a language of education. Other examples are available.

Indeed, the conflicts and changes calling forth language planning have most frequently led to an increase in the social and economic value of knowing and using an international language, usually English. In recent years, language planning, and national policies concerning which languages should be taught and learned through the state educational system, have thus combined to fuel the explosive growth of English worldwide. Crystal (1987:359) estimates the total number of English-users at 1.6 billion. Since only some 350 million of these have English as their mother tongue, several implications appear:

1. More than three out of four of the world's population capable of some use of English have learned it through instruction, or have "picked it up";

2. The large numbers of people who have been learners of English in recent years have created a strong economic demand for instruction, which, in turn, has generated financial resources for research on and development of more effective ways of learning and teaching;

3. The teaching of English as a foreign or second language has been relatively successful;

4. The popular opinion about whether an individual can reasonably hope to learn a foreign language has been influenced by the positive experiences of many EFL/ESL learners;

5. By definition, all the one billion or more non-native users of English are multilinguals;

6. It can be argued that the last major populations of monolinguals are the native speakers of English, i.e., the British, Americans, Australians, etc. (Strevens 1988); and

7. In a world in which the ability to handle more than one language is increasingly the norm, those populations that can make use of only their own language—even if that is the predominant international language—are at a disadvantage.

4.3. Speech-Communication Research

In the early postwar years, it became clear that progress in communications technology required sophisticated linguistic awareness. The first computers, for example, were originally regarded by computer engineers as "obviously" capable of producing automatic translation through the simple device of matching dictionary entries from different languages. Machine-translation projects in the United States and Britain soon found it necessary to engage the services of specialists in linguistics as language-related complexities quickly overwhelmed them; these projects are thus examples of applied linguistics.

In another area of speech-communication research, bandwidth-compression research (roughly, how to put more conversations on a single telephone circuit), telecommunications engineers sought the collaboration of those specialists in phonetics who could bring knowledge of the articulation and acoustics of speech into the consideration of information theory and electrical and electronics engineering. Today, every major communications-research laboratory and project makes such use of applied linguists. Their participation is especially notable in projects dealing with the automatic recognition of speech, the automatic synthesis of speech, automatic translation, man/machine communication, artificial intelligence, and similar fields.

4.4. Specialized Occupational Languages

As is common knowledge, airline pilots and air traffic–control personnel have long been required, for reasons of safety and following international agreements, to use English for aircraft-operational purposes, and to abide by rigorously controlled procedures, phraseology, and conventions. This operational use of English has created many applied-linguistics projects in countries where English is not a native language. A similar recent project, dealing with the language of radio communications at sea, was perhaps a paradigm example of applied linguistics in this domain (Strevens and Weeks 1985; Weeks, Glover, Strevens, and Johnson 1984).

Collaboration between two master mariners, both of them specialists in maritime communications, and two applied linguists with knowledge of seafaring, produced SEASPEAK, a regularized subset of English specifically designed for use over VHF radio, ship-to-ship, and ship-to-shore, where special difficulties and constraints exist. Among the characteristics of the new procedures is the rule that every message must be introduced by a 'message marker' that states in advance what kind of message immediately follows. Message markers include: QUESTION, INSTRUCTION, ADVICE, REQUESTS, INFORMATION, WARNING, INTENTION, and response markers appropriate to these. Thus, a message to the effect that dredgers have completed their work in the harbor entrance, but have not yet gotten clear might be transmitted as: "INFORMATION: Dredging now completed in the harbor entrance. WARNING: The harbor entrance is not yet clear." Other linguistic devices have been incorporated to increase the listener's expectancies of correctly identifying what has been said, to reduce the number of propositions that are transmitted before the listener is permitted to check what he/she thinks has been said, and to eliminate ambiguity as far as possible. SEASPEAK was officially adopted in 1988 by the International Maritime Organization of the United Nations.

4.5. Speech Therapy

The origins of much of the treatment and rehabilitation of speech and language disorders, in Britain at least, lay in the somewhat antiquarian, invented, and elitist concepts of elocution, the teaching of diction, and the subject often labeled "normal voice and speech." In recent years, the treatment of patients with speech disorders, and above all the vocational preparation of speech therapists, has been revolutionized through the incorporation of applied linguistics (though not necessarily under that name) into many of the courses of professional training. Linguists and applied linguists themselves have been involved in the study and treatment of various aphasias (e.g., Crystal 1984). Psycholinguists and neurolinguists have been working for years to understand how language is processed in the brain, and how various brain injuries affect both language memory and language production. It has been determined that ASL (indeed any sign language) has all the features of natural language, and that the teaching of ASL to people in an English-speaking environment is exactly analogous to the teaching of ESL to hearing students. Much has been learned about the similarities and differences between first- and second-language learning. The application of these discoveries to patient treatment constitutes a classic example of applied linguistics.

4.6. Lexicography and Dictionary-Making

During the past decade, the making of dictionaries has changed its nature as a consequence of technological changes in printing and publishing that have opened new practical possibilities in dictionary-making. Dictionary-making is now a much more rapid process, and one which can link into cognate areas such as the creation and harmonization of terminology and the large-scale library database networks now spreading across the world (Kaplan 1983).

Simultaneously, a new generation of lexicographers has emerged whose affinities and allegiances, instead of being rooted in philology, as has typically
been the case in the past, now lie with linguistics. Lexicographers of this mold
are in fact engaging in applied linguistics for at least part of their task.
Sinclair's (1987) *Cobuild Dictionary* is a principal example of the way applied
linguists contribute to lexicography (see also Hartmann 1985).

4.7. Translation and Interpreting

The fully automatic production of reliably authentic written text in language
B from the input of written text in language A, without human intervention,
remains an elusive goal, despite repeated stories in the popular press. Improvements in what can be achieved do occur from year to year; after 40 years
of intensive research, it is now possible to produce reliable translations within
certain registers of particular languages. In general, however, the goal remains
elusive due to a number of factors: among others, the influence of the context;
the tendency of authors to playfulness, irony, and the use of idiom; the constant creation of original metaphor; and the fact that some semantic ambiguity
is inherent in natural language. Such factors render it necessary for human
editors to check the output text from automatic-translation devices. The task
of achieving further improvements is one shared between computing engineers and applied linguists. The task of training translators and interpreters
has changed dramatically over the past two decades and now often includes
training in applied linguistics.

4.8. Language and the Professions

The primary goal of language-use research in professional domains is to improve delivery of services and to resolve problems of miscommunication that
might otherwise have serious consequences. In a simple sense, one may see
this domain of study as the facilitation of communication between specialist
and citizen. While there are many professional contexts for such study, two
examples will serve to illustrate this domain of applied linguistics: doctor-
patient discourse and language use in legal contexts.

In Britain, in the context of the recruitment into the British health and
hospital service of large numbers of medical doctors from overseas countries
such as Pakistan, Malaysia, Hong Kong, etc., it was quickly found that, although their medical training and experience might be entirely adequate, difficulties arose in understanding their patients and in being understood by
them. Thus, although a doctor from Pakistan might be perfectly capable of
reporting that "the patient presented with severe abdominal pain," he would
first need to have understood the patient's saying to him, "Ee doc, I've an
awful pain in me gut." Applied linguists, notably from Lancaster University

under Christopher Candlin (Candlin et al. 1976), were able to diagnose the nature of the language problems involved, propose remedies, and devise tests of language attainment pertaining to these professional contexts (see also Fisher and Todd 1986; Maher 1986a; Pettinari 1988).

Language in the legal system has similarly become a growing area of study over the last ten years. The use of language in legal contexts affects not only how a lawyer makes his or her case in the courtroom, it also affects the perception of a witness's veracity, the choice of jury members, the understanding of directions to jurors, the transcribing of trail records, the admission of evidence in trial, and the strength of expert testimony. An example of the role of applied linguistics in this domain is Roger Shuy's (1987a, 1987b) studies of the ways in which the language used in legislation and public administration in the United States is either ambiguous or deliberately obscure, to the detriment of the citizen's interests. This important work shows that we err if we take it for granted that 'lawyers' language' is always: (a) precise; (b) understood by other lawyers; and (c) irrelevant to nonlawyer citizens except when court cases supervene (see also Fisher and Todd 1986; O'Barr 1982; Penman 1987).

5. RELATIONS BETWEEN THEORY AND PRACTICE

Applied linguists often experience a tension between two contrasting paradigms distinguished by differing roles assumed within each for theory, research, and practice. A *theory-dominated paradigm* starts from the suppositions:

1. That a current 'best' theory exists that is based in linguistics;
2. That the most important task of the scholar is to contribute to the development of that theory;
3. That the theory determines what research is needed; and
4. That practice should be confined to the validated results of that research.

This is essentially the ethos that drives most second-language acquisition (SLA) research, and in consequence, when SLA research is invoked in aid of practical language teaching, classroom considerations are often held, tacitly or overtly, to be a little account. A *pragmatic paradigm*, on the contrary, starts from the existence of a massive tradition of practical teaching—imperfect, but improvable. Research in this context is essential in order, for example, to find out why some techniques are more successful than others; the validated results of research will contribute to a greater understanding of theoretical issues.

The theory-dominated paradigm assumes also that its basis lies not in just any theory, but as far as possible in a single, unified theory; and this is held to justify an exclusive, disparaging attitude toward other theories, and especially toward nonunified ('eclectic') theoretical positions. The pragmatic paradigm, by contrast, is skeptical of the opinion that a single, unified theory is possible or even appropriate in view of the multiple perspectives of human language, and regards it as desirable for the scholar to construct his/her own synthesis, seeking aspects of the theoretical truth wherever they may be found. These polar differences of view confront each other particularly in research relating to language learning and teaching. SLA research in particular, derived from transformational-generative (TG) psycholinguistics, expects to instruct the teacher in better practices because "the theory predicts and research confirms" that such practices are effective. Classroom research, on the other hand, based in pragmatic applied linguistics, encourages the teacher to analyze the short-comings of practical learning and teaching, to devise directly relevant research into these problems, and to use the results both for improving classroom practice and for a better understanding of the principles and theories that underlie it (Allright and Bailey 1989).

A further philosophical viewpoint on the relations between theory and practice, and one which sheds light on the foregoing discussion, is provided under the concept of social construction, well summarized here by Bruffee:

> The tendency to classify our knowledge into "theory" and "practice" has its source in the cognitive understanding of knowledge. Cognitive thought assumes a vertical, hierarchical relation between theory and practice. It regards theory or concept making . . . as the more privileged, more powerful level of thought. And it regards practical application . . . as less privileged and less powerful. Theory is said to 'ground' and sanction practice. Practice is said merely to be ways of behaving or methods of doing things that are grounded and sanctioned by—that is, are the 'consequence' of—theory. The categories "theory" and "practice" implicitly express, therefore, what Stanley Fish calls "theory hope." "Theory hope" is the belief that whatever a theory sanctions us to do is surely correct, whatever we learn under its aegis is surely true, and whatever results we get using its methods are surely valid. (1986:781–82)

A radically different approach is then described by Bruffee, one based in social-construction theory. As Bruffee explains:

> Concepts, ideas, theories, the world, reality, and facts are all language constructs generated by knowledge communities and used by them to maintain community coherence. (1986:777)

This point of view reduces the distinction between 'theory' and 'practice' and hence takes away the justification for regarding the one as superior to the other. From this point of view, theory is no more than a socially accepted perspective of a group of people, having no independent validity or claim to knowledge.

6. INTELLECTUAL EXCHANGE
IN APPLIED LINGUISTICS

Many of those who work in applied linguistics also work in other theory-'bounded' disciplines—for example, in general linguistics for a greater or lesser portion of their professional time. For some of them, there is a contrast, not to say at times a conflict, between the essentially pragmatic, polysystemic, goal-oriented nature of their applied linguistic work and the theoretical, monosystemic, and self-sufficient nature of much of their linguistics research. To point out this contrast is not to denigrate either of these philosophical outlooks, but it does bring a problem to the surface. The desire to seek a unified theory expressed within some theoretical positions in linguistics is modeled on physics, and on the belief that the universe can be fully explained in terms of a small number of forces and the rules that govern their interaction. "We hope to explain the entire universe in a single, simple formula that you can wear on your T-shirt" (Lederman, quoted in Davies 1987:13). With such an outlook, it is not surprising that theory seems to possess a value not shared by more mundane practicalities. The concept of social construction, in contrast, provides an appropriate counterbalance for applied linguists.

Physicists and cosmologists are currently engaged in an internal debate that not only touches on the relationship between theory and practice, but may also offer to applied linguists some illumination of a problem central to language study. The issue is whether the fundamental laws of physics apply to all events in nature, without exception—in which case the whole history of the universe is, in principle, 'knowable' and its future predictable—or whether some events are by their essence disorganized, chaotic, and thus unpredictable. In addition, those within this debate who regard the orthodox view, paraphrased by Lederman in the above quotation, as no longer adequate for the total explanation of the universe, point to the existence, within apparently chaotic and unpredictable events, of rules of self-organization. Systems that operate in a predictable manner are known as linear systems; those that produce unpredictable events are nonlinear systems.

The concept of nonlinear systems, in which hugely complex and essentially chaotic activity nevertheless becomes subject to rules of self-organization, is a subtle one. A simple example is seen when we heat a pan of water on a stove. Paul Davies (1987:42), an eminent physicist and cosmologist, describes the events thus:

> At first, the temperature at the bottom of the pan is only slightly higher than at the top. The water remains uniform and featureless. The system is in a state of smoothly increasing disorder, with the water molecules slowly conducting heat up through the liquid—the system is close to thermodynamic equilibrium. . . . If, however, we heat the pan more strongly, we drive the system far away from equilibrium. Eventually, the

temperature difference between the bottom and the top layers reaches a critical value, and something dramatic starts to happen. The liquid becomes unstable and starts to convect. Under properly controlled conditions, the convection motion spontaneously organizes itself into a highly regular pattern, which may take the form of rolls of hexagonal cells.

Turning to experimental attempts to simulate brain activity by means of networks of interconnected nodes, Davies (44) describes some of the unexpected results of starting up such a network and leaving it to evolve according to its simple on-off connections. Instead of:

> impenetrably complicated behavior of little interest . . . , remarkable things can occur. Coherent patterns of activity swirl around the net, organizing themselves into stable cycles. Self-organization may occur even from random input. Moreover, the patterns are highly robust; severing a link in the net leaves them essentially undisturbed. Many physiologists believe that these processes reflect the neural activity of real brains.

The point, then, is that the brain is neither a simple device nor linear in its mode of operation. And the question for linguists is whether human language, generated in the brain, is the product of a linear or a nonlinear system. If of a linear system, then research into human language output can assume a linear relationship with input. Such a view might accord reasonably well with a theoretical position that holds a largely deterministic view of the development of language, for example, entailing a predictable sequence of learning events. But experienced teachers, and applied linguists, are aware that there is a discrepancy between input-for-language-learning and output-of-language-actually-learned. If the brain is a nonlinear system, then the learner's output is dependent not only on the nature of the language input, but also on the precise, idiosyncratic 'wiring' of the learner's neural connections, which in turn includes the effects of interaction with other human beings—and thus also with the learner's entire learning history. This would seem to offer strong confirmation of the applied linguist's view that the progress of language learning in an individual is the result of many different influences, some of them linear and knowable, others from nonlinear sources whose rules of self-organization are as yet far from understood.

A further example of illumination from other disciplines can be seen in the phenomenon of psychological 'flow', i.e., the total absorption in a satisfying task that occurs in musical performance, or rock climbing, where an artist is engrossed in creation (Flaste 1989). This mental state, with its heightened cognitive processes, can be induced also in language teaching/learning by high-grade teaching. Thus, the psychology of task performance provides a plausible explanatory theory for a previously mysterious aspect of language learning.

[Editors' note: In October 1989, Strevens wrote to the editors, saying "I have recently been fired by reading about the phenomenon of 'flow'. . . . It seems to me to answer exactly one of the most intractable questions in language teaching: how can we explain the very great difference between the rate of learning achieved by the best learners, in contrast to that of the worst? (I put the difference, in the extreme, 'best-case' examples, at around a factor of 100). . . . I recognize [such features as] absorption in the task, the element of a challenge, the tension between boredom on the one hand and anxiety on the other, with high-gear cognitive operations in the ground between." He enclosed with his letter an article by Richard Flaste from the "Good Health Magazine" of the *New York Times* (8 Oct., 1989) which describes the work of University of Chicago psychologist Mihaly Csikszentmihalyi on the notion of 'flow'—"a state of concentration that amounts to absolute absorption in an activity." The brief review notes an environment, the polar extremes of which are:

High challenge and high skills = Flow

Low challenge and high skills = Boredom

High challenge and low skills = Anxiety

Low challenge and low skills = Apathy

It was apparently Strevens' notion that 'flow' was characteristic of successful language learning. Unfortunately, he died before being able to elaborate on this notion.]

7. CONCLUSION

In a certain sense, the simplest definitions of applied linguistics remains that it is what applied linguists do (Kaplan 1980b). The first applied linguists were linguists who were prepared to give their attention to language-related problems outside linguistics. Now applied linguists are being created by taking graduates, usually with subsequent experience as a teacher or in some other profession, and giving them a broad training in a number of disciplines, of which linguistics is the inescapable core.

With this broad multidisciplinary background, applied linguists, working in a number of different domains, help to spread awareness of linguistics, the nature of language, and its importance in society. In addition, they constitute a channel for the introduction of concepts unfamiliar to linguists at large. Some of these concepts, as for instance philosophical and cosmological ideas such as social constructivism and self-organization within chaotic events, are likely to affect the nature of applied linguistics, the attitude of applied linguists, and the rate of change within this discipline bridging between science and the humanities.

NOTES

1. This is, of course, a complex and vexed question. Like anthropologists, applied linguists should not become involved in the affairs of the people whose language(s) and language needs are being studied; yet, when an applied linguist proposes a language plan or a teaching method, or a set of teaching materials, s/he is by definition becoming involved in the affairs of the people receiving the recommendations. A language plan may advocate the use of some language(s); a methodology may be based on some set of assumptions alien to the culture in which it will be introduced, and a set of teaching materials may mask a set of cultural practices unacceptable to the people being taught. An applied linguist can only act within the constraints of his/her knowledge and beliefs; s/he must strive not to do harm to the target population. In sum, s/he must behave in as ethical a manner as possible and must be prepared to deal with unexpected and undesirable consequences.

The following annotated bibliography provides the basis for a clear understanding of the link between applied linguistics and language teaching over the past quarter century. The editors take the view that applied linguistics is much more than that relationship, and rightly so, but there is little question that no larger understanding of applied linguistics is possible without taking account of that relationship.

ANNOTATED BIBLIOGRAPHY

Allen, J.P.B., and S.P. Corder (eds.) 1973–1977. The Edinburgh course in applied linguistics. Vol. I, Readings for applied linguistics, 1973; Vol. II, Papers in applied linguistics, 1975; Vol. III, Techniques in applied linguistics, 1974; Vol. IV, Testing and experimental methods, 1977. Oxford: Oxford University Press.
These four volumes established a framework for postgraduate studies of applied linguistics in relation to language teaching. Although the pace of recent developments means that *The Edinburgh Course* is now somewhat dated, it remains an excellent overview of the field.

Brown, H.D. 1987. *Principles of language learning and teaching.* 2d ed. Englewood Cliffs, NJ: Prentice-Hall.
More recent than Allen's and Corder's Edinburgh Course, but filling only a single volume. Brown's *Principles* provides a good summary, with copious quotations, of current applied-linguistics views on language teaching.

Crystal, D. 1987. *The Cambridge encyclopedia of language.* New York: Cambridge University Press.
A remarkable work of reference and a mine of information about matters concerned with language, languages, and linguistics, compiled from a broad applied-linguistics perspective.

van Ek, J.A., and L.G. Alexander. 1980. *Threshold level English.* New York: Pergamon Press. [For the Council of Europe Modern Languages Project]
The first and most influential of the "threshold levels" published for most languages of Europe. Having identified as its target the adult worker needing a language for pur-

poses of work and leisure, the book specifies the situations for which language is needed, the language functions to be covered, and the notions that the learner will need to express. The language forms for each of these are given, together with a lexicon and grammatical inventory for English. *T-level English* is a unique source book for the textbook writer.

Halliday, M.A.K., A. McIntosh, and P. Strevens. 1964. *The linguistic sciences and language teaching*. London: Longman.
Addressed to language teachers with little or no knowledge of linguistics, the book was one of the first to attempt a broad survey of how phonetics and linguistics (the "linguistic sciences" of the title) could make a contribution to the improvement of language learning and teaching.

Howatt, A.P.R. 1984. *A history of English language teaching*. New York: Oxford University Press.
Less restricted than its title might suggest, this book is an excellent treatment not just of the historical development of English-language teaching and applied linguistics, but of the main threads of intellectual development also. It includes a valuable monograph on H.E. Palmer; his grounding in the Reform Movement of nineteenth century–language teaching, and his apprenticeship in academic phonetics under Daniel Jones, laid the foundations for Palmer's remarkable contribution to the understanding of language teaching. His work predated modern linguistics, but Howatt shows that Palmer's career provided continuity of thought from the end of the philological era to the beginning of applied linguistics.

Kaplan, R.B., ed. 1980. *On the scope of applied linguistics*. Rowley, MA: Newbury House.
Although only a slim volume, this is a good introduction, by one of the American founders of the discipline, to the attitudes of AL and the range of topics applied linguistics covers. The contributors include many of the leading figures in applied linguistics.

Kaplan, R.B. et al., eds. Since 1981. *Annual Review of Applied Linguistics*. New York: Cambridge University Press.
Published annually since volume one in 1981, this series of publications provides an authoritative picture of the extension of evolution of applied linguistics, with articles on the major themes written by leading specialists. *ARAL* is the principal source book on applied linguistics for the past decade. Volumes one (1981), five (1985), and ten (1990) offer broad surveys of the entire field; volume two (1982) takes as its theme "Language and Language-in-Education Policy"; volume three (1983), "Written Discourse"; volume four (1984), "Literacy"; volume six (1986), "International Bilingual Communities"; volume seven (1987), "Language in the Professions"; volume eight (1988), "Communicative Language Teaching"; volume nine (1989), "Second-Language Acquisition."

Mackey, W.F. 1965. *Language teaching analysis*. London: Longman.
Mackey's seminal work provided the first attempt at a comprehensive and usable analysis of the language teaching/learning process. It was written early in the history of applied linguistics, but it remains an invaluable source of reference today.

Richards, J., and T. Rodgers. 1986. *Approaches and methods in language teaching: A description and analysis*. New York: Cambridge University Press.
While this book is concerned largely with the methodology of language teaching, and in particular with teaching English as a second or foreign language, its standpoint is an

intellectual one, and it looks closely at the historical roots and origins of the profession, in ways that are consonant with applied linguistics. The book considers the various competing methods and approaches in use today, but each "is considered in terms of its links to more general linguistic, psychological, or educational traditions."

Rivers, W. 1981. *Teaching foreign language skills.* 2d ed. Chicago, IL: University of Chicago Press.

Following her earlier book, *The psychologist and the foreign language teacher* (1964), Rivers became one of the most influential leaders in applied linguistics, and this book is among her most valuable publications, written, as they all are, with the realities of the classroom always in mind.

Savignon, S. 1983. *Communicative competence: Classroom practice and theory.* Reading, MA: Addison-Wesley.

Savignon, another leading American AL specialist, has concentrated on the promotion of language teaching as a communicative activity; her orientation, and that of the series in which this volume appears (Addison-Wesley's *Second Language Professional Library*), falls squarely within the domain of applied linguistics. This book provides a wide-ranging introduction to the field for the language teacher.

Savignon, S., and M. Berns, eds. 1984. *Initiatives in communicative language teaching.* Reading, MA: Addison-Wesley.

This is a volume in the same series as Savignon (1983), and complements that work with a range of chapters on different aspects of language teaching seen from an AL standpoint. (The term *communicative* does duty in these two books, as it frequently does in the work of American researchers, as a synonym for *applied linguistics.*)

Spolsky, B. 1989. *Conditions for second language learning: Introduction to a general theory.* New York: Oxford University Press.

This important work proposes 74 minimal conditions that are relevant to language learning. In so doing, Spolsky's book illustrates all the main features of applied linguistics: it looks pragmatically at the central question (of how foreign/second languages are best learned); it takes theory as an inescapable basis for the solution; and it makes use of theoretical ideas from several disciplines, including linguistics, in proposing a solution.

Steele, R., and T. Threadgold, eds. 1987. *Topics in language: Essays in honor of Michael Halliday,* 2 vols. Philadelphia, PA: John Benjamins.

The 68 articles in these two volumes provide a state-of-the-art conspectus of the entire field of AL. It is unusual for a Festschrift to be a major work of reference, but this one is, and is a tribute to the personal influence of Halliday, whose contributions to AL go back to the earliest days of the Edinburgh School of Applied Linguistics.

Stern, H.H. 1983. *Fundamental concepts of language teaching.* New York: Oxford University Press.

This monumental work by the late David Stern is a repository of wisdom and knowledge addressing both theory and practice. It presents the learning and teaching of languages from an applied-linguistics standpoint.

Strevens, P.D. 1977. *New orientations in the teaching of English.* New York: Oxford University Press.

The main sections of the book deal with principle and theory in language teaching, methodology and teacher training, English for specific purposes, and varieties of

English, including British and American English. The 'new orientations' throughout are those of applied linguistics.

Widdowson, H.T. 1979. *Explorations in applied linguistics.* New York: Oxford University Press.

Widdowson, H.T. 1984. *Explorations in applied linguistics 2.* New York: Oxford University Press.

These two volumes are by one of the leading theorists in applied linguistics, and they display intellectual vigor in discussing most of the current issues in applied linguistics. There are few more challenging or convincing AL texts than these two books.

QUESTIONS FOR FURTHER DISCUSSION

1. Given the long history of the relationship between applied linguistics and language teaching, particularly second-language teaching, and given the emergence of several paradigmatic changes relating to language testing and second language–acquisition research in the recent past, what might be the predicted relation between applied linguistics and language teaching in the future? Are there any trends that might help to develop this relationship?

2. Why is it that applied linguistics as a field study should develop independently in two English-speaking countries at approximately the same period in time?

3. Lexicography, translation, and speech therapy are not typically considered "mainstream" domains of applied linguistics. Why might this be the case? Why should these fields be seen as domains of applied linguistics?

4. How is the SEASPEAK project a good example of applied linguistics?

5. Why does Strevens make use of the notion of social construction, the recent findings in physics, and the study of nonlinear systems as arguments to develop a theoretical basis for applied linguistics?

6. How does Strevens' concept of "domain of applied linguistics" tie in with the discussion of applied linguistics as an interdisciplinary field in the introduction?

7. How is Strevens' perspective on applied linguistics distinct from that set forth in the introduction?

8. In what ways does Strevens' chapter extend the discussion of training applied linguists as presented in chapter 14, by Grabe and Kaplan?

9. Compare the views of applied linguistics expressed by Davies (chapter 7) and by Strevens; note that Strevens does not include testing as one of his domains of applied linguistics.

10. Strevens does not discuss computer-assisted instruction or the use of computers at all. On what grounds might the editors have decided to include in this volume a chapter devoted to computer uses?

An Introduction to
Applied Linguistics and Linguistics

Linguistics is the eponymic discipline of applied linguistics—an obvious statement perhaps, but the connection is too often minimized in applied-linguistics training programs. Two consequences arise as a result. First, linguistics tends to look on applied linguistics as a field without a theoretical foundation; second, applied linguists are often trained to distrust the seeming irrelevance of linguistic theory for their more practical concerns and needs. Both consequences are unfortunate. Applied linguistics, if anything, suffers from too much theoretical foundation rather than too little, drawing on theory from psychology, education, anthropology, and sociology, as well as linguistics. Applied linguists, then, may choose to emphasize other research perspectives above current theoretical linguistics. The danger in this is the misperception that linguistics is treated too minimally by applied linguistics generally, and the more accurate perception that certain applied-linguistics training programs do not emphasize linguistic research sufficiently. The second consequence (related to the first) is that applied linguistics perceives theoretical linguistics as offering little in the way of practically useful knowledge. While it is the argument of Grabe's chapter that such is not the case, there are, nonetheless, enough reasons for this perception to be held by some applied linguists.

This chapter argues that such perceptions are too narrowly conceived. Linguistics, in fact, is a vast terrain with many contending notions and theoretical orientations. Linguistics is far from being a united discipline with the basic ground rules for participation already sorted out. Rather, linguistics offers many options for applied research, and many branches or theories of linguistics are strongly oriented to the resolution of practical language issues. Through an overview of the various major approaches to linguistics, this chapter highlights the many ways in which linguistics and applied linguistics come together productively. It also argues strongly that linguistics is the eponymic discipline of applied linguistics for good reason. There would be little of importance in the work of applied linguistics if linguistics itself were ignored. Linguistics has much to offer to applied linguistics. It is for the applied linguist to be aware of these offerings and use them in the most appropriate contexts. But the point must be made that the relationship between applied linguistics and linguistics is symbiotic.

There are many accounts and overviews of the field of linguistics. In each case there is necessarily a bias evident in the telling of them. For some writers, the bias is toward a particular theory or orientation to the study of linguistics. For others, it is the bias to stress the importance of a particular subfield of research. This chapter, it is fair to say, is little different in this respect. In this case, the bias is toward the potential of linguistic theory for application to real-world uses. It is also entirely reasonable that this chapter, if written by another applied linguist, would stress different issues and pieces of research. In fact, a comprehensive treatment of the topic would require its own book. Nevertheless, because Grabe's overview is quite broad, attention is given to a wide range of theories, issues, and points of contention. It needs to be recognized that linguistics has many branches and theories, and that each has important insights of offer. Grabe's chapter strongly emphasizes such a view.

Applied Linguistics and Linguistics

William Grabe
Northern Arizona University

Linguists don't seem to know where they've come from, so how can they know where they're going.

—An anonymous rhetorician

1. INTRODUCTION

The rapid growth of the field of applied linguistics over the last twenty years has led to a general observation that applied linguistics must be viewed as an interdisciplinary field; indeed, it is probably impossible to do applied linguistics without incorporating expertise from some related discipline, be it anthropology, psychology, education, sociology, psychometrics, or some other field. The role of linguistics itself in applied linguistics has, however, at times been underestimated. It makes little sense to maintain such a designation as *applied linguistics* without recognizing the centrality of the core discipline. The fact that such a relation has come into question at all suggests the sometimes less-than-ideal interaction between the divisions of the field. This question is further magnified by the many competing fields and research theories within linguistics and the sometimes-strident debates accompanying the competition.

It is the purpose of this chapter to sort out the various theories within linguistics and to provide an overview of linguistics as it relates to concerns of applied linguistics. This overview will begin with a brief history of twentieth-century linguistic research and will subsequently review the various areas within linguistics as they relate to concerns of applied linguistics. It should also be noted at the outset that it is not the goal of this chapter to provide specific descriptions of the various theories mentioned; rather, the goal is to provide a sort of map to help the reader understand where linguistics has been, how it has influenced applied linguistics, and the direction or directions in which applied linguistics may nudge linguistic theory in the future. This overview will therefore be a sketch of main events and personalities; of course, the true history of modern linguistics is much more complex. It is the task of other books and course work to expand on this history, explain the specific theories, evaluate them, and comment on their applications (e.g., Horrocks 1987; Newmeyer 1988a–d; Bright, forthcoming).

2. HISTORICAL BACKGROUND

Modern linguistics necessarily begins with the work of Ferdinand de Saussure and his *General course on linguistics* (1916). His systematic structural approach to language has been a foundation for virtually all of linguistics since that time. The central continuing notion is that language is a closed system of structural relations; meanings and grammatical uses of linguistic elements depend on the sets of oppositions created among all the elements within the system. To take a simple illustrative example, *slush* is a notion that depends on the existence of terms such as *rain* and *snow* for its specific meaning and use—it is understood because of its opposition to the other terms. In addition, de Saussure introduced distinctions such as synchronic (at a single specific time) vs. diachronic (historical) analyses of language, and *langue* vs. *parole* (cf. competence vs. performance). These latter two influential notions evolved from the structural assumptions on the nature of language. de Saussure's work had a powerful impact on various structural-linguistic groups that emerged across Europe, including the London School of Linguistics, the Geneva School of Linguistics, the Copenhagen School of Linguistics, and the Prague School of Linguistics (cf. Robins 1989; Sampson 1980).

The Geneva School and the Copenhagen School gradually waned, though for different reasons (cf. Lamb's stratificational grammar 1966; Robins 1989; Sampson 1980). The Prague School and the London School are still important sources of linguistic research, and both have had a considerable influence on later developments in American linguistics. The Prague School, begun in 1926, provided the foundations for most later phonological theory and created the now commonplace notion of *distinctive features* in their analyses. They also explored functional uses of language in sentences and discourse and had a significant impact on Chomsky's later theories through Roman Jakobson. The London School was primarily the product of J.R. Firth, who in 1944 became the first professor of linguistics in Great Britain. Based on a tradition of anthropology and of functional approaches to language use (in particular, on Malinowski's anthropological research), Firth proposed a systemic linguistics which made major contributions to phonetics and phonology as well as to the study of language use in its situational context. Firth trained Halliday (as well as many other leading British linguists), who later developed systemic linguistics into a major approach to language analysis. Through Halliday's work, the London School is also currently having a profound effect on work in applied linguistics.

2.1. Growth of American Linguistics

American linguistics has been historically central to the emergence of the discipline generally as synchronic descriptive research on many languages received its greatest academic support and research funding in the United States. The growth of American linguistics began when European anthropological linguists arrived in North America to study and record native-American languages before many of those languages disappeared. The leading figure in this migration was Franz Boas, who first came to North America in the 1880s. Boas established American descriptivist linguistics and trained the leading American structural linguists, in particular Sapir and Bloomfield. Sapir, with perhaps the most enduring legacy of these early scholars, wrote a highly influential book, *Language* (1921), which foretold many of the assumptions guiding current linguistic research. It was Bloomfield, however, who has had the most immediate impact on American linguistics.

Bloomfield wrote a book, also called *Language* (1933), which profoundly changed the course of American linguistics for the next 30 years. Bloomfield combined insights from anthropological linguistics with the then-pervasive views of behavioral psychology and with philosophical empiricism and positivism, to develop American Structural Linguistics, a linguistic theory that dominated American research from the mid-1930s to the mid-1960s. The anthropological influences were seen in the -etic/-emic distinctions in data collection and analyses (externally- vs. internally-oriented analyses), in the primacy given to oral language, in the assumption that all languages are equally complex and of equal value, in the assumption of endless diversity among languages, and in the emphasis on field-research methods.

Psychological emphases appeared in the beliefs that the mind began language learning as a *tabula rasa*, a blank slate, that only what was observable could be used as evidence—intuitions and semantic evidence would be misleading and unreliable—and that there could be developed a mechanical discovery procedure for doing linguistic research. Philosophical positivism and empiricism also led Bloomfield and others (e.g., Markwardt, Fries, etc.) to influence language teaching in accordance with the research findings of scientific linguistics. Thus Bloomfield was a strong proponent of the new basal reading series; Fries applied structural linguistics to the development of both first- and second-language teaching (including audio-lingual approaches; cf. the chapter by Morley in this volume); and Markwardt wrote "scientifically based" linguistic grammars for freshman writing students in U.S. universities.

The strong dominance of American structural linguistics was finally challenged in the mid-1950s by a young linguist named Noam Chomsky.

2.2. Generative Linguistics

Chomsky's theories represented, and still represent, both a strong break with American structural linguistics and, at the same time, a basic continuity with ideas traceable back to de Saussure and beyond. The major changes introduced by Chomsky's theories were:

1. To challenge basic discovery procedure for linguistic research deriving from behavioral assumptions;
2. To reject the belief that language acquisition is habit formation;
3. To include intuitions and semantic information as admissible linguistic data;
4. To center linguistic research on syntax;
5. To reject an item-arrangement approach in favor of an item-process approach (e.g., with transformations and the assumption of a deep-structure syntactic level);
6. To devise a set of criteria for evaluating competing grammars; and
7. To propose as the goal of linguistic research the search for linguistic universals, the discovery of which could then represent arguments for the biological predispositions that humans appear to have to learn language structure.

At the same time, Chomsky retained the structuralist notion of language as an internally defined system, as well as the basic phrase-structure approach to syntactic analyses and the categorization of language units in traditional parts-of-speech units (e.g., nouns, noun-phrases, verb-phrases, etc.). In his book *Syntactic structures* (1957), Chomsky first outlined his theory, which he later solidified in *Aspects of the theory of syntax* (1965). In this second work, which became known as the "standard theory," Chomsky first devoted considerable time to the notions of competence and performance (what a speaker knows about language vs. how a speaker performs at any given moment using the language), arguing that the appropriate goal of linguistic research lies in explaining linguistic competence. The effort to account for a speaker's linguistic competence points to a very different level of description for a grammar. Instead of presenting relevant examples of major construction types in a language and a list of exceptions, now the goal of a grammar was to describe every potential sentence of a language and rule out all ungrammatical sentences (or to answer the question: What is it we know when we know the grammar of a language?)

This goal of explaining linguistic competence is closely related to Chomsky's arguments for a generative theory—a theory which proposes that humans are able to generate a potentially infinite number of sentences by means of a finite system of well-definable rules. A linguistic theory that is psychologically based must capture such an insight, and Chomsky's goal of explaining linguistic competence was intended to capture the generative capacity of human language—*how* we can generate all and only the grammatical sentences of a language, and *what* explicitly defined rule systems combine to create such a grammar. He also developed his ideas on language universals by proposing a universal grammar (UG), a possible set of underlying principles and constraints on language applicable to the learning of any natural language. Finally, he argued that his theory had psychological reality; the components of the standard theory in some way described the mental representations of the language-processing mechanisms.

The claim of psychological reality, proposed in the early 1960s, provided a strong impetus for the field of psycholinguistics (language processing and first-language acquisition). Through the late 1950s and 1960s, processing experiments were designed to test the transformational derivations of sentences from deep structure to surface structure, as well as to provide tests of constituent structure (Garnham 1985; Greene 1972). This pursuit of language processing was also fueled by the need for MIT-based linguists (colleagues and followers of Chomsky) to carry out numerous investigations of machine translation and artificial intelligence for which they had received grants (which explains why the linguistics department at MIT began as a component of an engineering department; cf. Newmeyer 1986). By the early 1970s, however, psycholinguists interested in language processing broke away from Chomsky's theory and focused their attention on general cognitive strategies to explain language processing. This break is emblematic of the tumultuous period in American linguistics from the late 1960s to the late 1970s.

The broad acceptance of the standard theory by the late 1960s also led to a number of related linguistic theories that were more semantically (rather than syntactically) based. In the standard theory, Chomsky has introduced semantics as an important component of the grammar. A number of researchers combined the importance of semantics with the idea of syntactic deep structure to propose that language is initially generated from a semantic (or logical) deep-structure level. This fundamental change led to theories of "case grammar" (Anderson 1977; Cook 1981; Fillmore 1968, 1977; cf. Gruber 1976; Jackendoff 1972) and "generative semantics." For almost a decade, generative semantics was quite popular since it was based on an intuitively appealing notion. However, such an approach quickly became unmanageable; deep-structure trees became wildly abstract, and transformational rules multiplied daily. It soon became apparent that this theory provided little constraint on what anyone could propose as an addition to the theory.

2.3. Current Generative Theory

Chomsky quickly recognized the limitations of early semantic-based approaches, and from the late 1960s to the late 1970s, he argued for a theory of grammar that was first known as the "extended standard theory" (Chomsky 1975; Jackendoff 1972; Newmeyer 1986), and later as the "revised extended standard theory" (Chomsky 1977a, 1977b). Chomsky's goals were to focus on the conditions and constraints that influenced grammatical structure generally—to restrict the power of theoretical grammar so that it would conform to these conditions and constraints operating on language (and not allow endless specific ad-hoc rules), and to explore fundamental principles underlying language structure rather than to describe particular transformational rules (operating on particular constructions); the more generally applicable a principle would be, the more powerful constraint it placed on the form that any grammar could have. The overall research goal was to restrict the power of the grammar so that rules could not be added endlessly for essentially arbitrary reasons. If Chomsky were to work toward the goal of UG, he would need a theory that was potentially learnable by a child, not a theory with an endless list of different deep structures and transformations. Since learnability concerns represented a major motivation for UG, a theory of grammar would have to be sufficiently constrained so that a child would be able to construct the right grammar based on the available environmental evidence. The revised extended standard theory of the late 1970s managed to cut away much of the transformational superstructure and uncovered principles with broad application cross-linguistically. However, there were serious shortcomings in the theory, as it had retained many assumptions and ideas from earlier versions while trying to incorporate newer insights (Horrocks 1987).

In 1979 Chomsky departed from the revised extended standard theory (REST) in a series of lectures known as the Pisa lectures. The general theory to emerge became known as "government-and-binding" (GB) theory and was first presented in book form in *Lectures on government and binding* (1981). This major revision of his approach to grammar was an attempt to account for principles and conditions on language in general within a framework that could explain the outlines of UG and also provide a learnable grammar for child language acquisition. Chomsky wanted to develop a grammar that would not only describe the language competence of adults, but would also explain why language competence has the particular framework that he proposes.

A brief description of this now current theory is necessary since it is having a profound impact on second-language acquisition research, as well as on general linguistic theory. Chomsky retained the notion of deep structure and transformations, though the set of transformational rules was reduced to one generally applicable rule named "move alpha" (i.e., all constructions and language-specific conditions were done away with). The rule simply states "move anything to anyplace" (commonly discussed in terms of two complementary transformations, NP-movement and WH-movement). The conditions and constraints operating on the grammar, however, interact in such a way as to rule out all but the appropriate movements allowed in the grammar (of any language). The maintenance of a transformational level still provides an elegant way of explaining long-distance relations in syntactic structures. For example, how it is possible to understand that a WH–question word originated in a perceived gap somewhere lower down in a complex sentence and to account for this intuition. Thus, in the following sentence, a transformation of WH-movement helps to link the WH-word at the beginning with the gap occurring later in a subordinate clause.

(a) The man thought [I was going to find *what* in the closet]?

(b) *What* did the man think [I was going to find ____ in the closet]?

A strictly surface-structure grammar has difficulty explaining how a speaker intuits the relations between the WH-word and the perceived gap.

In the current government and binding theory, the deep-structure level still retains a lexicon (the mental listing of morphemes and words) and a minimal framework of phrase-structure rules (X-bar theory), as well. The major difference from previous versions of Chomsky's theory lies in the superposition of a set of general systems of principles that operate at deep- and surface-structure levels to determine the grammaticality of every sentence generated by the system. Chomsky outlines seven such systems of principles: government theory, binding theory, bounding theory, theta theory, case theory, control theory, and X-bar theory (Horrocks 1987; Newmeyer 1986).

The truly radical departure in this current theory is that these principles represent general parameters that allow some variation in how they work in different languages (parametric variation). They may be seen as universal principles operating in all natural languages and thus become the basis of Chomsky's theory of UG. The larger claim is that these sets of principles, since they are universal to the human species, are not consciously learned anew by children; rather, they are given as biological predispositions that begin to operate appropriately when they develop and when children are given enough exposure to a natural language. It should be pointed out that Chomsky does not claim that everything speakers know about language is biologically predisposed; only certain general principles that seem to help organize all natural languages are so predisposed. (Further discussions and introductions to this theory are readily available; e.g., Chomsky 1986, 1988; Cook 1989; Horrocks 1987; Newmeyer 1983, 1986; Radford 1980, 1988; Reimsdyk and Williams 1986; Sells 1985.)

Much as Chomsky's theories in the 1960s generated competing grammars, so have his theories of the late 1970s. Two theories in particular are providing strong competition: *generalized phrase-structure grammar* (GPSG) and *lexical-functional grammar* (LFG). Both theories center around the basic problems of how to explain long-distance relations in sentences (e.g., the relation between the fronted WH-word and the perceived gap lower in a complex sentence); how to generate all and only the grammatical sentences (e.g., generative capability); and how to provide a good account of grammatical relations cross-linguistically. GPSG and LFG each give rise to a different initial set of assumptions. Both argue that deep structures and transformations are unnecessary; rather, they argue, a theory of grammar should be developed by reference only to the surface structure ("what you see is what you get"). Each theory then moves in a different general direction. GPSG creates a more complex system of phrase-structure rules with a set of formal interpretive principles and a more complex lexicon as another way of accounting for long-distance relations in sentences (cf. *head-driven phrase-structure grammar*). LFG instead chooses to expand the power of the lexicon greatly and attributes much structural information in sentence building to the particular lexical items themselves. In brief, then, one theory elaborates the phrase-structure rules to take the place of transformations; the other elaborates the lexical entries to take the place of transformations. A major strength of both theories is their computational adaptability to processing models. Since they are surface-structure grammars with only one structural level of representation, they are more easily converted to computer applications. Unfortunately, this very adaptability may mean that both theories are more formally grounded than GB, and less directly related to natural-language data than GB (complex introductory discussions are given in Horrocks 1987 and Sells 1985). While these three generative theories have moved closer together in recent years, it is not appropriate to consider them variations of a single general theory (McCloskey 1988).

Before leaving formal generative theories of syntax, it is important to note that these theories are exerting important influence on other areas of formal linguistics. Phonology and morphology have been influenced (both directly and indirectly) by changing syntactic theory (Newmeyer 1988). Recently, morphology has become an increasingly important concern in syntax, as syntactic theories attempt to incorporate highly inflectional languages into their general theories of grammar. For example, how does a theory of government and binding handle a language like Navajo, in which so much grammatical information is signaled by various prefixes and suffixes, and in which a complex verbal form could translate into an entire sentence in a minimally inflectional language like English (cf. Baker 1988).

Semantics has also undergone significant changes in the last fifteen years. From its origins in philosophical logic, it has now been steadily growing as an important component of current theories such as GB, GPSG, and LFG. In the 1970s most linguists were not as concerned with the semantic component, and most semantic research proceeded somewhat independently (e.g., Montague grammar: Dowty, Wall, and Peters 1981; Partee 1976; logical-types semantics: Keenan and Faltz 1985; situational semantics: Barwise and Perry 1983; cf. Ladusaw 1988). In the 1980s the incorporation of semantics as an important component of grammar has meant changes in semantic theories, and currently these theories are in a state of flux. The major point, however, is that semantic integration into modern syntactic theories will continue to increase in the near future (Enç 1988; May 1985).

The research field of psycholinguistics has also been greatly influenced by the generative theories of the 1980s. From their dissatisfaction of the early 1970s, researchers interested in language processing have become more interested in the translation of current theories into processing models for both comprehension and production. In its turn, psycholinguistics is now providing additional evidence for the nature of grammatical organization and adding important constraints on the possible form of grammatical theories (Carlson and Tannenhaus 1988; Garnham 1985; Tannenhaus 1988). Research on language acquisition is also providing additional sources of information about generative grammatical theories. In government-and-binding theory, the claim for language learnability as a criterion for the explanatory adequacy of a grammar is a major focus of certain acquisition research (Hyams 1986; Pinker 1989; Roeper 1988).

3. DESCRIPTIVE SYNTAX

The descriptivist approach initiated by de Saussure and developed in the United States under Boas did not disappear with the rise of the behavioristically oriented American structural linguistics. In Europe, synchronic descriptions of English were developed by Jesperson, Curme, and Poutsma in the 1920s and 1930s. In the United States, many anthropological linguists continued descriptive research on native-American languages (e.g., Sapir, Whorf), with the behavioristically oriented linguists representing only part of the range of research, though the most influential at the time. Many of these linguists were not drawn into generative linguistics, and instead either pursued research as part of typological or functional linguistics (e.g., Greenberg 1966; cf. section 4 below), or contributed to the development of sociolinguistics (e.g., Gumperz and Hymes 1964; cf. section 5 below). In Great Britain, the descriptive tradition continued in the 1950s and 1960s with the work of Palmer and Quirk. Much of the British descriptive research was applied to dictionaries and pedagogical reference grammars, two enterprises that greatly influenced language standards and language instruction at all levels.

During the late 1960s and early 1970s, these British grammarians/linguists developed major corpuses of the English language which were used, in turn, as resources for an extremely influential modern descriptive grammar of English, *A grammar of contemporary English*. A number of other shorter volumes resulted from this research as well. A second version of the grammar, *A comprehensive grammar of the English language,* appeared in 1985. In the last ten years, these volumes and this line of linguistics research have taken on greater importance on both theoretical and practical levels. The use of language corpuses to create grammars that are based primarily, or solely, on usage represent a strong reaction to purely intuitive data collection and research. In part, this reaction has been motivated by the fairly unusual sentence data used in generative-linguistic arguments—sentences that were marked by a grammaticality that was difficult to assess, and that were unlikely to be uttered in any case. Descriptive grammars of the type developed from corpus data filled a void left by generative grammars for grammatical reference materials that could be used by many other researchers in education, sociolinguistics, psychology, etc.

At the present time, this line of linguistic research is becoming more popular as the use of computers in analyzing the corpuses increases. Sociolinguistic research comparing oral and written varieties of language make extensive use of descriptive grammars (e.g., Biber 1988). Lexicographers and grammarians base their dictionaries and reference grammars on the results of corpus data bases, particularly in England (Leech and Beale 1985; Sinclair 1987). A considerable amount of computational linguistics in Europe is devoted to analyses of English linguistics based on results of corpus data and involve descriptive explanations of the data that provide new insights into the English language (various issues of ICAME journal, Aaarts and Meijs 1984; Garside et al. 1987; Johannson 1982; Meijs 1987).

4. FUNCTIONAL AND TYPOLOGICAL THEORIES

An outgrowth of descriptivist traditions in the United States and of Halliday's systemics in Great Britain and Australia, functional theories of grammar have never left the stage, though they had been pushed to the side in the United States for a long time. The most consistent proponent of a functional grammar, one which explains its central role in communication and its adaption to this purpose, is Halliday's systemic functional theory (e.g., Halliday 1985). Language has been adapted to the needs of humans to communicate, and grammars reflect this adaptation. For Halliday, each language element chosen plays a meaningful role in furthering communication in that its choice represents a binary decision not to say something else. The systemic aspect of his theory is this set of binary (branching) choices through every subsystem (Berry 1975; Butler 1985c). The functional aspect of his grammar is best captured by the division of grammar into ideational, interpersonal, and textual components and by his typology of language uses (instrumental, regulatory, interactional, personal, etc.).

From the beginning, Halliday insisted on incorporating discourse concerns into his theory, since an explanation of grammar without an account of how language is actually used seemed pointless, and dysfunctional, to him (a reason to consider his approach an essentially sociolinguistic perspective). One of the great current appeals of this theory, particularly for applied linguists, is the emphasis on discourse and language function in actual use (as opposed to a theory that distinguishes competence from performance). It would be impossible to give an adequate description of his theory here. There have been a number of recent descriptions of this theory that are accessible introductions, and that should indicate the relevance of this approach to applied-linguistic concerns (Berry 1975; Butler 1985c, 1989; Fawcett and Young 1988; Halliday 1985; Halliday and Fawcett 1988; Halliday and Hasan 1989; Steele and Threadgold 1987).

Halliday's influence has increased greatly in the last decade as a result of the strong emphasis on discourse and communication now prevalent in applied linguistics (Halliday 1973, 1975, 1978, 1985; Halliday and Hasan 1976, 1989; Halliday, McIntosh, and Strevens 1964; Hasan 1989; Hasan and Martin 1989; Kress 1976), as well as of its compatibility with sociolinguistic research (Kachru 1985a), cognitive-strategy research, composition research (Couture 1986; Martin 1989; Rafoth and Rubin 1988), educational research on emergent literacy (Christie 1989; Fine and Freedle 1983; Glazer 1989; Goodman 1986; Harste, Woodward, and Burke 1984; Jagger and Burke-Smith 1985), communicative approaches to language teaching (Brumfit 1984; Brumfit and Johnson 1979); and computer-programming applications for natural discourse (Benson and Greaves 1985a, 1985b; Mann and Thompson 1986, 1988).

Other functional theories with less applied concerns have developed in the 1970s as researchers, many of whom were trained in generative linguistics, became discouraged by the absence of discourse influences and the abstraction away from communicative functions of language by formal generative theories. Leading functional linguists interested in the shaping influences of discourse include Chafe (1980), Comrie (1988), Givón (1979, 1983), Hawkins (1983, 1989), Kuno (1986), and Thompson (1985). (For accounts of European research on functional linguistics cf. Dik 1978 and Firbas 1986.)

These researchers also form part of a larger group of linguists who investigate linguistic structure from a typological perspective rather than focus on a single major language as the basis of their research. Based primarily on the typological and universals research of Joseph Greenberg and other major American descriptivist linguists of the 1940s to 1960s (Greenberg 1966, 1974; Hawkins 1979, 1983), these researchers study how languages differ from one another, what generalizations may be made cross-linguistically based on the data analyzed, and how universal statements about language structure may be derived from the patterns of typological variation (Comrie 1988; Hawkins 1983, 1989). This approach is not to be equated with Chomsky's universal-grammar perspective.

Among the best known of these universal principles is the accessibility hierarchy of Keenan and Comrie (1977; Comrie 1989; Comrie and Keenan 1979). They arrived at their universal principle after examining data from hundreds of languages, a fairly typical approach for typological linguists. This hierarchy captures the generalization that grammatical relations (such as subject, object, indirect object, etc.) are more accessible to use in constructions, particularly relative clauses in this case, and more productive as they are higher on the scale (SUB > OBJ > IND OBJ > OBLIQUE OBJ > OBJ OF COM-PARISON).

While this group of functional linguists is concerned about discourse, their interest lies primarily in examining how discourse exerts influence on the shape and frequency of occurrence of syntactic constructions in various contexts (e.g., Prince 1988). They are primarily syntacticians and would not call themselves discourse analysts; with the exception of Thompson (Thompson 1985; Mann and Thompson 1988) and Givón (1983), they do not, in general, study discourse structure or propose theories of discourse analysis. Modern Prague School linguists, in contrast, are well known for their research on discourse structure and their theory of functional sentence perspective (see Vande Kopple 1986 for a good overview).

There is one final group of functional linguists who examine how language is used in terms of its pragmatic functions. The primary impetus for this research direction is from research on semantics and the philosophy of language. Beginning with the 'language-use' philosophers, such as Austin (1962), Searle (1969, 1979), and Grice (1975, 1978), research on language semantics has explored how language use creates meanings that are conveyed by the context of utterance more than by the literal meanings of the words. What originated as a challenge to formal truth-functional theories of meaning evolved into a major field straddling linguistics and philosophy. While pragmatics has received considerable support from sociolinguistics, it is primarily a formal approach to language meaning in use (cf. Gazdar 1979; Horn 1988; Kempson 1988; Leech 1986; Levinson 1983; Sperber and Wilson 1986). And while it is a discourse-based research field, it is more constrained by its formal approach to language than is common in sociolinguistics.

5. ANTHROPOLOGICAL LINGUISTICS AND SOCIOLINGUISTICS

A fourth line of linguistic research, pursued mainly in the United States, has led to the emergence of modern sociolinguistics. As already noted, the early history of American linguistics does not follow as neat a linear chronology as might be assumed from the description given in section 2. Again, the development of descriptive research provides the foundation for yet another linguistic approach. In particular, certain anthropological linguists, grounded in European structuralism and influenced by Sapir's later work, expanded their research interests to include the study of discourse uses of language in various social contexts, as well as the study of language change resulting from contact among languages and dialects. In the 1950s, a prominent group of these linguists began to formulate an approach to language which was discourse-based and centered around analyses of speech events and variations in the uses of language in changing contexts. Leading linguists during this time, such as Bright, Ferguson, Fishman, Gumperz, Haugen, and Hymes, became founders of a new research field now known as sociolinguistics.

A major impetus for the then-emerging field of sociolinguistics derived from the reactions of Hymes and others to Chomsky's notion of competence and performance in the 1960s. Responding to the idealization of language data and the limiting of research to the sentence level, Hymes proposed that the real object of linguistic research should be the study of communicative competence; that is, linguists should study how language is performed in different contexts, with different people, on different topics, for different purposes. Writing in the 1960s, Hymes argued that performance-based research agendas should be organized around communicative events and should focus on various aspects of the event, including addressor, addressee, channels, codes, setting, message form, topic, and the event itself (Hymes 1972, 1974).

Other sociolinguists have built upon this foundation, and by the mid-1970s sociolinguistics was recognized as a major alternative discipline to 'formal' approaches to linguistics (phonetics, phonology, morphology, syntax, and semantics). Researchers such as Fasold (1984, 1990), Labov (1966, 1972a, 1972b), Shuy (1979, 1984, 1987a, 1988), and Trudgill (1974, 1983, 1984, 1986) helped define sociolinguistics as the study of language variation and its relations to different social contexts, thus building upon and greatly expanding earlier research on dialect variation and language-contact phenomena. The notion of variation, central to sociolinguistic research, has since been extended to the study of different language use based on age, occupation, gender, situation, relative power, and various languages-in-contact situations.

The mid-1970s also saw the emergence of sociolinguistic research on close discourse interaction. Earlier ethnographic research of this sort was more typically thought of as falling in the domains of anthropology, sociology, and education. Research by Gumperz, Hymes, and others led to the training of scholars identifying themselves as interactional sociolinguists. This line of research examines oral-discourse interaction and focuses on how language use reflects social meaning (as opposed to variation research, which is primarily concerned with how social factors influence specific linguistic forms; cf. Heller 1985). Important scholarly work by Milroy (1980, 1987), Ochs (1988), Philips (1983), Schiffrin(1987), and others has contributed to the growth of interactional discourse analysis. In the 1980s the increasing importance given to social networks (e.g, Milroy 1987; cf. Heller 1985) as a source of explanation for specific linguistic and social behavior provided a bridge between variationist and interactionist research. At the same time, interactional research began to diversify as subfields broke away from the ethnography-of-speaking-umbrella, and as sociolinguists began identifying themselves as ethnomethodologists, conversational analysts, conversational stylists, and generally as discourse analysts.

While most sociolinguists would identify themselves as discourse analysts, there are limitations that they impose on this term. In general, sociolinguists are still not very interested in the study of written discourse, though Chafe (1982, 1985) and his colleagues have devoted considerable research to the comparison of oral and written forms, as has, most recently, Biber (1986, 1988, 1989). Written-discourse analysis has more often been the domain of applied linguistics, European text linguistics, and systemic-functional linguistics. It is important to note that these two views of discourse analysis represent an important indication of the distinction between sociolinguistics and applied linguistics. Written-discourse analysis and the larger question of literacy development is most often seen as a language problem and a language-training issue. Only recently have some sociolinguists decided that questions of literacy development center on the same issues guiding other sociolinguistic research; the variation of language use both influences social processes and depends on social-class origins (Cook-Gumperz 1986; Heath 1983; Stubbs 1980).

While the distinction between sociolinguistics and applied linguistics sometimes appears blurry, and some researchers are seen as both (e.g., Ferguson, Fishman, Kachru, Saville-Troike, Shuy, Tannen, Wolfram, and Wolfson), they are in fact distinct fields. Sociolinguists may investigate socially related language uses that have great importance in terms of language-based problems to be studied, and sociolinguists, like applied linguists, often turn their research in the direction of practical application. One particular area of considerable overlap has been the study of language use in professional contexts. The connection with studying language variation in many professional and occupational contexts is almost invariably tied to certain language-based problems and their resolution. Research in language and the law, language in medical contexts, language and bureaucracy, language in business contexts, language in scientific and technical contexts, etc., all center around problems created by negotiation failure, nondelivery of services, legal misrepresentation, or misunderstanding through miscommunication (Kaplan, et al. 1987). When sociolinguists extend their research in applied directions, it is possible to talk of applied-sociolinguistic research (Trudgill 1984), and the distinction between sociolinguistics and applied linguistics is not clearly defined. At the same time, however, many sociolinguists see themselves primarily as basic researchers examining patterns and generalizable behavior in language in its many social contexts. And much like formal research, the ultimate goal is the furthering of basic knowledge about language rather than the explicit application of research findings to the resolution of language-based problems.

In general, then, there are many research areas that are solely sociolinguistic and other research areas that are solely applied-linguistic in nature. Within sociolinguistics, there is also a modicum of ambivalence about research on certain issues in languages-in-contact phenomena, such as language spread, language maintenance, language shift, and language choice. It is sometimes argued that these fields are more the concern of sociologists and social psychologists than of linguists and sociolinguists. This debate typically centers around the distinction between sociolinguistics, on the one hand, and the sociology of language on the other; this distinction is sometimes discussed in terms of microsociolinguistics vs. macrosociolinguistics as well (Fishman 1980, Wardhaugh 1986). These particular research issues, along with issues of language policy and planning and bilingualism, are studied much more intensely by applied linguists and educational researchers. This is due to the fact that many of these issue are problem-driven rather than theory-driven; that is, these issues manifest themselves as language-based problems which require some resolution. Applied linguists, of course, also explore many areas which are not within the domain of sociolinguistics at all: language teaching and language learning; second- and foreign-language teaching/learning; language testing and evaluation; language therapy, lexicography; translation, etc. It may soon be the case that applied linguists, sociolinguists, and education researchers will move closer on a number of issues tied to language teaching, language learning, and language testing.

6. LINGUISTIC RESEARCH AND APPLIED LINGUISTICS

One might assume from the above description that there are a number of very distinct lines of research that have evolved throughout the twentieth century without significant overlap. In fact, this review has highlighted research distinctions that perhaps exaggerate the differences in some instances. It is the case that certain typological and functional linguists accept the generative goal of accounting for the generation of all sentences in a language, though they are concerned with other issues as well, and may not be as concerned with a learnability criterion as Chomsky is. Sociolinguists, as well, cross over to generative approaches, as indicated by Labov's creation of variable rules following the general format of phonological and syntactic rules in transformational-generative grammars. Sociolinguists often make use of descriptive research as a resource for analyzing their data; in their turn, descriptive researchers make use of sociolinguistic research to explain stylistic variation in their corpus data. Nevertheless, most linguists, if pressed, will express allegiance to one of the four approaches to language analysis described above.

There are other possible approaches that could be added, most notably tagmemic grammar (Pike 1982; Pike and Pike 1982; Robins 1989). While tagmemic grammar developed out of American structural linguistics and does not represent any major innovations of the structuralist base, it has been the major system for describing uncommon languages around the world. Tagmemics has been the primary language-analysis approach used by the Summer Institute of Linguistics (SIL) researchers in their efforts to produce resources for Bible translations in every language around the world (for workers in the Wycliffe Bible Translators movement). Tagmemic theory was also among the few approaches that stressed the importance of discourse analysis, having an impact on American rhetorical theory and the teaching of composition at the tertiary level (Young, Becker, and Pike 1970). While limitations of this chapter preclude technical discussion of this important approach, its contributions to applied linguistics (via discourse-analysis research) have been significant, as have its extensive production of descriptive analyses of uncommon languages (cf. Grimes 1976; Longacre 1983; Sampson 1980).

The four major approaches highlighted in this chapter provide the theoretical basis for most applied-linguistics research. In the many subfields within linguistics (e.g., phonology, morphology, syntax, etc.), each approach has made a contribution of which applied linguists make use. A review of these subfields of linguistics will highlight the pervasive influence of linguistics as the core discipline upon which applied linguistics draws.

6.1. Phonetics and Phonology

Phonetics and phonology have undergone a number of changes over the last 25 years, and phonology in particular has been subject to major theoretical revisions (Basbøll 1988; Beckman 1988; Kaye 1989). Despite these changes, it is the more traditional articulatory phonetics and phonology that still make the greatest contribution to applied linguistics. Transcription of speech is still a major undertaking for oral-discourse analysis of language in the professions, as well as among speech therapists and in certain educational research. Speech problems and rehabilitation needs are still discussed in terms of the more traditional articulatory framework, as opposed to more recent approaches, such as autosegmental phonology, metrical phonology, or the SPE (the sound patterns of English) system (Crystal 1984; cf. Anderson 1985; Goldsmith 1990; and Kaye 1989 for overviews of phonology). Moreover, the traditional articulatory approach is still the basis for most discussion of pronunciation and oral language instruction generally in second-language contexts (Swan and Smith 1987). The situation is much the same in current second-language acquisition research on pronunciation (Hammarberg 1989;

Ioup and Weinberger 1987; James and Leather 1987) and the transcription of oral-language interaction.

6.2. Morphology

Linguistic research on morphology and on the organization of the lexicon (e.g., Anderson 1988) has not initiated any great changes in practical research over the last twenty years. Applied-linguistics research on lexicography, terminology development, second-language acquisition, and language teaching (particularly vocabulary development) is still employing descriptive approaches that have been in use for some time (Carter 1987; Carter and McCarthy 1988; Gass 1989). This state of affairs is not necessarily a problem, since straightforward descriptive terminology is best understood across disciplines and is most transparent for application.

6.3. Syntax

Three approaches to syntax appear to have an influence on applied-linguistics research activities. Chomsky's GB theory has induced a number of second-language acquisition researchers to examine acquisition in terms of possible UG parameters. The goal is to see if, and to what extent, such parameters would play a role in second-language acquisition (cf. Cook 1989; Felix 1987; Flynn 1987, 1988; McLaughlin 1987; White 1989). Chomsky's earlier approaches to syntax are still proving influential in that many introductions to syntax courses in applied-linguistics programs are modification on both past and current Chomskean linguistics (e.g., Baker 1989; Radford 1988). Similarly, other graduate-level texts on syntax combine a transformational approach with a descriptive approach (e.g., Celce-Murcia and Larsen-Freeman 1983).

Descriptive approaches to syntax have had a strong influence on applied linguistics over the last decade, both with regard to the training of graduate students and teachers, and in terms of research. Descriptive research such as that by Greenbaum (1988), Leech (1971), Leech and Short (1981), Leech and Svartvik (1975), Palmer (1986, 1987), Quirk et al. (1972, 1985), Quirk and Greenbaum (1975), and Sinclair (1987a, 1987b) may be considered typical. The descriptive syntax texts have been used for grammar courses and for resource references in language policy and planning—particularly in the development of language standards in schools, in second-language acquisition, in discourse analysis, in computational stylistics, and in lexicography.

The third major syntactic approach having a strong influence on applied linguistics is the functional-systemic approach of Halliday. Many applied linguists have received their basic syntactic training in this approach (particularly in England, India, and Australia) and regularly pass this approach on to their students. Since much linguistic stylistics and literary stylistics is done in

England, this field also has been heavily influenced by the functional-systemic approach. Perhaps the greatest impact of this approach, though, comes in the fields of language arts teaching and written-discourse analysis.

In Australia, Canada, Great Britain, New Zealand, and the United States, the movement to have schoolchildren write from the earliest grades, commonly referred to as the *whole language approach,* has drawn support for its ideas at least in part from the work of Halliday. From his own research on child language learning, and drawing on the research of Basil Bernstein, Halliday (1973, 1978) has argued that children learn language when its use has a meaningful purpose for them. In educational contexts for children, Halliday's explanation that language is learned because it serves functional purposes becomes the basis for early writing and reading. Such an argument translates into providing meaningful learning activities in a context in which all four language skills are regularly practiced, as each contributes in a search for meaning and communication (Enright and McCloskey 1987; Goodman 1986; Haley-James 1981; Harste, Woodward, and Burke 1984; Jagger and Smith-Burke 1984; Rigg and Enright 1986; Strickland and Morrow 1989). A similar influence is felt in educational efforts in Australia and New Zealand to have students use all language skills in the first grades (Clay 1975; Graves 1983; Martin 1989; Walshe 1981).

The second major influence of Hallidean linguistics comes in the area of discourse analysis. Halliday's theory was the first to emphasize strongly the importance of discourse to a theory of language. Both the interpersonal and textual level of his functional grammar focus on discourse and communication. His work on 'theme' and 'rheme' (what introduces a clause, and what follows) and 'given-new' relations in text analysis has been the source of much later research in text linguistics, applied linguistics, and composition research. His work on cohesion with Hasan (1976, 1989) similarly continues to be influential in all fields of written-discourse analysis (e.g., Benson and Greaves 1985a, 1985b; Couture 1986; Fawcett and Young 1987; Steele and Threadgold 1987).

6.4. Semantics and Pragmatics

Semantics, particularly the area of lexical semantics, has been important to applied linguistics. Research in second-language acquisition and lexicography have both used lexical semantics as a resource for research on how words may be related, and on how they differ in various ways. These same concerns become important issues in vocabulary development as well, in both the teaching of language arts and the teaching of second languages. Another area of semantics that has been examined extensively in second-language acquisition contexts is the tense-modal-aspect system in various languages and its influence on learning second languages (Dittmar 1989).

Pragmatics, a historical development out of semantics, has had a much greater impact on applied linguistics, primarily because the issues raised and the theories developed directly inform discourse analysis. While pragmatics can take on formal characteristics (as the area of language meaning not addressed by semantics), many interpretations of pragmatics amount to an exploration of the uses of language in discourse contexts and the study of the intentions of speakers underlying the literal message. Important concepts developing out of pragmatics include speech-act theory, Gricean maxims of conversational management, and the concept of relevance as the overriding criterion in interpreting discourse interaction (Sperber and Wilson 1986).

The term *speech acts* refers directly either to sets of verbs that do things when uttered in the right context (e.g., I now *pronounce* you man and wife; I *sentence* you to ten years hard labor) or to the use of utterances in order to convey messages that are only inferrable from a combination of the context and the literal words (e.g., "there's a fly in my soup" means COMPLAINT: "get me a different bowl of soup"—and don't expect a tip). Gricean maxims are typically presented as:

Quantity—say as much and not more than you need to
Quality—tell the truth
Relevance—stay on the topic
Manner—be clear and direct

These maxims are important not only as principles for conversational management, but also for explaining indirect speech-act inferences through the purposeful violation of particular maxims. For example, a one-line letter of reference consisting of the statement: "Mr. Jones is a friendly person," typically violates the maxim of quantity and becomes a bad reference letter. A more extensive listing of possible conversational principles is proposed in Leech (1983). More recently, the notion of relevance has been proposed by Wilson and Sperber (1986) as the single essential feature of pragmatic message interpretation. In conversation, listeners are compelled to make sense of what a speaker is saying and will attempt to impose a relevant message interpretation on even marginally coherent utterances (cf. discussion of coherence by Brown and Yule, 1983).

7. SOCIOLINGUISTICS AND DISCOURSE ANALYSIS

By far, the most important area of research for applied linguistics is the field of discourse analysis, and the contributions of discourse analysis made by sociolinguists are central. The most powerful foundation for applied research has been the development of the notion of communicative competence. Since it was first introduced by Hymes in the 1960s, it has influenced virtually all areas of applied-linguistics research. For the last ten years, it has been a major focus of language teaching, curriculum design, language testing, classroom-centered research, and the study of language use and language problems in professional contexts (Duran et al. 1985; Canale 1988; Spolsky 1989a; Taylor 1988; Widdowson 1989; Wolfson 1989). The general concept has become the source for most recent language-teaching innovations coming under the heading of communicative approaches to language teaching (Kaplan et al. 1988; Savignon 1983).

In the last decade, efforts have been made to create a definition of communicative competence that would be directly applicable to various sorts of applied research. Canale (1983) proposed an explanation of communicative competence as involving grammatical competence (rules of grammar), sociolinguistic competence (principles of appropriate language use sensitive to different contexts), discourse competence (principles of connected discourse such as cohesion and coherence), and strategic competence (ways to correct communication failure or enhance communication). It is important to state that definitions and explanations of communicative competence are not all compatible, and any assumption of a single notion agreed upon by applied linguists must be treated with some reservations, particularly when language-instruction researchers and materials developers make very strong claims (cf. Hymes 1989; Spolsky 1989a; Widdowson 1989).

Other direct contributions from sociolinguistics to applied-linguistics research include the fields of conversational analysis and conversational style. Both of these research areas developed out of Hymes' ethnography of speaking and represent ways of investigating oral discourse. Conversation analysis includes research on interactional structures such as turn-taking, topic initiation, conversation closing, etc., all of which would come under the heading of ethnomethodology. It also includes research on linguistic features of oral interaction such as tense alternations, discourse markers, and speech acts (Schiffrin 1987, 1988).

Conversational analysis also encompasses research on conversational style, though the topic is often recognized as a distinct area of research. Beginning from Gumperz's research on cross-cultural interaction (Gumperz 1982a, 1982b, 1986), conversational-style analysis has been extended into male-female miscommunication (Tannen 1986), interethnic miscommunication (Tannen 1984), and student-teacher miscommunication (Michaels 1986; Cazden, Michaels, and Tabors 1985). The basic premise of this research is that conversation is made up of many organizing assumptions and principles, most of which are difficult to observe except when communication breaks down for some reason. Then principles may be extrapolated by examining how and why the interactants miscommunicated. Both conversational analysis and conversational style have played important roles in second-language acquisition research in classroom settings (Allright 1988; Chaudron 1988; van

Lier 1988), as well as in the analysis of utterances by naturalistic learners of second languages (Klein 1986; Scarcella 1989).

While oral discourse analysis had been influential in applied linguistics, and particularly in second-language acquisition research, the emphasis on written discourse analysis is even greater. The stress placed on discourse analysis by sociolinguistics, the emphasis given to written discourse analysis by Hallidean functional linguistics, and the emerging interest in language-comprehension research in cognitive psychology have all combined to focus applied-linguistics research on problems and issues in the analysis of written discourse. Prague School research on functional sentence perspective, and given-new relations in discourse has been translated into analyses of written texts and student writing which have provided interesting insights into text organization and writing quality (Vande Kopple 1986; Witte 1983). For example, it seems to be the case that students were judged as better writers when they organized their writing in patterns where given information in sentences (and in the text overall) regularly appeared before newly introduced information in the sentence (Vande Kopple 1986).

A second discourse approach (also applicable to oral language data) used in applied linguistics was developed by the functional linguist Givón and given its fullest treatment in his book *Topic continuity in discourse* (1983). The essential idea is that there are markers in discourse that help the reader maintain the topic of the discourse, or that help a reader recall a topic. For example, the use of a pronoun in a subject position is a weak topic reassertion marker because the topic being referred to is close in the preceding text material. A full noun-phrase as the subject, however, either reasserts a topic from the previous text material which is not as easy to remember, or asserts a new topic for the discourse. This tracking of the subject elements in texts is a mechanism used in discourse to help readers keep to the topic of discourse and recognize new topics when they appear. (See Givón 1984 for applications to second-language acquisition research.)

Another major research tool used by applied linguists in the analysis of discourse is the system of cohesion developed by Halliday and Hasan (1976) and developed into a theory of cohesive harmony more recently (Butler 1989; Cox et al. 1990; Halliday and Hasan 1989; Pappas 1985). Cohesion is due to the system of surface signaling devices in texts that allow the text to hang together and assist the reader in deriving a coherent interpretation of the text. Cohesive devices include pronouns, substitution and ellipsis markers (e.g., so does x, one), definite-article reference to an earlier noun (e.g., he brought a book; *the* cover was torn), repetition, transition devices (e.g., first, next, therefore, however), and lexical collocation. Cohesive harmony is a more recent innovation that combines the analysis of cohesion devices with the continuous reference to major topics in a text (topical chains). The interaction of the two indicates ways in which a reader may develop a coherent interpretation of a given text.

The study of coherence in text has been an elusive though important concept in applied linguistics, as well as in cognitive psychology and composition research (e.g., de Beaugrande and Dressler 1981; Grabe 1985; Johns 1986; Phelps 1985). However coherence is defined, it must include a set of major organizing principles that tend to sort out texts into different types. Kinneavy (1971) argued that such organizing principles ('discourse aims' in his theory) would guide the interpretation of the entire text. Research in text analysis has shown that a notion of this sort does seem to influence the reading of texts, though probably not as strongly as Kinneavy has claimed (cf. Martin 1989). This research on top-level organizing predicates (Carrell 1984; Horowitz 1987; Meyer 1975, 1985) has shown that writing quality and recall of text information depends on the overall signaling of text organization. Similar research in England by Hoey (1983, 1986) has explored how the general organization of a text contributes to the reader's sense of a coherent interpretation.

Another important area of discourse-analysis research in applied linguistics has been the study of contrastive rhetoric. Kaplan (1966) developed this notion in trying to understand how international students speaking different languages could organized their English writing in predictably different ways. Since that time, research has continued to examine the cultural influences on rhetorical patterning (Connor and Kaplan 1987; Grabe and Kaplan 1988; Kaplan 1988; Kaplan et al. 1983; Kaplan and Grabe in press; Purves 1988). One example of this line of research is Hinds' research on differences in expository organization and business letter writing in Japanese and English (Hinds 1983b; Jenkins and Hinds 1987).

A final area in which discourse analysis is having a major impact on applied linguistics lies in language-based problems in professional contexts (Kaplan et al. 1987; Maher, in this volume). Whether there is a problem in the training of scientists in English as a second language, in equal access to legal rights, in appropriate provider care in medical clinics, in securing government-welfare or social-security assistance, or in understanding failures during business negotiations, applied linguists rely heavily on the research tools and concepts developed for discourse analysis, some developed by applied linguists, some by sociolinguists, some by functional linguists, some by composition researchers, some by education researchers, and some by cognitive psychologists. Research in discourse analysis is now at the heart of applied-linguistics research, reflecting the need to examine real language use and its varying situational contexts and purposes.

8. CONCLUSION

The purpose of this chapter has been to provide an outline of linguistic research and indicate the various areas where linguistic research has had a direct and ongoing impact on applied linguistics. It should be evident from this discussion that linguistics, generally speaking, is indeed the core discipline for applied linguistics, even if formal research theories appear to have less to offer than functional linguistic theories and sociolinguistic research. And while there are strong arguments for maintaining a distinction between linguistics and applied linguistics—a distinction that should be evident from the extensive interdisciplinary contacts in applied-linguistics research—there is an equally strong argument for viewing linguistics as *the* major resource for applied-linguistics research. By extension, applied linguists must be trained linguists. At the same time, this chapter has demonstrated that linguistic training is considerably diverse, and the mix of different training and research approaches available to applied linguistics makes linguistics an almost inexhaustible source of ideas that can be applied to the resolution of language-based problems in the real world.

SUGGESTIONS FOR FURTHER READING

Since the purpose of this chapter has been to acquaint readers with the wide spectrum of linguistic research that can be called upon in applied-linguistics activities, its primary goal is to lead the reader to further sources in all areas of linguistics. At the same time, it is possible to recommend readings which will provide a broad foundation in linguistics as a starting point from which to move on. General introductions to linguistics that are accessible include Akmajian, Demers, and Harnish 1984; Crystal 1987; Finegan and Besnier 1989; Fromkin and Rodman 1986; O'Grady et al. 1989; and Robins 1989. Broad introductions to sociolinguistics (e.g., Chaika 1988; Fasold 1984, 1990; Wardhaugh 1986; Wolfson 1989) and discourse analysis (e.g., Brown and Yule 1983; Saville-Troike 1989; Stubbs 1983; Wardhaugh 1985) are also readily accessible. First introductions to psycholinguistics (Garnham 1985), language acquisition (Bennett-Kastor 1988; Fletcher and Garman 1986; Foster 1990), and applied psycholinguistics (Oakhill and Garnham 1988; Perera 1984; Rosenberg 1987) also add important linguistic information. Finally, a thorough overview of linguistics from an applied-linguistics perspective is offered in Stern (1983).

QUESTIONS FOR FURTHER DISCUSSION

1. Why should an applied linguist be conversant with current theory in linguistics?

2. Is it also the case that a general linguist ought to be aware of the current issues in applied linguistics? Why or why not?

3. Does second-language acquisition (SLA) research fall within the concerns of applied linguistics? of general linguistics? of both? of neither? Comment on what Strevens has to say about SLA research.

4. Why has language testing moved away from both general linguistics and applied linguistics? See comments in the essays by Davies, Kaplan, Grabe, and Strevens.

5. Grabe shows the gradual evolution of the TG theory. Have any of the stages of this theory contributed importantly to applied linguistics? Which? How?

6. Compare Chomsky's theoretical conceptualization with that of Halliday and suggest which has had the greater influence on applied linguistics and why.

7. Why wouldn't it be possible for an individual to be a successful applied linguist without ever studying any formal linguistics?

8. Should a competent language teacher have a good basic knowledge of linguistics? Why or why not? If so, then how much?

An Introduction to
Second-Language Learning

Both Kaplan and Morley point out that a number of questions have driven applied linguistics through most of the twentieth century, and that changing answers to these basic questions account for the pendulum swings in language teaching and learning. The questions involve the nature of language, the grounds for choice of what to teach, and the problem of how to teach what has been chosen. There is, however, a different set of questions that is equally important. Teachers are intuitively aware that there appear to be major differences among individuals with respect to the relative ease with which they learn. Quite a lot of effort in recent years has been invested in the successful language learner. In part, this interest has been stimulated by the shift from the teacher-centered to the learner-centered classroom, but it has also been stimulated by the assumption that, if the behavior of the good learner can be analyzed, then aspects of that behavior may be inculcated into less successful learners, thereby improving their language-learning skills. The research in this area has followed a number of different models. McLaughlin and Zemblidge first review a number of approaches that include explorations of intelligence, personality characteristics, cognitive styles, and motivation and attitude. They look carefully at first-language influence in second-language learning, showing along the way that much research on second-language learning has been influenced by developments in first-language research, and giving particular attention to the studies of acquisition sequence and their relation to notions of universal grammar; they also review the pidginization hypothesis.

The second half of the chapter is devoted to the development of an argument for the cognitive approach—an approach that sees second-language learning as the acquisition of a skill marked by the development of automaticity and the ability to restructure information (that is, to improve organization of it). This is quite different from earlier approaches oriented to 'person variables.' And the authors argue for the integration of studies of the internalization of procedural knowledge with studies of natural acquisition sequences, thereby avoiding the problems implicit in the assumptions of deterministic, biologically determined and specified rules for language learning.

The determination of how and why individuals learn either first or second languages is central to the concerns of applied linguistics. Such knowledge to a large extent underlies the specification of what parts of a language can be taught and determines to a significant degree how the identified parts of a language can be taught. It is possible that the cognitive approach advocated by McLaughlin and Zemblidge can eventually help to short-circuit some of the current concern about diversifying instruction for specific audiences, if the approach can isolate general learning strategies that would apply to a variety of student populations. Should further research support the notion that adult second-language learning is less like child first-language learning and more like other adult modes of skills acquisition, that information would have important implications for syllabus development for adult second-language learners (cf. Yalden 1987).

Second-Language Learning

Barry McLaughlin and John Zemblidge
University of California, Santa Cruz

1. INTRODUCTION

Second-language learning is a critical task for millions of immigrants in the United States, Europe, and developing countries. In recent years, an increasing number of researchers have directed their attention at the question of how individuals acquire a second language. People working in this field are convinced that what they are doing is important: the economic and social well-being of a great many people throughout the world depends to a considerable extent on how well they learn a second language.

Historically, a variety of disciplines have been involved in research on second-language learning. Initially, the field was dominated in the United States by educators concerned with questions of teaching and learning languages. This tradition continues, although in recent years most of the research appearing in journals and presented at professional meetings has been concerned with more linguistic issues. Presently, developments within the area of cognitive science are beginning to influence the field of second-language research.

2. FIFTEEN YEARS OF SECOND-LANGUAGE RESEARCH

As we know it today, the field of second-language research dates from the early 1970s. For the last fifteen years, a number of issues have been dominant. A brief sketch of some of these issues follows. More detailed treatment is available in Brown (1987), Ellis (1985), Kaplan et al. (1989), McLaughlin (1987), and Spolsky (1989).

2.1. Factors Influencing Language Learning

A traditional area of concern in second-language research is the question of why some individuals seem to learn languages with apparent ease and others have great difficulty. This has been formulated as the "good language learner" question; what are the characteristics of good language learners that distinguish them from others? A number of variables related to this question have received attention in the literature.

Some researchers (e.g., Carroll 1981; Pimsleur 1966) have argued that intelligence is an important predictor of language-learning aptitude. However, intelligence appears to play a greater role in analytic and literature-oriented courses than it does in more audio-lingual and practically oriented courses (Carroll 1981). This suggests that it is more the method of instruction and evaluation than the task itself that demands a higher level of intelligence for success.

Another set of factors that have been studied relates to personality characteristics. For example, it has been suggested that empathy, defined as "a process of comprehending in which a temporary fusion of self–object boundaries permits an immediate emotional apprehension of the affective experience of another" (Guiora, Brannon, and Dull 1972: p. 116), is directly related to language-learning ability. Similar claims have been made for freedom from inhibition (Guiora et al. 1972a), self-esteem (Heyde 1977), extroversion (Chastain 1975), and spontaneity (Oskarrson 1975). In each of these cases, however, the results have been mixed. What relationships exist seem to be small and unreliable, in large part because of the weakness of the measurement techniques used to assess these personality variables (McLaughlin 1980).

The same is true of variables of cognitive style. Claims have been made for a relationship between successful second-language learning and tolerance of ambiguity and field independence (Naiman et al. 1978). The data, however, show correlations only with some aspects of second-language learning and only for some learners. Strong and consistent relationships are lacking.

The work of Gardner and Lambert (1972) on motivation and attitudes has perhaps had the greatest impact on theory and teaching. These investigators concluded that a critical distinction could be made between two general classes of motivation for language learning: "integrative" motivation and "instrumental" motivation. Integrative motivation, based on positive attitudes toward the target-language group and the desire to integrate oneself into the culture of the target-language group, was seen as strongly related to successful second-language learning. In contrast, if a person attempts to learn a language to attain some instrumental goal—to obtain a job, pass an examination, etc.—the prognosis is not as good.

Other investigators have conducted numerous studies on integrative and instrumental motivation, and the conclusion of this research is that for some learners, in some contexts, integrative motivation is predictive of success, but for other learners, in other contexts, instrumental—and not integrative—motivation is predictive of success (Brown 1987). Furthermore, second-language learning is rarely motivated by only one of these supposedly dichotomous variables. The dichotomy is a theoretical one that is rarely so clear-cut in individual cases.

In general, research on the factors that lead to successful second-language learning has produced disappointing results. A central problem has been the difficulty of measuring the affective or cognitive variables thought to predict success. The notion of stable personality type, independent of situational contexts, is itself disputable. Finally, there is the question of the possibility of developing a model of the good language learner that is sufficiently complex to incorporate all relevant variables. In the last decade or so, researchers have taken a different tack. The trend in more recent research—as we shall see shortly—is to examine language learning *as a process*, and to investigate the strategies that learners employ that lead to success.

2.2. The Influence of the First Language

In the early 1970s, as the field of second language learning began to engage the energies of an increasing number of investigators, there was a great deal of excitement about research findings and their bearing on instructional practice. This early work came as a reaction to the behavioristic-structuralist position. The traditional doctrine stressed the role of transfer from the first language. The language learner, like any other learner, was thought to build up habits— old habits interfering with the acquisition of new ones. There was increasing evidence, however, that led some researchers to conclude that transfer from the first language played a minor role in second-language acquisition.

Specifically, researchers found that contrastive analysis did not predict what errors learners made in acquiring a second language. Contrastive analysis, based on linguistic comparisons of languages, both overpredicted and underpredicted the difficulties of second-language learners. It overpredicted because learners made errors that could not be explained on the basis of transfer between languages.

The evidence for these statements came from the examination of learners' errors. For example, Dulay and Burt (1972, 1974a) found that the majority of errors that children made reflected the influence of the target second language more that the influence of the child's first language. Data from Spanish-speaking children who were learning English showed that the majority of errors were developmental in nature—that is, most errors were of the type that monolingual children make when they are acquiring English (Dulay and Burt 1972). Studies of adult subjects (e.g., George 1972; Lance

1969) also indicated that errors based on first-language constructions were relatively infrequent, and that many errors were like those made by mono-lingual children acquiring the target language.

However, it became clear that it is difficult to be certain precisely what type of error a second-language learner is making, or why the learner makes it (Schachter and Celce-Murcia 1977). A particular error can sometimes be attributed to developmental mistakes found in monolingual speakers and also to transfer from the learner's first language. Indeed, this may not be an either–or proposition: there is evidence that some errors are the result of the inter-action of both factors (Andersen 1978).

Hakuta and Cancino (1977) noted that researchers who have found a predominance of developmental errors in a second-language learner's corpus usually score the omissions of high-frequency morphemes—such as nouns and verb inflections and the verb to be—as developmental errors. Because transfer errors often involve large constituents or changes in world order, Hakuta and Cancino maintained that the relative opportunity of occurrence of the two types is not equivalent. Furthermore, it may well be that second-language learners simply avoid certain linguistic structures in which they would be likely to make errors (Schachter 1974). It is conceivable that such avoidance tendencies reflect structural differences between their first lan-guage and the target language. The rejection of contrastive analysis by re-searchers such as Dulay and Burt now appears to have been premature. Re-search on transfer has led to a richer and more sophisticated view of the goal of contrastive analysis (Zobl 1983, 1984). It has become apparent that both the target language and the first language affect the course of interlanguage de-velopment.

2.3. First and Second Language Compared

Much second-language research has been influenced by developments in first-language research. As more became known about how children acquire their first language, researchers and practitioners in the field of second-language acquisition began to ask how the findings of first-language research and theory applied to their field. One "spin-off" of first-language research were the so-called morpheme studies based on the work of Roger Brown (1973). Brown had found that children learning English as first language follow a common "invariant" sequence in the acquisition of fourteen functor words— such as noun and verb inflections, articles, auxiliaries, copulas, and preposi-tions. In a number of studies of children, Dulay and Burt (1973, 1974b) found that second-language learners, regardless of their first language, followed a similar developmental sequence.

Dulay and Burt (1973, 1974b) used the Bilingual Syntax Measure (Burt, Dulay, and Hernandez-Chavez 1975) to elicit speech samples from children of different ages and linguistic backgrounds. Even though the various groups differed in their exposure to English, they showed roughly the same patterns in their use of the functors in obligatory contexts. These patterns were similar, but somewhat different, from the pattern Brown had observed in monolingual children. Dulay and Burt attributed the differences to the difference in cognitive abilities of children at various stages of their development.

Research with adult subjects (Bailey, Madden, and Krashen 1974; Larsen-Freeman 1975) indicated that the pattern in the use of functors obtained in cross-sectional studies of children was found for adults as well. Although there were differences due to the subjects' first language and the types of tasks they were engaged in (Larsen-Freeman 1975), the variation was generally not marked enough to obscure the common pattern in the accuracy order. Statistically significant correlations were found between learners from various first-language backgrounds, suggesting a ("natural-order") developmental sequence common to both first- and second-language acquisition.

It was not long, however, before this conclusion was challenged. Serious methodological flaws were found in the research showing similar developmental sequences in first- and second-language acquisition, and new research indicated that transfer from the first language does play a role in second-language acquisition. Another criticism of the morpheme studies is that the findings were not, strictly speaking, related to acquisition sequence, but rather to accuracy of use. Critics noted that the studies were cross-sectional in nature and measured the percent of times subjects of different ability levels supplied morphemes correctly in obligatory contexts. Thus, this research examined accuracy at one point in time, rather than acquisitional sequences across time. Furthermore, several longitudinal studies have yielded orders of acquisition that did not correlate with the orders of accuracy of use obtained in cross-sectional research (Hakuta 1976; Huebner 1979; Rosansky 1976).

The trend in current research is not to look for similarities in first- and second-language acquisition, but to look for the unique aspects of second-language development. For example, the followers of Chomsky have adapted ideas from his recent writings and applied them to second-language phenomena. Terms such as bounding nodes, pro-drop parameters, and preposition stranding have begun to appear in the literature.

Contemporary Chomskyan theory, or universal-grammar theory, argues that there are parameters in every language that have to be fixed according to the particular input data of the given language. These parameters describe the characteristics of the language, and the learner's task is to discover which of the various options pertain to the target language. The rules of a grammar may be marked or unmarked, according to their degree of complexity. Unmarked rules are thought to be less complex than marked. The interlanguage of the language learner is thought to be constrained by universal grammar, and there is some evidence that second-language acquisition proceeds by mastering the

easier unmarked properties before the more difficult marked ones (Mazurkewich 1984). There is also evidence to suggest that, when the second-language
rule is marked, the learner will turn to the first language, especially if it has an
equivalent unmarked rule (Flynn 1983). For a fuller treatment of these issues,
the reader is referred to Cook (1985, 1989) and McLaughlin (1990). Critiques of
the universal-grammar approach can be found in Bley-Vroman and Chaudron
(1988) and in Clahsen and Muyskens (1989).

   Thus, developments in contemporary linguistics have led some researchers to make predictions about the ease of acquisition of various constructions.
The question driving this research is no longer the question of the relationship
between first- and second-language development, but that of how a given
second-language learner, with a specific first language, learns to set the parameters for the target language.

2.4. The Process of Second-Language Development

We would like to turn now to another approach to second-language learning.
In the late 1970s and early 1980s, concerted research attention began to be
given to the social context of adult second-language learning. This work has
generally come to be known as the acculturation approach. Schumann (1978b),
for example, argued that the degree to which a learner acculturates to the
target-language group will determine the extent to which that person acquires
the second language. In this view, acculturation—and hence second-language
acquisition—is a function of the social and psychological "distance" between
the learner and the target-language culture. Social distance is the result of a
number of factors: (1) domination vs. subordination; (2) assimilation vs.
adaption vs. preservation, enclosure, size, congruence, and attitude. Psychological distance is the result of various affective factors that concern the
learner as an individual. (These factors would include resolution of language
shock, culture shock and culture stress, integrative vs. instrumental motivation, and ego permeability.)

   Schumann (1978a) argued that the early stages of second-language acquisition are characterized by the same processes that are responsible for the
formation of pidgin languages. When there are hindrances to acculturation—
when social and/or psychological distance is great—the learner will not
progress beyond the early stages of acquisition of the target language, and his
or her interlanguage will stay pidginized. Schumann documented this process
in a case study of a 33-year-old Costa Rican immigrant, Alberto. As a member
of a group of Latin-American working-class immigrants, Alberto was seen as
socially and psychologically quite distant from the target-language group. He
showed very little linguistic development during the course of a nine-month
longitudinal study. His interlanguage was characterized by many simplifications and reductions:

1. Use of the general preverbal negators: 'no,' 'don't'
2. No question inversion
3. Lack of auxiliaries
4. No inflection of possessives
5. Use of unmarked forms of verbs

Schumann saw these simplifications and reductions to be a form of pidginization that leads to fossilization when the learner no longer revises the interlanguage system in the direction of the target language.

Further evidence for the acculturation hypothesis was reported by the Heidelberg Research Project for Pidgin German (1976). In this project, 48 Italian and Spanish immigrant workers were studied as they acquired German without formal instruction. The investigators developed an index of syntactic development that was in turn related to several social factors: leisure contact with Germans; age upon entering Germany; contact with Germans at work; length of education; mother tongue; and sex. Each of these variables except the last two was significantly related to language development, age yielding a negative relationship. Leisure contact with Germans was found to have the highest correlation with syntactic development, suggesting that social proximity is a critical factor.

Two members of the Heidelberg group (Dittmar 1982; Klein 1981) reported on the speech of a Spanish immigrant worker who had been living in West Germany for five years, but whose knowledge of German had fossilized at a rudimentary level. Like Schumann's Alberto, this learner had very limited social contacts with native speakers. His language had the following characteristics:

1. Extensive use of the general preverb negator: "nicht"
2. No use of copulas
3. No use of auxiliaries with the infinitive
4. Active language based mainly on nouns; few function words
5. No use of inflection

These simplifications and reductions are similar to those Schumann found in his subject, and were seen by these investigators as evidence of a similar process of pidginization.

Another German research project studying immigrant workers, the Zweitspracherwerb italinerischer und spanisher Arbeiter (ZISA) project, also attempted to link social-psychological and linguistic aspects of second-language development. These researchers (Meisel 1980; Meisel, Clahsen, and Pienemann 1981) argued from their data that there was no single path to second-language acquisition. They advocated a multidimensional model in which groups of learners form different paths to the target language. In this model, the learner's position relative to the target language is defined by two dimensions: the learner's developmental stage and the learner's social-psychological orientation. The developmental stage is defined on the basis of linguistic criteria, but within a stage learners may differ because of their social-psychological orientation. Specifically, Meisel (1980) proposed that learners vary along a continuum that ranges from a segregative to an integrative orientation, depending on how favorably they are disposed to speakers of the target language.

Thus, a learner whose social-psychological orientation is segregative may have attained the same level of syntactic development as another learner whose social-psychological orientation is integrative. The segregative learner, however, is more likely to fossilize at that level than is the integrative learner, who has a better chance of learning the target language well. The advantage of the integrative learner comes from the use of different learning strategies. Whereas segregative learners are more likely to use an early strategy that involves the omission of elements and morphology, integrative learners are more inclined to formulate and correct hypotheses about the rules that apply in the target language and hence make greater progress.

To summarize, second-language researchers working in the acculturation framework are alike in their emphasis on the role of social and psychological factors in second-language development. Fossilization occurs in naturalistic adult second-language acquisition because of a combination of social and psychological factors relating to acculturation. The common theme in this work is that acculturation is a determining variable that controls the level of success achieved by second-language learners.

3. THE COGNITIVE APPROACH

At this point we would like to turn to a relatively new approach to second-language learning, one that derives from developments in the field of cognitive psychology. Although most writings and research on the role of cognitive processes in second-language acquisition have appeared in the last few years (e.g., Hulstijn and Hulstijn 1984; McLaughlin, Rossman, and McLeod 1983; O'Malley and Chamot 1989; Pienemann and Johnston 1987a; Segalowitz 1986), many of the ideas were anticipated by Levelt in an article that appeared in 1978.

From the cognitive perspective, second-language learning is viewed as the acquisition of a complex cognitive skill. To learn a second language is to learn a *skill* because various aspects of performance must be practiced and integrated to achieve fluent performance. This requires the automatization of component subskills. Learning is a *cognitive* process because it is thought to involve the internal representations that regulate and guide performance. In the case of language acquisition, these representations include procedures for selecting appropriate vocabulary, grammatical rules, and pragmatic conventions governing language use. Performance improves through the constant reorganizing and restructuring of information contained within the internal representation. This allows the language learner to simplify and unify linguistic information, and to gain increasing control of language behavior (Karmiloff-Smith 1986). These two notions—automatization and restructuring—are interdependent and are central to the cognitive perspective.

3.1. The Routinization of Skills: Automaticity

The acquisition of the skills involved in any communication task involves the assessment and coordination of information from a multitude of perceptual, cognitive, and social domains. The speaker must communicate the intended message unambiguously and must learn to obey a large number of conversational conventions. Such a task requires the integration of a number of different skills, each of which must be practiced and routinized to reduce the processing load.

Several researchers (Hasher and Zacks 1979; LaBerge and Samuels 1974; Posner and Snyder 1975; Schneider and Shiffrin 1977; Shiffrin and Schneider 1977) have conceived of the difference in the processing capability necessary for various mental operations in a dichotomous way: either a task requires a relatively large amount of processing capability, or it proceeds automatically and demands little processing energy. Furthermore, a task that once taxed processing capability may become, through practice, so automatic that it demands relatively little processing energy.

Following Shiffrin and Schneider (1977), we refer to the two processing modes as *automatic* and *controlled processing*. Automatic processing involves the activation of a learned response that has been built up through the consistent mapping of the same input to the same pattern of activation over many trials. Because an automatic process utilizes a relatively permanent set of associative connections in long-term storage, most automatic processes require an appreciable amount of training to develop fully. Once learned, an automatic process occurs rapidly and is difficult to suppress or alter. the second mode of information processing, controlled processing, is not a learned response, but a temporary activation of a response sequence under attentional control of the subject. Because attention is required, only one such sequence can normally be controlled at a time without interference. Controlled processes are thus capability-limited and require more time for their activation. The advantage of controlled processes is that they are relatively easy to set up, alter, and apply to novel situations.

In order to function effectively, humans develop ways of organizing information. Some tasks require more attention; others, which have been well practiced, require less. The development of any complex cognitive skill involves building up a set of well-learned, automatic procedures so that controlled processes will be freed up for new tasks. In this way, limited resources can be spread to cover a wide range of task demands. The notion of a capability-free (automatic) process provides an explanation for improvement in performance. Because human learners are limited in their information-processing abilities, only so much attention can be given at one time to the various components of complex tasks. When a component of the task becomes automatized, attention can be devoted to other components of the task and a previously difficult or impossible task becomes possible.

3.2. Restructuring

There is more to learning a complex cognitive skill than automatizing subskills. The learner needs to impose organization on information that has been acquired. As more learning occurs, internalized cognitive representations change and are restructured. This restructuring process involves operations that are complementary to those involved in gaining automaticity.

In acquiring complex skills, such as those involved in using second languages, learners devise new structures for interpreting new information and for imposing a new organization on information already stored. Cheng (1985) has proposed that improvement in performance results from a restructuring of the components of a task, so that they are coordinated, integrated, or reorganized into new units, thereby allowing the procedure involving the old components to be replaced by a more efficient procedure involving new components.

The most detailed treatment of the restructuring process has been provided by Karmiloff-Smith (1986), who argued that children and adults attack new problems by going through the same recurrent phases. Phase one is data-driven; components of the task are mastered, but there is no attempt at overall organization. Organization is imposed at phase two when behavior is dominated by "organization-oriented procedures," which result from the learner's attempts to simplify, unify, and gain control over the internal representation. Phase three involves the integration of data-driven, bottom-up processes that guide phase one and the internally generated top-down processes that guide phase two. This integration results from the restructuring at work in phase two, which, once consolidated, can take environmental feedback into account without jeopardizing the overall organization.

Restructuring occurs because learners go beyond the success of phase one and attempt to control and link previously isolated procedures into a unified representational framework. As Karmiloff-Smith states:

> my argument has been that the human organism (both linguistic and cognitive) incorporates a drive to have control not only over the external environment (the input stimuli) but also, and importantly, over its own internal representations and finally over the intricate interaction between the two. (1986:175)

Once the procedures at any phase become automatized, become consolidated, and function efficiently, learners step up to a "metaprocedural" level that generates representational change and restructuring.

3.3. Research on Automaticity and Restructuring in Second-Language Learning

We would like to turn now to some research evidence for the processes of automaticity and restructuring in the second-language literature. A number of studies have been discussed elsewhere (McLaughlin 1987); here we will discuss two examples. As we mentioned earlier, there has been a long tradition of concern with the "good language learner" in second-language research. Most research in this tradition has looked at person variables—intelligence, personality, cognitive style, and attitudes—as they relate to success in second-language learning. In a more process-oriented study, Nation and McLaughlin (1986) decided to examine the way in which the performance of multilingual subjects on a language-learning task differs from the performance of persons who have had less experience with languages. Anecdotally, at least, once a person has learned several languages, the process of language learning becomes easier.

Nation and McLaughlin (1986) carried out an experiment in which they compared information processing in multilingual, bilingual, and monolingual subjects learning a miniature linguistic system. They wanted to see how "expert" language learners (multilingual subjects) compared in their performance with more "novice" language learners. Subjects were asked to learn a miniature linguistic system under conditions in which they were merely exposed to the system without instructions to learn it (implicit learning), or under conditions in which they were told that the system was rule-based, and that they should learn the rules (explicit learning). Multilingual subjects were found to learn the grammar significantly better than bilingual or monolingual groups when the instructions call for "implicit" learning, but not when the instructions called for "explicit" learning. Nation and McLaughlin argued on the basis of error patterns that the superior performance of the multilingual subjects on the implicit-learning task is the result of better automated letter- and pattern-recognition skills, and of greater flexibility in exploring different routines and heuristic strategies. Similar results were found in another study using a miniature artificial linguistic system; Nayak, Hansen, Kreuger, and McLaughlin (1989) found that multilingual subjects showed more flexibility in switching strategies than did monolingual subjects. Such cognitive skills, rather than personality variables, were seen to characterize "the good language learner."

The second study involves research that bears on the notion of restructuring. It comes from work done on adult second-language reading. McLeod and McLauglin (1986) analyzed the errors of beginning and advanced ESL students reading aloud in English and found that the errors that beginning ESL students made were primarily nonmeaningful, which was seen to be due to these students' focusing on the graphic aspects of the text. Their command of the syntax was also not secure enough to allow them to make accurate predictions in reading, as evidenced by a cloze test. Advanced ESL students were significantly better at making predictions on the cloze test and made significantly fewer errors in reading than did the beginning students. However, there were no differences between advanced students and beginning students in the proportion of meaningful errors in their reading.

Successful readers interact actively with the test—adding, deleting, and substituting words where appropriate. They use the cues available to seek the most direct path to meaning, drawing on prior conceptual and linguistic competence to predict what might plausibly come next. A number of authors have made the point that fluent reading requires going beyond the "mechanics" of the reading process, which involves attention to graphic and orthographic information, to extracting meaning from words (e.g., Gibson and Levin 1975; Goodman 1968; Smith 1971). Some poor readers apparently have mastered the mechanical aspects of reading, but continue to process the text word by word, not using contextual semantic relations and syntactic information to comprehend meaning (Cromer 1970).

McLeod and McLaughlin argued that this was the problem that the advanced ESL students in their study were having. Analysis of the errors they made indicated that they were not utilizing semantic and syntactic cues as well as they could have. They were not approaching the task as a "psycholinguistic guessing game," a process in which graphic cues are used to make predictions about what the printed text means—even though the evidence from the cloze test suggested that they were quite capable of making such predictions. Their increasing syntactic and semantic competence enabled them to make nearly twice as many accurate predictions as the beginners on the cloze test. Yet they had not applied this competence to their reading behavior.

It seemed that the advanced subjects had not yet reached the point in their reading performance where restructuring occurs. That is, they were using old strategies aimed at decoding in a situation where their competencies would have allowed them to apply new strategies directed at meaning. Their performance on the cloze test indicated that they had the skills needed for "going for meaning." Presumably they read this way in their first language. But they had not yet made the shift (restructured) in their second language. In this language, they did not make strategic use of the semantic and syntactic knowledge at their disposal.

To summarize, there is evidence from some recent research that the cognitive approach is a fruitful line of investigation to pursue phenomena of second-language learning. In all likelihood, this approach will become more popular in the coming years as researchers begin to explore in more depth the process (as opposed to the product) of second-language learning. However, we would not argue that this approach provides the whole answer.

4. CONCLUSION

Many authors in the field of second-language research are convinced that learners follow acquisitional sequences, and that these sequences are determined by the nature of the internal linguistic system. The second-language learner's utterances are seen to be a natural outcome of the internal system. Thus, universal-grammar theory stresses the regularity in learners' acquisitional processes and postulates that language learners approach the task endowed with innate, specifically linguistic, knowledge that is biologically determined and specialized for language learning.

Rather than stressing internal, predetermined linguistic processes, the cognitive approach focuses on the internalization of procedural knowledge that accounts for how learners accumulate and automatize rules, and on how they restructure their internal representations to match the target language. Within this framework, it is possible to incorporate natural acquisitional sequences if one assumes that some acquisition involves the development, in predictable sequences, of routines that are already automatized when they emerge (Sajavaara 1978). Thus, it would be necessary to posit two acquisitional routes: (1) a route that is highly determined by linguistic constraints, that is predetermined and automatic, and that follows natural acquisitional sequences; and (2) a route that is not determined, but that requires automatization through controlled processing. Such an assumption provides a way for a cognitive approach to deal with the constraints of linguistic phenomena. In a similar vein, Felix (1987) has proposed that the principles of universal grammar are available to the adult second-language learner, but that they are highly constrained by more general cognitive processing strategies.

We believe that such an integration of a cognitive and a linguistic perspective is necessary if we are to come to grips with second-language phenomena. By itself, for example, the cognitive approach cannot explain such linguistic constraints as are implied in markedness theory, or that may result from linguistic universals. These specifically linguistic considerations are not addressed by an approach that sees learning a second language as involving the acquisition of a complex cognitive skill.

Learning a second language does involve the acquisition of a complex cognitive skill, but it involves the acquisition of a complex linguistic skill as well. Thus, a cognitive approach is only one way of looking at language learning. It becomes more powerful if it is complemented by linguistic research. For example, understanding the process of restructuring is a central concern of contemporary cognitive psychology, but a more thorough understanding of restructuring in second-language acquisition requires the analysis of linguistic data. Thus, the work of Bickerton, Schumann, Stauble, and others on restructuring in decreolization and late second-language learning enriches our understanding of the linguistic details of the restructuring process.

Similarly, an account of transfer phenomena requires linguistic considerations. From a cognitive perspective, transfer occurs because the speaker has incorrectly activated an automatic routine based on the first language. Such errors occur because learners lack the necessary information in the second language or the attentional capability to activate the appropriate second-language routine. But such an account says little about why certain linguistic forms transfer and others do not. Here a theory of markedness may generate detailed predictions that are more specific than the cognitive account, which does not make predictions that are as explicit about when transfer will occur.

Finally, there are social-psychological considerations. It goes without saying that language learning takes place in a social context. No account of second-language learning is complete without consideration of the learner's attitude and motivation. As Meisel (1980) has pointed out, different attitudes toward the target language can drastically affect the course of language development. Language cannot be separated from its social matrix. We need this perspective, just as we need the linguistic and the cognitive perspective, if we are fully to understand second-language learning.

SUGGESTIONS FOR
FURTHER READING

There have been quite a number of recent volumes on second-language acquisition; most notable among these are: Beebe 1988; Ellis 1985; Kaplan et al. 1989; Klein 1986; Krashen 1985; McLaughlin 1984, 1985, 1987; Scovel 1988b; Spolsky 1989b; and White 1989. An extensive range of research publications is available in the Newbury House *Second Language Research* series. Second-language acquisition from a bilingual perspective is presented in: Cummins 1986; Edelsky 1986; Goldman and Trueba 1988; Hakuta 1986; Homel et al. 1987; and Vaid 1986. A number of journals are primarily devoted to second-language acquisition, including: *Language Learning, Studies in Second Language Acquisition, Second Language Research, Applied Linguistics,* and *NABE Journal.* Other journals that regularly publish research on second-language acquisition include *Applied Psycholinguistics, TESOL Quarterly, Modern Language Journal, Canadian Modern Language Review,* and *Foreign Language Annals.*

QUESTIONS FOR
FURTHER DISCUSSION

1. Discuss how the various research models involving person variables (e.g., intelligence, personality characteristics, cognitive styles, motivation, attitude) have had

an effect on teaching methods and approaches. It may be useful to look at the chapter by Morley to recall the various contemporary approaches.

2. Several contributors to this volume have suggested that the so-called humanistic approaches do not have an anchor in either linguistic or learning theory. Is there anything in McLaughlin's and Zemblidge's survey of person-variable approaches that can supply a theoretical basis for the humanistic approaches?

3. Is there any argument implicit in McLaughlin's and Zemblidge's survey of the research that might explain why transformational generative grammar has not made a significant contribution to language teaching?

4. Can such notions of automaticity and restructuring be worked into language teaching syllabi?

5. What is the relationship between the notion of automaticity as developed by McLaughlin and Zemblidge and the earlier notion of "overlearning" that is part of the audio-lingual method?

6. Do McLaughlin's and Zemblidge's reservations about Schumann's pidginization hypothesis have important implications for syllabus specifications?

7. What kinds of error analysis seem to emerge as useful from McLaughlin's and Zemblidge's discussion? Would such error analysis be of use in other areas of applied linguistics?

8. McLaughlin and Zemblidge posit certain assumptions about bilingual individuals. Compare those assumptions with the ones in the chapter by Macias.

An Introduction to
Current Directions in Second-Language Teaching

As both Strevens and the introduction to this volume point out, applied linguistics grew out of a concern for language teaching and language-teacher training. While applied linguistics has been substantially restructured and expanded over the past twenty years, it has an abiding interest still in language teaching. Within applied linguists' concerns with language teaching, there have also been significant changes. The audio-lingual method (ALM) has fallen into some disrepute, though it persists in many areas of the world, and a variety of other approaches and methodologies have been developed and have challenged its place. There has been a gradual and important shift from an emphasis on teaching and a teaching-centered classroom to an emphasis on learning and a learner-centered classroom, and there has been a shift from a focus on structure to a focus on communication. In some instances (e.g., some of the so-called humanistic approaches and natural language learning), the focus on the learner may have gone to an extreme, advocating perhaps too much control of course context by the student.

ALM may be said to have represented the still center of the pendular movements among methodologies. It offered a teaching approach fully synchronous with a compatible linguistic theory and a comparable learning theory (structuralist linguistics and behaviorist psychology, respectively). In more recent years, there has been a proliferation of teaching approaches ranging from some that have no clear anchor in either linguistic theory or learning theory, to others that are more heavily dependent on one or the other or both.

The concern in the development of language-teaching theories has been with several basic questions:

1. What is language, and how can it best be described?
2. How do learners learn, and what do learners need?
3. On what grounds is it possible to select what is to be taught?
4. How is the selected material to be taught and learned?

As the answers to these questions have gradually changed, owing to paradigm shifts in learning theory and in linguistic theory, there have been radical swings of the pendulum in language teaching. At present, important work in research on second-language acquisition, in ethnographic research into the events that occur in classrooms, and in the area of discourse linguistics has contributed to a better understanding of what is involved in language learning and in language teaching. While the work in the several theoretical areas is not all within the scope of applied linguistics, the coalescence of that work in relation to language learning and teaching is the concern of applied linguists.

Morley looks carefully at the contributions of various theoretical notions in linguistics and in learning, and at the shift from the teacher-centered classroom to the learner-centered classroom in which the teacher functions as a manager of learning rather than as the source of knowledge. Throughout, she maintains a focus intended to help working teachers, offering an overview of principles and practices of language teaching that are likely to shape future instruction for some time.

Current Directions in Second-Language Teaching

Joan Morley
University of Michigan

These are the best of times and the worst of times in the profession of foreign language teaching.

—H.D. Brown (1987:xi)

1. INTRODUCTION

Never before in the history of language teaching has there been such a variety of resources available to us. At the same time, we recognize now more than ever how far we are from answers to many difficult questions we have been asking. One answer which is clear is that second-language learning is no simple unidimensional reality, but a very "slippery" domain, indeed (Brown 1987).

Abundant evidence of changing perspectives on language learning and teaching (LL/LT) is to be found in the wide array of approaches, methods, materials, and techniques that have appeared in the language-teaching profession over the last 25 years. Richards and Rodgers observed:

> The proliferation of approaches and methods is a prominent characteristic of contemporary second and foreign language teaching. (1986:iv)

They went on to note that, while some may see this as a strength of the profession, others view the wide variety of method options currently available as indicative of confusion, that methods appear to be based on very different views of what language is, and how language is learned.

In order to assess current directions in language teaching, then, it is essential to look at underlying assumptions and concepts that influence perspectives on language learning. Such an assessment must necessarily consider the impact of three domains: linguistic backgrounds, learner considerations, and teacher choices. The second section of this chapter will review linguistic backgrounds. The third section will examine six learner considerations. The fourth section will discuss various aspects of teacher choices. The concluding section will draw together some overall comments on current directions in language learning and language teaching.

2. LINGUISTIC BACKGROUND

For many second-language professionals, linguistics has been and continues to be central to second-language theory and practice. Clearly, many of the changes in language learning and language teaching over the past 50 years have reflected changes in linguistic models. However, Wardhaugh (1972:295) reminded second-language teachers of Bolinger's (1968) caution that "language teaching is not linguistics, any more than medicine is chemistry." Concurring with Bolinger, Wardhaugh commented that linguistic knowledge must be thoroughly integrated with contributions from disciplines other than linguistics and with an awareness that language teaching is not the exclusive domain of any single discipline. The need for considering language teaching as interdisciplinary and the recognition of the close relationship between linguistics and language teaching gave rise in the 1940s to the field of applied linguistics.

2.1. Applied Linguistics

Van Els et al. (1984:10–11), observe that *applied linguistics* is a fairly recent term, and one whose first use appeared specifically in connection with foreign-language teaching (FLT), at least in Western Europe and the United States. They cite Engels (1968) as reporting that applied linguistics was recognized as early as 1946 as an independent subject at the University of Michigan. Engels also observed that it is likely that the term originated there, and noted that its use was certainly propagated from there. Specifically, it was disseminated from the English Language Institute (ELI) that occupied itself with teaching English to foreigners and, in 1948, originated the first journal to carry the term *applied linguistics* in its title, *Language Learning: A Journal of Applied Linguistics.*

In the meantime in Europe, although precisely the term *applied linguistics* may not have appeared so early (but see Strevens' chapter in this volume), certainly the British work in English-language-teaching (ELT) programming earlier in this century reflected careful linguistic analysis in its detailed focus on vocabulary and grammar patterns. Significant works included the vocabulary list for the teaching of English as a foreign language by Faucett et al. (1936); West's *General service list* (1953); the Palmer grammar substitution tables and *A grammar of spoken English,* (Palmer and Blandford 1939), and Hornby's *A guide to patterns and usage in English* (1954).

In sum, the 'application' of 'linguistics' to language matters of practical concern in second-language teaching has been a continuing feature of the field for a long time. Some applications have been indirect; some have been direct, and there have been 'misapplications' from time to time; but, overall, linguistics was and is an important source discipline for language teachers. (See van Els et al. 1984: ch. 2, for a detailed discussion of the term *applied linguistics* and its history; see also the chapter by Strevens in the present volume.)

2.2. Linguistic Models and Language Theory

Language teachers have been drawn to the field of linguistics as a source of language information for a long time. Like language teaching, the field of linguistics—the scientific study of language—has undergone profound changes over the last several decades. It has gained stature as an important intellectual academic discipline with increasing numbers of universities offering degrees in linguistics since the early 1960s. Grammar is at the heart of linguistics. The term *grammar* in the linguistic sense encompasses the entire system of rules that mediate between sound and meaning in a given language. Thus, the linguistic specialties of phonetics, phonology, morphology, syntax, semantics, pragmatics, and discourse analysis are all resources that can be accessed to inform language teaching. We would expect a review of current language-teaching theories to include information and concepts from some, but perhaps not all, of the subcategories of linguistic study listed above. In addition, an analysis of language-teaching theories probably would reveal the assumptions of one (or more) of four different paradigms of linguistic analysis as the basis for selecting, sequencing, contextualizing, and presenting language items:

1. Traditional linguistics
2. Structural linguistics
3. Transformational-generative linguistics
4. Systemic linguistics

A traditional model of grammar is based primarily on classical and prescriptive linguistic notions. Traditional language analysis focuses on the 'rules of usage' that are 'correct', for written language in particular. Traditional grammars are termed prescriptive or normative in that they dictate 'correctness' and make value judgements about language usage. It has been and continues to be, in large part, the basis for the grammar-translation method of language teaching. McArthur summarizes the explicit focus on "classical" grammar and its impact on language teaching:

Firstly, those who used and developed classical grammar believe in it as a descriptive device, but they were well aware that a grammar with its rules and paradigms is not the language itself; it is a model, an aid towards appreciating and using that language. They were also basically concerned with reading and writing; speech was a secondary consideration for people who wanted to train scribes, clerks and scholars, or readers of a revered foreign literature. Those were the primary goals, and for such goals the grammar-translation method worked adequately for centuries. (1983:59)

A structural model of grammar is also known as a descriptive model. It features structural language analysis with a focus on spoken rather than written language. Unlike traditional-prescriptive linguistics, structural-descriptive linguistics concerns itself solely with describing *what is actually occurring* in language use, not with making value judgements about *what should be occurring* in language use. It focuses only on recording and analyzing observable surface forms—particularly sound patterns and grammatical patterns—without recourse to the meaning they carry.

Structural linguistics gained popularity in the United States in the 1920s as a "new linguistics" movement; a heated battle raged between the prescriptive dicta of traditional grammarians and a then-new breed of structural linguists dedicated to descriptive grammatical analysis. In 1939 Charles C. Fries, a structural linguist at the University of Michigan, convinced the U.S. State Department to accept his ideological basis for a government project of English-language teaching, one that featured a linguistically based approach, instead of a system of basic English with pictures proposed by I.A. Richards. Subsequently, Fries established the first English Language Institute (ELI) in the United States and developed materials and methodologies for teaching oral language to nonnative speakers of English. Ultimately, as noted by J. Richards:

> The Michigan approach and the Michigan materials became nothing less than the 'American way,' the orthodox methodology of American English specialists in both the United States and abroad. (1985:40)

Before leaving structuralism, it is important to note Crystal's comment (1987:347) that this approach can instill considerable fluency in conversation, in both listening and speaking, in a relatively short time. Crystal also points out the importance of the special focus on contrastive sound and grammatical patterns in the first language and the second language, which was a hallmark of structural-descriptive language analysis.

Transformational-generative (T-G) grammars quickly superseded structural grammars beginning in the early 1960s. The development of ideas emerging from transformational-generative theory has exerted a powerful influence on language study since its rise to pre-eminence. The theory has created a revolution in how linguists view language description, language processing, and language acquisition. The tenets of the T-G revolution in theoretical linguistics were introduced, and have been elaborated, by Chomsky in a series of publications (1957, 1965, 1975, 1981, 1986). Since the early publications, there have been reformulations by others within the T-G paradigm. Some of these developments follow Chomsky's lead; others are radical departures from his ideas; and some are clearly reactionary developments in relation to his concepts. But whether one agrees or disagrees with Chomskyan linguistic principles, certainly no one can ignore them. (See the chapter by Grabe in this volume.)

Scovel provides an important pedagogical implication regarding T-G theory:

> Second language teachers cannot continue to base their grammatical insights on outdated models of linguistic analysis, and if teachers have not been introduced to TG grammar during their university studies, then it is important for them to try to get some training in TG analysis, especially in Chomsky's extended standard theory, which I believe to be more amenable to pedagogical practice than other competing generative models that are currently popular in linguistics. (1988:176)

Systemic linguistic approaches provide one of the few viable and productive alternative theoretical perspectives to T-G theory, particularly with respect to its influence on LL/LT. Systemic linguistic principles follow from the work of Halliday, which, in turn, draws upon the teachings of Firth. Systemic linguistics is sometimes referred to as Hallidean or neo-Firthian linguistics (see Berry 1975; Butler 1989; Hasan 1987; Halliday 1970, 1973, 1978, 1985; Halliday and Hasan 1989, Halliday, McIntosh, and Strevens 1964; Steele and Threadgold 1987). Basically systemic linguistics, as developed by Halliday in the 1960s, conceptualizes grammar as a network of systems with interrelated contrasts; the language analysis regards a language as being a system of systems with hierarchical categories. Of particular importance, Halliday's focus on semantic and pragmatic aspects of language analysis has been widely studied and "applied" in language teaching. His seven "functions" of language are well known: instrumental, regulatory, representational, interactional, personal, heuristic, and imaginative (as elaborated in *Explorations in the functions of language*, 1973). A second area of special influence in language teaching has been the work of Halliday and Hasan in discourse analysis and in text cohesion as discussed in *Cohesion in English* (1976) and other publications.

Traditional, structural, transformational-generative, and systemic theories have all had a prominent influence upon the second-language teaching field. The merits of each, relative to "application" to language teaching, continue to be the source of ongoing and lively discussion and debate.

3. A FOCUS ON LEARNER CONSIDERATIONS IN SECOND-LANGUAGE TEACHING

This section on current directions in LL/LT will review some of the recent research and trends in learner considerations. The influence of linguistic research, as discussed in the previous section, will be apparent in each of the following six main topics:

1. Learners as active creators in their learning process;
2. The learner's language and what it may reveal about the language-learning process;
3. The individuality of learners and individual learning styles and strategies;
4. The conscious intellectual involvement of learners in the learning process;
5. The cultural, social, and affective dimensions of language learning, and "humanistic" considerations; and
6. The needs of particular groups of learners and language for specific purposes (LSP) to meet those needs.

3.1. Learners as Active Creators in Their Learning Process

The notion of active participation in a creative process is perhaps the cornerstone for the single most fundamental change in perspective on the nature of language and language learning in recent years. We cannot begin to examine developments in this area without turning immediately to the contributions of Noam Chomsky, Roger Brown, and S. Pit Corder. The position that the learning of language is an active process, coming onto the academic scene in the late 1950s and 1960s, was a radical departure from a notion of first- or second-language acquisition as a behavioral phenomenon attributable to habit formation, to stimulus, to response, to conditioning. Conceptual frameworks of behavioral psychologists such as Skinner were challenged, and views of earlier cognitive psychologists were re-examined—especially notions on learning as an active process, one enriched by interaction, Some of the writings of Vygotsky and Piaget from the 1920s and 1930s were sought out and studied with renewed interest in the 1960s, 1970s, and 1980s.

    Chomsky (1959) rejected the structuralist approach to language analysis and the behaviorist theory of language learning. He argued that such a learning theory is not a plausible model of the way human beings learn language, since much of human language use is not imitative behavior, but novel creation based upon underlying knowledge of abstract rules. This position, along with data from Brown's explorations (1973) into first-language learning from a creative-process perspective (i.e., one in which children work out "rules" from the input available to them), and the work of those who followed, moved the field to a point where it no longer found tenable a concept of the student role in language learning as primarily one of passive repeater of forms and patterns. Students were recognized as the active prime movers in their own learning process. S. Pit Corder observed:

> Efficient language teaching must work with, rather than against, natural processes, facilitate and expedite rather than impede learning. Teachers and teaching materials must adapt to the learner rather than vice versa. (1976:10)

This orientation toward learning and learner processes constituted a major shift in the second-language field. Theretofore, the preoccupation had been with teaching, inasmuch as habit-formation learning afforded little in the way of interesting intellectual exploration. An important part of this shift has been the postulated duality of language learning; that is, the acquisition/learning concept introduced and elaborated by Krashen (1978, 1981). Krashen has modified his positions from time to time, and his notions certainly have generated continuing controversy, as well as a number of adjusted and some original alternative models. The latter include models by Schachter (1983; 1989), who looked at the resemblances between concept learning and second-language learning in adult learners, and by Bley-Vroman (1988), who takes the view that adult language learning bears a closer resemblance to general skills development than it does to language learning in children.

While views on the role of the language learner have been greatly influenced by linguistic research, both in the area of formal language theory and in the area of language-acquisition theory, the array of learner variables that may affect the language-learning situation has also claimed more and more attention from those investigating language learning and language teaching. In order to treat this topic in more detail, the following sections of this chapter will examine a number of these learner considerations.

3.2. The Learner's Language and Language Learning

It was not so many years ago that the learner's language, and especially the learner's mistakes, were not considered to be very interesting. They were looked upon as aberrant products resulting from a breakdown in the teaching methodology. Corder (1971) noted that it was not surprising that structuralist/behavioralist teachers showed little interest in the study of a learner's idiosyncratic sentences for at least two reasons:

1. To them, errors were evidence that the correct automatic habits of the target language had not yet been acquired;

2. Theoretically, if the teaching process had been perfect, no errors would have occurred in the first place.

Corder (1976) also observed that if, instead, language learning is conceived of as some kind of data-processing and hypothesis-forming activity of a cognitive nature, then "errors" have a three-way significance:

1. For teachers, they indicate how far toward a goal the learner has progressed;

2. For learners, they represent a device that the learner uses in order to test hypotheses about the nature of the language being learned; and

3. For researchers, they provide evidence of how language is learned, the strategies or procedures employed in the learner's "discovery" of the language.

Over the years, the focus of study on the learner's language has shifted from the prominence of contrastive analysis in the 1940s and 1950s, to error analysis in the 1960s and 1970s, and to interlanguage analysis in the 1970s and 1980s. Interlanguage analysis, growing out of the work of Corder (1967) and Selinker (1971), is marked today by a variety of investigations looking at different aspects of language learning related to less-than-exact target-language use. Research studies range across a wide spectrum of factors that appear to be reflected in the second-language learning process (Kaplan et al. 1989). These include areas as varied as universals, transfer from the first language, specific aspects of the second language, individual learner strategies, input, language variation, the learning environment and learner interactions, and the influence of the teacher and of teacher strategies. Recent state-of-the-art reference texts in this area of study include Beebe (1988), Gass et al. (1989), Kaplan et al. (1989), and Spolsky (1989b).

3.3. Individual Learning Styles and Strategies

With a focus on the centrality of the learner's role as active creator in the language-learning process, not as passive recipient, comes the corollary that both similarities and differences will be observed in the way individual learners go about the task. In the last ten years, more and more research has focused on learner characteristics in the learning process. One area of research interest has been the study of features that seem to separate good language learners from not-so-good language learners (cf. McLaughlin and Zemblidge in this volume).

Two kinds of learner characteristics are *styles of learning* and *strategies of learning*. Brown (1987) presents useful definitions and clear descriptions of these characteristics, summarized as follows. Styles of learning are made up of an individual's consistent and rather enduring preferences related to general characteristics of intellectual functioning and personality type. Involved are factors such as greater or lesser tolerance of ambiguity, more or less reflectiveness/impulsiveness, more or less field dependence/independence, orientation more or less toward logical/analytical information, orientation more or less toward imagery and holistic information, etc. Strategies of learning are measures taken by language learners to facilitate their own language learning. They are tactics employed by an individual in attacking particular problems in particular contexts. Strategies of learning are of two types: learning strategies, per se, are learner measures relating to input while communication strategies are learner measures relating to output. Strategies of learning are important as they provide additional explanations to account for different degrees of success in language learning. They provide, and will continue to provide, a strong focus for research because: (1) studies show that learning strategies can be improved or modified through training; and (2) successful language learners tend to use 'good' strategies more often then unsuccessful language learners.

Two important articles on good-learner characteristics appeared in 1975, and since that time there has been an increasing number of studies on these topics. Rubin (1975:45–48) reported the following seven characteristics exhibited by good language learners:

1. They are willing and accurate guessers;
2. They have a strong drive to communicate;
3. They lack inhibitions (are willing to appear foolish);
4. They pay attention to form;
5. They seek opportunities for practice;
6. They monitor their own and others' speech; and
7. They pay attention to meaning (look beyond the surface structure).

At the same time, Stern (1975) outlined ten characteristics, many of which were quite similar to those identified by Rubin. These became part of the Toronto/ OISE study on characteristics of good language learners (Naiman et al. 1978). In the last decade, much new research has appeared that refines the earlier research. Work by Chamot et al. (1987), Faerch and Kasper (1983), Oxford-Carpenter (1989), O'Malley et al. (1983, 1987, 1989), Wenden and Rubin (1988) extends and elaborates on theories of learner styles and strategies.

3.4. The Conscious Intellectual Involvement of the Learner

Specific attention to various kinds of intellectual involvement of learners in the learning process has become an increasingly important feature of LL/LT in recent years. One kind of intellectual involvement was noted briefly in the preceding section—learning styles used by learners, with individual styles reflecting both intellectual functioning and personality type. Most learners are largely unaware of the characteristics of their personal stylistic approaches to language learning, unless they are made aware by teachers. Instruments such as the *Myers-Briggs Type Indicator* (ascertains psychological types) (1963, 1975), which have been introduced into some programs (Brown et al. 1988; Ehrman 1986), apprise learners (and their teachers) of preferences in areas such as introversion, extroversion, sensing, intuition, etc.

A second kind of intellectual involvement of learners, with its roots earlier in the history of the field, was that related to cognitive-code theory, which made an appearance as an alternative to behaviorist learning theory in the late 1960s and early 1970s. Carroll described it as a modified up-to-date grammar-translation theory in which language was viewed as:

> a process of acquiring conscious control of the phonological, grammatical, and lexical patterns of a second language largely through the study and analysis of these patterns as a body of knowledge. (1966:97)

The intellectual involvement in cognitive-code called for intellectual focus on the *product,* in an item-by-item analysis of the language. The grammar text *Modern English,* by W. Rutherford (1968, 1975, 1977), is an example of a careful cognitive-code analysis of English grammar for ESL/EFL learners. Although a clear methodological format was not developed for the field of language teaching as a whole, useful applications were made in English for science and technology.

A third kind of active intellectual involvement that has appeared as a significant development over the past two decades is learner- and teacher-concern about the *process.* Especially in classes for teenaged and adult learners, there has been increased attention to encouraging learners to 'intellectualize' about their language work in order to help them gain insights into:

1. *What* they are doing (i.e., the process);
2. *How* they are doing it (i.e., the procedures); and
3. *Why* they are doing particular things (i.e., the outcomes and the values that accrue to them).

Learner involvement and attention to guiding the learner into being an intellectual partner in the language-learning setting has become a component of many ESL instructional materials and some FLT materials in the 1970s and 1980s. Research has shown that self-involvement is one of the primary characteristics of the effective learner. Learner involvement cannot be left to chance, however; it must be actively directed and shaped by the teacher, the learning activities, and the materials.

3.5. Cultural, Social, and Affective Dimensions of Language Learning

A focus on the relationships among language, society, and culture has been an integral part of the field of second-language teaching for a long, long time. Historically, perspectives on the questions of the cultural 'what' and 'how' have ranged across a spectrum of topics as varied as: nonverbal features of communication (Hall 1959, 1966), attitudes, acculturation, anomie (Gardner and Lambert 1972), attitudes and success (Oller et al. 1977); acculturation and social distance (Schumann 1976, 1986); culture shock and the traumas of learners (Bateson 1972, Clarke 1976); empathy and second-language learning (Guiora et al. 1972a, 1972b), etc. Papers in Valdes explore just such issues by examining "the difference between interacting with another culture and entering it . . . [and] understanding a new culture without embracing it." (1986:iv)

The social dimension of language learning is defined by the interdisciplinary field of sociolinguistics, which deals with relationships between social and linguistic behavior. Studies of the 'roles' and 'rules' in conversational interactions by Grice (1967, 1975), Schegloff (1972), and Sacks et al. (1974), and those who followed them, provided information about interactional expectations between two native speakers of a language. Research on second-language acquisition (SLA) is exploring aspects of both native/nonnative (N/NN) and nonnative/nonnative (NN/NN) interactions and meaning negotiation, and their influences on second-language acquisition (Gass and Varonis 1985; Long 1983; Scarcella 1989).

In the affective dimensions of language learning, perhaps the place to begin is with two of the shared characteristics of the 'humanistic' approaches to language learning that developed in the 1970s:

1. Placing much of the responsibility for learning on the learner, not the teacher, and

2. Making students more receptive by providing a nonthreatening environment in which they are not 'on the defensive.'

Reflecting the influence of humanistic psychologists, such as Rogers (1951, 1969), Maslow (1970), and others, the theoretical view of these approaches can be termed an 'interactional' view of language, one in which language is seen as a vehicle for the realization of interpersonal relations and for the performance of social transactions. Representing a British perspective, Strevens (1986) referred to these approaches as representations of what he termed the 'mystique-dominated' paradigm in language learning and teaching. Taking a more sympathetic view, Stevick (1976, 1980) introduced many language teachers to the concepts of the humanistic approaches, particularly in his book *A way and ways*, in which he brought to our attention counseling-learning (Curran 1972, 1976), Silent Way (Gattegno 1972), and Suggestopedia (Lozanov 1979).

Quite apart from the specific 'humanistic' approaches of the last twenty years, there has also been a keen interest in the wider dimension of affective factors and the ways they influence the language learner and learning. Specific areas of work included a focus on theoretical affective issues by Brown (1973, 1987), Schumann (1975), Scovel (1978), and Tucker et al. (1976), as well as on classroom procedures by Moskowitz (1978). Finally, it is necessary to underscore the idea that 'affect' is not a recent discovery in language instruction. Sensitive language teachers have long been aware of the influence of affect on learning. Although many teachers do not follow a humanistic interactionist philosophy, most take into serious account: (1) placing more of the responsibility for learning on the learner; and (2) providing a nonthreatening environment so that learners' anxiety levels are reduced.

3.6. The Needs of Particular Groups of Learners

Language for specific purposes (LSP) has been a strongly and steadily growing development in the field of second-language teaching. It comes in many forms, as one would expect, and is found worldwide. Language for specific purposes is concerned with the development of language programs for groups of people who need a language to meet a predictable range of communicative needs. If one includes early maritime phrase books for entering foreign ports as LSP, then one can find documentation for the use of special language books by German sea captains as long as 200 years ago. And special language guides for clearing customs and passport control were used for English/French travel as much as 400 years ago (Strevens 1977a). As an institutional activity, however, LSP began to develop as a special focus on language teaching in the early 1960s, although Widdowson has been quick to point out that, as early as 1921, Palmer expressed an LSP view:

> We cannot design a language course until we know something about the students for whom the course is intended, for a programme of study depends on the aim or aims of the students. (1983:14)

The preceding statement captures the general sense and the breadth of scope that underlies 'special' versus 'general' LL/LT. The controversial areas lie in the decisions that must be made about what constitutes 'special' needs, uses, purposes, and language items as distinct from a 'general' course of study. Clear rationale and specific criteria must be established for the selection of language, use and usage, and methodology.

Swales (1989) suggests that a three-stage process be carried out in planning an LSP program. The process must begin with an analysis of the target situation and identification of the roles of the participants. If possible, this should include an ethnographic study of the real-life setting. The second stage focuses on characterizing the language that expresses these roles. A linguistic analysis must be carried out, including a study of pragmatics and discourse in order to understand the texts, both oral and written, in the situation. Stage three follows up with the construction of curricula and language-learning activities that allow the specified language to be acquired efficiently and effectively. Communicative language teaching with a focus on task-based learning is then recommended for a narrowly targeted rapid-learning LSP program.

Historically, the first institutional development of LSP probably was in English for specific purposes (ESP), which in large part focused on English for science and technology (EST). The event that signaled the beginning of this specialty was, according to Swales (1984), the work of Barber (1962). From the beginning, in addition to EST, ESP has also focused on English for academic purposes (EAP) and more generally on English for professional purposes (EPP) (Pugh and Ulijn 1984). EAP has been of particular concern in the United States where steadily increasing numbers of foreign students have been enrolling in undergraduate and graduate college and university programs. Many of the old generalist intensive courses have been called upon to deal, instead, with the special language problems of regularly enrolled students in EAP and in a variety of ESP areas. With swelling enrollments of international students in graduate programs has come an increase in the number of international teaching assistants (ITAs) involved in undergraduate instruction. A number of institutions now direct special programming to the preparation of ITAs in pedagogical, cultural, and language aspects of college teaching in the United States. Useful resources for this aspect of LSP include Ard and Swales (1986), Bailey et al. (1984), and Byrd, Constantinides, and Pennington (1989).

A second LSP focus has been that on special language needs in the workplace and in occupational- and vocational-training programs in business and industry. The Council of Europe project for adult LSP developed programs and instructional materials for dozens of occupational categories (Trim 1978; van Ek 1975). In the area of English for special purposes, extensive government and/or private-foundation funds have provided for the development of programs in England, Canada, New Zealand, Australia, and the United States. This has resulted in the preparation of both vocational English as a second language (VESL), and survival English (SE) programs and materials, particularly for adult refugees and migrants. Useful resources in this area include Crandall and Grognet (1982), Crandall (1987), Jupp and Hodin (1975), and Savage and Dresner (1986).

4. A FOCUS ON
TEACHER CHOICES

The various areas reviewed above that have to do with learner considerations all indicate a strong connection to linguistics and to linguistic interdisciplines. This section on teacher choices is influenced to some degree by linguistics, but also (perhaps more so) by the related interdisciplines of psychology and education. The focus on teacher choices will examine current directions in language learning and teaching from the perspective of the teacher. The preceding discussion of learner considerations in second-language teaching said little about the role of the teacher (or for that matter, the role of the curriculum planner). This section on teacher choices will begin with some comments on the teacher's role as a manager of learner experiences. Next, the development of methods and syllabus design in language teaching will be discussed briefly, highlighting the gradual change from teacher-centered to learning-centered instruction, and also indicating the changes in types of teacher choices to be made. The final portions of this section will then discuss the incorporation of recent insights from linguistic research and advances in learning theory as they influence teacher choices. Teacher choices will focus on the following seven topics:

1. Teachers as managers of language-learning experiences;

2. Teaching methods and syllabus design;

3. Language function as well as language form;

4. Communicative language teaching and the components of communicative competence;

5. Interactive modes of communicative classroom instruction—modes that foster creative interaction among and between learners;

6. Content-area language learning and language teaching; and

7. Creative use of technology in language learning and language teaching.

4.1. Teachers as Managers of Language-Learning Experiences

The radical changes in both language theory and language-acquisition theory have had a strong influence on the role of the teacher in the language classroom. Once again we must refer to the work of Corder (1976), whom we already noted as encouraging language teachers to *facilitate* rather than impede learning, a term also closely associated with the work of Curran (1976). Although this direction in teacher orientation is clearly a sign of the times in second-language teaching, many teachers still are struggling with their role as facilitator. They are seeking ways to carry out that role in order to provide the most effective guidance and support for learners.

With the shift of the field toward a focus on learning and learner processes, there was something of a pendulum swing away from serious attention to teachers and teaching processes. Now there appears to be emerging a
renewal of interest in teaching styles and strategies and in language-teacher
education. Higgs observed:

> Little if any . . . literature seriously considers the preferred style of in-
> structors. In general, teachers are more effective when they are confident
> about their own abilities and feel free to capitalize on their perceived
> strengths while minimizing their weaknesses. A native-speaking instruc-
> tor of the target language usually feels more comfortable giving copious
> examples of the language, spontaneously creating them in response to a
> given situation. Nonnatives, however, usually feel more secure explaining
> materials already presented in text materials. The affective environment
> in the classroom may well be more influenced by a teacher's feeling of
> confidence than by externally imposed considerations of methodology.
> (1984:4)

While the direct influence of linguistic theory is not evident, the indirect
impact of linguistics on teacher approaches is clearly traceable through theories of language learning. The question of what appropriate teaching choices
are, and how teachers should most properly be trained is now assuming a
larger role in teacher-education considerations. Thus, research into teacher
education is becoming a concern in many second-language settings.
Bernhardt, in a discussion at the 1988 TESOL conference in Chicago observed:

> Without some basic research into what is going on in teacher education,
> we cannot possibly meet the demands for reform in teacher education.

In the not-too-distant future, an inventory of primary instructional features by
which the field of second-language teaching can best be characterized many
well include a special focus on the individuality of teachers and individual
teaching styles. The concern with teacher choices and teacher influence will be
given more in-depth consideration in the following sections.

4.2. Teaching Methods and Syllabus Design

The history of teaching methods has a centuries-old tradition dating back to
the early records of the Greeks (Kelly 1968; McArthur 1983). In fact, most of
what has been proposed as sets of new ideas for language teaching in the
twentieth century can be discovered in written records somewhere in the past
(except, of course, CALL—computer-assisted language learning). It is safe to
say that, for the most part, language teaching was represented by a dominant
'traditional' method well into the twentieth century (cf., Krashen and Terrell
1983; McArthur 1983). Grammar-transalation instruction had great status as

the approach to language teaching, for a number of reasons, until the rise of behavioral psychology and structural linguistics in the 1920s and 1930s (Bowen, Madsen, and Hilferty 1986; Chastain 1976; Rivers 1981). As noted earlier, the audio-lingual method (ALM) arose in the 1940s and 1950s as a scientific approach to language theory—one that presented a strong underlying language and learning-theory basis (see Strevens' chapter in this volume). It is important to note that both of these language-teaching methods are strongly teacher-centered; the teacher plans the daily lessons, typically dependent on a carefully structured textbook sequence. Language is treated as discrete information to be passed on to the passively accepting vessel, the student.

For a variety of reasons, teachers and students alike experienced dissatisfaction with both the grammar-translation and the audio-lingual approaches. Most students did not become adept language users in accordance with their perceived needs; after all, students were never asked what they felt they needed to know. Teachers were similarly dissatisfied with approaches that locked them into a set sequence, and that did not allow them to exploit specific learning occasions and contexts. The direct method and the audio-visual method provided greater interaction, as they were less tied to preset scripts for language use. However, they did not provide answers to many of the problems that were troubling researchers and teachers. In the 1970s, a more general counterapproach emerged—one that incorporated aspects of T-G linguistic theory, a learning theory derived from cognitive psychology, and humanistic psychology (Brown 1987; Chastain 1976). These perspectives were combined under the label of *cognitive learning-code theory*. The general views proposed under this theory offered more options for teaching techniques in the classroom, accorded the learner greater responsibility as an active and creative partner in the learning process, and allowed teachers and researchers to consider other ways of addressing issues in language teaching. This approach, however, ran into difficulties of its own; the main difficulty, soon recognized, was that this approach did not provide a coherent framework for particular methods and techniques organized in specific ways to address either student or institutional needs.

The cognitive–learning-code approach quickly evolved into a number of other approaches, both generalized and specific. A number of 'innovative' approaches developed in combination with learning and humanistic psychology: Community Language Learning; Silent Way; Total Physical Response; Suggestopedia; and the Comprehension Approach, among others (Blair 1982; Larsen-Freeman 1985; Oller and Richard-Amato 1985; Richard-Amato 1987; Richards and Rodgers 1986; Stevick 1980). While there are a number of major differences among these various methods (cf. Scovel 1983, who pointed out the "neoaudiolingual" features of the total-physical-response and comprehension approaches, which both feature delay of oral production), they all exhibit certain common features that may be seen as an outgrowth of ideas from cognitive–learning-code theory, as well as of research in cognitive psychology and learning theory. In all cases, students are recognized as individuals with creative learning capability; further, students have to take responsibility for their learning—they are not passive *tabula rasa*. Finally, these approaches all assume some similarity between learning a first language and learning a second language. Since all L2 learners are successful at learning their first language, a common goal is to tap into the same set of conditions and learner strategies that worked the first time around. Not the least among these is the need to make language learning more learner-centered.

A second general approach that developed out of similar assumptions is the Natural Approach of Terrell (1977, 1985; and later, Krashen and Terrell 1983). A distinction between this approach and the above approaches is that it has come to rest on a very specific set of theoretical arguments, above and beyond the common features noted above, which derive from Krashen's Monitor Model (1981, 1982, 1985). In this case, once again, linguistic research, first language–acquisition research, second language–acquisition research, learning-theory research, and teaching method all converge to support the Natural Approach. In fact, more recent discussions of the Natural Approach incorporate many of the techniques of the other innovative approaches when they are supportable by Krashen's theory and compatible with Natural Approach methods (Krashen and Terrell 1983; Richard-Amato 1987). This approach is very learner-centered, depending on the contexts created by the learners in the classroom for many of the teaching and learning activities.

As with all other methods, the Natural Approach has a number of limitations that have prevented its general acceptance/adoption. First, the Natural Approach, perhaps, tries to be all things to all people—a shortcoming of most general approaches to language teaching developed in the United States. There are, in fact, many contexts in which such an approach is not appropriate, even for general language learning; for example, the Natural Approach requires that the nonnative-speaking language teacher have extraordinary second-language skills. In many EFL contexts, such skills are not common. Further, the Natural Approach has limitations, in that it is oriented to certain types of learning strategies and styles. Students whose learning styles and strategies are not compatible with this approach will not fare as well. Third, the Natural Approach, much like other general approaches, is less well articulated for advanced language learners, particularly students who need to develop literacy skills for postsecondary study in L2 contexts. Despite these, and possibly other, limitations, the Natural Approach has become a widely adopted language teaching approach. It has clear advantages over many other methods when in the hands of a skilled teacher, and it has the advantage of being usable with both adults and young children.

Another general teaching approach, one that has gained the widest application to date, is the communicative approach (Communicative Language Teaching). This approach emphasizes the centrality of communication in language use and in language learning. The goal of instruction using the communicative approach is to develop contexts for real communication and interaction, using, if not real language for purposeful activities, then realistic language (Harmer 1983). Its foundations are somewhat different from those discussed above. While it incorporates a number of the insights of cognitive–learning-code theory, its roots can be traced to other sources, principally to sociolinguistic research, systemic linguistics, and British notional-functional approaches (Wilkins 1976). Drawing on discussions of communicative competence as a foundation for sociolinguistics (Hymes 1972) and functional uses of language (Halliday 1973, 1978), researchers in language teaching proposed that language learning could be more effective if the focus of learning was on language tasks that were meaningful to the learner and functionally appropriate (Breen and Candlin 1980; Paulston 1974; Savignon 1983). The result has been the range of teaching approaches falling under the umbrella of communicative language teaching. The openness of this approach to variation and the charge of unprincipled eclecticism has been a major criticism (but see Brown 1987 for notes on "principled eclecticism"). Another drawback to communicative approaches is that the notion of communicative competence is not an agreed-upon theoretical notion (cf. Canale 1983; Canale and Swain 1980; Hymes 1972, 1989; Widdowson 1989; Wolfson 1989). A reaction to these limitations among researchers on language teaching has been to turn from teaching methods to issues of syllabus design and curricula as a way to focus instruction more effectively, though the question becomes more one of *what* to teach than of *how* to teach.

Syllabus design, following early attempts to energize the field (Munby 1978; Richards 1984b; Robinson 1980; Wilkins 1976; Yalden 1983) and to break out of the ESP straightjacket that had constrained it, has become a major concern in the development of current approaches to language teaching. Three trends in particular merit comment. The first is the movement away from structural syllabuses: instead of sequencing instruction according to ordered bits of language (either grammatical or notional-functional), syllabus designers considered task-based syllabi in which the focus was on learning certain skills rather than certain pieces of language. A second alternative was the development of a problem-based syllabus in which learners have to solve a sequence of problem activities, activities which called upon the use of language for accomplishing the tasks (Beretta 1987b, 1989; Crookes 1988; Prabhu 1987). Finally, there has been a strong focus on the development of content-centered instruction. The goal in this case is to build in natural motivation and natural information along with meaningful language task (Brinton, Snow, and Wesche 1989; Cantoni 1987; Crandall 1987; Johnson 1989; Mohan 1986; Nunan 1988; Shih 1986). Such approaches tie in well with the strong push in elementary instruction for integrated curricula (Enright and McCloskey 1988; Rigg and Enright 1987; Wallerstein 1982), with whole-language instruction (Edelsky

1986; Goodman 1986), and with both 'sheltered' and 'mentored' university-course formats (Brinton, Snow, and Wesche 1989).

This brief overview of methods and syllabus design is not intended to be complete, but rather to emphasize certain trends in language teaching, particularly in the last twenty years. Its purpose is to focus the following discussion of teacher choices and to provide a frame of reference for the various critical issues that are now facing language teachers as they shape instruction and provide the learning environment for students. Each of the following five sections treats in more detail particular issues that will give rise to research and instructional decisions into the 1990s.

4.3. Language Function and Language form

Instruction that concentrates on helping students master grammatically correct structures, but fails to give them any experience in putting such structures to purposeful use in appropriate communicative contexts is often criticized for teaching language *forms* without *functions*. A widely held belief that "form equals function" was challenged by Austin (1962). His theory of speech acts and his classification of language functions, followed by Searle's model of the use of speech-act theory in discourse analysis (1969), drew the attention of the language field to a number of concepts including "proposition" and "illocutionary force." The various distinctions that emerged from speech-act theory have been instrumental in discussion of how language is used in its literal sense, and how it conveys speaker messages. This distinction is essential to Widdowson's distinction between the terms *use* and *usage*:

> If it is the case that knowing a language means knowing what signification sentences have as instances of *usage* and what value they take on as instances of *use*, it seems clear that the teacher of language should be concerned with the teaching of both kinds of knowledge. (1978:19)

Widdowson also observed that concentrating on *usage*, and assuming that learners will eventually "pick up" the necessary knowledge of *use* on their own may be too optimistic a view to take.

Building upon the theoretical notions of speech acts and emphasis on language use, Brumfit (1980) proposed a syllabus design that used the grammatical system as a core in a series of ladderlike stages, with appropriate notional, functional, and situational material wrapped around it in a spiral-like pattern. As noted in Widdowson and Brumfit, the core "contains the linguistic structures for expressing the varied curricular content found in the spiral, [and this model] . . . has the merit of recognizing that some parts of the syllabus can be systematised, while others cannot be so." (1981:208)

Over the years a variety of inventories of language functions and notions have been proposed, including, in particular, the one by Halliday (1973) referred to earlier, which delineated seven critical language functions (personal, interactional, instrumental, regulatory, representational, imaginative, and heuristic). Another rich resource for notional/functional guidelines has been the project work of the Council of Europe language-teaching programs begun in 1971. These have led to such landmark studies as that of Wilkins (1976), which contains an extensive specification of notions and functions; of van Ek (1975), which provides a wide variety of comprehensive inventories; and of Munby (1978), which presents a model for the analysis of language needs.

Finally, one can find today dozens of language texts that purport to be functional and/or notional texts. But let the buyer beware! Many are not precisely what they claim to be. As Campbell observed, "We must be sure we are not getting structural lamb served up as notional-functional mutton." (1978:19; see also Quinn in Kaplan et al. 1985)

4.4. Communicative Language Teaching and Communicative Competence

To understand the notion of communicative competence, one must go back to the early writing of Chomsky (1965), who called our attention to the notions of 'competence' and 'performance.' His purpose was to define the goal of theoretical linguistics as the study of ideal underlying rule systems of language rather than trying to account for all the features of language use, including errors, misstatements, hesitations, etc., which are more matters of how we perform the language than reflective of the underlying knowledge we possess. Other linguists, such as Hymes (1972), reacted to this simplification by saying that we need to have a theory as well of how we actually use language for various purposes. Hymes (1972) therefore coined the term *communicative competence* to refer to the rules of language use without which the rules of grammar would be pointless. Paulston (1974) reiterated this position specifically for second-language teaching and learning contexts. The concept of 'communicative competence' (and its practical offspring: communicative language approaches) has now assumed central importance in discussions of language learning and teaching (see Breen and Candlin 1980; Kaplan et al. 1988; Savignon 1972, 1983; Widdowson 1978).

Canale and Swain (1980; Canale 1983; cf. Taylor 1988) proposed a model of communicative competence that brought together a number of viewpoints in one linguistically oriented and pedagogically useful framework. They argued that communicative competence minimally includes four areas of knowledge and skills: (1) grammatical competence; (2) sociolinguistic competence; (3) discourse competence; and (4) strategic competence (cf. Canale 1988; Duran et al. 1985). Cummins (1979, 1980) has also distinguished types of language use as part of his general theory of second-language development in children, drawing attention to differential proficiency in children's acquisition of: (1) basic interpersonal communicative skills (BICS); and (2) cognitive/academic language proficiency (CALP).

Another force active with regard to 'communicative' and 'competence' concepts has been the American Council on the Teaching of Foreign Languages (ACTFL). In particular, the ACTFL yearbook, *Curriculum, Competence, and the Foreign Language Teacher* (Higgs 1982), included a number of important papers in this area. The year 1982 also saw the publication of the *ACTFL Provisional Proficiency Guidelines*, which are sets of descriptions of proficiency levels for speaking, listening, reading, writing, and culture in a foreign language. These guidelines are having a significant influence on foreign-language teaching in the United States (cf. Savignon in this volume).

Finally, it is important to review two 'forms' of the notion of communicative language teaching that have emerged. A 'weak' form of communicative language teaching (and one in regular practice today) concentrates on "providing learners with opportunities to use their English for communicative purposes and, characteristically, attempts to integrate such activities into a wider program of language teaching" (Howatt 1984:279). A 'strong' form claims that "language is acquired through communication," and that learners must *use* English to learn it. Allright sums up these two positions succinctly with the question: "Are we teaching *language* (for communication) or are we teaching *communication* (via language)?" (1979:166; cf. Kaplan, et al. 1988)

4.5. Interactive Modes of Communicative Classroom Instruction

It was not so long ago that the primary kind of interaction between learners in language classrooms was either exchanges or memorized dialogues or chaining exercises in which the interaction went something like this:

> A: I like to swim. What do you like to do?
> B: I like to ski. What do you like to do?
> C: I like to . . .

While a few creative alternatives, particularly for grammar practice, were formulated in the 1960s and 1970s, and led to the search for more effective language-practice techniques (cf. Rivers 1964, 1972, 1981; Paulston 1971, 1974; Rutherford 1968, 1975, 1977, for these earlier innovations), most classrooms were dominated by grammar drills; there was very little communicative classroom exchange at all between or among students. The basic patterns to be found were: (1) teacher-to-student(s), requiring a form to be repeated or transformed, or a question to be responded to; (2) student(s)-to-teacher, performing the appropriate operation on the form; and (3) student-to-student, performing set situational dialogues. Research in California as early as the late

1960s showed that ESL teachers were using upwards of 80 percent of available classroom time talking to students, rather than letting the students talk. This extreme situation may also be found in some EFL classrooms, particularly in classrooms where class size is great (70 to 100 students); recitation time is very limited; teachers are not native speakers of the target language; not all students have textbooks; and the duration of instruction is short.

But classroom practices are changing and, in many situations, increasing portions of the available time are regularly reserved for a variety of interactive activities in which students have opportunities to use language for communicative purposes. Some of these activities fall into the category noted earlier as a 'weak' form of communicative language teaching; others clearly are designed to give learners opportunities to use language in order to learn it—the 'strong' form of communicative language teaching (Long and Porter 1985). Task-based activities for pairs and small groups highlight information exchange and often make use of special interactive pair-practice material in which each member-set has missing material to be found in the partner's set. An 'information gap' created by this kind of activity, and the interactive exchange that it stimulates, is one the most fundamental concepts of the strong form of communicative language teaching. The belief is that the transfer of information that is thus provided for involves the learner in *real communication* (not pseudocommunication) with *real negotiation of meaning* taking place (cf. Johnson and Morrow 1981; Harmer 1983).

4.6. Content-Area Language Learning and Teaching

From one perspective, it appears quite reasonable to say that the concept of 'content' LL/LT is not new, that it has been around for a long time. It might seem to be the case that a person learning 'new' information (i.e., content) in a nonnative language is, of necessity, engaged in content-area language study as well. By such a definition, anyone who has been placed in a sink-or-swim situation in which language is 'foreign,' but with content that must be mastered and transmitted in that language, is in such a learning situation (perhaps 'predicament' is a better word). And by such a gross definition, any bilingual immersion program might seem to qualify for inclusion in the content-area LL/LT category. This, however, is not true. To qualify as true content-area LL/LT instruction, a program must integrate language instruction and content instruction in a principled manner (Brinton, Snow, and Wesche 1989; Enright and McCloskey 1988).

Historically, in the development of LL/LT, several dimensions of language instruction have emerged that focus on issues involving content (e.g., needs analysis and the preparation of LSP curricula), communicative language teaching, and 'forms and functions' (i.e., the 'uses' and 'usages' of the particular language) involved in the communication centering around specific situations and the roles of interactants. In this regard, Widdowson and Brumfit note:

> True communicative teaching may depend on our stressing language as a means to acquire knowledge, rather than as an end in itself. . . . If the teaching of a subject were to be carried on through the medium of a foreign language, many problems associated with communication would disappear. (1981:197)

And in recommending procedures for designing adult LSP courses, Swales (1989) stresses the importance of analyzing the target setting, the roles of the participants, and the language texts involved, after which analysis the preparation of a syllabus of task-based communicative activities can be undertaken.

In the last several years, increased attention has been given to content-based second-language instruction for elementary and secondary school–aged children. Mohan (1979, 1986), in particular, has long argued that teachers should integrate language development with content learning. However, Mohan cautions that there must be systematic planning for language learning, that language is not to be dealt with randomly. And Curtain has noted:

> The integration of language and subject content has successfully been accomplished in immersion programs and has emerged as a feature of sheltered-English programs [courses in content areas matched with language courses that cover the same material] for Limited English Proficient (LEP) students. (1986:11)

In focusing on language, content, and the effect on the school-aged child, clearly much more is at stake than a narrowly conceived concept of second-/foreign-language learning. More general concerns involving student cognition, student motivation, student drop-out, classroom and school practices, the learning and teaching of content, teacher decision-making, the stratification of educational opportunities, institutional change, and much more have implications for LEP students (Crawford 1989). As noted in a previous section of this chapter (4.4), Cummins (1979, 1981) has discussed the very significant difference between basic interpersonal communication skills (BICS) and cognitive/academic language proficiency (CALP) and has estimated that it requires around one to two years to develop the former, but five to seven years to develop the latter (see also Collier 1987, 1989). Carefully constructed content-area language-teaching programs are a sign of the times in second-language teaching today, in widening varieties of both LSP instruction and school-aged second-language instruction. In her introduction to a discussion of content-area instruction, Crandall has observed:

> Content-based ESL courses—whether taught by the ESL teacher, the content-area teacher, or some combination—provide direct instruction in the

special language of the subject matter, while focusing attention as much or more on the subject matter itself. (1987:7)

4.7. The Creative Use of Technology in LL/LT

The use of technology has long been a feature of language teaching around the world—used sometimes more and sometimes less creatively. The very word conjures up a host of visions of audio, video, film, and computer materials, broadcast language laboratories, self-access self-study audio and video learning centers, giant-screen TV viewing rooms, computer banks, shortwave radio, satellite TV, and much, much more. Ranging further afield, through technology, ESL/EFL has reached out to learners everywhere through special English-teaching radio and television programs (BBC 1975; ELTB 1987). Both Australia and New Zealand, for example, are engaged in 'distance education,' broadcasting language instruction (among other instructional materials) to isolated populations, respectively, in the Outback and in the Polynesian Islands over which New Zealand has jurisdiction.

But it is as true today as it was in the earliest days of language laboratories that the primary concern is not with the equipment that modern technology can provide, but with the educational principles that underlie the development and use of instructional materials and the nature of the contribution technology can make to the total language-learning experience (Morley 1979, 1985). There are many questions to be asked and many decisions to be made, whether one is using 'old' technologies or 'new' ones.

What of computers and language learning and teaching? Is it possible to involve learners in purposeful instructional activities in which they are active/interactive participants? Cummins (1986b), in a paper on computer use in teaching French and English in Canada, offered a number of observations that are focused on computer use, but they give us some considerations that can be explored as well with regard to new developments and uses of both audio and video instructional materials and learning activities. Cummins discussed computer use in relation to two pedagogical models:

1. The *transmission* model, based largely on behaviorist psychology, sees the computer as a 'tutor' that can assume the role of the teacher in transmitting information, knowledge, or skills that are programmed so that the student plays a *passive* role, simply receiving the knowledge.

2. The *interactional* model sees the computer as a tool that students use in the *active* pursuit of a goal they wish to achieve; the student thus is 'generating' knowledge rather than receiving it, and the computer can provide guidance, facilitation, and support to help students achieve their goals.

In addition to the strong potential of the computer for interactive language learning, another promising direction is in use of state-of-the-art video technology for language learning and teaching, particularly the development of the video disc (Flint 1989b). Recent projects in the teaching of modern Hebrew by means of video discs have been reported by Coffin (1988). In one pilot project, Coffin has taken one-hour programs from Israeli television and constructed ten hours of interactive instructional activities built around each program. In another project, a courtroom drama in Hebrew was recorded on videotape in the studios of the University of Michigan; then student-interactive activities were added that encouraged vocabulary acquisition and listening-comprehension skills.

The Athens Language Learning Project at MIT, with a $1.4 million sponsorship by the Annenberg/CPB Project, has a number of projects underway. The project's aim is to develop computer-based materials which make use of the capabilities of networked stations to develop natural language processing, interactive video, and digitized speech applications. Noblitt (1988), at Cornell University, has developed a very sophisticated student-interactive computer program for use in French composition instruction and writing practice: *System-D: Writing Assistant for French*, an innovative software package that provides a word processor that incorporates a bilingual dictionary, a concise reference grammar, complete verb conjugations, and examples of usage.

New computer-program speech-analysis systems that can transform speech input into a visual display on the computer screen have been developed and used in ESL programs as reported by Browne (1988) and Molholt (1988). Using a voice analyzer, according to Browne, "the computer takes a student's speech input from a microphone and portrays directly on the screen the frequency and amplitude distribution of what a person has said" (1988:1). She notes that this visual feedback mode is very helpful in speech/pronunciation instruction.

Overall, the 'old' language lab, long the home of language drill of the 'listen and repeat' format, is changing. As Ronoff notes, "The phonetic incantations of beleaguered students in cramped carrels are giving way to a more modern vision of motivated learners typing responses at interactive video workstations" (1988:30). Indeed, more and more language programs have access to new technology that can facilitate certain aspects of language instruction as never before.

5. CONCLUSION

This chapter has examined a range of issues that influence any decision making relating to second-language teaching. The issues treated here are by no means comprehensive in covering all the important concerns facing language teaching; indeed, many book-length descriptions do not provide a comprehensive account. Rather, this chapter has highlighted certain areas that represent current trends and directions in the field.

Part of the discussion focused on linguistic influences and rightly so; as much as scholars talk of learner-centered instruction and communicative approaches, language teaching cannot deny its essentially linguistic foundation. And the more that teachers are aware of the linguistic foundations of language, the more effective they are as informed decision makers and resource persons in the classroom. Language teachers have a responsibility to understand what the component structures of language are, and how language works as it is used in various contexts.

The second set of issues addressed in this chapter presents important aspects of recent approaches to teaching—a focus on learner characteristics. It is now widely recognized that learners do not approach the learning task neutrally; rather, they are influenced by motivations, attitude, individual learning style and strategy, interaction style of the teacher, degree of involvement in the learning, and sociocultural factors, among other matters. The third set of issues addressed what many teachers might consider, at the outset, the main purpose of this chapter: teaching methods, syllabus-design issues, and innovative teacher choices for instruction. In fact, this section bypasses a simple listlike inventory of options in favor of addressing rationales for informed teacher choices. There are many books and chapters that focus almost solely on listing specific options in methods, techniques, and syllabi. In the short space allotted to language teaching and applied linguistics in this volume, it is more appropriate to present underlying motivations that guide informed teacher choices and to inform the reader of current directions that will influence teacher choices for some time to come.

SUGGESTIONS FOR
FURTHER READING

Linguistic influences on language teaching can be explored from a number of perspectives. Historically, Howatt (1984) and Stern (1983) provide good overviews of linguistic and language teaching. An older collection of articles on the relation between linguistics and language teaching by Allen and Corder (1973) is still well worth reading. The impact of functional linguistics and sociolinguistics on language teaching is discussed in Savignon (1983), Steele and Threadgold (1987), and Wolfson (1989).

The study of learner variables is explicitly discussed in a number of sources such as Brown (1987), Chamot et al. (1987), Oxford-Carpenter (1989), Spolsky (1989b), and Wenden and Rubin (1987). Research on learner variables is also a part of the overviews of second-language acquisition by Beebe (1988) and McLaughlin (1987), and is important in Edelsky's (1986) study of writing development in bilingual children.

Teacher variables are discussed in Kaplan et al. 1988, Richard-Amato (1987), and Richards and Rodgers (1986). Recent perspectives on curriculum issues are presented in Brinton, Snow, and Wesche (1989), Johnson (1989), and Nunan (1988, 1989), and for young children in Cummins (1986a, 1989) and Enright and McCloskey (1988).

QUESTIONS FOR FURTHER DISCUSSION

1. Morely cites Richards and Rodgers on the proliferation of approaches and methods in contemporary second- and foreign-language teaching, and then suggests that this proliferation may be seen either as a strength of the field or as a sign of deep confusion. What is the case? Is the field to be seen as rich in many alternatives, or as basically confused and lacking in direction?

2. Widdowson has several times noted the difference between *usage* and *use*, between the needs of linguists to describe all and only the possible structures of a language (or of languages) and the needs of language users to communicate in what some have called "a rough and ready manner." If Widdowson's claim is correct, what contribution *can* linguistics make to language teaching and learning?

3. It is now generally accepted that learners are not *tabula rasa*, passive recipients of teaching, but instead are active participants in the process. It is also generally accepted that listening and reading are not at all passive skills as was held in ALM, but very active participants in the creation of meaning. How are these two notions related to each other, and what implications do they have (individually or collectively) for what happens in classrooms, not merely in terms of teacher and student behavior, but also in terms of lesson content and even of the uses of physical space?

4. How does Morley's account of the scope of applied linguistics accord with the views of Strevens?

5. How does Morley's account of second-language learning accord with the view in the chapter by McLaughlin and Zemblidge?

6. What role can contemporary technology play in language teaching? How does the use of technology accord with the notion of a learner-centered classroom?

7. Compare what Morley has to say about technology with the views expressed in the chapter by Biber.

8. Morley has little to say about assessment. Given the views of Davies, what might be said to working teachers about classroom assessment of language learning?

An Introduction to
Current Directions in Foreign-Language Teaching

The development of foreign-language (FL) teaching, particularly in the United States, closely reflects the evolution of applied linguistics as a discipline. As described by Strevens and Morley, applied linguistics began to influence language teaching in the late 1950s and the 1960s. Early enthusiasm for new and scientific views of language behavior and language learning promoted a move away from grammar-translation methods and supported the introduction of foreign-language learning into elementary-school curricula. Most FL instruction in the United States, however, did not make the transition as rapidly as did FL teaching in Europe and elsewhere, or as did ESL/EFL instruction more generally. Continuing until the 1980s, the large majority of FL teachers in American universities and secondary schools were primarily teachers with a literature background who were put into language-learning classes to meet basic course demands. As a result, FL teachers were often uninterested in teaching methodology, and FL instruction meant little more than working through a set of literature-oriented grammar-translation texts.

At the same time, FL instruction advanced considerably in Europe and other countries around the world. In the 1970s the Council of Europe developed a wide range of curricular and instructional resources for FL teaching with its unit-credit scheme. The goal has been to promote a uniform approach to FL teaching among the member countries of Europe; each European foreign language should be taught in similar ways, following general curricular guidelines, with student progress certified at specific proficiency levels. While the project is incomplete, a major outcome has been a large volume of FL research on language learning as well as state-of-the-art perspectives on language teaching and curriculum design.

Similar advances are now taking place in FL teaching in the United States. In the following chapter, Savignon outlines the developments in FL teaching in the United States over the last three decades. Beginning with its emergence in the late 1950s, Savignon traces the influence of applied linguistics on FL teaching. While the 1960s offered much hope and many promises, little of lasting effect developed in FL teaching. In the 1970s the insights from sociolinguistics and systemic linguistics led to a greater emphasis on communicative aspects of language use. Savignon and a number of other researchers promoted communicative orientations to FL learning and teaching, leading to the development of communicative approaches to language teaching in the late 1970s and early 1980s. In the 1980s, FL teaching underwent a number of significant transformations. Research on FL learning, both within and outside of classroom contexts, is beginning to have an influence on FL teaching generally in the United States, and research is now providing a solid foundation for instruction and curriculum design. No longer is FL teaching guided by simple approaches and outdated commercial texts; instead, FL professionals are making significant contributions to applied linguistics and language-learning theory, and these contributions are reflected in current FL teaching methods and curricula.

As any field develops and matures, new issues and controversies are bound to arise and lead to healthy scholarly debate. In the final section of Savignon's chapter, she highlights a number of these issues specific to FL teaching that will shape future trends into the 1990s, including: the social contexts of FL learning; the importance of FL learning research in classroom contexts; and the advantages and disadvantages of uniform proficiency guidelines for all FL learners. The vigorous debates over these and other issues are a sure indication that the field of foreign-language teaching and learning is a vital contributor to applied linguistics.

Current Directions in Foreign-Language Teaching

Sandra J. Savignon
University of Illinois at Urbana-Champaign

1. INTRODUCTION

At the close of the 1950s, few American foreign-language teachers had ever heard of applied linguistics, let alone guessed the influence that this new field was about to have on their profession. The application of linguistic theory to foreign-language teaching was soon to bring dramatic changes to classroom methods, materials, and testing. The "New Key" in language teaching, as it came to be known, would be a systematic, principled approach based on some of the best current descriptions of language and language behavior.

The story of applied linguistics and American foreign-language (FL) teaching has its beginning, then, in the 1960s when audio-lingual theories of language changed the nature of language classrooms around the country. In the decades since those early years, theories of language and language behavior have evolved. Subsequent research into the nature of language acquisition has brought with it new insights and raised further questions. What has not changed, however, is the concern for a systematic, principled approach to teaching, that is, teaching practice grounded in theory. Along with their ESL colleagues, FL teachers look to applied-linguistic research for insight and innovation in curriculum, methods, and evaluation. The relationship of applied linguistics and foreign-language teaching is thus well established. This chapter will review briefly the history of this relationship and then go on to look at specific current issues.

2. THE 1960s: CONTRASTIVE ANALYSIS AND AUDIO-LINGUALISM

The 1960s proved to be an important decade for foreign-language teaching for two major reasons. First, the launching of Sputnik, the first man-made satellite, by the Soviet Union in 1957 alarmed the United States. This show of Soviet technology led directly to the appropriation of massive amounts of federal funds to improve secondary education in those fields deemed critical to national defense: mathematics, science, and foreign languages. The National Defense Education Act of 1958 provided money for upgrading teacher competence in foreign and target languages, as they came to be called, given the defense focus of the time, and equipped schools across the nation with the latest audio equipment. Overnight, language labs brought the spoken language into the classroom. Second, the growth of the field of applied linguistics in the 1940s and 1950s had prepared a cadre of scholar practitioners who were ready to give their attention to the development of methods and materials suited for a comprehensive reform of foreign-language teaching in American schools.

In her contribution to this volume, Morely has documented the origin of the term *applied linguistics* at the University of Michigan, a world-known center for the teaching of English as a second or foreign language. In 1948, a new scholarly journal originated on that campus, *Language Learning: A Journal of Applied Linguistics*. A few years later, in 1957, the publication of *Linguistics across cultures: Applied linguistics for language teachers* by University of Michigan professor Robert Lado provided the first systematic statement of contrastive linguistics as the basis for the preparation of language-teaching materials and tests. It provided new insights for teaching not only English, but other modern languages as well.

Lado's study outlined procedures for making systematic comparisons of native and foreign (L1 and L2) phonology, grammar, and vocabulary. Two years later, in 1959, the Center for Applied Linguistics was founded in Washington, D.C. Among its early projects was a series of studies contrasting English with the more commonly taught foreign languages in U.S. schools: French, German, Italian, Russian, and Spanish. Intended to provide a basis for the development of audio-lingual teaching materials, these studies served to establish contrastive analysis as the most visible early application of linguistics to FL teaching.

The structural linguists brought to language teaching the skill of isolating the phonological and morphosyntactic features of the spoken language. That isolation, in turn, provided the basis for the systematic introduction of phonemes and morphemes in the illustrative dialogues and pattern practice that were the hallmark of audio-lingual materials. Scores of FL teachers were introduced to applied linguistics through the courses with that title that were an integral part of the many National Defense Education Act (NDEA) summer FL institutes that were offered in the early 1960s. Organized by language and by level of language ability, their aim was to bolster both the linguistic and pedagogical competence of classroom teachers.

Under the general editorship of Simon Belasco, and with funding from the U.S. Office of Education and Pennsylvania State University, a series of manuals were assembled to acquaint the participants at these summer institutes with "New Key" procedures. (Grammar-translation methods were described as "rusty old keys" that failed to unlock the door to language learning.) *Applied linguistics: French*, by Albert Valdman (1961), was one such manual. Emphasis was on the kinds of phonological and morphosyntactic difficulties an American student was likely to encounter and on the use of classroom drill for acquisition of basic L2 patterns.

Similarly, Politzer's 1960 book, *Linguistics applied to the teaching of French*, stated that its aim was to develop an awareness of the pattern conflicts between French and English and of the remedies that a "linguistic" teaching method can offer. Politzer characterized the most important contributions of linguistics to language teaching as those that led to the preparation of teaching materials and influenced classroom practice. In his view, teaching materials would be improved by: (1) systematic comparison of the native language with the language to be studied in order to highlight the difficulties encountered by the learner; (2) simplification of linguistic description for the sake of learning ease; and (3) the inclusion of rules of spoken language for use in an audio-lingual phase to precede the introduction of reading and writing. In actual classroom practice, linguistic theory served to distinguish between learning language through performance (behavior) and simply learning rules of language. Slow, systematic presentation and drill of the component elements ('building stones') identified by linguists were seen as the route to L2 proficiency:

> The major contribution [of linguistics to teaching] lies in its systematic comparison of English and French and the application of a teaching methodology which, through systematic drills, attempts to build up the student's knowledge of the structure of the foreign language, while at the same time eliminating those errors which are caused by the patterns of the student's native English. (Politzer 1960:3-4)

Brook's *Language and language learning* (1960) was also widely regarded as a guide to classroom teaching. He presented the basic concepts of American structural linguistics that, together with prevailing behaviorist theories of learning, provided the theoretical justification for the audio-lingual method. The basic tenets of this method adopted for FL teaching may be summarized as follows:

1. L2 learning begins with the spoken language.
2. L2 learning goes from the simple to the complex—sound discrimination (e.g., sun/soon, back/pack, heat/hit) precedes structural manipulation, which, in turn, precedes communication.
3. Nativelike pronunciation and fluency may be attained through memorization of illustrative dialogues and rapid oral drilling of the structural patterns they display.

The teacher's manual for *A-LM French: Level 1* represents the audio-lingual perspective by citing Brooks, who served as general editor for this popular series of classroom texts: "Language behavior is not a matter of solving problems but of performing habits so well learned that they are automatic" (1961:3).

Innovations in language testing soon followed. A concern with the 'objective' measurement of language proficiency began to grow in the 1950s and on into the 1960s, an impressive decade for L2 testing in view of the number of large-scale standardized test programs that were initiated. Clark describes what he terms this "golden age" of standardized development:

> The period extending roughly from 1960–67 may be considered the "golden age" of generally available standardized test development in the foreign-language field. Under contracts from the U.S. Office of Education, and using NDEA funds, two major standardized test batteries were developed through the collaborative effort of the Modern Language Association of America and Educational Testing Service. The first of these, the MLA Foreign Language Proficiency Tests for Teachers and Advanced Students, consisted of separate skills tests (listening comprehension, reading comprehension, speaking, and writing), each in two parallel forms, for five different languages: French, German, Italian, Russian, and Spanish. (1972:156–7)

The second of these was the MLA Cooperative Foreign Language Tests, a lower-level series of tests that was also developed with U.S. Office of Education funds and under MLA-ETS auspices.

Never since has there been such a large-scale effort to establish tests and norms for foreign-language study in American schools. It was during this same period that the *Test of English as a Foreign Language* (TOEFL) was launched. The psychometric-structuralist approach represented by these tests attempted to isolate discrete structural features of language and to assess learner recognition and discrimination through the extensive use of multiple-choice format.

3. THE 1970s: A FOCUS ON COMMUNICATION

By the 1970s foreign-language teachers, along with ESL teachers, were beginning to question the basic tenets of audio-lingualism. Despite massive teacher education efforts, a primary emphasis on oral expression ran counter to an established classroom focus on reading and writing. Even in the best of audio-lingual programs, moreover, the goal of nativelike syntax and pronunciation proved elusive. Results of an early attempt to demonstrate the superiority of audio-lingual methods over grammar-translation methods in a university setting (the University of Colorado) proved disappointing (Scherer and Wertheimer 1964). A large-scale study comparing teaching methods in Pennsylvania secondary schools was similarly disappointing (Smith 1970). Both studies suffered from the problems inherent in large-scale comparison of educational approaches when variables are numerous and both classroom procedures and learning outcomes are difficult to define. The theoretical underpinnings of the structural-behaviorist audio-lingual approach were further shaken by the Keating report (1963), which criticized the effectiveness of language laboratories, and Rivers' critique of behaviorist learning theory in *The psychologist and the foreign language teacher* (1964).

A subsequent small-scale comparative study of adult classroom learners of French (Savignon 1972) examined the audio-lingual tenet that communicative self-expression is best avoided at beginning stages of L2 learning. It distinguished between sentence-level morphosyntactic accuracy (grammatical competence), on the one hand, and a broader communicative competence on the other. By encouraging learners to participate in communicative events, to seek clarification, to volunteer information, and to use circumlocution and whatever other linguistic and nonlinguistic resources they have available to them to negotiate meaning, teachers invariably lead learners to take risks, to speak in other than memorized patterns. In the prevailing view of the times, this meant that bad 'habits' would result, and that structural accuracy would suffer. In fact, evaluation of learner competence at the end of the experimental eighteen–week, five–hours-per-week program showed that learners who had practiced communication in lieu of laboratory pattern drills for one hour per week performed with no less accuracy on discrete-point tests of structure. Moreover, their communicative competence as measured in a series of four unrehearsed oral tasks significantly surpassed that of learners who had had no such practice. Learner reactions to the test formats lent further support to the view that even beginners respond well to activities that let them focus on meaning as opposed to formal features.

The Savignon study introduced the concept of communicative competence into discussions of learner evaluation, underscoring the disconcerting practice in many programs of limiting evaluation of speaking to recitation of memorized dialogues. In the model of communicative competence that would subsequently be elaborated by Canale and Swain (1980), the Savignon study served to identify *strategic competence*, the need for learners to practice communication, to develop the strategies required to negotiate meaning. Other components of the expanded view of language behavior include *grammatical competence, discourse competence*, and *sociolinguistic competence* (Brown 1987, Savignon 1983). In addition, the Savignon study supported the findings of the Keating report having to do with the ineffectiveness of language-laboratory pattern practice in increasing structural accuracy. Another major finding was the lack of correlation between learner attitudes at the beginning of L2 study and level of achievement eighteen weeks later. Rather, the inverse appeared to be the more accurate hypothesis; success in L2 study seemed to bring with it positive attitudes toward learning. This latter finding further underscored the need to evaluate learners in terms of their overall communicative competence as opposed to a more narrowly defined structural accuracy.

The shortcomings of the audio-lingual methodology are now widely acknowledged. There is general acceptance of the need for learners to have the experience of communication, to participate in the negotiation of meaning. Newer, more comprehensive theories of language and language behavior have replaced those that looked for support to American structuralism and behaviorist psychology. The applied linguistic focus of the 1970s may be said to have shifted from the language to the learner. Error analysis (EA) replaced contrastive analysis (CA) as the framework for understanding acquisition. Spurred by research in L1 acquisition (e.g., Brown 1973), the rapidly emerging field of L2 acquisition began to document similarities in acquisition patterns among learners from diverse L1 backgrounds. In this volume, McLaughlin and Zemblidge have provided a brief sketch of L2 research. Among the issues they note are learner variables, first-language influence, comparison of L1 and L2 acquisition, social context of adult L2 learning (the acculturation framework), and the role of cognitive processes.

The preponderance of studies addressing these issues have looked at the acquisition of English, primarily in naturalistic settings. A notable exception was the work of Gardner and Lambert (1972) on learner attitude and the distinction between *instrumental* and *integrative* motivation in classroom learners of French. Thus, while L2 acquisition was talked about in some FL circles, few researchers were involved in the kinds of data collection and analyses that could be seen to have direct relevance to FL classroom contexts, and FL teachers felt removed, in the main, from what they perceived to be ESL interests. Learner errors did receive some attention, and teachers were sometimes encouraged to be more tolerant of nonnative forms and were provided with alternatives to outright corrections; e.g., rephrasing a learner utterance to reflect native norms (Hendrickson 1978, Savignon 1974). Audio-lingual concern for error avoidance persisted, however, in much discussion that claimed to encourage communication and the development of communicative competence. Communication was often viewed as something that came later, after rote memorization and mechanical drill to 'master' morphosyntactic features. For some methodologists, the term communicative competence even came to denote not the expanded view of language use described by Canale and Swain (1980), Hymes (1972), Savignon (1972), and Widdowson (1978), but a disregard for structural accuracy, a minimal 'survival' level of communicative ability ill suited to the goals for school programs. The term *proficiency* was introduced to reassert the importance of attention to grammar and error correction. (For discussion, see Savignon 1983, 1985.)

Notional/functional approaches to language description similarly received attention from the American FL profession in the 1970s. Council of Europe guidelines for the development of language-teaching materials based on notions associated with various language functions (Coste et al. 1979, Slagter 1979, van Ek 1975) were noted, and suggestions were made for providing functional practice in the use of grammatical patterns. Many state FL guidelines in the United States were rewritten to reflect functional, as opposed to structural goals. As an alternative approach to syllabus organization, however, functional, or meaning-based descriptions failed to gain widespread understanding or support. Whether owing to publishers' lack of courage or to authors' lack of convictions, FL textbooks throughout the 1970s remained virtually unchanged from those of the 1960s (Ruiz 1987).

4. THE 1980s: THE EMERGENCE OF A MULTIDISCIPLINARY RESEARCH AGENDA

Such inertia is no longer the story of applied linguistics and foreign-language teaching. The 1980s marked the beginning of many widespread efforts to modify and expand existing programs to make them more reflective of current linguistic and L2 learning theory. The decade has also marked the emergence of FL learning as a multidisciplinary research field supported by university language departments and professional organizations. A small group of FL researchers are beginning to address questions of classroom learning, while at the same time continuing to underscore theoretical issues in discussions of methodology. The remainder of this chapter examines these developments.

At present, there are immersion programs in U.S. public schools, many of them modeled on established Canadian programs (Anderson and Rhodes 1984; Stern 1984), and the interest in elementary-school FL study continues to grow (Curtain and Pesole 1987). There has been a modest increase in language enrollments at both secondary and tertiary levels, although figures remain below those attained in the 1960s. Citing both the need to expand foreign markets and to promote tolerance of cultural diversity at home, the state of New York has taken the lead in broadening enrollment at the secondary level by mandating L2 experience for all learners, not only the college-bound. Curricula have been revised to emphasize functional goals accessible to all learners with appropriate changes in teaching methodology (state of New York 1985). In college and university FL departments, bastions of tradition when it comes to language teaching, reassessment of goals, diversification of offerings to include commercial studies as well as literature, and increased student participation in study-abroad programs have led in some cases to more communicatively oriented teaching. Freed (1984) documents the establishment of a foreign-language requirement at the University of Pennsylvania based on level of communicative ability, not numbers of semesters of study.

Hopes remain high for the National Foreign Language Center, established in 1987 at Johns Hopkins University School of Advanced International Studies, Washington, D.C. In his statement of goals for the Center, Lambert cites the development of:

(1) prototypical teaching and learning systems which would integrate classroom and informal learning; (2) prepared text and authentic source materials, overseas and domestic instruction; (3) intensive and non-intensive study; (4) oral-aural and visual materials, and (5) teacher-delivered classroom instruction and machine-oriented individual learning strategies. (1987:4–5)

The Center proposal includes plans for establishing a "number of experimental classrooms and other research settings to evaluate the effectiveness of the new procedures and material." (1987:5)

Throughout the proposal, the need for cumulative empirical research in foreign-language teaching methodologies is emphasized:

[There is a] surprisingly weak tradition of empiricism in the search for what works and what does not work. In place of solidly grounded practice, we have wildly exaggerated claims for one or another way to teach a foreign language. In place of theory linked firmly to applied study, we have staunchly asserted opinions on how students learn. In place of carefully formulated relationships among practice, theory, research, and curriculum and materials development, we have teachers, theorists, researchers, and pedagogues each going their own separate way. (1987:2)

Researchers, for their part, are looking increasingly at the classroom as a language-learning environment, and responsible methodologists are careful not to make sweeping claims based on limited data. Thanks to the longitudinal data that have been collected in Canadian immersion programs, we now have a better understanding of the nature of learner-classroom L2 interaction and of the communicative ability that develops. Through the work of Beretta (1987), Breen and Candlin (1980), Chaudron (1988), Felix (1981), Krashen (1982), Lightbown (1983), Long (1981), and others, we are gaining a better understanding of what goes on in classrooms and how this particular learning environment can be modified in the interest of promoting acquisition. A collection of research papers devoted exclusively to classroom FL learning (vanPatten, Dvorak, and Lee 1987), the first such volume published in the United States, marks perhaps best of all the coming of age of FL classroom learning as a worthy research focus.

As a new research perspective has developed, a new generation of FL researchers and methodologists has pursued advanced study, not only in the language and culture they teach, but in linguistic, psycholinguistic, and psychometric concepts related to language and language learning. They do so often with great difficulty. To understand the effort that this involves, one has only to compare the master-level programs of graduate students in ESL with those in FL programs. While the former emphasize theory and research, in the latter, courses in linguistics, psycholinguistics, and language acquisition must compete with advanced-level courses in language, literature, and civilization. Moreover, the multidisciplinary nature of these programs, while intellectually challenging, often places upon degree candidates the additional burden of coordinating their own graduate studies.

Support for research-oriented programs in FL learning/teaching is increasing, however. The University of Illinois multidisciplinary SLATE (Second Language Acquisition and Teacher Education) doctoral program, for example, has brought together teachers, methodologists, and researchers from the departments of English as an International Language, French, German, Italian, Portuguese, Spanish, Linguistics, Psychology, and Education. The first such program nationwide, its success in terms of number and quality of graduates is due in no small part to the opportunity for students with an FL interest to learn from and interact with leading scholars in related fields, including ESL. Opportunities for publishing research findings are also increasing. In addition to the major journals of second-language acquisition and applied linguistics, several language-specific journals now include discussions of language-acquisition theory and research findings; e.g., *Unterrichtspraxis* and *Hispania*. Most importantly, FL departments around the country advertise openings for applied linguists or methodologists with a research interest in language acquisition. Coordinators of basic language courses, traditionally newly hired professors of language or literature seeking tenure, are being replaced by directors of language programs with a record of research in language acquisition.

The increasing number of specialized conferences are further evidence of the support within the FL profession for L2 research. The first national conference on second-language acquisition/foreign-language learning was held at the University of Illinois at Urbana-Champaign in 1987. Conference papers explored the relationship of second-language acquisition research to the foreign-language learning context (vanPatten and Lee 1990). Also in 1987 a symposium on the evaluation of foreign-language proficiency (Valdman 1987) was convened to examine issues in the evaluation of oral language ability. A 1989 conference at the University of Pennsylvania, "Foreign Language Acquisition and the Classroom," sponsored by the Consortium for Language Teaching and Learning (Freed 1990) attests to the interest of the broader FL profession in research issues. The support is welcome, for the agenda is challenging.

5. CURRENT ISSUES

It is, however, still true that not all methodologists maintain a research perspective. As within ESL, there remains the worrisome phenomenon of the researcher who turns promoter and makes unwarranted claims for a teaching method or manual. When product becomes more important than process, research suffers. With specific reference to the FL context, vanPatten notes that hardly has research on L2 input been initiated when there are grand claims made about what should happen in the classroom. "We get 'input methods.' What I find worthy of concern is that the FL community does not respond with a research agenda about input in the classroom, but responds instead with a consumer's eye focused upon instruction." (1990:20)

Similar criticisms have been leveled at the American Council of Teachers of Foreign Languages (ACTFL) for its wide-scale promotion of a test of oral proficiency developed by ACTFL in collaboration with the Educational Testing Service. The ACTFL Proficiency Guidelines and Oral Proficiency Interview (OPI), promoted as a national metric with implications for FL curriculum and teaching methods, have drawn criticism both as measures of communicative ability and as the bases for methods and materials development. Discussion focuses on the need to define communicative competence and to demonstrate the construct validity of tests that purport to measure functional language ability. Valdman sums up the situation as follows:

> Those involved in adapting the OPI to the college and high school levels have not shown any profound awareness of current research directions in SLA, particularly research devoted to the specific type of learning the OPI attempts to gauge. . . . As a result, it is fair to say that, although the OPI may be experientially based, its theoretical underpinnings are shaky and its empirical support, scanty. There is no denying that a reliable and valid standardized instrument for assessing FL proficiency is highly desirable. . . . However, the FL teaching profession is incurring a high risk if it prematurely institutionalizes an assessment instrument inadequately validated and lacking theoretical support. (1988:121–122)

Thanks to an infusion of funds from the U.S. Department of Education and other sources, however, the "proficiency movement," as it has come to be known, has gathered momentum and threatens to distance a sector of the American foreign-language teaching profession from the mainstream of L2 methods research and development. Kramsch has summarized the inappropriateness of the neobehavioristic perspective for American school programs:

> . . . the oversimplified view of human interactions taken by the proficiency movement can impair and even prevent the attainment of true interactional competence within a cross-cultural framework and jeopar-

dize our chances of contributing to international understanding. The suggested proficiency oriented ACTFL/ETS goals differ from interactional goals on three accounts: (1) they focus on behavioral functions rather than on conceptual notional development; (2) they have a static rather than a dynamic view of content; (3) they emphasize accuracy to the detriment of discourse aptitude. (1986:367)

Spolsky (1986a, 1989a) takes a similar view of the FL proficiency movement. Citing the complexity and diversity of L2 ability, Spolsky sees:

serious problems with any approach that hopes to develop a simple set of common standards such as those that from the base of the guidelines developed by the American Council on the Teaching of Foreign Languages. The ACTFL Guidelines assume that it is possible to set up a single monodimensional scale on which the appropriate behaviors can be ranked. (1986a:16)

Spolsky's critique raises an issue that merits attention in a discussion of applied linguistics and FL teaching today—the issue of linguistic norms. The ACTFL Guidelines make mention of the "native speaker" with reference to learner evaluation. The significance of structural errors in terms of their effect on a testee's global rating frequently depends upon whether or not these errors "disturb the native speaker." In his critique of the Guidelines, Barnwell (1989) observes that fluent, fully communicative New York Puerto Ricans risk receiving lower ratings on the ACTFL scale than do Anglo classroom learners because their variety of Spanish does not correspond to the idealized "educated native speaker" model of the test developers.

Berns (1990a) calls attention to the need for sociolinguistic as well as psycholinguistic perspectives in looking at language learning. Social contexts of learning influence both the languages to be learned and the particular models of those languages that classroom learners are to approximate. Native-speaker competence may not be an appropriate goal for a learner or group of learners. Similarly, Preston (1989) notes the instability and variation in language systems generally. Interlanguage systems show even greater instability, he points out, and concerns of identity and accommodation require the bilingual to construct a "variation space" different from that of the native speaker. Among learners, nonnative forms may be maintained to exhibit "learner" status. And the classroom as a social context with its own relations and identities provides a setting for symbolic variation. An understanding of sociolinguistic concepts of norm, appropriacy, and variability is thus important to L2 research.

Much applied linguistics has taken an invariant attitude to goals and models in SLA, but L1, L2, interlanguages, and the most successful learners' competent systems are not invariant. Watching such systems grow and accounting for them is the goal of general sociolinguistics. (Preston 1989:272)

The development of learners' competence systems in classroom settings has become the focus of some of the more promising recent FL studies. Analysis of classroom talk and an identification of the opportunities for developing not only grammatical, but discourse, sociolinguistic, and strategic competence are preliminary to describing any but the most general relationships between classroom practice and language development. Not until the nature of classroom L2 use under different conditions has been described more fully can this use be related to learning outcomes and recommendations made for classroom practice.

An early study of foreign language–teacher talk was conducted by Guthrie (1984) who found persistent form/focus confusion even when teachers felt that they were providing an optimal classroom acquisition environment by speaking only in the L2. Transcriptions of teacher/learner dialogue reveal the unnaturalness (i.e., incoherence) of much of the discourse. More recently, a study by Kinginger (1989) has examined the nature of learner/learner talk associated with a variety of task types involving small group or pair work. Conversations representing four distinct task types were observed in two different college-level French programs. The conversations were examined with respect to: (1) turn-taking and topic management; and (2) negotiation and repair strategies. Her data show that, when learners are constrained by formal considerations or provided with a structure-embedded 'text' as a basis for 'conversation,' their talk has many of the same characteristics as form-focused teacher talk. Analyses of talk resulting from other task types provide examples of ways in which the instructional setting can be managed to provide opportunities for discourse, the dynamic process of negotiation between participants.

Negotiation of meaning is similarly the focus of a study by Pica et al. (1989) in which native speaker–nonnative speaker pairs collaborated on three different communicative tasks. Participants in this instance were intermediate-level adult Japanese learners of English and native speakers of English with no teaching background. The native speaker–signal type was found to have a significant impact on the type of nonnative speaker response. The nonnative speaker was more likely to modify his or her expression when the native speaker signaled an explicit need for clarification rather than providing a model utterance for confirmation. Among the other interesting findings of this study was the influence of gender on the nature of the negotiation. Male nonnatives were much more likely to modify their expression, to interact in negotiation with the female native speakers participating in the study than were their female counterparts. This observation led the researchers to note that "[nonnative speaker] production of comprehensible output was not simply an outcome of a single factor such as task type, but a host of inter- and intrapersonal variables as well" (1989:84), and to recommend that both gender and ethnicity of participants be taken into account in the design of further research on learner expression and negotiation. Analysis of interaction of this kind represents a rich source of data, not only for understanding the nature of negotiation between native and nonnative speakers, as the researchers conclude, but also for understanding the potential for nonnative–nonnative negotiation in foreign language–classroom settings. The Kinginger study (cited above) represents a step in this direction.

6. CONCLUSION

Understanding of language and language behavior will continue to change as multidisciplinary inquiry advances. However, the implications for classroom teaching will not always be clear-cut. Sobered by the reassessment of the 1970s, FL methodologists in the 1980s generally have taken a more cautious position, advocating further research and experimentation in lieu of far-reaching educational reform. Among the basic questions that remain may be included the following:

1. What does it mean to know a language?
2. How does language competence develop within a classroom?
3. How does language competence develop outside a classroom?
4. How do linguistic, psychological, and social factors in second-language acquisition influence FL instruction?
5. What additional sociopolitical factors influence how teachers teach?

This brief overview has attempted to provide a sense of history and of current issues in applied linguistics and FL teaching. To be sure, the relation has been a dynamic one and has contributed in no small way to establishing FL learning as a research field in its own right. As increasing numbers of FL researchers enter the field, they no doubt will make their presence felt in the broader field of language-acquisition research. As the world continues to grow smaller, and linguistic and cultural boundaries become increasingly blurred, the day may even come when the distinction 'foreign' will no longer appear useful. In a multilingual perspective we may simply speak of language learning and teaching.

SUGGESTIONS FOR
FURTHER READING

Until recently, there was relatively little research oriented to FL learning and teaching (cf. Savignon 1983; Savignon and Berns 1984, 1987). In the last few years, however, a considerable amount of important research has been published. In particular, volumes by Berns (1990b), Freed (1990), Lantolf and Labarca (1987), Spolsky (1989), vanPatten et al. (1987), and vanPatten and Lee (1990) all focus on major issues discussed in this chapter and are representative of the rapid growth in FL research. Other research perspectives that emerge from the application of modern technology to FL teaching may be found in Flint (1987, 1989b). In addition, FL teaching and learning research is reported in a number of important journals: *Applied Linguistics; Canadian Modern Language Review; Foreign Language Annals; Language Learning; Modern Language Journal;* and *Studies in Second Language Acquisition.*

QUESTIONS FOR FURTHER DISCUSSION

1. In what directions has FL teaching evolved over the last three decades?
2. Why is it useful to distinguish ESL instruction from FL instruction in the United States?
3. Why does Savignon suggest that FL teaching may be more consumer-driven than research-driven, as indicated by the vanPatten quotation ("We get 'input methods'.")?
4. How does a sociolinguistic perspective on language learning and language teaching provide an argument against the use of an all-inclusive language proficiency–evaluation guideline (such as ACTFL) for curriculum development?
5. In what ways are the developments in U.S. FL teaching similar to, and different from FL teaching in other countries?
6. How does the overview provided by Savignon differ from the perspective on second-language teaching presented by Morley?
7. In what ways does the discussion of language learning by McLaughlin and Zemblidge provide a foundation for current perspectives in FL teaching?
8. Macias' chapter in this volume also presents a view of second-language learning in the United States. Why are the discussions in Macias and Savignon so different?

An Introduction to
Language Testing and Evaluation

A central theme in the Davies chapter is that paradigm shifts within linguistics, psycholinguistics, sociolinguistics, and applied linguistics have served to move language testing from a minor position within applied linguistics—one with a particularly practical orientation—to center stage within applied linguistics. It is now the case that research in language testing not only brings into question certain theoretical notions in language teaching, but also makes important contributions to curriculum design and materials preparation, as well as to such more theoretical areas as second-language acquisition research and research in discourse analysis. In short, the contributions of language testing to applied linguistics have become very significant and have been instrumental in the movement of language testing into a position of prominence.

When audio-lingual methodology was in wide use, thus when language theory, learning theory, and teaching methodology were in close coordination, testing was largely relegated to the role of selecting and arranging discrete points drawn from the language syllabus and serving to assess particular structures. But as attention has shifted from structural knowledge of language in the direction of communicative competence; as syllabus development has been separated from structuralist models of language and has moved through notional/functional designs to even less syntactically defined models; as materials development has moved from the assumption that slot-filler, substitution, or repetition drills taught language skills toward designs that attempt to involve the learner in meaning-creating activities; and as classroom focus has been redirected from the teacher to the learner, the function of testing has changed.

Testing, as Davies suggests, has actually become a very large research field; it is also a field that must address a number of practical concerns and issues. Questions of how to design an effective test are not only a matter for testing corporations but also for the classroom teacher (cf. Heaton 1976; Madsen 1983). Teachers need to consider what to test, how to test, and why to test the various skills and material introduced in their classes (Oller 1979; Savignon 1983). In the United States, the American Council for Teachers of Foreign Languages (ACTFL) has developed testing guidelines intended for use in curriculum development (see Savignon, in this volume). These guidelines are being adopted in many foreign language–teaching contexts, particularly in university curricula. To what extent these guidelines would be appropriate to various types of EFL/ESL instruction is an open question. The growing interest in communicative language teaching has also had an influence on language testing, not only in the classroom but also on a more theoretical level.

Oller (1979, 1983) and other scholars interested in testing have sought ways to tap both more communicative skills (e.g., through dictation tests, cloze tests, and other integrated language-use activities) and more universal factors underlying language learning (cf. Canale 1988; Oller 1981; McLaughlin and Zemblidge; Morley and Strevens, in this volume). More recently, the work of such researchers as Bachman (1989, 1990) has begun not only to contribute to new views of measurement, but also to contribute algorithms which researchers in discourse analysis must take account of. For example, Bachman devised a taxonomy of functions that atomizes text in tests into a complex set of presupposed features constituting analyses of, among other things, test facets, text length, propositional content, contextualizations, topic, lexis, syntax, etc. More sophisticated statistical procedures have opened the door to the analysis of more complex structures and conceptualizations, and have provided validation of new ways of looking at assessment generally (e.g., using factor analysis, item response theory [IRT], causal-path analysis [LISREL]. Changing views of the definition of language and of the definition of what can be taught have placed new demands on test development. Thus the notion of discrete-item multiple-choice questions gave way to cloze-procedure tests, which in turn gave way to holistic measures.

Davies positions language testing in relation to applied linguistics generally and then goes on to identify three basic problems in contemporary language testing: communicative language testing, testing language for special purposes, and the question of the unitary-competence hypothesis, all of which he explores in depth. He also explores the problem of validity and reliability in relation to tests devised for different purposes—achievement tests, proficiency tests, and aptitude tests—and contrasts practices that have grown up in Britain, the United States, and Europe. He concludes that the role of language testing is to provide a viable research methodology and to raise central theoretical questions by operationalizing theories as testable hypotheses. He also comments on the role of computers in testing, noting both their uses and their limitations.

Language Testing and Evaluation

Alan Davies
University of Edinburgh

1. INTRODUCTION

In the last twenty years, applied linguistics has developed as a coherent discipline by identifying those areas of linguistics, sociolinguistics, psychology of language, and education that inform our understanding of the processes of language learning, notably in institutional settings; that is, with particular reference to language teaching. In doing so, it has gone from fragmented attempts to provide a framework for rational discussions of language teaching to a more theoretical approach to language teaching and to language use. So far, the greatest effort in applied linguistics has been in relation to language teaching and (to a lesser extent) language pathologies; but the way is now open for a more dynamic applied linguistics which will inform, and in due course, explain other aspects of language use. As part of the development over these two decades, the discipline has properly and necessarily developed its own experimental procedures that permit the testing of hypotheses drawn from the theoretical statements. It also provides descriptive apparatuses by which to examine the linguistic data in terms of analyses demanded by the theories.

The three main sources for the experimental and descriptive developments have been: (1) language testing; (2) second-language acquisition studies; and (3) discourse analysis. Of these, the most applied is language testing, in that it so obviously takes its origin in practical issues of language demands and selection requirements. But as Lado's key study (1961), which set the agenda for work on language testing over the following twenty years, made clear, language-testing provides both practical solutions to language-teaching problems and an examination of central applied-linguistic concerns: the nature of language proficiency, language aptitude, and the delineation of language-learning stages.

There is a proper dynamic in the growth of a discipline. As it develops, its parts grow and prosper at different rates and jostle for the high ground. In so doing, their very success can take them away from the center of the discipline that they inform to a potentially separate existence, thus creating, or threatening to create, a new discipline. Second-language acquisition is a striking example of such a trend. Growing out of the practice of error analysis as a methodology for contrastive studies, and thereby providing one explanatory theory at the heart of earlier applied linguistics, it has now become so important as a theoretical study in its own right, dislodging contrastive analysis from its explanatory status to being a mode of description, developing its own methodology and analyses, and now its own set of theories (often conflicting), that second-language acquisition regards itself as no longer part of applied linguistics, but as a discrete discipline.

While such a trend is normal as disciplines grow and develop, it is, in fact, unnecessary in terms of the second-language acquisition–applied linguistics relationship. It can only be true that second-language acquisition is not part of applied linguistics if applied linguistics concerns itself solely with language teaching. But applied linguistics itself has, as we have suggested, moved on during the period of growth in research on second-language acquisition to reorient itself to concern with language learning, a wider and more basic study than language teaching, and will, if our prediction is correct, move on to become the theoretical and descriptive study of language in use. That being the case, second-language acquisition should still be regarded as part of applied linguistics. Its disassociation from applied linguistics is unnecessary and destructive both of itself and of applied linguistics, since applied linguistics needs research in second-language acquisition as a major set of explanatory and descriptive apparatuses. Similarly, the study of second-language acquisition needs applied linguistics to give it context and purpose.

2. LANGUAGE TESTING AND APPLIED LINGUISTICS

The development of language testing over the same period (roughly the last twenty years) exhibits a parallel dialectic. At the time of the Lado publication (1961), language testing was peripheral to applied linguistics, curiously so since language testing had always been so closely linked to language teaching. Language testing was thought to be hardly linguistic and very nontheoretical. However, research in language testing in the last twenty years has moved it into a commanding position within applied linguistics because it has confronted major questions of language learning and language use by articulating viable research methodologies. In short, what language testing has done in the last twenty years has been to move itself from a practical to a theoretical status within applied linguistics. As such, it has gained academic respect (which is always given more readily to theoretical studies) and has begun to develop explanatory power. At the same time, it has lost some of its practical force and development value in language teaching: while its theoretical modeling has developed very fast, its practical applications have not kept pace even with developments in language teaching.

Once again, this may parallel the development over the last twenty years of research in second-language acquisition, with the research element moving forward from contrastive analysis and the practical link to language teaching, but gradually weakening as the theoretical/research aspect becomes stronger. This trend has progressed to the extent that some current scholars of second-language acquisition claim for their discipline as much—or as little—concern with language teaching as, say, theoretical linguistics. And when one such scholar (e.g., Krashen 1985) makes a direct connection (with his input hypothesis) between language teaching and his acquisition-learning distinction, the insights provided for language teaching are but momentary and the gain in methodology nonexistent. It is also of particular interest to our present discussion that there are signs in certain current thinking about second-language acquisition that there is a need for a rapprochement between the investigation of second-language acquisition and language testing (e.g., Brindley 1986; Long 1987; Pienemann and Johnston 1987b).

The paradox we face, as illustrated above by testing and second-language acquisition, is that development in applied linguistics is away from language-teaching concerns and interests. At one level, this must be inevitable. What starts as a subject (teaching courses for selected groups of students, often vocational students in the case of applied linguistics) typically develops into a discipline, an area institutionally defined by named posts (professor of _____), journals, degrees, etc. Eventually, the subject-become-discipline acquires a momentum and, hopefully, a coherence of its own. Thus, applied linguistics loses its original subject-like direct link with language teaching.

Again, it is indeed true that applied linguistics has made serious attempts over the last twenty years to extend its range of relevance beyond language teaching and especially beyond foreign- and second-language teaching and the teaching of English as a foreign (second) language.[1] It has rapidly moved into the pathologies (speech production, hearing, sight, etc.), translation and interpreting, language policy and planning, lexicography, speech synthesis and computer modeling, literary stylistics, and a range of areas of language use in social contexts (where the label is often 'language and/in/of _____)'; e.g., language and medicine, language and the law, language in science, the language of propaganda). While applied linguistics has made some inroads in some of these areas (notably the pathologies and lexicography), and while there is always some ambiguity about the categorization of sociolinguistics, psycholinguistics, and so on, yet, inevitably, there is always a special concern for language teaching, if only because applied linguistics, in spite of its growth as a discipline, is vocationally oriented, and the largest single vocation for which applied linguistics is (thought to be) relevant to language teaching.

But the assertion of our paradox does not stand up to scrutiny. For the move in applied linguistics that we have characterized as being toward theory and research has not in reality taken it away, except at a very superficial level, from language teaching. What has happened, as we see it, is that applied linguistics has attempted to explore the underlying structure of language teaching, to consider its aims, demands, processes, in a more abstract way, and to provide explanations for the behavior of language teaching (and, more generally, to incorporate the other areas of language use which we have cited). As such, it does not purport to 'solve' immediate problems of language teaching nor to improve that teaching directly. What it does, rather, is provide a rationale for the activity, in all of its manifestations, which we know as language teaching. This must have profound implications for the vocational training that applied linguistics set out to provide, and it has been suggested that a more appropriate designation would be *education* in applied linguistics rather than *training* in applied linguistics (cf. teacher education and teacher training). The assumption, which we fully accept, is that an education in applied linguistics provides a combination of theoretical understanding and general methodological skills that are of relevance across a very wide range of language-teaching (and indeed language-use) situations.

3. CURRENT TRENDS IN LANGUAGE TESTING

We can document a similar progress in language testing. As with applied linguistics in general, so with language testing in particular, a subject matter has become a subdiscipline with named posts—in research if not in teaching—textbooks, at least one international journal, and qualifications (at least one university certificate). The effect of this move from subject to discipline has certainly meant greater coherence, but as we have already seen, it also means more research and more theory that may not appear to be of indirect relevance to language teaching. Hence the common complaint from language teaching that 'academic' language testing has nothing to say about, for example, communicative-language testing. The fact is that applied-linguistics language testing has a great deal to say about relevance to language teaching and indeed to communicative-language testing, but usually in terms of fundamental issues (cf. Alderson and Hughes 1982) rather than in terms of communicative-language tests for classroom use (cf. Savignon 1983). In other words, the relevance is indirect.

Language testing has also extended its range of relevance beyond its earlier focus in two ways. First, it has developed measures other than quantitative ones (basically a growing realization of the need to value validity—what a test claims to measure—more than reliability—how well the test measures across students and across time), so that qualitative measures of judgment, including self-judgments and control and observation, are included in the tester's repertoire. Second, it has extended the scope of testing to include evaluation of courses, materials, and projects, using both quantitative and qualitative measures of plans, processes, and input, as well as measurement of learners' output, the traditional testing approach.

As with the more general case of applied linguistics, again the paradox of moving away from the vocational mainstream is more apparent than real. The research and theoretical development of language testing has led, it is true, to a less direct concern with the writing of language tests, and here critics such as Morrow (1977) are correct. But it has also led to a much clearer view both of the nature of language testing, of the ways it can be instrumental in applied-linguistics research, and also of the role of language testing within applied linguistics. What we see is that Alderson's plea (Alderson 1982) has already been answered, and that our own doubts about the connection between language testing and applied linguistics, with language testing on the periphery, were always misguided. Language testing was, in reality, always a chief way of applying linguistics, perhaps more so than most other activities in applied linguistics, in that the selection of material for language tests and the statements made about or on the basis of the results achieved were always of linguistic import, making statements about the nature of language and of language learning (see also Bachman 1989, 1990).

This view is best realized in the volume edited by Alderson and Hughes (1982), which indeed represents a resource for making the field more coherent in reporting recent language-testing research in applied linguistics. Moreover, it provides a systematization of language testing that could have been made in a speculative manner (i.e., without, as we have said, the recent empirical research) twenty years before (e.g., Lado 1961; Harris 1969; Valette 1978). In the Alderson and Hughes (1982) volume, three main areas are designated and discussed in depth, with published papers used for discussion, followed by discussants' written comments and an account of the seminar discussions that followed the papers and the discussants' papers. The three areas regarded as chiefly relevant to language testing in applied linguistics are:

1. Communicative-language testing;
2. Testing language for specific purposes; and
3. The unitary-competence hypothesis.

In all three cases, the discussion is theoretical, but, equally in all three cases, the implications are practical and have (no doubt indirect) relevance to language learning and teaching.

The first topic, communicative-language testing, raises the issues of communication, of authentic language use and evaluation, of language samples as representing language proficiency, and of abstraction in language sampling, as well as of direct vs. indirect tests, and the relationship within linguistics (and language teaching) of structural systems and their realization and uses (competence vs. performance). All of these are of equal importance in linguistic and eventually in language teaching, and it is the role of applied linguistics to tease out and seek to explain those issues that bridge language theory and language use.

The chief role so far for applied linguistics in relation to communicative-language testing seems to be that of providing critical theory as in, for example, the critical framework provided by Canale and Swain (1980) following on the sociolinguistic ideas of Hymes and Gumpers. The upshot to date still seems to be that communicative-language testing means not communicative testing of language, but the testing of communicative language. This follows the views of Morrow (1977), who has pointed out that what critically distinguishes communicative-language testing is the introduction of real-language input rather than some new methodology of testing. As a result, those few tests of communicative language that have been developed (The Royal Society of Arts n.d.; Savignon 1983) focus on one small area in which there is reasonable agreement that the input is direct language. To choose a large amount of input would give hostages to the fortune of contrived or redundant (and therefore untestworthy) data.

The second topic treated in the Alderson and Hughes (1982) volume, testing languages for specific purposes, concerns at one level the very practical need in many situations for assessing learning programs of instruction in languages for specific purposes, usually those related to specific academic subjects or to vocational training (English for engineering students, English for flight attendants). At the same time, in order to make sense of the demand for LSP testing, the discussion examines the status and validity of systems for the analysis of language needs, as well as the more fundamental linguistic question of accounting for differences in language varieties. LSP teaching assumes that discrete language varieties can be established and described for learners. The role of language-testing research—precisely applied-linguistic research in language testing—is both to examine the methodology of such assessment demands and also, and more profoundly, through operationalizing the question, the idea, speculation, or theory (i.e., by making testable hypotheses), to query the claims and the status of specific language varieties (vs. general English) and therefore of the teaching and testing of LSP as a separate approach.[2]

The third topic, general language proficiency, concerns the seemingly least practical issue connected with language testing, that is, the nature of linguistic competence—whether it is unitary or multiple. Using multivariate statistical procedures, researchers are exploring whether various language skills converge, statistically, as a single underlying construct, or whether there are a number of distinct language subskills that need to be considered independently (cf. Oller 1981, 1983; Bachman 1989). At first sight, this has little relevance for language teaching and appears to be trying to resolve a theoretical question about linguistic competence through statistical analysis. However, the topic and its discussion show how the issue is of central importance to applied linguistics in that they demonstrate, by extensive discussion of experiments in language-testing research, that an elegant research methodology is possible in applied linguistics, through language testing, and that the issue addressed is important to applied-linguistic ideas of language learning and the relationship among the modalities (e.g., listening, speaking, and writing). As such, it is also of practical interest, by implication, for language teaching; the issue is raised whether or not language learning can be achieved generally by focusing only on certain language-learning skills or classroom procedures. Similarly, for the design and choice of language tests, the issue is raised as to how many separate language tests are needed to assess proficiency—the 'one best test' question.

All three of these important issues: communicative-language testing; testing English for specific purposes; and general language proficiency testing, remind us that applied linguistics necessarily focuses on matters of central concern to language learning. Communication, with its emphasis on the role of meaning and the importance of purpose in language learning; English for specific purposes and its attempts to operationalize the pragmatic reality of selected language learning; and general language proficiency, which seeks evidence for the factorial structure of language learning, are all central language-learning issues and, therefore, of importance in applied linguistics. All that is surprising here is that the form of investigation being undertaken on behalf of applied linguistics into these three current central issues of language learning is that of language testing. It is no wonder that language testing is now regarded, as has been suggested in this chapter, as firmly within the main area of applied linguistics.

The role of language testing in relation to all three issues, then, is twofold: (1) to provide a research methodology; and (2) to raise central theoretical (and eventually practical) issues by operationalizing the theories, making them into testable hypotheses. What is clearly needed in the further development of language testing in applied linguistics is a closer link in theory and research between language-testing concerns and research in second-language acquisition. While second language–acquisition research is uniquely concerned with, and equipped to examine, language-learning processes over time (e.g., McLaughlin and Zemblidge, in this volume), language testing provides the methodology for, and the interest in, the assessment of product. The two together might—if a union could be made—offer productive insights into, and explanations of, the relation between process and product that we currently lack, again providing both theoretical and practical results.

4. VALIDITY AND RELIABILITY IN TESTING

Developments in language testing move over time between thesis and counter-thesis, first maximizing validity (what the test measures), then maximizing reliability (how carefully the test measures). Rather than expect some kind of synthesis—an unacceptable stasis—it is probably good and inevitable that development should take the form of this reactive process, given the tension that necessarily exists between reliability and validity. The movement to communicative-language testing, or as Oller (1979) would have it, more performance-based tests, has been slow and painful for the reasons already addressed. Clearly, such a move is on the side of validity, in that it shifts the usually reliable, structuralist, objective, discrete point tests of the 1960s into a more communicative mode. That attempt has been most successful in achievement testing, less so in proficiency testing, and not at all in aptitude testing. And even before it has run its full course, we can already observe a countermovement back to an emphasis on reliability. We will examine these two stages of recent development.

4.1. Validity in Achievement Testing

The move to validity in achievement or attainment testing, i.e., it should be school-based with a typical control on previous learning, is found in the important work of the Council of Europe resulting in the unit-credit system (van Ek 1975). This scheme attempts to provide a uniform set of levels of attainment for learners of English throughout member countries of the Council of Europe (except, of course, for English L1 countries themselves), and by doing so implicitly and later explicitly to test attainment of those stages. In the United Kingdom, the schemes have been redesigned on a very similar mode for use with the teaching (and testing) of French, German, Italian, and Spanish, and it is reckoned (Clark 1987) that similar schemes could operate well in any language-teaching situation in which the language is, generally speaking, used only in the foreign-language classroom.

The motivation for the unit-credit system of the Council of Europe has been twofold (it could be argued that the two aims are two ways of saying the same thing): first, to provide a framework of equivalence for all member countries of the Council of Europe, and to do this by providing a similar set of stages; second, to make learning communicatively oriented. Successive attainment of stages is tested by appropriate tests, and since the second motivation has been to 'communicativize' learning through those stages, there is now the public assumption that communicative teaching and testing have become the norm. That is not the case. Much so-called communicative testing is so only in name, or lays too heavy a burden on the test administrator. We need to ask why there is so little success so far. Is it because of deliberate nonuse of communicative-language tests or because of the difficulty of their construction? In my view, it is largely for the second reason, though it is also due to a view stubbornly held by those responsible for testing that language tests are universally applicable; for many test administrators, the most efficient tests are believed to be indirect ones, since indirect tests are always at a remove from local contextual constraints. So it is for reasons partly of belief and partly of efficiency that indirect tests continue to be used so widely (e.g., grammar tests as surrogate communicative tests). It would be instructive to be able to argue for more communicative testing from data, and Savignon (1983) has tried to provide some. In the main, however, the argument in this area of testing is based on custom and belief.

As a result, such tests are not given much exposure but, more importantly, they are not widely available apart from the unit-credit system. Central to the philosophy of the unit-credit system is the view that teachers should be responsible for their own materials, including tests. The Council of Europe scheme is basically criterion-referenced (a mastery-levels philosophy) and, as such, the stages of attainment can be made good sense of the learner without necessarily becoming wholly routinized. However, it is agreed that schemes of the unit credit–system variety do lean heavily toward interaction routines, and the danger exists for teaching, as well as for testing, of tasks, projects, and activities that are so heavily routinized that they become rote-learned.

The test of the unit credit–system type is one of the more successful examples of criterion-referencing, which in recent years has come back into vogue for achievement testing. It must be the case, however, that criterion-referencing, much like all analyses of language learning, is of greater use at early stages; language criteria are more easily delineated at these stages. Advanced language learning simply is too complex for researchers to state (except in terms of broad partial coverage) exactly what must be achieved at every level of language learning. Criterion-referencing, as desirable as it may be educationally, has not found adequate support (and many would think should not) from research on second-language acquisition or from language testing proper, or indeed from linguistic and psycholinguistic analysis and description, so that it is making substantive progress beyond current uses.

4.2. Validity and Proficiency Tests

With regard to proficiency tests, language testing has been much influenced by Oller's investigations and arguments (Oller 1979), in particular by his views on pragmatic testing and the grammar of expectancy. Now it seems to be the case that the grammar of expectancy has a more psycholinguistic interpretation than a linguistic interpretation, and it might therefore be more appropriate to avoid using the term *grammar* and instead speak of *prediction* in the usual way. Nevertheless, Oller was ill advised in reminding us that prediction in language processing is central to proficiency, and that it both requires syntactic control and is at the same time not unlike a grammar in that it combines parts. Hence, in Oller's view pragmatic tests are likely to be those tests employing techniques that combine the simulated procedures of real-time processing of reasonably genuine texts. Dictation and cloze techniques have so far found most favor as pragmatic measures.

General proficiency tests have been influenced only partially by this search for greater communicative validity. The Test of English as a Foreign Language (TOEFL), which has been analyzed more extensively than any other proficiency test, has moved minimally toward a communicative mode and has changed only with regard to skill extension in its recent provision of a test of written production. There are two tests that have been much influenced by sociolinguistic discussion of communicative competence. The first of these is the open test offered by the Royal Society of Arts: The Communicative Use of English as a Foreign Language, which is interesting in three ways: (1) It provides for a profile-entry and a profile-scoring report. The test is available at three levels and in four skills, and candidates may offer any skill at any level. That flexibility has, it seems, not been made much use of. (2) The oral interview is made deliberately relaxed, and as much attention is paid to the interaction between candidate and speaker as in the Foreign Service Institute test (now the IART test). (3) The content of the reading materials in the reading component is intended to be real or genuine written English, and the tasks required of candidates are as authentic as is possible in a test situation.

The second test that has been influenced by sociolinguistic considerations, and is in a different way experimental in its approach, is the test constructed by the English Language Testing Service (ELTS) of the British Council/University of Cambridge Local Examinations Syndicate, which offers both general grammar and listening subtests, and specialist study-skills, writing, and oral subtests. The distinction of this test is that it really has attempted to make testing provisions for ESP needs and, according to the evaluation study (Criper and Davies 1986), has been judged to be reasonably successful in such a difficult area in which language varieties are not discrete—as we have already noted. Indeed, it could be claimed for the ELTS test that it is an example of language-testing research and development having implications, however tentative, for linguistic description, since a major problem of descriptive sociolinguistics has always been to demonstrate systematic differences among language varieties. The conclusion of the evaluation study made of the ELTS test is complex: variation does exist among learners, but it is not clear to what extent this variation is linguistic, and to what extent it is psycholinguistic.

The FSI Interview Scale has received the most extensive validation of any oral scale and represents one strong line of development that we have already noted in the case of the unit-credit system, namely, to provide distinct and clearly described stages of development for proficiency evaluation (see also ACTFL guidelines, ACTFL 1986; Higgs 1982). The advantage of the FSI scale is that it has been used so widely and thus (as is the case with all test instruments) has accumulated considerable validation information. The process of validation is, however, constantly in conflict with itself, since equal claims can be made both to maintain the same test instrument for the sake of accumulating data and to change to a new instrument for the sake of refinement conforming to current views of validity. As elsewhere in the field, a tolerant compromise is essential.

From time to time, suggestions have been made that there is a need to negotiate some method of test comparability that would presumably allow for this compromise. Such comparability is particularly desirable in the area of production tests, since without item matching of any kind, as is possible in receptive tests, the equivalence of one oral test to another or one written test to another may be a figment only of statistical sleight of hand. Both ELTS and TOEFL are currently making attempts to stabilize and make more explicit their writing and oral tests.

It must be noted that the Educational Testing Service (ETS, producer of the TOEFL) and the University of Cambridge Local Examinations Syndicated (UCLES) approach testing quite differently. Bachman points out that:

> the TOEFL is perhaps the prototypical psychometric/structuralist language test. . . . The Certificate of Proficiency in English (CPE) and the First Certificate of English (FCE), on the other hand, have been designed and developed largely on the basis of a consideration of language skills and abilities, with less emphasis on psychometric concerns. To oversimplify the distinction, we might say that the ETS tests represent language test development driven largely by measurement theory, while the UCLES tests represent language test development driven primarily by applied linguistic theory. (1988:2)

UCLES has commissioned a "Cambridge—TOEFL comparability study," which has as its main objective to examine the comparability of these two different testing batteries. The comparability study employs Lyle Bachman as the principal investigator, but the study is overseen by an international advising body including Braj Kachru, Gillian Brown, and several other scholars and researchers in applied linguistics and language testing.

Another recent approach to proficiency testing representing a deliberate attempt to inform proficiency testing with linguistic data is that associated with the work of Brindley (1986) and Pienemann and Johnston (1987b), which hazards that proficiency stages may be (perhaps should be) matched in some sense with stages of second-language acquisition (SLA). Inevitably, there are many problems here, problems of the status of SLA-research findings and of their applicability (particularly when the data are morpho-syntactic only) to proficiency which, says the counterclaimed, may be as much a matter of fluency as of accuracy. Nevertheless, the issue is an important one both for testing, which must answer the question whether indirect tests are in any sense equivalent to direct ones, and for SLA research, which must address the question to what extent the stage approach, the assumption of some kind of 'natural' order in second-language acquisition, is valid, whether it is possible to consider stages in terms of functions and discourse rather than forms only, and in any case, whether a natural order, if one exists, is relevant for any applied-educational or -testing concern.

4.3. Validity and Aptitude Testing

Language-aptitude testing has enjoyed periods of activity over the last 30 years but does not seem to have a permanent appeal. New aptitude tests are rare perhaps because they reflect a new linguistic or psycholinguistic model of language and learning. Even so, in terms of the influence of linguistics or psycholinguistics on test construction, there seems very little change from the early Carroll and Sapon experiments with the Modern Language Aptitude Test (Carroll and Sapon 1959). The extensions provided by Pimsleur (1966) and Skehan (1982) are essentially outside language rather than deeper inside language, although verbal-fluency tests (Davies 1971) have, on occasion, been used to tap a wider range of language skills, influenced, it must now be seen, by sociolinguistic notions of variety.

5. RELIABILITY, ITEM-RESPONSE THEORY, AND COMPUTERS IN LANGUAGE TESTING

The attempt to mak℈ language testing more valid, which has been briefly sketched, can be summarized in terms of attempts, of a very similar kind, to make language measurement more context-sensitive, to move it away from the earlier fixed idea that there is one type of measure suitable for all purposes. The results of the ELTS validation study indeed imply that what is needed now in proficiency testing is not more theory but a very large array of tests suitable for different purposes. Of course, the likelihood is that such an array will never be made available, since the interest of testing and certifying bodies is probably in maintaining a nearly unitary test provision for the sake of convenience and cost.

The search for greater validity through context-sensitivity is not necessarily wholly desirable, and the arguments against it are not only practical ones. It is argued that tests represent or set norms of the standard language, and therefore, any attempt to extend the range of norms through different standards can be seen as divisive, patronizing, etc. (cf. Prator 1968 for an early statement). However, if greater reliability goes with greater validity and more flexible testing, then such tests would be attractive. Much of the present development emphasis appears to be, in varied ways, on increasing test reliability through statistical methods. That is a generous view of the present situation. A more cynical view would be that the renewed interest in reliability comes from the rapid development of computer hardware and software. Thus, item-response theory (IRT), most often in its most accessible form, offered by Rasch, is used to produce tests of very high homogeneity (and therefore high internal reliability) which are, as far as possible, sample-free (that is, free of the requirement that all subjects respond to a large set of identical items; cf. Henning 1987; Larson and Madsen 1985; Woods and Baker 1985). Whether or not it is interesting or important to make language tests sample-free is a question rarely asked. It can be argued that sample-free tests are at the opposite pole from the search for context-sensitive tests, which more recent test development has been about (that is, a computerized testing procedure for all students vs. separate tests for different language specializations). No doubt one arguable view of reliability is that it is one component of validity; thus, improving reliability improves validity. This makes a strong argument for going far with attempts to improve reliability at whatever cost to validity. This is a seductive but dangerous view.

It must also surely be the case that interest in IRT comes in part from the increasing availability of computers, which, like other sophisticated machinery, have the capacity to dominate and not serve humanity. A serious drawback to IRT, the drawback of giving such test analyses maximum importance, is that IRT is really of value only with discrete-point tests. This is true also of current attempts to produce materials for computer-assisted language testing, which, at present, looks to be giving a backward rather than a forward direction to test development, since the only language tests so far available on computer are very traditional and quite noninteractive.

6. PROJECT EVALUATION

The relationship between course or project evaluation and testing has come under greater scrutiny within applied linguistics in the last decade. This reflects both the increasing importance given to process analysis as opposed to product analysis and the refining of tests themselves for more sophisticated (and therefore valid) purposes. Both influences, undoubtedly, stem from a general concern within the language disciplines, but also, more generally, are found among the social sciences seeking a less positivistic, more humanist approach, as well as a greater concern with the nondeterminist variation that permits individual cognitive differences. Such a paradigm is best observed in linguistics in the reassertion of the importance to language of social contexts and psychological processes; it is not surprising, therefore, that applied linguistics and then, in its turn, language testing and evaluation have extended their parameters.

The effect on project evaluation has been to extend the range of observation beyond the outcome (and the entry-exit) test and to include in the array of measurements questionnaires to participants, including those involved with input; ethnographic observation, including participant observation involving close analysis of discourse though transcripts; and self-assessment routines. In addition to process measurement, product tests are still much in use for project evaluation, including both integrated and discrete-point tests. The intention is to provide as full a picture of the project, course, or materials as possible. By such extensions, we acknowledge our general awareness that, as applied linguistics develops, we become more aware both of the complexity of language and of how inadequate our means are to describe and assess it. The extending of the types of observation used indicates our own recognition of the narrowness of any one measure.

The broadening, therefore, in project evaluation (Alderson 1985; Beretta 1987a; Brumfit 1984; Kennedy 1983) beyond quantitative to qualitative measures is another indication, in my view, of the growing maturity of applied linguistics, showing that it is now relaxed and confident enough to move with greater ease between quantitative and qualitative approaches to measurement, and to feel sure enough of itself so that its researchers do not have to choose between a positivist and nonpositivist approach.

7. CONCLUSION

I have argued that language testing is of importance in applied linguistics because it operationalizes hypotheses and provides practical scenarios. Language study contains many primitives that resist scientific-experimental definitions and remain at the level of imprecision. Language testing firmly tackles such concepts as 'native speaker,' 'level of proficiency,' 'criterion,' 'test,' and 'language,' all no-man's–land concepts in applied-linguistic discussions, and gives them definition and operational effect. By doing so, language testing acts as research methodology for applied linguistics and supplies data for model extension and building; thus, language testing extends and refines the view we take of applied linguistics in its relation to language learning and teaching.

NOTES

1. English as a foreign language (EFL) and English as a second language (ESL) will not be treated here as representing different fields of study, though they sometimes are.

2. We have referred here to LSP, but it should be observed that the best known example of LSP is that of English for special purposes (ESP).

SUGGESTIONS FOR FURTHER READING

Important overviews of language testing are found in Alderson and Hughes 1982; Bachman 1989, 1990a, 1990b; Canale 1988; Davies 1990; Hughes 1989; Hughes and Porter 1983; Oller 1979, 1983. More technical discussions of language assessment are available in Henning 1987 and Stansfield 1986, as well as in the numerous TOEFL research reports available from ETS. Reviews of standardized language tests are found in Alderson, Krahnke, and Stansfield 1987 and Madsen 1983. Coverage of more practical concerns in language testing are presented in Heaton 1976; Madsen 1983; Rivers 1981; and Savignon 1983. Finally, research on language testing is reported in the journal, *Language Testing*, as well as occasionally in *Language Learning*, *TESOL Quarterly*, *English Language Teaching Journal*, and *System*.

QUESTIONS FOR FURTHER DISCUSSION

1. To what extent does Davies' discussion of the role of testing contribute to Morley's view of language learning and teaching.

2. Davies does not discuss extensively problems related to testing in bilingual, multilingual, or multicultural populations (cf. Macias); what might those problems be, and to what extent does their omission constrain Davies' argument?

3. In his discussion of language policy, Kaplan suggests that the implementation of a language plan requires both assessment of learner achievement and evaluation of project-goal attainment and basic operation. Does anything in Davies' discussion support this view, and does Davies offer any practical approaches to the implicit problems?

4. In his introduction, Davies writes: "There is a proper dynamic in the growth of a discipline. As it develops, its parts grow and prosper at different rates and jostle for the high ground. In so doing, their success can take them away from the center of the discipline which they inform to a potentially separate existence." Discuss this view with respect to second-language acquisition research and textlinguistics.

5. In what ways has current research in language testing served to "operationalize theories as testable hypotheses"?

6. Davies notes that various innovations in applied linguistics have drawn the field away from language teaching. Assuming his observation is correct and accurate, comment on the implications of this change.

7. Compare Davies' view of second-language acquisition research with the view expressed by McLaughlin and Zemblidge.

8. To what extent does Davies' view of the position of language testing in applied linguistics accord with the descriptions of applied linguistics as a field given by Strevens?

An Introduction to
Applied Linguistics and Language Policy and Planning

The following article makes the claim that language-planning activity constitutes the prototypical example of applied linguistics. At one level this claim is accurate; clearly, planning language draws upon every kind of activity applied linguists normally engage in. At another level, there are other real-world activities—e.g., literacy programs, curriculum designs, etc.—that may also be considered prototypical examples of applied linguistics. To the extent that planning language involves the application of linguistic (and other related intellectual) activities to the solution of real-world problems, the claim is valid.

Language-planning activity has not always been perceived as connected to applied linguistics. Language planning is not a field in the sense that psycholinguistics is; rather, it is a set of practical activities driven by political and economic reality. Language planning has a very recent history. It is safe to say that 40 years ago, no one had conceived of it as it has evolved. Language planning came into existence without a theoretical base; it simply began to occur, and when it began to occur, it drew more heavily upon the field of planning than it did on the field of linguistics. The sort of theoretical notions discussed by Grabe in his chapter on the relationship of linguistics to applied linguistics has had relatively little direct bearing on language planning.

It is the case, however, that some recent language planning has been undertaken by the Center for Applied Linguistics (in some instances with funding from the Ford Foundation). It is also true that individuals with training in linguistics (and its various subdivisions) have played central roles in language-planning activities. But the association of language planning with applied linguistics is an outgrowth of events. The field of applied linguistics did not determine that there should be a field called language planning; rather, politicians and economists did such planning and it became apparent that a certain type of linguist, the applied linguist, was good at it.

Since the task has fallen to applied linguists, there have been increasing efforts to devise a theoretical base for language planning. While one has not yet been fully articulated, it is clear that the necessary base will come from a better understanding of language change and a clear perception of the ways in which language change may be stimulated in certain directions. This foundation will be supplemented by the accumulated accounts of actual attempts to direct language policy and implement language planning (e.g., Baldauf and

141

Luke 1989; Cobarrubias and Fishman 1983; Hagege 1983; Kennedy 1983; Paulston 1988).

In the end, language planning draws heavily upon an understanding of linguistics, but not only an understanding of linguistics. Indeed, the role linguistics plays is inversely proportional to the extent that the underlying motives are economically and politically charged. This reality makes the process of language planning problematic; the process is a two-edged sword that may cut either way, and individuals who wish to enter this arena should do so with some caution. However, it should also be noted that many people become inevitably drawn into activities which may be seen as aspects of language policy and planning such as curriculum planning, educational policies, literacy-development programs, and adult-education programs. Persons involved in these activities may well be engaging in language policy and planning, and they have an obligation to recognize such a connection in the activities they undertake.

Applied Linguistics and Language Policy and Planning

Robert B. Kaplan
University of Southern California

1. INTRODUCTION

Imagine that a country has newly emerged from an old colonial empire. The individuals responsible for the nurturing of this new polity seek the means to unify a diverse population and to create a 'history' that provides some sort of continuity and authenticity over time for the group of people who will now live together within the polity. But the new country is poor—it has limited natural resources, and it was constrained in its rate of modernization under the older regime. Thus, the new entity has an overwhelming need for education at all levels. The leaders believe that the modernization of the economy requires that the population be literate. It gradually becomes clear that the one device that can accomplish the objectives of unity, authenticity, and modernization is a national language. But the choice of a single language is complex, for a number of different languages are spoken by the citizens of the new country. Although one language is spoken by the largest number of people, the speakers of that language constitute only 40 percent of the total population, and, because they were a favored group under the colonial regime, they are not very popular. Many of the other languages widely spoken in the new country have no written form. The language of the particular colonial state itself might, of course, be chosen, but that language does not really contribute to the authenticity of the new polity. The leaders of the new polity are faced with a genuine language problem. This language problem requires some sort of solution.

Such a scenario is not uncommon, particularly since the 1960s when so many newly nonaligned countries achieved independence, and along with it the need to address a host of developmental problems. Looking back, it is clear that language policy and planning were issues widely recognized as deserving attention; it is equally clear that early efforts at such policy and planning were for the most part rather unsuccessful. In the decades intervening between the golden positivism of the language-planning experts and consultants of the 1960s and the more cautious policy/planning undertakings in the 1990s, it is possible to outline important principles of language-planning projects from around the world, and that represent an accumulation of trial and error knowledge on language policy and planning. Perhaps foremost among these slowly acquired principles is an organizational approach to language planning as an operational systems-design problem, one that begins with the basic questions: Who does what for whom? How is it done? And why is it done?

2. WHAT IS LANGUAGE PLANNING?

Generally speaking, a language problem occurs whenever there is linguistic discontinuity between segments of a population that are in contact. Such a discontinuity, of course, affects individuals as well as whole populations. A language policy recognizes the existence of such a discontinuity and proposes a principled solution to the discontinuity. A language plan is the vehicle for implementing a language policy; it tries to solve the problem by dealing with the individuals involved. In order to be effective, a language plan has to make it explicitly clear that adopting some other language behavior than that already practiced brings some palpable benefit to the individuals involved. If a language plan fails to recognize this relationship, it cannot succeed. Unfortunately, language plans tend to be couched in fairly altruistic terms; e.g., there is a tendency to try to motivate children to learn another language by telling them that doing so is somehow good for them. But an activity that promises a vague good in the distant future is not motivating. There is the additional problem of the level at which a plan originates and that at which it gets implemented. As in other areas, a plan may occur in a top-down fashion or in a bottom-up fashion; that is, a plan may be conceived by government as being good for the people and subsequently mandated downward to the individual, or a plan may be conceived at the level of an affected community, and subsequently government may be asked to help with it. It is difficult to generalize about the most successful approach, but if indeed the success of a policy depends upon its ability to deliver palpable benefits to individuals, it seems likely that bottom-up plans have a greater probability of success.

2.1. What Are Language Problems?

The above example illustrates one kind of situation in which language problems arise, but language problems may result from a vast variety of real-world events. For example, when one country invades another and occupies it, a language problem arises. When war, economic pressure, famine, or the weather create dislocations of populations, a language problem arises. When a particular in-group wishes to exclude a particular out-group in an existing polity, a language problem arises. The history of the world provides a vast range of examples. Using only contemporary history, one can point to countries like the Philippines, or Cameroon, or India after the Raj, as examples of the type of situation in which a national language had to be identified. The worldwide dispersal of Indo-Chinese refugees constitutes another kind of example—one in which the war-caused dislocation of large populations from Cambodia, Laos, and Vietnam has created language problems in Hong Kong, New Zealand, and the United States. A similar problem exists in the Southwest of the United States as the result of an influx of refugees from wars in Central America or from economic hardship in Mexico. The situation in Canada, where French-speaking Canadians reacted against domination by English speakers and have in fact reversed the language situation, so that, at least in Quebec, French speakers have dominance over English speakers, is an example of an in-group wishing to exercise some control over an out-group. When Japan invaded and occupied Taiwan, Malaysia, and Indonesia in the 1940s, a language problem was created there, and when the Nationalist government of China occupied Taiwan in the late 1940s, a different language problem was created. When the government of the People's Republic of China decided to choose Mandarin as the official language of China, a language problem was created, and when the same government changed its designation of first foreign language from Russian to English, a different language problem was created. When the newly emerged polity known as Israel elected Hebrew as its official language, a language problem was created. And the so-called English-only movement in the United States (cf. Judd in this volume) is creating a new language problem. There is a perception that language problems of the sort described here are all phenomena of the twentieth century. It has been claimed that the language problems of newly emerging nations are severe in part because these new nations are attempting to achieve in a decade what has evolved (implying accidental change) in nations with long histories over centuries. Neither claim is entirely true. Language problems have existed throughout recorded history, and the evolution of languages in nations with long histories was not as smooth as it appears in retrospect. In countries such as Spain and France, for example, where, respectively, Spanish and French are perceived to be long-established national languages, some groups are in revolt because, even now, they do not accept the domination of the national language. In Spain, the Basque people, and to some extent the Catalonian people, do not accept Spanish as their language and are demanding the recognition of their own languages in various sectors of the society, principally in schools. Only now are Catalonians being allowed to introduce their first language into the school systems of northeast Spain.

In France, where some Basque people also reside, there is a replication of the situation in Spain, though perhaps on an even greater scale. The Breton people are unhappy about the domination of their language by French. The speakers of Provençal and langue d'oc are unhappy about the imposition of northern metropolitan (standard) French in their southern regions. The Alsatian people are equally unhappy about the domination of their French/German dialect by French. In a country where over half the population were not speakers of standard French as late as the beginning of the twentieth century, the policy of the government has consistently been to develop the standard metropolitan variety of French at the expense of all other languages and French dialects. As late as the 1960s and 1970s, the language policy of the French government was one of brutal suppression of minority languages and dialects.

In Great Britain, there are ongoing efforts to maintain Welsh and Scots as living languages, though already in Great Britain Cornish and Manx have been lost, and Irish Gaelic is faltering despite heroic efforts by some concerned Irish scholars to reinvigorate it. In Soviet Azerbaizhan there is evidence that the Turkish minority is at present being victimized; again, this is not a new problem, but one based on an old migration. These are not twentieth-century problems; their roots lie far back in history.

2.2. What Are Language Questions?

The range of questions that can be addressed is vast. One set of questions deals with language preservation as the goal of language academies around the world (cf. language maintenance, which is primarily concerned with the preservation of minority languages/dialects). Much more is, of course, at issue. Perhaps by considering a few examples, one can determine the scope of language-policy activity. When the newly emerged state of Israel elected, for purposes of authenticity and unification, Hebrew as its official language, it was faced with a language which, though having a long written history, had become restricted in use largely to ritual functions. It was necessary to modernize Hebrew; to create within it whole new ranges of vocabulary, for example, to permit discussion of contemporary topics never dreamt of in classical Hebrew; to create mechanisms to permit the use of Hebrew in government, in auto mechanics, in the army, in banking, and so on. Some of the efforts were successful; some were not. In registers where a perfectly good non-Hebrew lexicon existed and was in common use among practitioners, the newly created Hebrew lexicon simply did not take hold (Hofman 1974, 1976). Similar problems were faced in Malaysia and Indonesia, as the language academies in those countries struggled to invent a greater lexicon in Bahasa Malaysia and Bahasa Indonesia to permit science and technology to be taught in those languages. In Japan, the problem was somewhat different; it was to permit the controlled entry of foreign lexicon into Japanese as the need for new lexicon in certain registers arose, and to control the way in which those new terms were written in the various orthographies of Japanese. In Japan, then, it was possible to make conscious decisions about areas that needed enhancement and to increase the influx in some registers and restrict it in others.

Language policy is not, however, only concerned with lexical development. In the Philippines, for example, where the population speaks some 250 languages, it was a political necessity to identify a national language. The 1976 constitution of the Philippines is a rather remarkable document; it recognizes a number of languages as having a certain status; e.g., Filipino and English are to be used for all official purposes (government documents, etc.), but a number of other Philippine languages (e.g., Ilocano, Cebuano, etc.) are recognized as having important status, and a number of smaller languages are recognized as simply existing. In addition, this constitution mandates as a national language a fiction—a language that does not exist. A language which, the drafters of the constitution believed, would come into existence over time—an amalgam of the languages of the Philippines—and which would be known as Filipino, was mandated as the national language.

This brief summary of language questions begins to suggest the range that may be subsumed under language policy and planning—the sorts of questions dealing with real-world problems that may be addressed. There are, of course, other kinds of issues that provide substance for planning and policy development.

2.3. Literacy, Numeracy, and Computer Literacy

In recent years there has been, both in developed and in developing countries, a great concern about literacy. In the minds of many people, literacy is equated with education, with intelligence, and with the notion of modernization and technical development. There are, of course, important questions to be asked in the context of literacy. Obviously, the first question is: "Literacy in what?" The answers to this question are not as obvious as they seem initially. In countries recently emerged out from colonial empires, there is a high probability that whatever literacy exists in the population is in the colonial language. When the colonial language is not chosen as the national language, some problems are created. In any circumstance, literacy implies that there is something to read; in languages recently elevated to prominence (or indeed, recently provided with an orthography), there is not likely to be anything to read. (That fact has created circumstances in which literacy painfully learned is rapidly lost because it has no significant function.)

There are other circumstances in which the written form of the language does not have a high intercorrelation with the spoken language. Written Chinese, for example, is not closely affiliated with many of the spoken varieties of China, and it has been observed that Cantonese-speaking children in Hong Kong attending English-medium schools are being asked to become trilingual: to control spoken Cantonese, written standard Chinese (which does not have a close affinity with spoken Cantonese), and English in both oral and written form. The nature of written Chinese simply complicates the problem; it has been observed that one must control seven or eight thousand characters to be considered really literate in Chinese and, as a consequence, staying literate in Chinese is like training for a boxing match.

But the issue of Chinese literacy raises an important additional question: "What does it mean to be literate?" Early definitions of literacy (e.g., those employed by UNESCO in the 1950s) tend to be fairly modest in their requirement, while the popular notion of literacy—usually the ability to read belletristic materials and to write letters, memos, and even books like this one—implies a very different standard. As the world has become more technologized, and as the quantity of available written material has increased at astonishing rates, the definition of literacy has changed. Furthermore, to what extent are literacy and numeracy intertwined? Is it a part of functional literacy to be able to read and manipulate numbers at some level? In the very recent past, developed societies have begun to discuss, in addition, something that has come to be called *computer literacy*. Is it reasonable to expect every high-school graduate to be able to manipulate numbers to a relatively high level of sophistication, to be able to decipher virtually any use of written text employing natural language, and also to be able to decipher and create text in computer languages? And is it further reasonable to expect the student to be able to do at least the first two kinds of activity in more than one natural language? These questions in turn raise important questions about the limits of human ability.

Given the preceding sample of various kinds of language-policy issues, it is necessary to introduce some sort of order into the activity. The sheer number and variety of issues is overwhelming. Without some sort of order—some system—the process would quickly become unmanageable. One way of introducing order is to categorize problems in some convenient way. One such categorization separates, at least formally, linguistic from political problems.

2.4. Corpus and Status Planning

Planning may occur either in a linguistic mode or in a political mode or both. Corpus planning is concerned with planning the language itself; that is, it deals with such issues as reaching standardization on questions of pronunciation, arriving at a means to represent the language orthographically (if it is not already so represented), arriving at an agreement on standardization of spelling, morphology, and grammar, and preparing and disseminating dictionaries and pedagogic grammars. Corpus planning begins with the current state of the language; to the extent that consensus already exists about the form of the language, that consensus constitutes the starting point for corpus planning. When, for example, it was determined that Bahasa Malaysia should be 'modernized' (to allow that traditional language to deal with modernization-related subjects, e.g., science and technology), a principal function of corpus planning became the creation of new Bahasa Malaysia terminology to permit discussion of science and technology and, subsequently, the compilation and dissemination of dictionaries containing that new lexicon. The development of new terms in turn created morphological problems that needed attention (e.g., appropriate pluralization rules for the new terms).

Status planning is, on the other hand, frankly political; it has to do with 'selling' new (or standardized) forms of a language to the language community. When Singapore decided to use Mandarin as the only standard and official variety of Chinese, it was necessary to persuade the Chinese-speaking community to accept that decision. That, in turn, required some understanding of the ways in which various dialects of Chinese were being used. Once understanding of the uses of different dialects of Chinese was understood, it became possible to devise a plan to encourage the Chinese-speaking community to switch to Mandarin. Such a plan requires the articulation of a set of reasons for changing and a set of rewards that would encourage the shift. (In some conditions, a set of sanctions may be imposed on those unwilling to make the shift.) Status planning receives by far the greatest amount of attention, and it is often a decision to create a status change that drives corpus planning. Like corpus planning, status planning requires research both to understand the existing situation and to rationalize a set of strategies that will enhance (or expedite) the desired change.

Both activities take a lot of time, require substantial investment, and necessitate constant back-checking to ascertain that the moves being made are in fact having the desired effect in the target population. Both activities are, in themselves, inadequate to ensure moderately rapid language change, in the sense that it takes more than a grammar text and a dictionary, and more than planned change to modify the behavior of a language community. Both corpus and status change must at some point result in planned enrichment; that is, lexicons must be available for all sorts of communication purposes; grammars must be available for all sorts of registers; and a genuine communicative need must exist. Once a language can be written, material must be written; a literature has to come into existence. The new language form must be used in the public media and in the educational system. Creating communicative need and disseminating the new form through every possible medium is still a function of status planning, but it is long-term status planning at a very so-phisticated level.

In principle, both corpus and status planning are value-neutral; in fact, neither ever is. All of the decisions underlying the inception of status planning are political: to include or exclude some segment of the population from the power structure. To the extent that corpus planning is driven by status plan-ning, it, too, is politicized. Even seemingly value-neutral decisions—e.g., the omission of some language from the inventory of languages to be taught in the official school system, when the omission is a genuine oversight or the result of budgetary (rather than political) considerations—take on value by virtue of being included in a language plan. Because language is so central to human behavior, any language policy, whether the outcome of formal plan-ning or of accident, takes on value at least for those whose existence as a language community is threatened. It is simply a fact that political motivations are not always altruistic; thus a planner may be faced with difficult ethical questions at the (any) point of involvement.

In sum, corpus and status planning are two basic activities underlying all systematic language planning (and some accidental language policy). The former deals with changing the shape of a language, the latter deals with changing the attitudes of speakers toward a language. Corpus planning draws more heavily upon linguistic descriptions; status planning is more clearly political, and it tends to drive corpus planning. Up to this point, the problem of defining language planning has been the focus of discussion. Assuming that language planning can be understood in terms of the illustrations devel-oped in the preceding pages, there is the question of who (or what) undertakes language planning.

3. WHO DOES LANGUAGE PLANNING?

Governments, typically, determine a policy to solve a problem and then de-vise a plan to implement that policy. With respect to language problems, one way of proceeding is to articulate a language policy and then devise a set of strategies—a language plan—for the implementation of that policy. But the determination of a policy requires a great deal of information. For example, what languages are spoken by whom in that community? For what purposes are these various languages used; that is, in what language does one pray, get married, buy groceries, vote, get a haircut, buy clothes, get sent to jail, hire a taxi, etc.? What kind of language talent (resources) does the country need for modernization, for regional trade, for international trade, to undertake scien-tific and technological development, to expand the educational system, to produce newspapers and books that people can (and will) read, to develop a radio/television network? What kind of language talent is already in place—for what languages are there teachers immediately available; how well do teachers control the languages they profess to be able to teach; what literary talent exists, and in what language is literature created? These are by no means all of the questions that ought to be answered.

The reality, of course, is that these questions rarely get asked. The fact is that politicians, not very sophisticated in matters linguistic, make the decisions, and they tend to make those decisions largely with respect to their own individual language loyalties. (Much the same could be said for bilingual-education implementation in many school districts in the United States.) Such decisions may or may not be unpopular, but the extent to which they are unpopular, or merely unimplementable, creates a new set of language problems. And the new set of language problems creates a new set of linguistic questions that must be answered before a policy can be articulated to solve that new set of problems. These various sets of questions are the proper concern of applied linguists, indeed, the solution of such real-world language problems is exactly the kind of work that applied linguists are supposed to do, and language-policy/planning questions are in a sense the prototypical activity of applied linguistics. Of course, as the questions suggest, it is unlikely that any one person can possibly know enough to undertake such an activity. Teams of specialists are normally involved in language-planning activities, teams including (and probably headed by) applied linguists, but also taking advantage of the talents of anthropologists, economists, historians, professional planners, sociologists, and the like. There are, in addition, a number of structures already in place in some language communities which function to make language-policy decisions, some of them very old.

3.1. The Role of Language Academies

In the seventeenth and eighteenth centuries, a number of 'language academies' sprang up across Europe. The original purpose of these academies was to preserve the purity of the languages over which they had authority and to prevent the perversion of those languages through the use of the languages spoken by uneducated peasants. The best known of the language academies is the Academie Française, but it is by no means the only such body. Language academies have been important shapers of policy throughout Europe, and more recently in the Middle East. In Portugal and Spain, these bodies have also influenced language policies in many Latin American countries and spawned language academies in a number of those countries. In addition, other nations have created their own language academies for various purposes in recent times; examples of these are the academies in Japan and Malaysia.

In the contemporary world, academies continue to strive to maintain the purity of languages, and they serve a pragmatic purpose by compiling dictionaries of the language and by acting as arbiters of correctness in grammar and usage. In Malaysia, the academy has been responsible for the creation of new indigenous lexicons in science and technology to assist in education and modernization. In Japan, the academy has been responsible for sorting out the limitations of the various orthographic systems that constitute written Japanese. Thus, they serve not only to keep languages 'pure,' but to promulgate rules regarding the 'right' use of the language. In a sense, the academies have authenticated private champions of taste in countries where academies do not exist. For example, in the United States there is a long history of individuals who have assumed the role of arbiters of standards and have written (indeed, fulminated) about decaying standards and about the importance of preserving stylistic beauties of the past. After all, a language that has a Shakespeare in its relatively distant history has a great tradition to look back upon.

3.2. Other Functionaries in Language Planning

Governments are engaged in language policy and planning in a number of other ways that go beyond the activities of both official and quasi-official language academies. It would perhaps be most useful to distinguish between activities that are externally directed by governmental agencies and offices, and other activities that are internally directed by such policy-creating units. Each type of activity has far-reaching influences in shaping the use and disuse of languages and dialect varieties. In modern times, the externally oriented agencies (both official and quasi-official) are units engaged in a kind of linguistic imperialism through their mission of language dissemination. The internally oriented agencies are more typically engaged in the dissemination of educationally oriented decisions (as in Morocco and Singapore), support for other languages within communities (e.g., minority/majority-language policies in the People's Republic of China and the Soviet Union), and the standardization of scientific and technological terminology and usage to improve production and effectiveness in research and business.

Examples of structures whose principle function is to assist externally with language dissemination are the German Goethe Institute, the British Council, and the Alliance Française. Through branch offices in other countries, they provide language instruction at relatively low cost and offer a variety of other 'cultural' services. The United States Information Agency (USIA; locally USIS) is a similar agency, though the language dissemination aspects of its mission do not receive nearly as high a priority. It does offer cultural services, but it does not to any significant degree engage in direct-language teaching, though it does support Binational Centers, which teach English, and provide teachers under the Fulbright-Hayes act, to local institutions that teach English. The government of Saudi Arabia, in the very recent past, without the creation of a special agency, has supported the spread of Islam and has funded Arabic-teaching operations in a number of countries.

Some governments have encouraged the flow of international students into their educational establishments, particularly their tertiary systems. Students entering the tertiary educational structures of developed countries are expected, as a matter of course, to learn the instructional languages of those countries. Hundreds of thousands of 'foreign students' have, since the end of World War II, learned English in tertiary educational institutions in Australia, Britain, Canada, New Zealand, and the United States; but the English-speaking nations have not really exploited the foreign-policy implications of international student exchange. The Soviet Union and the Federal Republic of Germany have, on the other hand, made explicit use of international students and of the resultant language dissemination as a vehicle of foreign policy. A recent entrant into this sphere of activity is Japan, which seeks to increase its 'foreign-student' population to 100,000 individuals by the end of the century. The preceding discussion suggests that all planning is a conscious activity of agencies of government. That is not the case.

3.3. Accidental Language Policy

There are instances in which governments and other organizations (often businesses) create language policy entirely by accident; that is, the functions of certain nonlanguage-related branches of government create implicit policy. An interesting case in point is the U.S. Bureau of Indian Affairs, long a branch of the Department of the Interior. This body (like those bodies in Australia responsible for the lives of Australian aboriginal people or those in New Zealand responsible for the Maori people) inadvertently created policy by establishing schools in which Native American pupils were inhibited from speaking their indigenous languages and were required to learn English. Other examples include the Census Bureau (which until recently has collected information only in English), the Post office (which has delivered mail only in English), the local agencies responsible for elections (which have permitted voting only in English), the local welfare agencies (which have permitted access to benefits only in English), the Department of Commerce (which currently is deeply concerned about what it considers a language-based "technology hemorrhage"), and even the Department of Defense (which expects all personnel to be able to function in English). Some of these practices have been liberalized in the recent past, but implicit language restrictions continue to exist in many governmental policies, and the English-only political movement growing in the United States will only strengthen this bias.

3.4. The Role of Religion in Language Planning

The earlier discussion suggests that language policy is a function of government; in contemporary times, it often is, but it is certainly not uniquely the province of government. An important actor in language policy is institutionalized religion. The Roman Catholic Church was, for hundreds of years, responsible for the preservation of Latin as a liturgical language; it was a conscious decision by the Church, in quite recent times, to abandon Latin in favor of vernacular languages. Both the decision to maintain Latin and the decision to abandon it in favor or vernacular languages are language-policy decisions. The preservation of liturgical Greek in the Greek Orthodox Church is another similar example, and the spread of Classical Arabic in relation to the spread of Islam is perhaps the most apparent example. But various institutionalized religions have also played major roles in relation to other languages as well. For example, as sub-Saharan Africa was colonized by European powers, one of the major subsidiary activities of colonization was the spread of religion by missionaries. In a relatively short time after initial colonization, in many areas of Africa, the missionary groups became largely or exclusively responsible for education. There was a major difference in the language attitudes of Protestant missionary groups from those of Roman Catholic missionary groups. Many Protestant faiths take as an article of faith the notion that personal salvation can be achieved through direct access to the Gospels; the Roman Catholic Church does not share this belief. As a result, Protestant missionary groups were (and continue to be) responsible for the translation of the Gospels into vernacular languages—an activity that sometimes has required the development of an orthography.

In many instances, it was the Bible translators who were initially responsible for the creation of orthographies in vernacular languages, and it was through the availability of the Bible in vernacular languages that those languages were preserved, were made languages of education, and eventually became candidates for national or official status in emerging nations. The work of the Summer Institute of Linguistics (SIL) is an important example. The SIL, a function of the Wycliff Bible Translators, has done significant work in linguistics in the description of little known vernaculars. The Church of Latter Day Saints (LDS; Mormons) has had an equally important function through its Bible Translating Mission. The Roman Catholic Church has not engaged widely in such activities, but has, on the other hand, played a powerful role not only in the preservation of liturgical Latin but in the spread of colonial languages (e.g., French, Portuguese, and Spanish) because of the language loyalty of the clergy doing missionary work in various colonial areas. As institutionalized religious bodies have selected certain languages for use (and therefore preservation and/or dissemination), they have deselected other languages; an interesting example of deselection is the resistance of some missionary groups to the spread of Swahili on the grounds that Swahili is affiliated with Islam.

3.5. Private Efforts in Language Policy

It is, however, not only through such formal structures that language problems are attacked on a large scale. There are a number of nongovernmental entities, made up of individuals dedicated to the presumed beauties of some language, which are to greater or lesser degrees engaged in actively disseminating a particular language beyond its normal sphere of influence; an example of such a group is the English-Speaking Union. It has branches in most English-speaking countries and has the stated objective of promoting the use of English through scholarships to study in English-speaking countries, through book donation programs, and through a variety of other mechanisms. A new phenomenon in language activity has arisen through the emergence in the late twentieth century of multinational corporations. Such organizations maintain operations in many countries, and, precisely because they have linguistically diverse employee pools, these organizations have internal language policies that define what language is spoken within the corporation, what proficiency in what language and to what degree can make an individual eligible for senior-management status, and what languages are used for doing business in what context. Such organizations are also responsible for the international sale of hardware—e.g., airplanes, ships, etc.—that brings with it maintenance manuals usually written in the language of the country of origin (or in some cases in the official language of the corporation) and that creates a language problem related to the maintenance of that expensive hardware. In multilingual nations, advertisers have begun to be concerned with choosing an appropriate language for advertising particular products in minority areas; at the present time, advertising agencies in the southwestern part of the United States are spending significant sums of money to determine whether Hispanic populations can be addressed most effectively in standard English, standard Spanish, or a nonstandard variety of either.

3.6. Science and Technology in Language Policy

In the contemporary world, perhaps the single most important area of language activity is that of science and technology. It is a fact that academic disciplines, particularly in the hard sciences and engineering, have been responsible for language dissemination and for language policy. Disciplines sometimes have internal 'language academies' that agree on the standardization of terminology for the things a particular discipline talks about. (This standardization also occurs in global functions, e.g., global maritime navigation and the global operation of commercial aircraft.) The key journals in each field take on important gatekeeping functions, since they determine in what language scholarly work may be published, and, even more important, they determine the conventions of presentation. The role of English in these contexts cannot be underestimated. At the end of World War II, a number of interesting accidents co-occurred to ensure the hegemony of English in the areas of science and technology: first, the United States was the only major industrialized nation to emerge from the war with its industrial and educational infrastructures completely intact and booming as a result of the war effort; second, the United States and Britain were on the winning side, and when the new international bodies (e.g., the UN, UNESCO, etc.) came into being, the United States and Britain had a voice not only in the way these bodies would be structured and would function, but also about the languages in which they would function. There is a truism in science, which of necessity is cumulative in its activities (that is, all new science depends on all previous science), that those who contribute most new information are also, of necessity, those who most use the information resources, and those who most use and most contribute to information networks come to own them. Thus, it is not merely the case that, according to the Fédération Internationale de Documentation (FID), 85 percent of all the scientific and technical information available in the world today is either written or abstracted in English, but it is also the case that the information in the world's great information-storage and -retrieval networks is coded under an English-based sociology of knowledge, and the key terms used to access the system are English terms.

3.7. Language-in-Education Planning

So far, the discussion has involved to some extent organizations and agencies that are aimed outward; that is, they are to some extent concerned with the dissemination of languages beyond the areas in which those languages have cultural significance. In every polity, of course, there are also bodies concerned with the promulgation of the indigenous (official, national) language among the citizens of that polity. These responsibilities typically fall to the education sector. Not only does the education sector determine the way in which the national or official language will be taught; it also determines the amount of time that will be devoted to national-language instruction in the curriculum (which, after all, has finite limits because children can only be required to go to school so many hours per day, so many days per week, so many weeks per year). More important, the education sector also determines what other languages will be included in the curriculum, how they will be taught, and what fraction of the curricular day will be devoted to the learning of those other languages; a corollary of this function is the implicit right to determine what and who will *not* be taught. The area under discussion here is called *language-in-education planning,* and this entire area is discussed at length in the chapter by Judd in this volume.

4. HOW DOES ONE DO
LANGUAGE PLANNING?

Although it is true that the various bodies (governmental or not) involved in making language-policy decisions do not often turn to applied linguists for information on which to base those decisions, from time to time they have.

Given that applied linguists have been involved, what precisely is it that they can do in such an environment? In order to deal with questions about language distribution and language use in communities, applied linguists have undertaken language-situation analyses through surveys. Language-use surveys attempt to establish who uses what language, for what purpose, under what circumstances in a given community. Basically, a language-use survey involves a number of steps that can be classified into three groups:

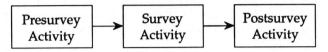

4.1. Presurvey

These activities fall basically into three categories: background research, instrument planning, and team training. For background research, Obviously, it is necessary to have some sense of the language situation to the extent that information is available. That requires doing background reading about the area, its culture, the ethnic groups who live there, and so on; but it also involves talking with as many people as possible who are in a position to be helpful; that group would include academic linguists and anthropologists who are at the time working (or have in the past worked) in the area, but it would also include individuals in the media, government officials, and others who are likely to have an overview of the situation. The information gathered in this way must be systematized, recorded, and analyzed; it will be used in shaping the survey instrument.

Survey work involves collecting data from a large population and therefore requires instrument planning. In order to collect data, one must decide not only upon what information to collect, but also upon the sorts of collection devices to be employed. It is sometimes convenient to use a written instrument, but obviously the use of such a form depends on the distribution of literacy in the population; if large segments of the population are not literate, written collection will not do, although it may be used among some segments of the population (e.g., government officials, teachers, etc.). If a written survey is to be used with any segment of the population, it is necessary to determine how the instrument will be distributed and collected; e.g., will it be mailed to respondents, and if so are the mails dependable, are the respondents likely to return the form, etc.? Or will it be handed out to the respondents in some convenient setting, and if so what setting? How will the survey-team members be sure that respondents fill out the form and do their own work rather than simply copying from some perceived leader in the group? And how will the instrument be retrieved? More important, if a written survey is to be used, what language will it be in? What variety of that language? Are there enough people in the survey team who can read and write that language to make such collection effective? How will the team be certain that the questions collect the desired information (since semantic variability can make nonsense of a question)?

If a survey must be conducted orally, what segment of the population can be surveyed, under what social circumstances? What numbers of surveyors will be required to conduct the oral interviews? Are trained surveyors available or will it be necessary to recruit and train an essentially naive group? What safeguards can be built into the system to assure that surveyors are asking the right questions in the right order, are recording their findings accurately, etc? Whether the survey is oral or written, can the instrument be structured in such a way as to facilitate data entry into some computer system? What system is available? Where is it physically located? How accessible is it? How secure is it? What will it cost to use it? What is the anticipated turnaround time for data analysis? Whatever sort of survey collection is chosen, it will be necessary to design a sample instrument and to try out that instrument on a sample population, making corrections and modifications on the basis of the trial data.

Team training depends upon a number of decisions deriving from the background check and the instrument design. In the first instance, before any work can be undertaken (even the background research), it is necessary to assemble the basic team. That is accomplished on the basis of the questions to be answered by the survey. Any team is likely to require members other than applied linguists. Once a basic team is assembled, and the team members understand the objectives of the survey task and the real-world constraints upon it, the background research can be undertaken, and once the background research has been accomplished, it is possible to begin to design the data-collection process, including the design and field testing of any data-collection instruments to be used. To the extent that the members of the basic team do not speak the local language(s), it will be necessary to augment the team with local specialists who can interview government officials, media people, and business leaders. These individuals need to be oriented to the project and trained in the method of conducting such interviews. Once instrument design is under way, it will be necessary to add translators sufficiently bilingual to be able to deal with the nuances of questions to be asked. The translators should be able to tell the team whether certain kinds of questions cannot be asked (that is, whether certain topics are taboo); how questions can be phrased in order to elicit reasonable answers; and how certain lexical items that may not have equivalences in the local language(s) can be dealt with. At the same time, it will be necessary to understand local experience with surveys in order to answer such questions as: How long (in time) can an oral interview be? What is the most likely site for an interview (e.g., in people's homes, in the marketplace, or in gathering places like bars or barbershops—and who is likely to gather in such places)? Can men and women be interviewed simultaneously? Where and under what circumstances can children be approached? If a written instrument is employed, how many questions can reasonably be asked? Can such techniques as semantic differential be employed?

Regardless of the type of survey to be used, it will be necessary to determine how large a segment of the population will be sampled. If field workers will be used, then, to distribute a written questionnaire or to administer an oral interview, such people will need to be recruited and trained. The overall timeline of the survey process will need to be calculated to permit for the time necessary to these recruitment and training activities. Care will need to be taken to assure that survey workers are paid a reasonable salary according to the standards of the local economy, and that they are employed for a sufficient period of time to permit both training and survey work. It is important that field workers be debriefed after the survey fieldwork to discover any problems they may have encountered and to get a sense of the cooperation of subjects. The instrument(s) will need to be field tested, and—once assumed to be ready—will need to be produced in sufficient quantity. If instruments are mailed, time must be to allocated to permit delivery and return, and it is likely that at least one reminder will have to be sent to recalcitrant subjects. The completion of these and other steps will lead to the survey itself.

4.2. The Survey

The survey process consists essentially of the data-collection process. Data collection may go on simultaneously in several different ways; that is, if a written questionnaire is to be used among literate segments of the population, distribution of that questionnaire can go on at the same time that oral interviewing of other segments of the population is occurring. Oral interviewing may take different forms; e.g., one group of interviewers may be working with "the man in the street," collecting data in people's homes, or in the marketplace, or wherever, while another group of fieldworkers (perhaps the members of the basic team) may be conducting interviews of various government officials (in the ministries of education, tourism, communication, foreign affairs, and commerce, in the military, etc.), of the police and representatives of the judicial and social-welfare systems, of those people responsible for national census data, of postal officials, of religious leaders, of leaders in the business community (including advertisers), and of other segments of the community where there are stated or implied language concerns. As information is received, it can be entered for computer analysis. As information is entered, it will need to be checked for accuracy and completeness. It is possible that, in the actual process of data collection, some hole in the database may be discovered; should that be the case, it will be necessary to devise a strategy to collect the missing data. The actual survey process is the most mechanical portion of the activity, but it cannot be assumed that it will run smoothly simply because it is mechanical.

Feedback loops need to be built into the system that will permit correction of the process at any time. For example, data entry may demonstrate that some single fieldworker (or some group of fieldworkers) appears to be encountering extraordinary difficulty; the cause of the difficulty needs to be determined, and corrective measures taken. It is possible that an entire process (e.g., a written questionnaire, a section of the oral interview) may be found not to be functioning properly; such a discovery requires corrective action even if such action necessitates redoing the questionnaire or some portion of it.

The survey stage may be said to be completed when all of the anticipated data have been collected and entered for analysis and when all of the entries have been reviewed for accuracy and completeness. One set of data that is collected right at the end of the process, but which is crucial to the process, is that deriving from the debriefing of fieldworkers. Information from that debriefing, too, needs to be quantified and entered. The last stages of the survey process involve making determinations concerning the statistical procedures that will be employed in data analysis. Presumably, that determination has been made early in the process and assumptions about statistical analyses have governed the design of the collection instruments. What occurs at this stage is a final check to be certain that the data is in a format such that the desired statistical procedures can be undertaken. If it is found that data is not appropriately entered, again, corrective measures need to be taken.

4.3. The Postsurvey Process

The postsurvey process can also be divided into three stages: data analysis; determination of recommendations, report writing, and report dissemination; and policy formation and implementation. Data analysis is exactly what the name implies; that is, the various preplanned statistical procedures are applied, correlations are developed, and the raw data is converted into a form that will have meaning. The basic team members must understand the data and must be able to perceive what the data suggest. As the data set is developed, it is important to use the knowledge of local experts in trying to understand the implications of the information that has been gathered. To put it in a slightly different way. the information gathered needs to be understood in terms of the local situation.

Determination of recommendations, report writing, and dissemination are done by the team as a whole. Once the data have been carefully analyzed, the members of the team can begin formulating recommendations. The recommendations, while they must be applicable to the local situation, should bring to bear on the local situation parallel experience of which the members of the team are aware. Each recommendation must be tested with local people to determine whether it is feasible and at lest potentially implementable in the local environment. There is no point in making a recommendation that will never be implemented; for example, if it is perceived that a local examination used to screen applicants to tertiary educational institutions is faulty, but it is known that the ministry of education is completely committed to the use of such an instrument for political and social reasons, it makes no sense to recommend the abolition of the instrument, but it may make some sense to suggest incremental modification.

As the various interpretations of the information collected and the various recommendations take shape, a formal report needs to be assembled. There arises the question of the language in which the report will be written; presumably, the initial contract will state the language in which the report is to be submitted, but it is useful to prepare the report bilingually. Preparing a two-language version of the report helps to assure that the report is accurate, and it provides a version the researchers can take away with them (assuming that the language in which the report is submitted is not the same as the native language of the team members).

The report and recommendations need to be confirmed informally with as many appropriate officers of government as possible while the report is being written. Indeed, by the time the formal report is submitted, it should contain no surprises; everyone concerned ought to be aware of precisely what the report has found the language situation to be, and of precisely what recommendations the report will offer.

The final report should be neatly printed and bound and, on a set date, simultaneously submitted to as many persons as possible. It is desirable to have some announcement of the availability of the report in the local media, and it is equally desirable to announce the existence of the report simultaneously in the professional journals. In making the submission, the basic team should indicate its willingness to answer questions about the report, but it should at the same time be fully prepared to disperse; in effect, once the report has been submitted, the work of the research team is finished. The purpose of a study and report is to provide information on the basis of which action can be taken; the work of the team is academic. Once the report is received, the conversion of the information and recommendations into action is a political process that is fully the responsibility of local authorities; the academic team should play no part in that process.

It is, however, appropriate for the report to include a section dealing with potential implementations; the policy-formation and -implementation recommendations. The members of the team will certainly have some thoughts on the staging of implementation, and it is important to build into the system feedback loops that will permit correction in the implementation process as the implications of various actions unfold over time.

It is sometimes the case that a report may be ignored by the government or governmental agency concerned. When that happens, it may be due to the fact that the report contains surprises—recommendations not anticipated by its recipients, or recommendations that are blocked by political or financial considerations. Proper review of recommendations in advance of the completion of the report will help to allay this problem. But it is also possible that, with the best of intentions on all sides, the government may be paralyzed by the magnitude of the task or by ignorance of how to proceed. When it is anticipated that such problems may be present in the environment, it is entirely appropriate that the report contain suggestions on the point at which implementation may begin, on the rate at which implementation may proceed, and on the sequencing of various stages in the process. Such discussion in the report probably should not seem to tell the government what to do, but rather should be couched as a number of alternatives available to the government as it moves to turn a team report into a viable plan, and the plan into a set of implementation stages.

A strategy that may be suggested as part of the report is the convening of an invitational conference, colloquium, or seminar at some point relatively early in the implementation process. Such a structure will permit some or all of the members of the team to return during implementation, and it will permit other language-planning experts to be invited to look at the report in a formal way, as well as look at the unfolding implementation process.

5. WHY LANGUAGE POLICY AND PLANNING IS DONE

Aside from these rather basic questions, there are other sorts of issues that motivate language planning. Most of the illustrations discussed above deal with the question of identifying a national language within a polity for purposes of authentication, unification, and modernization. But language-policy issues may be motivated by political and economic considerations as well. For example, in 1987 Australia enacted a National Language Policy. To a large degree, that policy is economically motivated, stressing policies that promote languages of trading partners, and it is only partially directed to solving internal language problems (e.g., providing access to speakers of minority languages, to hard-of-hearing persons, and so on). It is significantly motivated by the recognition that Australia's primary trading neighbors are not the states of the European Economic Community, where French and German might be useful, but its neighboring states, where such languages as Chinese, Indonesian, Japanese, and Korean are spoken.

To some extent, the Australian policy takes account of certain internal economic and political issues. There is evidence that the highest arrest rates and conviction rates lie among certain linguistic minorities, and there is also evidence that the greatest draw upon social-welfare services originates in those same linguistic minorities. In order to reduce the societal costs imposed on the welfare system and to the criminal-justice system, certain linguistic minorities need to receive linguistic help; i.e., to have greater access to majority-language functions. There are other examples of polities in which linguistic problems have important economic effects; for example, in some cases, the production and delivery of goods is impeded by the fact that different segments of the process are 'owned' by speakers of different languages or different varieties of a language. If, for example, produce is raised on farms whose owners speak one language; the produce is transported to market by a group speaking a different language or variety; and the retail distribution of the goods is in the hands of still a third linguistic minority, the entire process may be impeded.

In still other instances, a severe social problem can be created by differences between the language in which certain services can be delivered and the language of the population most in need of those services. This is most likely to occur in relation to medical services; it is often the case that medical practitioners are trained in a world language, but deliver medical services to populations who do not speak the language in which the medical practitioners were trained. Certainly that is the case in public-service medicine in places like Los Angeles, where medical practitioners are likely to be monolingual speakers of English, while their clients are likely to be speakers of Hmong, Korean, or Spanish. There is some evidence that a similar problem exists in much of sub-Saharan Africa in relation to AIDS. But the problem is certainly not unique to medical practice; it is equally an issue in relation to the law (cf. the article by Maher in this volume for a discussion of both problems).

The reasons why language policy and planning are done also point to an important aspect of how, and to what extent applied linguists become involved in language-planning activities. It would be preferable to report that language planners are regularly trained and recruited for such tasks as have been outlined in this chapter; in fact, however, the activity of language policy and planning is much more haphazard. As this section suggests, language policy and planning are most often undertaken for larger political and economic reasons; that being the case, the persons in charge of these activities are most often not applied linguists, but politicians and business executives. And if an applied linguist is called as a consultant to help formulate a plan, the choice of specialist is as much a matter of accident and referral by an unknown third party as it is of seeking out a highly qualified applied linguist specializing in language policy and planning. Of course, such a scenario also means that applied linguists wishing to specialize in language-policy and -planning activities will not find it an easy source of employment unless they are already working for the influential political and economic groups that motivate the policy and planning activities in the first place.

6. CONCLUSION

The process of information gathering, surveying, and policy creating in language planning as described in this chapter is, as noted early in this chapter, the prototypical activity of applied linguistics. In the course of doing a language survey within a language-planning context, a whole range of applied-linguistic activities are employed. Questions about who uses what language for what purposes under what circumstances in a particular linguistic situation—the basic research interests of applied linguists—are addressed; the tools of the applied linguist are employed to answer these questions (e.g., through written- and oral-use surveys), and the report deriving from that undertaking presumably contains recommendations dealing with applied-linguistic issues: changes in the basic code, modifications of the code in special circumstances (e.g., law, medicine, social-services delivery), and educational questions regarding changes in the code: questions of first- and second-language acquisition, of literacy, of materials development, of curriculum design, of methodology. If indeed applied linguistics is the application of linguistic and other strategies to the solution of basic real-world language problems, it is all here.

SUGGESTIONS FOR
FURTHER READING

Good overviews of the area are presented in Baldauf and Luke 1989; Cooper 1989; Fasold 1984; Kaplan et al. 1982; and Wardhaugh 1987. Important studies in the field include Beer and Jacobs 1985; Cobarrubias and Fishman 1983; Eastman 1983; Fishman 1972, 1974; Fishman, Ferguson, and Das Gupta 1968; Hagege (3 volumes) 1983; Haugen 1953; Kennedy 1983; Kloss 1977; Rubin and Jernudd 1971; Rubin et al. 1977; Weinreich 1953; and Weinstein 1983. There are a large number of country- or region-specific studies covering, for example, India, the Philippines, Canada, the Arab Middle East, East Asia, Australia, East Africa, Mexico, etc. Two illustrations of this broad genre are Ferguson and Heath 1981; McKay and Wong 1988.

There are also a number of important journals; e.g., *Language Problems and Language Planning, New Language Planning Newsletter, International Journal of the Sociology of Language,* and *Journal of Multilingual and Multicultural development.* In addition, there are various edited collections of the work of key figures like Ferguson, Fishman, Haugen, and others.

QUESTIONS FOR
FURTHER DISCUSSION

1. Kaplan makes a great deal of the distinction between corpus and status planning. Why is it necessary to pose this distinction? In practice, why can't the two kinds of activity be collapsed?

2. The discussion in this chapter touches upon the problem of literacy, but that problem is essentially dealt with in a separate chapter. Isn't it the case that lan-

guage planning is primarily and inevitably concerned with literacy? Why should the two areas be held apart?

3. Language-in-education planning is also treated separately in this volume. Isn't language planning exactly coterminous with language-in-education planning? Why should these two areas be held apart?

4. The discussion by Macias of bilingualism, multilingualism, and multiculturalism also invokes language planning. Isn't bilingualism an inevitable outcome of language planning? Why should these two issues be addressed separately?

5. It is claimed in this chapter that missionary religious groups have played an important part in language planning in some parts of the world. Is it the case that missionary groups have also played a role in language-policy development in the United States?

6. Kaplan makes the point that language policy sometimes is made by accident. What role, might one suggest, has the International Postal Union had in accidental language-policy development? Can other organizations be named that take part in accidental language policy and planning?

7. The point is made that unmotivated language change has little hope of success. Are there examples of language changes introduced in the United States that have not succeeded because they were inadequately motivated? (Consider the role of writers of "language purification" guides.)

8. The United States has not, to this point in its history, had an official language policy. What arguments can be developed to support the need for a policy now? What arguments can be developed against the need for such a policy?

An Introduction to
Language-in-Education Policy and Planning

This chapter addresses a topic which, on one level, is so obviously important to applied linguistics that its lack of careful treatment in the literature is surprising, but which nonetheless is seldom discussed. Language-in-education planning as a topic at times elicits questions indicating a basic unawareness among many applied linguists and education researchers. However, its ramifications for instruction are enormous. Policy and planning issues that are specific to educational contexts deserve to be viewed as a distinct branch of language policy and planning generally: first, language policy and planning itself covers many topics that are irrelevant to the educational context, such as graphization, creation of new terminology, dictionary writing, etc.; second, language-in-education policy often addresses issues of language policy and planning that are connected to other curricular and administrative matters; an educational policy may become a language-in-education policy, even though it would not be the recommendation of a language consultant, because it is the more appropriate decision overall, with language issues being only one of the variables involved. For example, the question of hours per week of foreign-language instruction in secondary schools might depend not simply on what would be the most effective curriculum for language learning, but on what other school subjects are competing for hours in the curriculum schedule at the school. Thus, language-in-education planning should be seen as an important and distinct domain of applied linguistics.

As noted in the section on language policy, language planning sometimes occurs in two stages; that is, a language-planning effort results in a series of recommendations, which in turn lead to policy decisions and the formulation of a language policy, which in turn leads to another plan: an implementation plan, the intent of which is to convey policy into practice. Once status and corpus efforts have gone beyond graphization, grammaticalization, and lexication—that is, once a language has been selected and its norms developed—then it is possible to be concerned with language dissemination and language cultivation.

Some significant portion of dissemination activity falls to the education sector. In that context, education authorities need to be concerned about the point of the curriculum at which the onset of instruction will occur, about the frequency and kind of achievement assessment that will be employed, about the content of syllabus and the relation between syllabus and assessment, and about the point in the curriculum at which the educational objectives will be assumed to have been met. Further, education authorities need to be concerned about the pool of teachers available for the task and the way in which teachers are selected and trained, about assessment of teacher performance and in-service training as a response both to needs revealed through assessment and to professional development, and about the remuneration and other motivational devices offered to these teachers. In addition, the education authorities need to be concerned about materials production and dissemination; that is, there has to be reasonable assurance that appropriate materials exist for each grade level involved and for each objective to be attained, that such materials are available in sufficient quantity that every pupil can have equal access, and that the materials are actually distributed to the schools and are available to teachers and students. These materials need to be appropriate to both the syllabi and the assessment instruments.

All these concerns are addressed through language-in-education planning, planning that mirrors at the level of the education sector the process elaborated at the national level—that is, there is a planning activity that leads to policy decisions that, in turn, lead to an implementation plan. However, language-in-education planning is dependent upon basic language planning and lags behind it, since language-in-education planning in specific contexts cannot begin until policy decisions have been formulated at the national level, if national-level policy is required. Of course, there is a further complication in language-in-education planning. It is often the case, that language-in-education planning is accidental or carried out in a haphazard manner with little conscious policy guidance. It is also the case that language instruction, whether in a first language or a second language, is typically done much less effectively in such educational settings. In contrast, an awareness of language goals in an educational setting leads to more effective instruction, curricular planning, and learning objectives. Why this might be so is revealed in the various topics addressed by Judd in the chapter that follows.

Language-in-Education Policy and Planning

Elliot Judd
University of Illinois at Chicago Circle

1. INTRODUCTION

As with any hyphenated topic, it is usually best to begin the discussion with a definition of terms, in this case, a definition especially of the terms *policy* and *planning*. Policy, as used here, refers to the set of statements, objectives, and/or commands explicitly or implicitly decreed by some agency, organization, or other body (usually governmental) with respect to any area over which that agency has jurisdiction. In this instance, the area of concern is language. A particular policy, which may have existed in the past and continues to exist, or which may have existed in the past and ceased to exist (or been substantially revised), or which may have been just articulated, may be clearly isolable and identifiable or may be buried in some larger policy package. Alternatively, it may not be explicitly stated at all but rather may constitute an implicit a priori assumption underlying some other policy. Usually, but not always, a policy has attached to it some sort of plan for implementation or some sort of set of procedures the apparent purpose of which is to cause something to happen that will lead to the attainment of the objective or the promulgation of the statements or commands. For example, a legislature may decree that the polity over which it has jurisdiction shall be a bilingual community; such a decree is a policy. It is then the function of various administrative bodies that derive their authority from that legislature to devise a plan to achieve the condition decreed by the legislature. Policy and planning normally go hand in hand, but one can conceive of a policy so broadly stated as to be impervious to planning; a case in point would be the Preamble to the Constitution of the United States.

Studies in language-in-education policy attempt to disambiguate what (governmental) programs exist (or do not exist), and how they came into being. Sometimes a policy is overt and can be easily identified; in other situations, a policy may be covert because it is difficult to isolate, or it may never have been clearly articulated in the first place. Policy may take the form of a positive pronouncement (e.g., to promote a given language or languages, or some variety of a language) or a negative one (e.g., not to promote a language or variety of a language, or censorship of certain materials). Planning, on the other hand, is future-oriented and represents a conscious attempt either to maintain existing policy or to alter it. In operational terms, planning is an attempt to systematize a course of action, or a direction, or a time sequence. Ideally, policy leads to planning, though in practice that is not always the case. Policy may occur in isolation and may never give rise to planning. In practice, however, planning may lead to a recognition of a need for policy and therefore to its articulation. If language-in-education policy changes without any attempt at orchestration, planning is not involved. Thus, based on the distinction made above, all countries have language-in-education policy, but not all engage in planning.

The domains within language-in-education policy/planning can also be subdivided. In certain situations, the issue involves the choice of the primary language or languages for educational instruction, which may or may not be the home language of the students receiving instruction. In other situations, the policy/planning deals with which variety of a language will be the 'standard' variety employed in the educational system—a variety that again can be either familiar or alien to any subset of students. Another area of language-in-education policy/planning relates to the choice made in second- or foreign-language subject instruction for students, both for new 'immigrants' as well as for those from older communities (the latter group may or may not know the second or foreign language).

Indeed, the semantic problem here is complex because a number of terms are employed on the assumption that the meaning of those terms is unambiguous. Educators talk of:

foreign languages	national languages
community languages	official languages
ethnic languages	educational languages
indigenous languages	literary languages

Thus, a Navajo-speaking child attending a bilingual school may be studying Navajo (described as an 'ethnic' or 'indigenous' language) while learning English as an 'educational' language through the use of English as a 'literary' language because English is the de facto 'national' language of New Mexico (where the child lives) although Navajo is the 'official' language of the

should be making language-in-education policy (Ashworth 1985; Baldauf 1989; Judd 1984; Weinstein 1983); educators are the ones who should implement the policy (cf. Baldauf 1989). Various people (educators, community leaders, academicians, writers and other cultural leaders, and the public in general) may articulate aspects of the policy or voice their dissatisfaction with policy and so influence politicians, but they do not make policy (cf. policymaking in the United States by state and local school boards). The relative influence of various societal groups is a function of the political structure of a given polity; in situations like those in the United States, politicians subject to election by popular vote tend to be rather sensitive to popular opinion, but in different political systems politicians may be more isolated from and more impervious to public opinion. It is even possible in some systems that the mechanisms to move public opinion to political consciousness simply do not exist. Whatever policy decisions are made, it is the educators who are expected to put these policies into operation.

One task for the researcher who is investigating language-in-education policy and planning, then, is to identify the exact sources influencing governmental policy, and the political motives that have led politicians to adopt that policy. While such policy decisions may be educationally beneficial, it is wise to view a policy as making political sense first and educational sense as a secondary benefit. Such a perspective allows researchers to understand why a language-in-education policy may be implemented even when it runs contrary to current educational/research wisdom (Edwards 1985). It should also be noted that changes of language-in-education policy are more often based on political and economic necessities than on educational ones.

A second corollary assumption is that language-in-education policy and planning are not neutral endeavors (Cobarrubias and Fishman 1983). It is a political act and has at its base certain ethical and moral assumptions (Judd 1984; Troike and Saville-Troike 1982). Anyone involved in the process (either in its formulation, revision, or implementation) is making a political statement. To support a policy, either actively or passively, is to voice agreement with the underlying political philosophy that the policy represents. To question the policy is to state some reservations about the underlying political assumptions. Questioning the policy also may challenge certain fundamental assumptions concerning how the rights of minority and majority members of a society interact, as well as the understanding of the obligations that those governing have to their citizens. As in all political decisions, choices are made and some groups gain disproportionate advantages. Claims of objectivity and neutrality in language-in-education issues are impossible to maintain; rather, such issues necessarily involve subjective perceptions of what is good or bad in and for a particular society. Often, the positions taken with respect to language-in-education policy and planning are only a product of more deeply seated philosophical inclinations (Edwards 1985).

3. THE UNITED STATES:
A CASE STUDY

To put things into a clearer perspective, the preceding general discussion will be exemplified through a case study of language-in-education policy/planning in the United States. The discussion focuses on federal policy (as opposed to state and local policy) in two areas: (1) policy that affects nonnative English speakers; and (2) policy on foreign-language education of monolingual English-speaking Americans. Excluded from the discussion is any consideration of policy regarding the use of varieties of American English (the use of some 'standard' vs. other varieties of English) or policy that extends beyond the schools (e.g., to the courts, health services, etc.), although these areas do merit study and have educational ramifications. What follows is intended to be illustrative, not comprehensive, and certainly does not provide thorough coverage of the topics under discussion.

Language-in-education policy in the United States can be divided into five periods. The first, from independence (1776) until the late 1880s, can be described as a period of linguistic toleration with relatively little governmental interference. The early leaders of the United States rejected designating English as the official language of the country. Their reasoning was both philosophical and pragmatic. In their view, freedom of choice and fear of control by the central government meant freedom to speak any language that an individual desired. Furthermore, the need to disseminate information to non-English speakers in the new country and a desire to attract new immigrants, many of whom were from countries where English was not spoken, also militated against any declaration of an 'official' language.[1] It was not because the early leaders of the country were anti-English or favored a multilingual country that they made this decision; the guiding principle was a basic belief in freedom of choice and individual rights with respect to language and other behavior. The early leaders also believed that citizens should acquire knowledge of other languages for cultural, intellectual, and pragmatic reasons (Heath 1976, 1977), although this view was related to foreign-language education for the elite, not for the masses. Indeed, in the European tradition, there has been a long-standing assumption that the educated man will be comfortable in several 'important' languages, usually including Latin, Greek, French, and German. Toleration of non-English speakers continued for some time and allowed the establishment of bilingual-education programs and non-English language schools in various communities, in both public and private education (Andersson 1971), as well as for classes to teach English to new arrivals. There were some periods of anti-immigrant feelings, but these were short-lived and did not affect the general trend of linguistic tolerance and freedom. In this period, the study of foreign languages by monolingual Americans was also encouraged (Heath 1977), but again, it was generally for the well educated, was often literary in nature, and was provided by tutors rather than as part of the regular school curriculum.

The second historical period began in the 1880s and continued until the mid-1950s. The early part was marked by a growing hostility to non-English language groups, part of a wider fear of immigrants and foreign ideas that reached its acme during World War I. A series of laws designed to require English literacy of new citizens and calling for English-only instruction in the schools was enacted with the general goal of 'Americanizing' the populace (in fact, English-language classes for new immigrants were often referred to as Americanization classes). Policy reflected a conscious attempt to realize the 'melting-pot' myth. At first, this trend did not affect foreign-language study for the elite; however, by World War I, there arose pressure to limit or abandon foreign-language study altogether, especially the study of German. Many states enacted laws to abolish use of languages other than English both inside and outside of the schools (Leibowitz 1976). The Supreme Court finally held these actions to be unconstitutional, most notably in Meyer vs. Nebraska (Appleton 1978), but the legacy of suspicion toward foreign-language use remained, as witnessed by the decline in the student enrollment in foreign-language classes. Coupled with the xenophobic reactions to non-English speakers, and particularly the fear of 'inscrutable' Orientals in the U.S. West (cf. the Asian Exclusion Act of 1882), the era can well be classified as the 'Dark Ages' of U.S. language-in-education policy.

The third era, the Sputnik era, was brief, lasting from 1957 to 1963. Although some educators and citizens were voicing concerns about the lack of American foreign-language proficiency prior to this time (McGrath 1952), it took the launching of Sputnik by the Soviet Union to spur policy-makers to pass legislation that supported foreign-language education. Known as the National Defense Education Act (NEDA), this legislation allocated money for science, mathematics, and foreign-language education on the rationale that such areas were crucial to national security and important for maintaining the international superiority of the United States (Grittner 1969; Huebener 1961; Ornstein 1962; Parker 1961; Roeming 1962; see also Savignon in this volume). Money for foreign-language education was allocated in the form of student scholarships, institutes for teacher training and study, provisions to help state departments of education train foreign-language supervisors, and for the purchase of equipment. It should be noted that this Cold-War legislation (including at first a loyalty oath to be signed by scholarship recipients) gave much less money to foreign-language study than to science and mathematics. Equally important is the fact that no mention was made in the legislation of the preservation of language resources in America's ethnic communities. The bill was directed at America's monolingual English-speaking population and to the educated elite. Nonetheless, the bill resulted in a temporary increase in the study of foreign languages, both common and 'exotic' (common = Spanish,

French, German, and Italian; exotic = everything else). During the Kennedy period, NDEA was translated into EPDA (Education Professions Development Act) without any real change in objectives, but with a diminished rhetoric.

The fourth historical period, "the Liberal Era," lasted from the mid-1960s to the late 1970s. The era began during President Lyndon Johnson's "Great Society" and the "rediscovery" of poverty in the United States. As a by-product of the civil-rights movement, growing assertions of ethnicity by minority groups, public support for educational lobbying groups, and the writings of various academic and social leaders, a belief developed that specialized educational programs could be designed to eliminate poverty and spur on economic and social opportunities for minority groups in the United States. A part of this flurry of educational and social legislation was the passage of the Bilingual Education Act of 1968 as Title VII of the Elementary and Secondary Education Act; this bill, and its subsequent amendments, marked a change in language-in-education policy toward non-English-speaking groups (Heath 1978a; Leibowitz 1980; Matute-Bianchi 1979; Pouncey 1981; Spolsky 1978a; Thernstrom 1980). For the first time, federal money was provided for bilingual education, allowing students to learn in their native languages while learning English as a second language (ESL). The bill, however, framed bilingual education as a "transitional" model, viewing learning in the student's native language as valid only until mastery of English was obtained. Furthermore, bilingual education was viewed as a "compensatory" strategy (as were other pieces of educational legislation during this period), with native-language learning viewed as necessary to overcome perceived deficiencies in lower-class children's backgrounds (cf. Bernstein 1972b; Edwards 1985; Ogbu 1987; Stubbs 1980). Thus, for the most part, bilingual-education programs were to be for poorer minority children, mostly Hispanic, and not for monolingual middle-class Anglo children, who were already fluent in English (Blanco 1978; Foster 1982a, 1982b; Lewis 1980)—that is, it was one-way bilingualism.

While certain academicians, educators, and minority-group spokespersons supported a 'maintenance/enrichment' model of bilingual education, in which native-language learning is continued after English proficiency is obtained, and all children, regardless of socioeconomic background, become bilingual, there was little support for this view either among legislators or in the courts (Applewhile 1979; Fong 1978; Grant and Goldsmith 1979; Rotberg 1982; and Teitelbaum and Hiller 1977). Neither allowed or mandated bilingual education as a remedy for unequal educational opportunities or as an effort to protect the civil rights of non-English speakers. Ironically, during this same period, foreign-language education for monolingual Americans almost disappeared as a policy issue, and the number of students studying foreign languages declined sharply, as did federal support for such programs (Hayden 1979). Toward the end of the period, there were calls for more studies of foreign-language and international education, most notably in the President's

Select Committee's study entitled *Strength through wisdom: A critique of U.S. capability* (1979); however, this report did not lead to the passage of any legislation that supported such efforts (Pincus 1980; Putnam 1981; Reinert 1981). It is important to note, in this regard, that the commission was appointed by President Carter, but the report was delivered as Carter was leaving office. The more conservative and anti-educational Reagan administration was profoundly disinterested.

The final period, beginning in the late 1970s and continuing to the present, can be described as that of the conservative reaction. It has been characterized by two types of reaction against non- and limited-English speakers. The first has been directed against bilingual education, claiming that children so educated have not acquired sufficient command of English, that being bilingual causes intellectual deficit and the inability to function in either language, that children only retained their native language and culture and/or that there are more effective ways of educating children who are not from English-speaking families (Baker and de Kantor 1983; Betchell 1979; Danoff 1978; Epstein 1977). While supporters of bilingual education have countered these claims (Baker 1988; Crawford 1989; Cummins 1983, 1986a; Fishman 1978; Hakuta 1986; Otheguy 1982; Troike 1978; Trueba 1979; Zappert and Cruz 1977), it is clear that policy makers are less supportive of bilingual education than in the previous era, and that some are in favor of limiting or abolishing programs (Levin 1982, 1983). A second type of reaction has been the movement to make English the "official" language of the United States on the grounds that English is not being learned by newer immigrants, that certain laws (including bilingual-education laws) induce the retention of non-English languages, and that people are less committed to the "traditional" values than they used to be (Judd 1987; Marshall 1986), those values being tacitly equated with English literacy. It is argued that foreign-language retention at the expense of English endangers the entire country and might lead to political fragmentation of the nation if not to absolute chaos. Certain states and municipalities have already passed legislation making English their official language. To make English their "official" language or "national" language of the United States will require an amendment to the constitution, but the Congress has not acted.

Although it seems unlikely that the amendment to make English the official language of the United States will pass, or that the Congress will totally abandon bilingual education, there has been an increase in hostility toward non-English users over the preceding periods (Pifer 1979; Vann 1978). With respect to foreign-language education, critics have continued to bemoan the lack of foreign-language proficiency on the part of most Americans and have argued that such a situation hurts the country with respect to both national security and international economic competition (Simon 1980). While few policy makers have voiced any opposition to these claims, there has been little real support in terms of specific legislation fostering foreign-language study and only modest support in terms of funding. There is evidence of growing isolationism, based in part on economic fears, in part on other, more clearly xenophobic considerations. The economic fears and xenophobia take several forms. The growing economic power of former defeated enemies, particularly Japan, is one basis of fear. This in turn has generated a concern for the protection of industrial patents and copyrights to prevent countries with less expensive labor forces from underselling the United States. A second phenomenon engendering feat is the continuing flow of cheap labor into the United States, largely from Mexico. There is the concern that illegal immigrants will take jobs away from U.S. citizens because they will work for less. There is also a 'fortress mentality' in the United States—a national paranoia that sees international communism as evil and as genuinely threatening to values deeply held by some segments of the population. A number of other social phenomena—the epidemic spread of substance abuse and of AIDS, for example—indirectly contribute to the economic fears and the growing xenophobia.

In summary, there has generally been favorable support for foreign-language education, at least on the philosophical level, for monolingual English-speaking Americans; however, attitudes toward the education of non-English users have vacillated, ranging from hostility and attempts at repression to toleration and encouragement (Kloss 1977). In both areas, language-in-education policy has been affected by factors beyond the educational system (Brisk 1981; Ovando 1983). Foreign-language education becomes an issue in times of threat, e.g., World Wars I and II, the Sputnik era, and during the current period of international and economic alarms. In times of relative tranquility, foreign-language education does not seem to be a major policy issue, and, while perhaps receiving passive support, it does not generate sufficient concern to influence policy makers to pass and fund legislation (Castro 1981). In the case of language-in-education policy for non-English speakers, factors external to the educational system have had a major impact on policy (Padilla 1984). From time to time, minorities, feeling more repressed than usual, organize themselves to seek social and economic mobility and the right to aspire to political power. When they do so, they threaten the status quo. That causes social perturbations and politicization on both sides—those who want to change and those who want (at best) to stabilize the environment (or, at the worst, to return to a mythic golden age when problems simply did not exist and the minorities knew their place). In these periods of heightened awareness, policy debate becomes more strident. Language-in-education policies, at such times, usually are justified on the basis of the societal goals that are desired, be they social equality, Americanization, national security, or whatever (Leibowitz 1971), rather than being justified on the basis of potential linguistic/learning benefits.

One question that could logically be posed is whether or not language-in-education policy in the United States is inherently contradictory; it supports foreign-language study while simultaneously discouraging use of non-English languages in the country's ethnic communities, many of whose members already speak the very languages that are being promoted in foreign-language study. From an educational perspective, the contradictions are obvious. There certainly are those who speak these languages—at skill levels far higher than the average foreign-language student is likely to achieve. Such foreign-language training policies also appear to be economically inefficient, since efforts are reduplicated (Gaarder 1964, 1978). However, from a wider perspective, the policy appears less contradictory. Foreign-language study is directed at the monolingual elite (Herron 1982), who have already been Americanized, while programs directed at non-English speakers are designed to achieve assimilation. Apparently, the underlying philosophy is that a person can study foreign language post-assimilation but not pre-assimilation. Once someone is acculturated, then foreign-language study can begin. In other words, assimilation and Americanization are the overriding concerns of policy makers; foreign-language study is secondary. In this way, the elite maintain control over the basic social, political, and economic institutions of the country and are not threatened by other groups. While this policy may be open to question from an educational/research point of view, it is logical from a political perspective. Sharing power through new policy pronouncements may endanger the status quo; it is far better to adopt policies that protect one's own position. Since policy makers have already "made it" in American society, it is to their benefit to enact language-in-education policy that serves their interests (Diamond 1980).

Predicting future trends in language-in-education policy in the United States is, at best, uncertain, because unforeseen factors can arise. Nonetheless, a few tentative generalizations are in order. With regard to foreign-language education policy, there seems to be a resurgence of interest caused by the belief that increased benefits in terms of national security and international trade will derive from greater proficiency in foreign tongues (Simon 1980). This has been coupled with a renewed call for higher academic standards for high-school and university students in all areas, including foreign-language study (Enwall 1977). This linkage will probably lead to some increase in foreign-language study. Nonetheless, long-term sustained support, especially in terms of financial outlays, is unlikely to occur. History has shown that support for foreign-language education has never been a high-priority item among U.S. policy makers (Gault 1980; Hawkins 1972). Especially if international tensions decrease and an improved foreign-trade balance is achieved, the interest in foreign-language study is likely to abate. Complacency lessens interest in foreign-language education, and, for the average American, it is hard to rationalize attention to or need for such study.[2]

With respect to policy on non-English speakers, it is hard to imagine any major change in the near future. The majority of policy makers do not show any support for maintenance and/or enrichment forms of bilingual/bicultural education, and most Americans still believe that people should learn English and abandon their native languages (Vazquez 1978). The mood about increased English-language abilities among the citizenry, both native and nonnative speakers, and the suspicion of, and fears concerning some minority groups have sparked a call for a return to the "basics," abolition of bilingual education, making English the official language, and competency testing of both students and teachers (including foreign university teachers and graduate assistants). While these proposals have appeared mainly at the state and local levels, and are unlikely to translate into national policies (owing in part to the fact that, constitutionally, the making of educational policy is, for the most part, a prerogative of the individual states), they mirror current national attitudes and make it difficult for national policy makers to legitimize increased use of languages other than English. On the other hand, transitional bilingual programs are likely to continue in some form. In the long run, increased support of languages other than English will depend on the political climate. If tensions, real or perceived, lessen, then such language usage will be tolerated, if not actively supported. If tensions remain, continued hostility toward other languages will form the basis of the policy. In short, history illustrates certain trends and attitudes in language-in-education policy in the United States, and, while similar events may not occur in the future because new factors arise, it is equally unwise to ignore historical evidence when making predictions (Edwards 1985).

4. THE SITUATION IN OTHER COUNTRIES

Language-in-education policy and planning varies around the world. Each country has its own particular set of issues caused by local conditions, making generalizations across countries problematic at best (Baldauf and Luke 1989; Cobarrubias and Fishman 1983; Edwards 1984; Fishman, Ferguson, and Das Gupta 1968; Kaplan et al. 1982; Kennedy 1983; Lewis 1980; Paulston 1988; Rubin and Jernudd 1971; Spolsky and Cooper 1977, 1978; Wolfson and Manes 1985). While solutions vary from situation to situation, certain key issues arise commonly and provide the basis for useful discussion.

One area of concern worldwide involves the selection of a national language or languages (Wardhaugh 1987; Nichols 1984; Santiago 1982). Such designations are difficult ones in and of themselves, for they not only represent linguistic decisions, but also affect people's economic, social, and political lives (Weinstein 1983). When one language is chosen as official, speakers of that language are at an advantage in terms of access to the major social institutions of that country, while others are often excluded (Weinstein 1983). It is not surprising that open hostility can arise between in-group and out-group members, leading in some cases to social and political problems and even to open hostility (Beer and Jacobs 1985; LaPonce 1987; Wardhaugh 1987).

One decision in language-status choice is whether to adopt an indigenous language as the national language or to select an international one. Such a decision, made by policy makers who are outside the educational system, greatly affects the language-in-education policy and planning in any country. If an indigenous language is chosen, speakers of that language have an advantage in terms of the benefits derived from being educated. On the other hand, those not speaking the chosen language have to acquire it as a second language and will encounter disadvantages relative to native speakers. In some situations, the choice of an indigenous language means that the language must become standardized for use in schools. Textbooks (grammars, dictionaries, spellers, etc.) will have to be written in that language, both for native speakers and for those who are acquiring it as an additional tongue. This process is not only expensive, but also requires expertise and may be impossible to achieve in practice (Edwards 1985). Furthermore, declaring an indigenous language to be a favored language in the schools threatens those who are already in power, especially if they have obtained their education and empowerment in a different language. In short, selecting an indigenous language may foster political unity by creating new nationalistic feelings; on the other hand, it may heighten differences and rivalries among groups, which would threaten national unity. Of course, the selection of an indigenous variety is no guarantee of political freedom or of equal opportunity for all segments of the population; the choice could be designed to foster or maintain existing advantages for one group over others in a society (e.g., the situation in Malaysia; cf. Fasold 1984; see also Weinstein 1983).

An alternative policy is to select an international language, usually that of the former colonial power, as the official language or co-language (LaPonce 1987; Wardhaugh 1987). On one hand, if such a language is chosen, no one internal group has an inherent native advantage (e.g., the situation in Kenya and India; Fasold 1984). In addition, international languages are in fact used for international communication, and, since they are often languages of technological and scientific communication, they provide an access to information necessary for modernization (Grabe 1988; Kaplan 1987). On the other hand, selection of an alien language may be in conflict with the desire to establish an independent political and cultural identity and to sever ties with the colonial or neocolonial past. In terms of language-in-education policy specifically, such a choice also implies massive second-language education for the majority of the population. Furthermore, since those in power may have already mastered the international language and also may have greater economic power owing to their status, the decision to employ an international language may serve to perpetuate the status quo. The schools may thus become an elitist training ground rather than an instrument for mass education (Kachru 1984; O'Barr 1984).

The issue of second and foreign languages affects many countries of the world (Ashworth 1985; Spolsky 1986b). The decision to teach another language to the indigenous population is often motivated by pragmatism—English and, to a lesser extent, French are major world languages and are studied more often out of need than out of loyalty. However, political reasoning also enters into the choice, as witnessed in the choice of the People's Republic of China's to switch its educational emphasis from Russian to English. The political importance of second-language study can be seen by the governmental support given by France (Weinstein 1984), Germany, and English-speaking countries to programs that spread their languages beyond their immediate borders. That is not to say that educational benefits are not gained in this process, but rather that the motivation of such governments may include the desire to obtain political and cultural allies. Sending students to study in another country also has political, as well as educational, consequences. It can be used to further a country's pool of knowledge, but it can also lead either to attempts to democratize the power base or to further perpetuation of the ruling elite's control. An additional, and often unforeseen, result of study abroad is that students encounter new ideas that may later threaten the political system. Thus, it is not surprising that governments are often selective in permitting some to go abroad to study (Judd 1984).

In many countries, there is also the question of education of new arrivals: short-term workers, refugees, and new immigrants. The decision as to how much socialization is desirable for members of these populations will affect language-in-education policy and planning. For example, Skutnabb-Kangas (1984) points out that short-term workers and their children in Europe receive inferior education because of hostility on the part of the majority population. Should they receive better education, they might obtain greater societal mobility, which would not only threaten the dominant group economically, but would have a negative effect on the source of cheap labor upon which the society depends. Thus, the decisions concerning how to handle the education of outsiders, in terms of both tolerance of their native language and teaching them the dominant language, is determined in the political arena and then given to educators to implement. What may be best educationally, in theoretical terms, may not be given serious considerations because of wider political considerations.

5. SUGGESTIONS FOR FUTURE STUDIES

Studies on language-in-education policy and planning exist (see annotated bibliography), but there is a need for far more research. Many countries have not been adequately studied, and those that have been examined can always benefit from re-analysis to confirm research findings, or to challenge them. Since language policy and planning always implicate ongoing phenomena, newer studies provide welcome additions to the literature. Based on the perspective offered in this essay, there are some basic questions that should be asked in the pursuit of such research. In keeping with the basic approach of this work, what is offered is meant to be suggestive, not comprehensive.

1. What is the existing language-in-education policy of the country? What factors, both internal and external, led to its formation?

2. Who has designed the policy? What groups have been influential in the policy formulation: educators, intellectuals, community leaders, politicians, bureaucrats, special-interest groups, etc.?

3. Who benefits from the existing policy, both as individuals and as members of certain groups? Who loses or is excluded because of the policy?

4. What are the underlying philosophical/moral assumptions of the policy: e.g., socialization, political unification, modernization, establishment of a new identity, maintenance of the status quo, etc.?

5. How is the school system viewed in relation to other societal institutions? What are the expectations of the schools with regard to implementation of the existing policy?

6. How effective is the existing policy in actually meeting the stated objectives?

7. What circumstances are currently at work that either support the existing policy or pose a challenge to it?

8. What plans have been offered for change in the existing policy? Who has suggested the changes, and what rationales are being put forth as justifications? How much power do the advocates of change have?

9. Who is likely to oppose any change? What are the stated and unstated reasons for their opposition? How much power do they possess to block changes?

10. What societal factors may influence the likelihood of change? What would be gained or lost if particular changes were implemented?

These ten questions are just starting points. It is important for researchers to look at other situations and other studies to see what has been done. However, care must be exercised when applying findings from one situation to another, since the interplay of factors will vary.

6. CONCLUSION

The underlying purpose here has been to examine language-in-education policy and planning from a power perspective (Kramarae, Schultz, and O'Barr, 1984). Questions of what is 'best' or 'fairest' or, for that matter, what is most beneficial educationally can be posed, but they do not necessarily explain what has happened or what is being planned. Things occur because those who control societal institutions allow them to happen. How a person reacts to these policies often depends on philosophical proclivities and personal perceptions of gain and loss. To cite one example, in viewing the issue of transitional vs. maintenance bilingual education in the United States, the position defended is often based on the person's view of assimilation vs. pluralism, and minority vs. majority rights (Cole 1980; Judd 1984; Kjolseth 1972; Padilla 1983; Valdez 1979). If a person favors pluralism (Fishman 1981), then s/he often will support a maintenance model; conversely, if assimilation is viewed as beneficial to society, transitional bilingual education (or no bilingual education) is the chosen stance. Similarly, the view that majority rights take precedence over minority freedoms leads to support of an assimilationist model, while the view that minorities should be protected from the tyranny of the majority causes a stance in favor of pluralism. Facts and studies rarely change people's positions, for these are highly emotional issues that may defy rational argument and counterargument. Those who are in education, who daily feel the impact of language-in-education policy and planning, must realize that factors that have led us to our current situations may not represent the best educational solutions, and may represent factors beyond the direct control of any set of contemporary actors. Language-in-education policy and planning affect our daily lives, and it is important to understand where these policies originate, how they can be understood, and how they will affect the lives of all those subject to such policies and plans.

NOTES

1. The founding fathers of the United States were galvanized by the notion of federalism at all costs and were therefore happy to permit non-English-speaking enclaves to exist within the new polity.

2. There is, at the same time, a certain amount of coincident hypocrisy in U.S. foreign-language teaching policies; for example, the United States is a signator to the Helsinki accords, promising to promote the learning of the languages of the group of signators. Since the signing of the accords, the U.S. education sector has not modified its policy in any way and thus is substantially out of compliance with the treaty.

   The following annotated bibliography lists a wide-ranging set of resources with which to pursue the issues of language-in-education policy and planning raised in this chapter. The sources cover such topics as language policy and planning, language disadvantage among minority-language users, bilingual-education studies in many contexts, and educational policy in the United States in particular.

ANNOTATED BIBLIOGRAPHY

Alatis, J.E. (ed.) 1978. *International dimensions of bilingual education* GURT 1978. Washington, DC: Georgetown University Press.

Proceedings of the Georgetown Round Table on Language and Linguistics dealing with international issues related to bilingualism and bilingual education, including theoretical studies, case studies from various parts of the world, and articles on teacher education and measurement issues written by some major authorities in the field.

Ashworth, M. 1985. *Beyond methodology: Second language teaching and the community.* New York: Cambridge University Press.
A book designed for educators dealing with the political issues that arise with second- and foreign-language instruction and with how educators can become aware of and deal with these forces.

Baldauf, R., and A. Luke (eds.) 1989. *Language planning and education in Australasia and the South Pacific.* Clevedon, Avon: Multilingual Matters.
A collection of articles reviewing language and language-in-education policy and planning in Australia, Southeast Asia, and the South Pacific. Articles provide numerous examples of the interaction, or lack of interaction, between governmental agencies and language-education planning.

Cobarrubias, J., and J.A. Fishman (eds.) 1983. *Progress in language planning.* New York: Mouton.
A collection of essays from an international perspective dealing with topics concerning decision making, codification, implementation, and evaluation of language policy.

Edwards, J. 1985. *Language, society and identity.* New York: Basil Blackwell.
An overall review of language-policy issues covering situations around the world, with chapters on language and nationalism, language maintenance and language shift, ethnic revival and new ethnicity, language and education, and language attitudes. It includes an extensive appendix on language issues around the world.

Edwards, J. (ed.) 1984. *Language minorities, policies and pluralism.* London: Academic Press.
A collection of articles and case studies on language-policy issues dealing with such topics as guest works, language minority groups, ethnic separatism, ethnic identity, and bilingual education.

Fishman, J.A., C. Ferguson, and J. Das Gupta (eds.) 1968. *Language problems of developing nations.* New York: John Wiley.
One of the first anthologies in the field containing articles on theoretical foundations of language and development, language planning, standardization, and education, with numerous case studies.

Grant, S.A. 1978. A language policy in the United States. *ADFL Bulletin* 9, 4:1–12.
A study commissioned by the MLA/ACLS Task Force on Government Relations that reviews language policy in the United States in terms of the role of English as the national language, bilingual education, law and court rulings, and foreign-language education.

Hakuta, K. 1986. *Mirror of language: The debate on bilingualism.* New York: Basic Books.
An overview of issues connected with bilingualism, including language acquisition in youngsters, the bilingual brain, second-language acquisition in both children and adults, societal bilingualism, and the debate over bilingual education.

Hartford, B., A. Valdman, and C.R. Foster (eds.) 1982. *Issues in international bilingual education: The role of the vernacular.* New York: Plenum.

A series of articles on vernacular education, cognitive development of individuals, evaluation and testing of bilinguals, teacher training, immersion programs, and case studies on language-in-education issues.

Judd, E.L. 1984. TESOL as a political act: A moral question. In J. Handscombe, R.A. Orem, and B.P. Taylor (eds.) *On TESOL '83: The question of control.* Washington, DC: TESOL. 265–273.
An argument that teaching English to non-English speakers often is a political issue and raises moral issues for anyone involved in the process.

Kaplan, R.B., et al. (eds.) 1982. *Annual review of applied linguistics, 1981.* Rowley, MA: Newbury House.
This volume of ARAL focuses on language policy in a variety of countries and also contains essays on language-in-education and literacy issues around the world.

Kennedy, C. (ed.) 1983. *Language planning and language education.* Winchester, MA: George Allen and Unwin.
This collection of papers combines classic articles on language planning with case studies of interactions between language planning and language-in-education planning.

Kramarae, C., M. Schultz, and W. O'Barr (eds.) 1984. *Language and power.* Beverly Hills, CA: Sage.
A collection of articles exploring the relationship between language and power, with examples from around the world; a number of the papers relate to language policy and planning.

Lewis, E.G. 1980. *Bilingualism and bilingual education: A comparative study.* Albuquerque, NM: University of New Mexico Press.
A discussion of bilingualism and bilingual-education theory and practice around the world, with especially good discussion of the situations in the Soviet Union, the United States, and Wales.

Paulston, C. (ed.) 1988. *International handbook of bilingualism and bilingual education.* New York: Greenwood Press.
A collection of papers providing a thorough overview of bilingualism and bilingual education in many parts of the world. Contributions are from many countries that do not regularly receive treatment.

Rubin, J., and B.H. Jernudd (eds.) 1971. *Can languages be planned?: Sociolinguistic theory and practice for developing nations.* Honolulu, HI: University of Hawaii Press.
General articles and case studies on motivations and justifications for language planning, including different approaches to and methods of conducting research in the field and discussions of how such research can be applied.

Schneider, S.G. 1976. *Revolution, reaction or reform: The 1974 Bilingual Education Act.* New York: Las Americas.
An in-depth case study of the 1974 Bilingual Education Act that describes the origins of the bill, how the bill made its way through the Congress, and issues that were discussed during the Congressional debate.

Spolsky, B., and R.L. Cooper (eds.) 1977. *Frontiers of bilingual education.* Rowley, MA: Newbury House.

A series of articles on various dimensions of bilingual education—historical, sociological, psychological, educational, philosophical—as well as issues relating to evaluation and language planning.

Spolsky, B., and R.L. Cooper (eds.) 1978. *Case studies in bilingual education*. Rowley, MA: Newbury House.
A variety of essays on bilingual education around the world dealing with issues of language education; bidialectism; and language maintenance, spread, and loss.

Wardhaugh, R. 1987. *Languages in Competition*. New York: Basil Blackwell.
An in-depth treatment of languages in contact with emphasis on multilingualism, language choice, language spread, language shift, and language maintenance.

Weinstein, B. 1983. *The civic tongue: Political consequences of language choice*. New York: Longman.
A book discussing how language decisions are influenced by the political environment, with emphasis on five areas: participation education, conflict, nation building, and world politics.

Wolfson, N., and J. Manes (eds.) 1985. *Language of inequality*. New York: Mouton.
A collection of essays on situations around the world, dealing with issues of social equality and language contact, language choice, language maintenance and shift, language standardization and educational planning, classroom language interaction, and multilingual functioning.

QUESTIONS FOR
FURTHER DISCUSSION

1. Early in the text, Judd articulates three preliminary assumptions: that language-in-education planning cannot be discussed in isolation; that the major goal of any educational system is the socialization of its citizens; and that education and socialization policy are segments of overall government policy.

    (a) Why are the second and third assumptions significant to language-in-education policy?

    (b) Why is it important that language-in-education policy not be discussed in isolation?

    (c) How do these three preliminary assumptions interact to underlie language-in-education planning?

2. Why should language-in-education policy be entrusted to politicians and the implementation of such policy relegated to educators?

3. Why do you think the United States has never had an official language? Is it important that it should or should not? Since the United States has managed without designating an official language, what has changed that might make it necessary now? Why does the establishment of an official language make more sense in certain other countries?

4. How useful are the questions listed in section five, "Questions for Further Discussion"? Are there questions that might be deleted because they are no longer

relevant? Are there questions that should be added to make the inventory more comprehensive?

5. Judd has a number of things to say about bilingual education; compare his views with those expressed in the article by Macias.

6. Judd has a number of things to say about literacy; compare his views with those expressed by Kaplan and Palmer in the article on literacy.

7. Judd writes: "Things occur because those who control societal institutions allow them to happen." If this is in fact the case, what is the point of planning at all?

8. In his second note, Judd observes that the United States is substantially out of compliance with the Helsinki accords. What does that mean in terms of language-in-education planning in the United States?

An Introduction to
Literacy and Applied Linguistics

Literacy may be examined from a number of perspectives; it may be seen as *opportunity*, as *resource*, or as *problem*. In the latter half of the twentieth century and in multilingual states, literacy has largely been perceived as a problem; that is, an equivalence has been assumed to exist between the extent to which a population is literate and the ability of the state in which the population resides to achieve and maintain an appropriate level of modernization—in Graff's (1987) terms, "the literacy myth." This underlying assumption has led to some pervasive secondary beliefs; e.g., that the absence of literacy is a societal ill that must be eradicated (like crime or communicable disease), and that it is the prerogative of states to 'combat' illiteracy, and that there are only two possible conditions: the presence of literacy or the absence of it.

These assumptions have in fact defined the behavior of states; governments have mounted campaigns to stamp out illiteracy (encouraged by UNESCO policy in many cases). It must be noted that the language used to discuss literacy is dominated by metaphors of military operations and disease; 'campaigns' have been organized following the military metaphor, while individuals who lack literacy have been treated like diseased persons. The 'problem' of literacy has become intractable. To a large extent, the 'problem' is a creation of the programs devised to deal with it, and there is an amazing circularity in discussions of literacy. One would not wish to claim that the matter can be ignored with impunity, but one could hope that the discussion might be more informed by economic, political, linguistic, and pedagogical reality.

The reality is that 'literacy' is not a point on a scale; rather, it is a set of practices that vary from context to context, depending on the functional uses required of literacy and the demands of the larger social structure. Thus, being literate is not simply a matter of more or less along an arbitrary scale, but of participating in the literacy practices of the community including, when appropriate, the literacy practices valued by the school system. Defining a literate individual can only be considered in relation to that individual's being a productive user of the literacy practices of a particular society. The criterion for determining literacy, then, may be seen as much in political and social terms as it is in linguistic or pedagogical terms, a view espoused by many current scholars of literacy.

The broad concern with literacy is an applied-linguistic concern because it implicates the solution to real-world language-based problems. Obvious questions arise around such issues as:

1. Literacy in which of the languages available to a society?
2. Literacy for what purposes in a given society?
3. Literacy in what registers in a given society?

There are additional fundamental questions: e.g., what are the particular literacy practices that may or may not be emphasized in particular contexts? Can we speak of different kinds of specific literacy skills, only some of which are valued in school systems? Further, to what extent does literacy implicate numeracy and/or other related skills (e.g., 'musical literacy,' 'computer literacy,' 'information literacy,' etc.)?

These questions in turn raise questions of language pedagogy; e.g., who will teach whom, in what physical facilities, with what methods and materials, over what duration, at what cost? And these questions place discussions of literacy in the domains of language planning and language-in-education planning. If the desired literacy occurs in a language that has only recently acquired an orthography, and/or that has yet to produce any significant body of material to read, the discussion may implicate corpus questions as well as status questions (that is, providing material for newly literate individuals to read). In any case, literacy issues are largely applied-linguistic issues, and they are of interest to a wide range of applied linguists: planners, curriculum specialists, writers of grammars and dictionaries, researchers in language acquisition, and others.

Literacy and Applied Linguistics

Robert B. Kaplan and Joe D. Palmer

University of Southern California and Concordia University

1. INTRODUCTION

There is a short story by Robert Fowles, "Poor Koko," in which he tells the story of an academic taking a holiday in a remote cottage in order to devote time to his life's work—"a definitive biography and critical account of Thomas Love Peacock." In the course of his stay, the cottage is invaded by a burglar. The burglar ties up the academic and in a needless act of vandalism, before the academic's eyes, burns his manuscript, page by page. The narrator, the academic, tries in retrospect to understand the event. "My sin," he writes, "was not primarily that I was middle-class, intellectual, that I may have appeared more comfortably off than I am in fact, but that I live by words." Fowles begins the story with an epigram in Old Cornish:

> Byth dorn re ver dhe'n tavas re hyr,
> Mes den hep tavas a-gollas y dyr.

and ends with the English translation:

> Too long a tongue, too short a hand;
> But tongueless man has lost his land.

This story, its epigraph, and its implications seem to constitute an appropriate beginning for a discussion of literacy and applied linguistics.

2. DEFINING LITERACY

Literacy is a tricky term; the dictionary is not much help in this area since it merely repeats the common misconceptions about the area. It defines literacy as the state of being literate, and then defines literate as an adjective (he is literate) meaning:

1. able to read and write;
2. educated, cultured; and
3. literary.

and as a noun (he is a literate) meaning:

1. one able to read and write; and
2. an educated person.

These definitions clearly equate literacy with intelligence and cultivation, though there is no absolute basis for such an equation. Nor is it clear to what extent literacy involves the ability to read and write; that is, the amount of reading and writing required to qualify as literate varies over time and across situations. In some situations, it is enough to be able to write one's name; in other situations, that minimal skill does not qualify its holder as literate. To some extent, the quantity of literacy may be a function of the relative difficulty of the orthographic system involved; for example, what control of how many Chinese characters qualifies one as literate, and how does that quantity compare with the requirements to be considered literate in an alphabetic language like English. It would appear that the amount of ability to read and write required to qualify as literate in England three hundred years ago (Cressy 1980; Resnick and Resnick 1977) is rather different from the amount required in the United States now. In sum, there is substantial confusion over the word literacy, not the least of which is terminological, and it may be useful to try to sort out that confusion.

2.1. Terms Employed in Discussing Literacy

There are a number of terms now in common use that substantially contribute to the problem because they are used interchangeably in common parlance. Table 1 should illustrate the fact that literacy is a complex phenomenon. It should also illustrate the fact that any definition of literacy has to be specific to the circumstances in which the term is to be used. What constitutes a perfectly acceptable set of criteria for literacy in one setting may not define literacy in another, and *setting* must be understood to include both a spatial and a temporal parameter (Graff 1987; Heath 1983; Mackie 1981).

2.2. Nonlanguage Symbol Systems

To complicate the matter somewhat, it is not clear to what extent the ability to deal with other symbolic representations plays a role in any definition of

TABLE 1: TERMS FOR VARIOUS TYPES OF LITERACY

In societies that have no system to represent the spoken language in graphic form (monolingual).	In societies that have an established method for representing the spoken language in graphic form (monolingual)
Nonliterate: individuals of any age who cannot read or write because there is no way to do so.	*Preliterate:* children who cannot read or write because they haven't yet been taught to do so.
	Literate: adolescent and older individuals who possess the ability to read and write in what is considered the normative range for that culture.
	Postliterate: adults who once knew how to read and write, but who have for any reason lost the ability.
	Illiterate: adolescents and older individuals who have for whatever reason not learned to read and write at all in the language of that culture.
	Functionally illiterate: adolescents and older individuals who are able to read and write, but do so at a level below the normative range for that culture.
	Highly literate: adolescents and older individuals who have the ability to read and write in the academic or other specialist registers appropriate to that culture.
In societies in which there are two or more languages, only one of which can be graphically represented.	In societies in which there are two or more languages, all of which can be graphically represented.
Nonliterate/preliterate *Nonliterate/literate* *Nonliterate/postliterate* *Nonliterate/illiterate* *Nonliterate/functionally illiterate* *Nonliterate/highly literate*	*Coliterate:* Adolescents and older individuals who have the ability to read and write in both languages at the normative level for both cultures.
	Biliterate: Adolescents and older individuals who possess high literacy in both languages.

[While there is no common term, it is possible to speak of individuals who are *triliterate* or *quatraliterate*; that is, who can read and/or write in three or four languages (e.g., French/Italian/Portuguese/Spanish, though the languages need not belong to the same family). Indeed, any of the terms above may be applied to multilingual situations; that is, an individual may be highly literate in one language, postliterate in another, and functionally illiterate in a third and/or fourth.]

literacy. Thus, there is a question to what extent numeracy may be a constituent of literacy. (*Numeracy* analogously refers to the ability to manipulate a system for representing numerical values.) If an individual is to be considered literate, should that individual be able to read, for example, signs in a vegetable market that convey the message: $0.30/lb., or $1.00@? Should a literate individual be able to add, subtract, multiply, or divide? If an individual can be expected to deal with such symbol systems as a function of being literate, obviously again in relation to particular situations, the individual may be expected to deal with much more complex symbol systems; e.g., *, %, &, +, #, $, @, =, 30303 Ganado Drive, Rancho Palos Verdes, CA 90274, etc. Certain symbol systems are so specialized that another set of terms is used to describe facility in their use; thus, one may speak of 'musical literacy' or 'chemical literacy.' A relatively new term in use in English, also formed and defined by analogy, is *computer literacy*—not the ability to type natural language words on a computer keyboard, but the ability to manipulate the special symbols that tell a computer what to do. And there are other types of manipulative skills that may be described as some form of literacy: e.g., 'information literacy'—the ability to manipulate information systems. The point is that these several literacies may be subsumed under the broader concept *if they constitute activity within the normative range in a given society.*

In certain societies the range of literacy uses may be limited or minimal. In those situations the uses of literacy skills and their development in educational contexts may be seen as an opportunity for advancement socially and economically. Not being literate in these contexts does not label any individual as somehow lacking or not contributing to the social structure of the community. For many countries in the world and in many communities, literacy as opportunity is the norm. In situations where a relatively high level of literacy use is considered normative, a very different set of relations develop. In these latter contexts (most developed countries of the world), it is expected that the citizenry have training in a variety of literacy skills; members function productively in their society in part because they have literacy skills. Persons in such contexts who do not have literacy skills are viewed as problems for society, and as deviant from the norm. Rather than literacy as opportunity, these contexts promote the view of illiteracy as problem. Most discussions of literacy are framed in the 'problem' context including, for the most part, the present chapter.

3. TYPES OF LITERACY PROGRAMS

In polities where the norms for reading and writing abilities are at a relatively low level, or where a large percentage of the population is illiterate, programs for the promotion of literacy (beyond the formal instruction available to

schoolchildren) typically involve governmentally sponsored literacy campaigns. Lesser efforts by churches, international organizations, and private
organizations do not have the resources to have a significant effect unless
funded consistently over a long period of time (e.g., the role of religious
institutions in language policy and planning; cf. Kaplan in this volume).
Large-scale literacy campaigns are not a recent invention, as such campaigns
have been undertaken in the past in Germany, Scotland, Sweden, and the
United States (see Arnove and Graff 1987). In the post–World War II contemporary period, literacy campaigns have most often been associated with governmental upheaval (e.g., in Cuba, Ethiopia, Guinea Bissau, Nicaragua,
People's Republic of China, Tanzania). The results of these literacy movements
in terms of greatly improved literacy skills for a large percentage of the
population, or in relation to the retention of literacy over time, are not clearly
defined, and there is continued debate over their effectiveness; nevertheless,
they represent a strong rallying point not simply for the development of literacy skills among the masses, but also as a political tool for mobilizing people
and making them aware of their condition (Arnove and Graff 1987; Mackie
1981; Wagner 1987). The study and careful documentation of these movements is a relatively new field of research. Since this chapter will focus more
on contexts of literacy development in which the societal norms are high, the
role of literacy in the above context will not be addressed in any detail.

In polities in which a relatively greater ability to read and write constitutes the norm, there are three types of literacy programs that may be supported in the education sector or in the society more generally. These are:

1. *Basic literacy programs*—educational programs that teach reading and
   writing to children through the established school system over the
   duration of several years, usually in the primary school years.

2. *Corrective literacy programs*—educational programs usually intended for
   adults who somehow did not learn to read and write in basic literacy
   programs, often provided outside the school system either by community organizations, churches, and other voluntary social groups or
   by a special postsecondary adult-education system, often having relatively short periods of instruction over a rather long duration.

3. *Additive literacy programs*—educational programs intended for adoles-
   cents and adults who have immigrated into the society at an age beyond that at which literacy is normally achieved, often administered
   through voluntary and community agencies and often characterized
   by fragmentary contact with the learners (a duration broken by periods
   of unemployment and other distractions that preclude the leisure for
   learning).

Basic literacy programs constitute part of the value structure of the society. It is assumed that all normal children will achieve literacy through such

programs and will, as a consequence, become contributing members of society. The definitions *literate* and *contributing member of society* are coterminus. That being the case, anyone who is not literate is not a contributing member of society. There are only two things that can be done with individuals who are not contributing members of the society; they may be made literate and thereby contributing members, or they may be excluded from society. Both approaches have been tried. Minorities made up of individuals who are otherwise undesirable (e.g., for reasons of race, religion, etc.) are easily excluded from the society (e.g., by being put in special geographic locations, sometimes called *ghetto*, sometimes *reservation*, sometimes *concentration camp*, sometimes *gulag*—the term varies with polity, time, type of government, etc., but the end effect is the same). That is the way in which various minorities in the United States (e.g., blacks, native Americans, Latinos, etc.) have historically been treated. The other alternative is now being pursued in the United States with respect to many of the groups that were formerly excluded. The other alternative has become acceptable and attractive in part because the groups have become too large to confine. In part, in a society that claims to be democratic, social consciousness requires that nonproductive individuals be made productive so that they may contribute to, rather than be dependent upon, the commonwealth; in short, it has become too expensive to support groups that do not contribute.

Corrective and additive literacy programs are provided for such groups. It is important to note that such programs often occur outside the mainstream, perhaps because there is a perception that public monies intended for education should not be used for these purposes. After all, if these were 'good' people, they would have become literate in the normal way; since they did not, life cannot be made too easy for them. That is, there is an element of public punishment (or at least of stigma) in corrective and additive literacy programs. The populations to which such programs are applied are often powerless either to protest the stigmatization or to demand somewhat better treatment. The fact remains that, being unable to manipulate literacy at the normative level for the particular society, such populations cannot vote, cannot find other than menial employment, and find themselves in other ways at or near the bottom of the class structure (however it may be defined).

It is, of course, the case that the lines between these several types of literacy-giving programs become blurred. Perhaps the case of bilingual education in the United States is the best case of such blurring; school children are placed in corrective and additive programs of many different types, though most are labeled as bilingual-education programs. One cause for the difficulty in devising appropriate programs is that students who may need special assistance may not need the same assistance in each case. For example, there are young children of immigrant parents, required to attend elementary school with their age peers, who have not acquired literacy at all because they come from nonliterate or preliterate environments in their home countries. Other students may be children of parents who do not have literacy skills, even though they come from a country that has a tradition of literacy among a large proportion of the population. Yet other students, children of minority-language parents, may have difficulty in acquiring literacy partly because their parents may be illiterate, even though they are not immigrants into a country with a high literacy norm. These students must all be dealt with somehow, but they do not fit neatly into any of the program categories suggested. Such children end up in what are, for the most part, euphemistically call bilingual programs—programs intended as bridging mechanisms in which children may get some instruction in their native language, but in which the real objective is to move them as rapidly as possible into mainstream literacy so that they can pass through the rest of the system together with their age peers.

Bilingual programs in a public-school setting, at least in the United States, have been the subject of major controversies. The results of bilingual programs have been mixed (cf. Cummins 1984; Genesee 1987; Hakuta 1986; Kaplan et al. 1986; Swain and Lapkin 1984). The only conclusion that is safe to state is that specific context variables for specific bilingual programs seem to have a major influence in the success or failure of bilingual programs, and generalizations from specific program contexts is a risky undertaking. Thus, the Canadian experiences with French and English do not explain performance in the United States by many Spanish and English, or Navajo and English students. The evidence is accumulating that children who grow up bilingual and function well in each language appear to gain some, perhaps minor, cognitive advantages; but this set of findings should not be taken as support for specific approaches to bilingual instruction. Bilingualism as a general cognitive ability cannot be equated with specific bilingual-education programs as educational enterprises. There are many explanations for the mixed results reported for bilingual programs and the confusing recommendations of many different scholars. The issues are too complex to be presented in the space of this chapter, and interested readers should pursue references to these issues in Macias (in this volume).

3.1. Relative Success of Adult-Literacy Programs

In general, many of the programs discussed above tend not to be enormously successful, partly because the affected minorities are in some other sense 'undesirable' and therefore do not have access to better employment even when they have taken the trouble to become literate, and partly because the effort is by definition stigmatized and scattered—that is, sufficient funds, facilities, resources, and manpower are rarely available to permit the affected minorities the leisure (the relief from the effort necessary for basic survival) to undertake serious learning or to afford them the environment in which effective learning can occur. Still another reason why such programs may fail is that they are simply misdirected. Announcements of literacy classes are *printed* and distributed to people who cannot read; classes are held in timeframes when the target populations cannot attend because they must accept employment at the most undesirable hours, and instruction is delivered through well-meaning but ill-trained volunteers. Most importantly, such programs may fail because the target populations do not perceive (or perceive only dimly) that there is any benefit to be gained from the personal investment required to achieve reading and writing skills at the normative level.

3.2. Literacy and the Culture of Poverty

As populations lacking the appropriate reading and writing skills have increased in size, they have begun to make demands on the culture in which they find themselves embedded. Like all people, they seek upward social mobility and the right to aspire to political power: these desires are particularly noticeable in consumer-based societies. The nonprint public media— billboards, radio, television—constantly present a profusion of consumer goods to which the affected populations also aspire, but from which they are cut off because their differentiation from the 'contributing' society makes it impossible for them to have the necessary purchasing power. Further, such 'noncontributing' populations are often disproportionately represented in the 'control' functions of the society: they tend to be more often arrested, more often convicted of crimes against the state, more often incarcerated, more often subject to substance abuse, more often calling on welfare and medical services. In other words, these populations tend to be locked into the culture of poverty. Given these characteristics, it is an easy step to the equation noted above: if they are poor, it is because they are illiterate; if they draw heavily upon the welfare services supported by tax monies, it is because they are illiterate; and if they are noncontributing members of society, that is so because they are illiterate. If these equations are correct, then all of the ills of any society may be corrected merely by making the entire population literate.

Recent research, however, has made it clear that such simple equations are far from correct. Graff (1982, 1987) and Street (1984, 1987), among others, have addressed such facile notions as the presumed correlation between literacy and quality of living as one among a number of literacy myths. Serious ethnographic and historical research has demonstrated that literacy, in and of itself, does little to change the social and economic standing of most newly literate groups in a literate society. Literacy can only be, at best, one among a large number of factors that determine the likelihood that certain group members will achieve some modicum of social mobility.

4. DEMOGRAPHY, LITERACY, AND
SECOND-LANGUAGE LITERACY

The problem of literacy is further complicated by the way it is reported. In the United States, for example, when literacy demographics are compiled, they tend to reflect only English literacy; that is, literacy in other languages is rarely counted. Hispanics in the United States may in fact be literate in Spanish, but if they are and simultaneously are illiterate, functionally illiterate, or postliterate in English, they are counted as illiterate—their Spanish literacy does not count. In the case of Native American languages, individuals may be nonliterate in their native languages (because not all Native American languages may have graphemic forms, or because, though graphemic forms exist for a given language, they have no reality for its speakers) and fall into some category of illiteracy in English, causing them to be counted as illiterates though they may be participants in a rich oral tradition.

A complex problem is posed by children categorized in this manner, because they may be preliterate in any language (e.g., Spanish and English) or preliterate in their native language and illiterate in English (perhaps for lack of opportunity to become literate, owing to years lost through poverty, war, refugee status, etc.). Such children are often required to become literate in their second language; that is, native speakers of Spanish, preliterate in Spanish, may be required in the United States to acquire literacy in English. This situation presents some obvious difficulties. To the extent that literacy depends on the development of sound-symbol correspondences, an individual who speaks the language of literacy with an accent is under some disadvantage. (This phenomenon has been observed among speakers of other languages designated 'foreign.') To the extent that the ability to read involves the ability to decode syntactic structures, the individual who is not very familiar with the syntactic structures of the language of literacy is under some disadvantage, and one may enumerate a number of other ways in which the nonnative speaker is disadvantaged in acquiring literacy in a second language.

5. LITERACY AND WAYS
OF THINKING

The literacy literature is filled with debates about the relation between literacy and thought. The strong form of the Whorf-Sapir hypothesis claims an absolute relationship between language and thought; indeed, takes the deterministic view that language absolutely determines thought processes. The weak version of the hypothesis merely recognizes that language and thought are to some extent mutually influencing; that is, while it is possible to say anything in any language, it is easier to say certain things in some languages than in others. It has been contended for example that, if Aristotle had been a

Mexican, the history of Western thought would have been entirely different. For example, as a speaker of an Indo-European language, one may say:

(1) I see you.

(or some superficially different set of words, differing only in surface structure from language to language). The proposition has a number of underlying assumptions. It may be assumed that the speaker *(I)* is an actor, that the speaker wills things to happen *(see)*, and that other beings and objects are recipients, the patients, of the speaker's action *(you)*. Still further, it must be assumed that this speaker lives in a universe in which such a set of presuppositions can co-occur. But there are languages in the world in which the nearest one may come to the intent of the given proposition would be in some such structure as:

(2) You appear to me.

(in which the differences from (1) are not now trivial surface differences but underlying differences). This proposition also implies a number of underlying assumptions. In this instance, the speaker *(me)* is not an actor causing things to happen; rather, s/he is a passive recipient of actions caused by forces unknown (and perhaps unknowable). Other beings and objects also are not actors. In example (1), I see you because I will to do so, and because you cannot escape being seen (excepting by willing not to be seen and taking action to prevent it). In example (2), no will is involved at all: I do not will to see you, and you do not will to be seen (or unseen). The seeing simply occurs because you and I find ourselves in a condition in which the seeing may occur. The underlying propositions in example (1) give rise to the kind of culture characteristic of most Western populations; these populations believe that they may for example exercise noetic control over nature and shape the environment to their needs. The underlying propositions in example (2) give rise to a quite different universe—one in which participants simply coexist with nature. It is apparent that these are significantly different world views (see also Kuno's discussion of empathy restrictions in Japanese 1976, 1978, 1986).

6. ORATE VS.
LITERATE CULTURES

Differences such as those described in terms of the restrictions of different languages are not directly related to the question of literacy. It has been argued, by Ong for example, that literacy causes a different way of looking at the world, that literacy plays a role in restructuring the functional uses of language as these functional uses expand into the written medium, that the differences between orate and literate populations is of the same order as the differences between speakers of different languages, that literacy causes a different way of looking at the world. Some scholars, such as Goody (1977), Havelock (1982), Olson (1977), and Ong (1982), have espoused a strong version of this notion, and others have argued that literacy creates cognitive differences between the literate and the orate individual, differences caused by the fact of becoming literate. While the logic of these arguments is appealing, the empirical evidence does not support such strong claims. In their ground-breaking study of literacy among the Vai, Scribner and Cole (1981) did not find evidence of general cognitive differences caused by literacy acquisition alone. Gough (1968) and Graff (1987), arguing from historical evidence, have not found evidence that literacy promoted differences in the cognitive structuring of individuals. Graff (1987), Heath (1983, 1986b), and Street (1984, 1987) all argue that the notion of a dichotomy between orate and literate itself does not hold up in the face of accumulating ethnographic evidence that multiple types of literacies exist and emerge differently in various times and in various communities. These more complex perspectives invalidate the idea that literacy can be discussed in such simple terms as orate vs. literate (though the descriptive designation is still useful for formulating more careful theoretical questions, particularly about the effects of literacy acquisition on social structures).

Recent discussions of the possible cognitive influences of literacy on the individual are couched in much more cautious terms, and appropriately so (e.g., Goody 1987). At the present time, it is only safe to say that the debate continues, with both sides taking more moderate and reasoned positions on the basis of the extant evidence and the careful interpretation of such influential psychologists as Vygotsky and Bruner (Langer 1987; Scribner 1987; Wertsch 1985b). It is, perhaps, possible to relate this debate to the strong and weak versions of the Whorf-Sapir hypothesis. Some initial positions may have been too deterministic—overstatements of the relationship that obtains between language and thought; other positions have been modified to accept the idea that literacy contexts probably have some effect on the individual, though that effect may be minimal, indirect, and difficult to measure. Given the history of the development of written language, the recognition of some literacy influence, however minimal, is not difficult to accept.

6.1. History of Written Language

Human beings and their immediate ancestors have been using elaborate call systems for about four and a half million years. The Australopithecines, living in the region of the Oldovai Gorge in Africa were, according to the evidence, organized into communities: territorial, nomadic, and group-hunting. On the basis of observation of contemporary species that share those characteristics (e.g., wolves), it can be assumed that they engaged in certain activities:

1. Group hunting, for example, requires an ability to communicate across distance; individual members of the hunting party must be able to signal their position relative to the game, the direction in which they are moving, and the speed at which they are moving. That complex of information requires a fairly sophisticated call system understandable to all the members of the group.

2. Nomadic existence in combination with territoriality requires the ability to recognize a territory, to recognize changes in the territory as the territory is moved with the nomadic group, and to share that knowledge within the group. It may be that early ancestors of man marked territory as wolves do, by scent; there is no clear evidence, and in the absence of evidence it may be presumed that a call system played some role in marking borders and in communicating about a shifting territory, as it does among monkeys.

3. Communal existence also requires some sort of communicative ability. In addition, human species are blessed with the most slowly developing young in the animal kingdom. Communal life combined with a slowly developing offspring would seem to require specialization within the community to free some individuals to participate in the hunt and to commit others (perhaps the aged, pregnant women, and disabled individuals) to care for the slowly developing young. Both activities require the ability to communicate.

These several behaviors may have created an evolutionary pressure in favor of the development of human language (as opposed to a sophisticated call system) and in favor of the development of human culture. Whether that is the case or not, the fact remains that, something on the order of 100,000 years ago, human beings did develop the brain capacity and the configuration of the buccal cavity permitting human language as it is presently understood. The ability to speak is universally distributed throughout the human species; indeed, it is so pervasive that malfunctions in the speaking system have historically defined the individual as outside the norm. Deaf-mute individuals were long regarded as marked, and a common punishment associated with banishment was the cutting out of the tongue. To speak is to be human.

Much later—something on the order of 10,000 years ago—some subsets of human beings invented written language. At no time has written language been universally distributed through the species. It is evident that contemporary policies regard the distribution of written language as an important feature of modern societies and carefully report the numbers of people within a polity who are possessed of the ability to read and write at some level; at the same time, the absence of the ability to read and write has come to be stigmatized only very recently, within the past few decades and only in some environments. It is entirely possible for human beings to live quite normal, full lives without acquiring literacy. Some rather long time after the invention of writing, some still smaller subsets of human beings invented printing, and printing gave rise to the possibility of mass literacy (cf. Eisenstein 1985). Still more recently—within the lifetimes of some readers of these pages—still smaller subsets of human beings invented electronic word processing, the full impact of which has yet to be determined. While it is true that to speak is to be human, no such claim can be made for literacy.

In the earliest periods when writing was available, its use was restricted to special segments of the population, and its functions were severely restricted. The restrictions were to some extent a simple function of the media then available: when language was inscribed on stone or wood, the process was slow; even the use of some form of paper and ink was slow because everything had to be laboriously written out by hand; in addition, the inks were poor and the paper was impermanent (Goody 1987).

The relationship between written language and religion is important. Among the early functions of writing was the recording of oaths, blessings, and curses. The clergy were a segment of the population that tried to reserve literacy to itself (Goody 1987; Graff 1987; Pattison 1982); until relatively recent times, even kings were not necessarily literate, but set their seal on documents and depended upon the clergy to keep their records for them. Among the masses, some feared that the writing of their names gave others special power over them.

It was not until after the invention of printing and a massive change in Christian theology that mass literacy became possible in Western cultures (Gawthrop 1987; Graff 1987; Lockridge 1974). The Protestant sects believed that individual access to the Gospels was the means to salvation, though many sects also controlled literacy through standardized catechism guides. This important change created a need for literacy. The Protestant settlers in the New World were among the most literate groups in history, and among their earliest acts was the establishment of schools to teach literacy (Kaestle 1985; Resnick and Resnick 1977; Stevens 1987). It is important to note that Protestant missionary groups have been responsible for the spread of literacy to non-Western cultures as well, because those missionary groups have translated the Gospels into hundreds of languages or taught literacy in the native language of the missionary groups to the unenlightened so that they might have access to the Gospels (see Kaplan's chapter on language planning in this volume).

6.2. Differences between Orate and Literate Populations

In orate populations, information is held in living memory. That fact has two major implications. On the one hand, the holding of information in memory means that retrieval is variable, depending on the condition of the owner of the memory, the audience for whom retrieval is undertaken, and the circumstances in which retrieval is achieved. In conditions in which retrieval is variable, text is fluid. It is possible to speculate that under these conditions, facts are also variable, and truth mutable (Goody and Watt 1963; Goody 1987). On the other hand, the need to hold text in memory has an effect on the structure of language, stimulating the development of devices that facilitate memory. For example, it is likely that syntactic structure in memorized text would have a smaller range of complex structuring, and that the language would include such devices as rhythms, rhyme, repetition, fixed expressions (e.g., Homer's "wine dark sea") and other memory-aiding devices (Ong 1982).

In literate populations, text is preserved in writing. This phenomenon in turn creates certain conditions. First, text becomes independent of time and space; for example, given the ability to read Classic Greek, it is now possible for an Englishman to read Plato's text exactly as it was written 2000 years earlier and hundreds of miles away from England. Second, text becomes fixed in content and form; it is not different at each retrieval. As text becomes fixed, it is possible to speculate that facts become invariable and truth immutable. Third, because text becomes invariable, it becomes possible to comment not only on content but also on form (cf. the vast commentary on the Bible or on the works of Shakespeare). Finally, written text functions to create a new set of structural needs (Halliday 1985, 1987); it becomes possible to create longer and more complex syntactic structures, and the language takes on more features of linearity while memory-aiding devices diminish in significance (de Beaugrande 1984a, 1984b). (It should also be noted that there are a number of negative consequences that are derivable from the development of literacy; cf. Goody and Watt 1963.)

Given these differing sets of characteristics of text, it is also the case that the group of knowledge gatekeepers changes with the introduction of literacy. In the orate situation, the owner of the memory is the absolute arbiter of who shall have access; s/he has the power to decide to whom information will be given, and what information will be given. Once text is written, it becomes available to anyone who can read; the gatekeepers then are those who teach literacy. As noted above, in earlier times of societal literacy, the clergy exercised dominion over literacy and decided who would read. In contemporary societies, governments usually attempt to make literacy widely available, but gatekeeping functions are still evident in the fact that some subgroups are accidentally or intentionally excluded from access to literacy, or to certain types of literacy. In contemporary literate societies, teachers and librarians assume a gatekeeping function (even though the former often have little control over the curriculum that they teach). In general, literacy is learned in school, and schools assume a gatekeeping function (in more senses than this one).

Further, as literacy exists over time, written language begins to diverge from oral language; written language takes on special functions (as in this text, which is in important ways different from either a conversation about literacy or a lecture on literacy). In complex societies, the functions of written and spoken language are to a very high degree diversified. This diversification causes changes in the structure of written text and in the domains in which written text (as opposed to spoken text) is used. Research has demonstrated that there are significant structural differences between written and oral text. While the research is not yet extensive, there is common-sense evidence that spoken and written language occupy different domains (e.g., one is not likely to talk a novel, though one may be read aloud).

Because oral and written texts have taken on different functions, other differences have developed. In a conversation, one normally has visual contact with one's conversational partner. If communication is breaking down, there is visual evidence of the breakdown in eye contact, body posture, gesture, proxemic distance, various phonological features, and the like. In other words, there is a large and important secondary channel of information that permits the speaker to adjust what s/he is saying. This secondary channel generally does not exist in the case of the written language because the communicants are not in seeing distance of each other (and because the act of reading may occur at a time quite separate from the time of the act of writing). The writer has to develop objective mechanisms to assure that s/he is maintaining reader interest, and that communication is occurring; the writer has no secondary channel to assist him/her. The writer cannot ask questions that constitute checks on the flow of information; so the writer has to develop other mechanisms to assure its uninterrupted flow.

When an individual acquires literacy, that individual not only has to establish sound-symbol correspondences so that s/he can recognize sounds and words on the written page, but also has to learn to manipulate the varying syntax of written language and the special features that mark written language as appropriate to its registers and domains. A common problem for beginning writers (particularly those acquiring literacy in a second language) lies precisely here; they do not recognize the domains for which writing is appropriate, the differences between the semantic and syntactic registers of written as opposed to oral language, and the greater personal distancing normal to written language. In some interesting recent research, Montaño-Harmon (1988) has demonstrated that the writing of Chicano students in English is extraordinarily marked with conversational devices like direct and indirect speech; it is possible that these writers have not recognized the differing domains of written language or the difference between private speech and public discourse in writing (see also Bereiter and Scardamalia 1987; Flower and Hayes 1980; Graves 1984; and Hillocks 1986 for similar first-language writing difficulties among low-level writers).

The widespread use of oral media introduces another complexity. Television watchers have the illusion that the characters in a soap opera are talking to each other, that they are engaged in spontaneous speech acts; in reality, of course, they are delivering scripted language, carefully written out by a script writer in simulation of spontaneous speech. The same is true of the anchor-person doing the news and of the characters who appear in advertisements. Not only do the media create the illusion of spontaneous speech, they also diffuse the need to be literate. If one can acquire all necessary information by listening to television, there is little incentive to read; if one can send one's correspondent an audiotape, there is little incentive to write. This condition is what Ong designates as "postliterate oracy." The often decried failure of the educational system to teach literacy to children may not be the result of serious weaknesses in the teaching of literacy, but may rather be a function of expanding postliterate oracy.

7. APPLIED LINGUISTICS
AND LITERACY

It should be clear from the preceding discussion that the question of literacy is only partly linguistic; it is to a large extent also political. Questions about who will have access to the literacy-teaching system and in what language(s) literacy will be delivered are largely political questions having little to do with the nature of language. Admission to literacy (or exclusion from it) is political in the sense that it defines who is a member of the power structure, and who is excluded from power. It is to a great extent the nature of groups to wish to preserve their coherence and to exclude individuals who will in some fashion threaten the group of its authenticity. The discussion now ongoing in many societies concerning literacy is not significantly a linguistic discussion; rather, it is very much politically oriented.

It has been suggested above that the use of language (or of a simpler call system) may be a function of the territorial imperative; that is, language may serve as a mechanism of territorial defense. There is ample historical evidence that human beings use language to identify the intruder (cf. the story of *shibboleth* in the Bible, or the use of 'linguistic' passwords in military history; e.g., the use of English words containing the sounds /r/ and /l/ during the Pacific war on the assumption that Japanese speakers would have difficulty with these sounds, as in the pronunciation *Flank Royd Light*). The demographics of any major city demonstrate the 'fit' of this assumption in the sense that borders between ethnic groups (including the linguistic majority) are clearly linguistically marked, and urban gangs often use speech recognition to identify their colleagues. To put the notion in the simplest terms, it is the enemy who talk funny: one's friends talk as one does oneself. There are many cultures that believe that only a full-blooded member of the community can possibly learn its language; indeed, it would be dangerous to try to teach the language to outsiders or to permit them to learn it. (Kaplan once encountered an elder in an Australian aboriginal community who explained that the young people in that community had fallen so far away from the ways of the group that they did not deserve to know the group's language.)

At the same time, it has come to be understood that discussions of literacy have their roots in linguistics. It is necessary to have an understanding of the structure of language and of the ways languages are learned in order to design a literacy program for any population. In the latter half of the twentieth century, many governments and some international bodies have supported literacy programs. They have done so largely on political grounds, to assure certain freedoms (or to restrict the same freedoms). The relative success of literacy programs does not depend on their political motivation; it depends to a high degree on their linguistic and pedagogic soundness. And it may be said that the persistent setting aside of linguistic information in the making of political decisions about language accounts for the relatively low degree of success in literacy programs.

However, such issues as:

1. The basic definition of literacy (specific to a particular place and a particular time;
2. The definition of the rewards to be associated with the achievement of literacy;
3. The motivation for a population (or an individual) to pursue literacy; and
4. The mechanism through which literacy instruction will be delivered and the source funding to pay for literacy instruction, teacher training, materials, and a body of literature to be read when literacy is accomplished

are political questions having little to do with the structure of language or with an understanding of language acquisition. On the other hand, questions having to do with:

1. Understanding motivational devices to enhance learning;
2. Understanding what sound-symbol correspondences implicate;
3. Understanding what language content and structure can be taught; and
4. Understanding how a given language content and structure can be taught

are linguistic questions. Issues of empowerment—of giving (or denying) people access to social mobility and the right to aspire to political power—are political questions. It is a regrettable fact that the political questions appear to be uppermost in the minds of decision makers while the linguistic questions remain largely unattended. A few writers (e.g., Friere) have attempted to combine a discussion of the political and the linguistic issues, but to a large extent they are isolated in the literature on literacy.

It is the position of literacy research, squarely between the political and the linguistic, that makes it the business of applied linguists. It is not our intent to suggest here that the political questions are not relevant; on the contrary, they are not only relevant but critical to the well-being of certain populations. It is not our intent to suggest here that only the linguistic issues are relevant, though they certainly are to some degree. Rather, it is our intent to suggest that the political and the linguistic considerations are equally part of the solution to any literacy problem. As several of the other chapters in this volume suggest, applied linguistics is a discipline concerned with the solving of real-world language problems by bringing to bear on such problems not only relevant linguistic information, but also information from any of a number of related disciplines. Like the broader concern with language planning generally (and literacy constitutes one kind of language planning), literacy research is applied linguistics precisely because it requires both the application of linguistic information and the application of information from learning theory, from political theory, from psychological processing theory, and from other related areas.

SUGGESTIONS FOR FURTHER READING

Good general overviews of literacy issues are contained in Kaplan et al. 1984, and Kintgen, Kroll, and Rose 1988. National literacy campaigns are reviewed in Arnove and Graff 1987. Historical overviews are covered in Clanchy 1979; Cressy 1980; Goody 1987; Graff 1987; Houston 1988; Kaestle 1985; and Resnick and Resnick 1977. Social/ psychological issues are examined in Cook-Gumperz 1986; Gee 1986; Goody 1987; Scribner and Cole 1981; and Street 1984. Educational issues are treated in a now overwhelming literature; in particular, see Bloome 1987, 1989; Boggs 1985; deCastell, Luke, and Egan 1986; Edelsky 1986; Haley-James 1981; Heath 1983; Langer 1987; Schieffelin and Gilmore 1986; and Scollon and Scollon 1981. The 'problem' orientation, and its political implications, is discussed by Coe 1986; Pattison 1982; Street 1984; and Trueba 1989.

QUESTIONS FOR FURTHER DISCUSSION

1. A number of national and/or international bodies have mounted literacy campaigns. Relatively few of these campaigns have enjoyed great success. Why have so many well-intentioned programs not succeeded? Are there any common characteristics among programs that have been relatively more successful?

2. One approach to literacy problems has been a kind of program known as "book flood." What are the assumptions underlying such programs? Have they been successful?

3. In multilingual environments (e.g., Ethiopia, India), what sorts of problems are most commonly encountered by literacy programs? Are these problems the same ones that would be encountered in a multilingual context such as the United States?

4. Is it likely that 'illiteracy' will ever be completely eradicated? What definition of *illiteracy* must be assumed in order to respond to this question?

5. How has the definition of literacy changed in United States since c. 1900? Why has it changed? (A reading of Kaestle 1985, or Kaestle and Stedman 1987 will provide a useful overview.)

6. Why do most social historians, anthropologists, and comparative-education researchers view literacy as a technology and define it as basic encoding and decoding skills? How else could literacy be usefully defined to allow comparison across cultures, social contexts, and time?

7. Why does it seem to be virtually impossible to find demographic data on biliterate or triliterate individuals? How widespread is biliteracy?

8. Find information on the planning for the 1990 census of the population of the United States. What plans did the Census Bureau make for collecting literacy statistics in the United States?

9. Is it possible to formulate one coherent definition of literacy for the United States at the beginning of the twenty-first century? What might be the principle components of such a definition?

An Introduction to
Bilingualism, Multilingualism, and Multiculturalism

There are chapters in this volume on language planning, language-in-education planning, and literacy; it has been thought useful to include also a separate chapter on bilingualism, multilingualism, and multiculturalism. This is so because to a significant degree discussions of planning and of literacy tend to presuppose a stable monolingual environment, despite the fact that such environments are not easy to find. The fact that an individual speaks two or more languages, or that a society subsumes within itself speakers of many languages only complicates the problem. And since more than half the world's population deals, to one degree or another, with more than one language in the school environment (as well as in the larger societal context), problems and issues in bilingual and multilingual contexts are major concerns of applied linguists.

A major problem in discussions of bilingualism is that societies are to some extent victims of complex terminological confusion. It is important to note that the very same language may be an official language, a national language, an educational language, a literary language, a liturgical language, a language of wider communication, a first language, a second language, and a foreign language to various individuals in the same community (e.g., English in the United States). For most people living in the United States who are bilingual or multilingual, English is of necessity part of that bilingualism or multilingualism. The problem lies in the fact that monolingualism was for so long seen as a desirable condition; as a consequence, bilingualism came to be viewed as aberrant. In reality, of course, the parents of many present-day U.S. citizens learned English relatively late in life and were 'bilingual' to some degree by virtue of having some degree of control over English and the language(s) they brought with them when they immigrated to the United States. It is only in the relatively recent past that people have questioned the hegemony of English and have recognized that it is not evil to know another language. In fact, in virtually every country in the developed world, individual skill in a second (and even a third) language is a basic assumption of the educational system. The United States is one of the few countries that adheres to a monolingual educational policy as a basic curricular assumption.

These social and educational conditions make the study of bilingualism particularly important. Not much is known about how children acquire one language, let alone two, and work on how adults acquire a second language is still to a large extent in its infancy. Aside from these fascinating questions, however, it is important to understand how the ability to use two or more languages affects the individual socially and psychologically; how that ability affects other learning and individual capabilities to adapt to a changing environment. Furthermore, because it seems likely that the ability to use more than one language is very broadly distributed among the human species, there is considerable research to be done on the ways in which that ability affects whole communities and what effects that ability has on language contact, language change, language spread, language diversity, language maintenance, and a variety of other societal phenomena.

Macias explores the social and psychological perspectives of bilingualism and, like Judd, uses the United States as a case study for examination of educational, political, and economic perspectives. The discussion makes clear the problem that bilingualism is not a crisply defined notion, nor is likely to be so at any time in the near future. What, in fact, does it mean to say that an individual is 'bilingual'? How much of each of two languages does such an individual possess, or need to possess? How do the two languages interrelate in the individual? Is there a quantum of language that one person can know so that, after some point, increase in knowledge in one language means loss in the other? Is there some language threshold beyond which one language provides metalinguistic assistance for the development of the second (cf. Collier 1989)? Are there social factors that enter into the equation? How does one (or does one) divide various functional registers among the languages one commands? There is a large number of questions that can be (and that often are) raised by the study of bilingualism; Macias' article discusses many of these questions and raises yet others for consideration.

Bilingualism, Multilingualism, and Multiculturalism

Reynaldo F. Macias
University of Southern California

1. INTRODUCTION

In order to discuss the relationship of applied linguistics to bilingualism, it is necessary to formulate an 'operational definition' of applied linguistics more generally. Although others have spent much time discussing and defining applied linguistics (Kaplan 1980), this paper assumes that applied linguistics refers to applied research and applying research related to language. It begins with a question that derives from real-world concerns related to language, but not necessarily circumscribed by language, and ends by generating knowledge that answers that question, or attempts to address the circumstances that generated the question in the first place. This broad approach calls attention to many issues as it is applied to bilingualism and multiculturalism.

The organization of this field called *bilingualism* (language contact, multilingualism, language diversity) has drawn particular modern attention since Weinreich published his *Language in Contact* monograph through the New York Circle of Linguistics in 1953 (cf. Haugen 1956; Mackey 1972). More recent publications have extended this earlier research with new questions, new data, and new research methods (cf. Appel and Muyskens 1987; Cooper 1982; Fasold 1984; LaPonce 1987; Lehiste 1988; Paulston 1988; Wardhaugh 1987). This essay reviews some of those attempts to bring order to the field of bilingual studies and the research dealing with bilingualism and social issues, psychological issues, educational issues, political issues, and economic issues.

2. DEFINING THE TERMS

There are three levels at which *bilingualism* has been described if not defined: the individual, the group, and the nation (or, more specifically, the territorial basis). Much of the literature and research on bilingualism over the past 40 years has concentrated on defining and delimiting the 'bilingual' individual. Definitions range from "being able to utter a meaningful phrase" in two languages to "native-like ability in two languages, including reading, writing, speaking, and understanding at a highly educated level." Suffice it to say that psychologists in particular have been obsessed with definitional measurement, conceptualization of language proficiency, and related notions. Whether one is concerned with second- or foreign-language teaching, bilingual education, or delivery of services to communities or individuals speaking a nonstandard or nondominant language, the popular understanding of a bilingual person takes in persons with a *wide* range of abilities in the two (or more) languages of concern. It also very often includes individuals with varying abilities in more than two languages (multilingualism). The research on social aspects of individual bilingualism has tended to focus on language use, while research on group bilingualism has paid greater attention to life-cycle and intergenerational changes in language abilities and use (such as in studies of language maintenance and shift, acquisition, and loss). National bilingualism (or multilingualism) has generated issues of language policies, planning, and politics.

In addition to the concern for multiple languages, there has been a concern for the cultural embedding of the individuals and groups who use those languages. The relationship between language and culture has a long history of debate (Carroll 1956; Fishman 1985) and is a key conceptual linchpin in understanding ourselves as human beings (cf. Kaplan 1980a).[1]

The term *linguistic minority* has been used more recently to refer to a number of groups variously identified as minority-language groups, nationality groups, immigrant groups, and ethnic groups. It is currently in vogue in the United States as a name for those groups of individuals who do not speak English well, or at all, and who rely on another common language. It sometimes includes all members of a racial, ethnic, or nationality group who live as a bilingual community, whether or not all of the individuals in the group speak English or are bilingual (e.g., Chicanos, Navajos, Vietnamese, Blacks). Its use very often tends to de-emphasize the social/cultural embedding or racial characteristics of the group in favor of the distinguishing language characteristic. Internationally, the notion of linguistic minorities is becoming more popular as the movement grows for more firmly establishing the 'language rights' (as one of the basic human rights) on nondominant groups throughout the world.

3. THE SOCIAL PERSPECTIVE
OF BILINGUALISM

The general delimitation between social issues and psychological issues of bilingualism is whether they are related to an individual (psychological) or group (social) level of concern and analysis. The social aspects of bilingualism (as the study of group-language attitudes, choices, and uses) generate a great variety of issues for applied linguistics. It is the nexus between social structure and process, and language. Some of the more salient issues addressed in this area include: (1) the social valuation of specific languages, specific language varieties, and their speakers (language status, language attitude); (2) the distribution of language abilities within a population (language demography, diglossia, domain analysis); (3) group processes of language change over time (measured as life-cycles and generations; language spread, maintenance, and shift); and (4) communication between and among groups with different languages (languages in contact, language choice, intercultural communication, translation, code switching).

Language attitudes have been studied from both the social and psychological perspectives, and particularly by the interdisciplinary field of social psychology.[2] The study of language attitudes and of the social evaluation of specific languages in social interactions has contributed to knowledge of the role of language as a mediator or symbol of social-group relationships. It has also provided useful evidence for evaluating the nature of miscommunication between members of different speech communities (Fasold 1984; Shuy 1977). Further, it has helped to explain the influence of language on social relations (Leibowitz 1969; cf. Hymes 1971, especially the introduction to Part 3).

The study of language maintenance and shift has benefited greatly from the application of sociological and demographic research methods to language data, particularly language-census data, allowing wide-scale analyses of *group* maintenance or loss of languages. National language-census data increased dramatically after 1950, partly as a result of the emergence of new multilingual nations in the Third World from the breakup of European colonial jurisdictions. National language profiles and formulas for national multilingualism were created and promoted through the 1950s and 1960s to describe and understand the multilingualism of populations more effectively (Fasold 1984). Immigrant nations (i.e., those admitting speakers of other languages) like the United States became concerned with understanding the process of language adoption (spread) by the various immigrant language groups who entered them, while other nations were concerned with establishing national languages for their multilingual populations. *Language loyalty* was the term one group of researchers (Fishman et al. 1966) used in discussions of the maintenance of non-English languages in the United

States, while *anglification* was used to describe the adoption (spread) of English in the United States and Canada (Veltman 1983). *Language renewal* and *language spread* were two terms other scholars used to refer to the increase in the number of speakers, or the spread of speakers of a specific language over a territory and over time (Cooper 1982; St. Clair and Leap 1982). Much of this demographic/census data allowed analyses of national (or territorial) multilingualism, but it sometimes only collected data about *current* language abilities and individual bilingualism (Fishman 1985; Veltman 1983). Very often, the presentation and use of these data fueled discussions on language policies (Ohannessian et al. 1975).

Language change and variation have been of interest to linguists for a long time. Initially, the field was seen as historical linguistics (the diachronic change in language) and as dialectology (the synchronic changes or variation in language). Twentieth-century linguistics generated new frameworks for looking at language change (cf. Carroll 1956). With the breakthroughs in research methodology and analyses of sociolinguistic data of the 1960s, variation theory addressed language change *in progress* and associated it with social structure (patterned variability). The initial analyses using variation theory focused on vernacular black English in urban centers (Labov 1966, 1972b; Shuy et al. 1968).

The bulk of work done in bilingual communities focused on code switching (the alternating use of two languages within the same discourse event) and on the bilingual abilities of members of an ethnolinguistic group, as those abilities related to their position in the social structure.[3] One major longitudinal study of Puerto Rican Harlem in New York City concluded that those adults who switched codes the most were the most skillful at code switching (e.g., they did not violate the grammatical rules of either language when they switched) and were the most proficient in each of the languages (Center for Puerto Rican Studies 1984). One of the only studies on the acquisition of code-switching behavior also suggested that there was a sequence and age-developmental pattern for the acquisition of specific code-switches (McClure 1977).

The need for communication across interacting language groups should be self-evident. Very often this is done by and through bilinguals serving as interpreters or translators. Unfortunately, there has been very little systematic research attention paid to this area. Laws providing for bilingual education, court interpreters, and bilingual electoral and governmental services in the United States and other countries have sometimes called for criteria and standards of adequate and effective bilingual performance. Often, the criteria and standards are absent (or at best vague), and so translation and other related services and activities are weakened. Although issues of document design, plain language, and readability have been raised for English in the United States and Britain, especially in connection with governmental and legal documents, there has been little generalization to translated documents or bilingual documents for linguistic minorities, and only slight attention has been given to these issues for diplomatic purposes (i.e., comparability of dual-language documents such as treaties).

4. PSYCHOLINGUISTIC PERSPECTIVES ON BILINGUALISM

The psycholinguistic issues addressed by applied linguistics have been domi-nated by second-language acquisition and learning, particularly as it relates to second-language teaching and to the teaching of English (cf. Homel et al. 1987). The area of second-language acquisition has been followed by studies of language-proficiency assessment, usually of proficiency in English, some-times of a second/foreign language, and only rarely of bilingual or relative language proficiency (cf. McLaughlin 1984, 1985; Vaid 1986; Verhoeven 1987).

Second-language acquisition studies have been very important to the field of applied linguistics, especially as a reflection of the need to develop and understand better language-teaching methods. In a number of different ways, this area of research has provided the space for competing theories, providing an indicator of the academic and 'intellectual' maturity of the field (Krashen 1981, 1982; McLaughlin 1987). Unfortunately, it has also been fragmented, reflecting the different political and practitioner traditions of programs for English as a second language and of bilingual education in the United States. The bulk of second-language acquisition studies have been concerned with English and with adults. They have tended to ignore the relationship between the native language and the target language (partly in reaction to earlier con-trastive linguistic studies), as well as the different language-acquisition pat-terns at earlier ages (cf. Edelsky 1986).

It is important to attend to the different language-acquisition patterns: monolingual language acquisition and bilingual language acquisition, which can be subdivided into dual or simultaneous language acquisition, and se-quential language acquisition. This last category can further be subdivided into early sequential bilingual acquisition (roughly between the ages of five years and puberty) and late sequential bilingual acquisition (roughly after puberty). 'Second languages' are often spoken and used in the learning/ teaching location or environment (e.g., in a multilingual nation), while 'for-eign languages' are generally absent from the teaching/learning environment. It is important also to remember that acquiring a *second* language results in a bilingual person.[4]

Bilingual acquisition and cognition studies have continued to contribute to the knowledge of language acquisition and development, academic achievement, and cognitive 'strategies' (Cummins 1981; Cummins and Swain 1983). The development of the threshold hypothesis (positing a minimum level of proficiency in a language needed to take advantage of the cognitive benefits of bilingualism), and the interdependence hypothesis (positing a positive relationship between L1 and L2 transfer, and memory), has also spurred the development of a broader framework for child bilingualism and its implications for teaching and learning (cf. California Department of Education 1986; Edelsky 1986; Wong-Fillmore 1986).

Research on the assessment of language proficiency has been motivated by the intellectual need for defining language and proficiency, on the one side, and on the other side by the practical concerns for measuring effectiveness or success in second, foreign, and bilingual instruction. There have been two broad approaches by applied linguists in this area: one concerned with assessment of proficiency in a single language (as in second and foreign languages); and one concerned with assessment of two languages (as in bilingual education). Bilingual assessment research distinguishes between dual language assessment (where the two languages may be assessed independently), and relative language proficiency assessment (that is, of the level of language proficiency in one language relative to, or compared with, the same or similar measures of proficiency in another language). This latter type of assessment is necessary to construct the language dominance of the bilingual individual. Research issues have included the question of whether language proficiency is a unitary global ability or a collection of many subcomponents/subskills (Davies in this volume; Oller 1979); the comparability of measures of dual language proficiency; grammatical/structural vs. communicative/functional approaches to language-proficiency assessment (Carrol 1980); and the relationship between language proficiency, achievement, and intelligence as measured by standardized tests (Rivera 1984a, 1984b, 1984c, 1984d).

The development of bilingual-education programs in the United States during the late 1970s and early 1980s gave a boost to the need for accurate and well-conceptualized assessment instruments for younger children and youth. Bilingual-education programs have also provided the motivation, if not the need, for the assessment of adult professional standards of non-English language and bilingual abilities, as well as of English-language proficiency (for ESL), as parts of teacher-certification procedures (especially in the states with larger language-minority populations; e.g., California, New Mexico, Texas). The U.S. Court Interpreters Act of 1978 provided a similar motivation for the development of criteria and procedures for assessing the bilingual proficiencies of translators. This act applies to interpreters and translators in Federal Court criminal proceedings involving defendants who are not sufficiently proficient in English to participate in the court proceedings, or who are profoundly or partially deaf.

5. EDUCATIONAL PERSPECTIVES
ON BILINGUALISM

There are many educational issues that can be addressed, and have been addressed by applied linguists. Three of the most frequently addressed issues are language teaching, literacy instruction and acquisition, and classroom interaction patterns and organization (especially those described through micro-ethnography). The three categories of language teaching (bilingual, second-language, and foreign-language instruction) are distinguished by whether or not they foster (additive) bilingualism as a goal or utilize two languages only as media of instruction. Foreign-language instruction has the longest history, although until the turn of the nineteenth century it could be seen as a form of bilingual education in which the goal was achieved through instruction in the second/target language. It was not uncommon in much of the world for the elite to be self-taught in another language, or to acquire the language through reading. As the 'common school' movements in different countries succeeded in achieving universal free/public schooling, the organization of the curriculum for these schools involved making two critical decisions regarding language(s): what should be the language(s) of instruction? and what language(s) should be studied? These two questions have been addressed by applied linguists at different levels. As policy questions they have been tied to language demography, planning, and the status of the languages involved. In some instances, as with smaller language groups who have no standardized orthography for their languages, there are issues of implementation and development that must be addressed first, such as the development of a writing system in order to be able to teach literacy in the language. In multilingual areas, it is important to consider the sequencing of the languages as subjects of study as well as how many languages can be used effectively as media of instruction.

The United States provides an appropriate example of how these various factors can interact together. Until the turn of the nineteenth century, a number of school districts allowed or provided for the use of languages other than English (principally French, German, and Spanish) as the medium of instruction, sometimes exclusively, sometimes bilingually, and almost always with English as the subject of study. Around the turn of the century, most states adopted laws that mandated English as the medium of instruction in public (and sometimes private) schools, and restricted the teaching of non-English, 'foreign' languages to the middle grades or after 10–12 years of age.[5] The teaching of English as a second language got its greatest boost through the Americanization and literacy programs of the early twentieth century. At first these programs concentrated on adults; later they were made available to children through the public schools.

Bilingual instruction was revived in the 1960s in response to the educational needs of Cubans in Miami and Amerindians and Chicano students in the Southwest. Bilingual-education programs were developed principally as transitional bilingual programs (subtractive bilingualism) rather than maintenance programs (additive bilingualism). The national Bilingual Education Act funded demonstration programs in bilingual education (monies were provided to school districts that applied voluntarily for them in competition against other school districts in order to experiment with bilingual-instruction programs), not as mandatory or service programs that have as a goal providing bilingual instruction for all students who 'needed' it (who were of limited English proficient—LEP). It has also been credited with encouraging states to remove their laws mandating English only as the medium of instruction in order to be eligible for these federal funds. Very quickly, several states developed bilingual-education laws that were more stringent than the federal law (particularly California, New York, and Texas). The educational principle upon which these laws were based is that a student has the right to understand the language of instruction, and the school district has an affirmative (minimal) responsibility to teach these students the English language.

With the enactment of federal civil-rights laws supporting this educational principle (*Lau v. Nichols*, 1974; *Aspira v. NYC Board of Education*, 1974), students in need of these 'special language services' were generally identified on the basis of their limited English proficiency (including orality and literacy), or by the fact that their dominant language was not English (relative language proficiency). Although instruction in English as a second language (ESL) became a defining characteristic of these public bilingual-education programs, foreign-language instruction (and additive bilingualism) generally did not.

Schooling and literacy are very closely intertwined as issues for applied linguists (as well as for others). As the level of schooling achieved by national populations rose beyond the primary grades, reading and writing became more important. For bilinguals, literacy received uneven attention that was partly distorted by the national concerns regarding the question of what language should be used for initial literacy instruction. To understand this unevenness it is helpful to keep in mind three kinds of literacy-acquisition patterns: native-language literacy, second-language literacy (implying no literacy in the native language for a bilingual), and biliteracy (literacy in two languages).

Since the various reports issued by UNESCO in the 1950s bringing world attention to illiteracy and the need for native-language literacy for language minorities, much effort and many resources have been directed at teaching reading to adults and improving elementary schooling for children throughout the world (to assure early acquisition of literacy). Writing acquisition and instruction very often went hand in hand with reading instruction, but it was not given much explicit and direct attention. Research in these areas lagged behind practice. For many of the new nations of the Third World, literacy instruction and school development in the national language constituted a high priority.

Similar literacy efforts were only sometimes directed at native language literacy for language minorities. The Summer Institute of Linguistics and the Bible Translation Society have probably engaged in the greatest linguistic effort to date, describing languages of usually small groups of language minorities (many of them indigenous to their regions, and located throughout the Third World). These groups have engaged in basic descriptive-linguistic research for the purposes of developing (generally phonemically-based) writing systems for languages that did not have them. Subsequent to this initial work, basic literacy materials have been developed for instruction and general schooling.

Whereas the linguistic axiom is accepted that every normal child acquires a language pretty much in a similar fashion (similar sequence of structures and rates) throughout the world, regardless of the language, there has been no corollary for literacy. Literacy was and is generally taught formally through schooling and is not associated with age and social development in the same way as oral ability in a language. This difference allowed the development of a debate over which language in a bilingual community should be used for initial literacy instruction. This initial literacy very often was in the national language for language minorities, which meant that they developed second-language literacy. The effectiveness of these campaigns has been severely criticized. Their rationales have been called political, their goal being the imposition of the national language rather than educational development.

More recent research indicates that greater school success and cognitive benefits are derived from initial native-language literacy instruction, and that there is a sequential transfer to literacy in a second language; the findings of their research argue for coherent programs of instruction in biliteracy (Baker 1988; Cummins 1989; Hakuta 1986).

Other areas of research in literacy have to do with the relationship of the writing system and information processing and memory. The acquisition of literacy across different writing systems (especially those that are phoneme/ alphabet-based vs. syllable-based vs. ideogram- or logogram-based) is of particular concern to applied linguistic researchers studying bilingualism (cf. Tzeng and Hung 1981). The transfer of the cultural-semantic-discourse patterns acquired in and associated with the native language (both sociolinguistic norms and literacy) to second-language literacy usage attracted great attention from applied linguistic researchers and practitioners (especially those concerned with English as a second/foreign language), particularly after the 1960s when methods and techniques of discourse-level analysis were developed and refined.

A third area that has begun to receive attention from applied linguists is the organization of the classroom for teaching and learning. Although different research methods have been used, the most frequent methodology is that of ethnography of communication. Researchers have described participant structures (Philips 1972), varieties of teacher talk (Heath 1978b), interaction patterns that facilitate language and literacy learning (Moll and Diaz 1985; Wong-Fillmore 1986), and other elements of the teaching/learning situation characterized as a series of linguistic and communicative interactions (Cazden 1988).

6. POLITICAL PERSPECTIVES ON BILINGUALISM

It is not always easy to distinguish political perspectives of bilingualism from social issues related to bilingualism. It may be easier to identify the political perspectives and issues that involve language use in the administration of government (embracing the executive, legislative, and judicial functions), as well as those issues generated when one studies how language is used for political purposes (the relationship between power and language).

Language and the administration of government has generally been identified as a matter having to do with language policy and planning. Policy issues usually focus on changes in the status of a language, including whether or not it has any official designation (official or national language), or on the functions of a language, including how it is to be used within the government and nation, for what purposes, and by whom (allocation of the language resources). They may also focus on corpus planning, or the forms and structures of the language itself, including the standardization of a language variety, creation of new words, or the development of a new or different writing system. Each of these types of language issues requires the application of different linguistic and language knowledge and resources.

Language-policy decisions are usually embedded within the sociopolitical structure of the nation. As such, they are part of the cultural politics and polemics of the country. Generally, those who make policies or implement them are referred to as language policy makers, while those who attempt to influence those policies and practices have been called language policy strategists (Weinstein 1983).[6] The interaction between these two kinds of political participants can be called language politics. In most of the nearly 200 countries of the world, there are language politics, generally involving multilingual issues generated by indigenous language minorities, transnational migration of peoples, or the former colonial heritage of a new nation-state in which a number of different languages are spoken as well as the colonial language. An example of these issues and language politics can be seen in the United States.

In 1980 there were approximately 23 million persons in the United States who spoke a language other than English (out of a national population of 226 million). More than half of them (81 percent) also spoke English, while about 4.3 million were monolingual in a language other than English. About 11 million were Spanish speakers (48 percent) with 75 percent of these also speaking English. Some 2.8 million were monolingual Spanish speakers (cf. Wagonner 1988). The concentration of non-English monolinguals and bilinguals can be much greater at the local level (that is, they were not evenly distributed throughout the nation).

Language diversity, coupled with prior language-based discrimination, has been the basis for: (1) the development of governmental services in non-English languages; (2) the provision of bilingual and/or translator services (cf. the Court Interpreters Act of 1978); and (3) the provision of instruction in English as a second language. Prevention of language-based discrimination has taken the form of inconsistent attempts to protect the civil rights of members of language minorities by extending, or defining, discrimination on the basis of national origin to include discrimination because of language. The 1965 Voting Rights Act suspended the use of English-literacy tests as a basis for voting, while the 1975 amendments to the act provided that, in certain circumstances (where there had been prior schooling and language-based discrimination), English-only elections were a violation of the fundamental right of Spanish speakers, Asian-language speakers, and Amerindians as citizens to vote.

The language issues raised in the United States have been principally status issues when the language in question has been English. For many of the Amerindian languages, particularly Navajo (St. Clair and Leap 1982), they have been status and corpus issues.

The current attempts to make English the official language of the United States is primarily motivated by a view of what the national culture and racial fabric ought to be. English-language unity is promoted as the basis for political unity (Macias 1988). The arguments are squarely rooted in the English-language ideology of the country (Macias 1985). This call for language homogenization is in concert with the calls for 'cultural literacy'; the identification and promotion of a common core of cultural knowledge that all 'good Americans' should and must know (Bloom 1987; Hirsch 1987). As with most national polemics, there is more than one side. The other part of this dialectic involves the promotion of bilingualism and celebrates the cultural diversity found within the United States. It is known as English-Plus. Still others have promoted a foreign-language and international-education policy (Simon 1980) that calls for the improvement of foreign-language instruction in the nation for diplomatic, international-commercial, and national-security reasons. These issues of Americanization, the melting pot, and cultural pluralism are not new and, in varying degrees, reflect the human drama played out through much of the world.

In international human-rights activity, a 'principled approach' to a national language policy is promoted through two standards: an individual's right to be free from discrimination on the basis of language, and an individual's right to learn his/her home language as well as the language(s) of the community, the state, and the nation.

At a different level, the relationship between language and power has been explored as it is manifested in forms of speech between interlocutors of different status—those associated with gender and perceptions of powerful and powerless speech (which is associated with authority, veracity, and accuracy). Although many of these small-group and individual speech studies have not focused on bilingualism, when they are placed within the studies of language status and politics, there are strong parallels. The linkages between levels of analysis in these studies become important for understanding sociolinguistic norms, membership in speech networks, and negotiated speech events as they draw on language ideologies of and across speech communities.

7. ECONOMIC ISSUES AND BILINGUALISM

The relationship between bilingualism and the economy has drawn attention from applied linguists in several ways: how does individual bilingualism affect the workplace; how do economic units (i.e., businesses) utilize bilingualism, and what is the relationship between national or group multilingualism and the economy of national development. It is difficult, if not impossible, to analyze sociolinguistic issues without a notion of 'social structure.' It is equally difficult to analyze economic issues and bilingualism without a notion of economic structures and how they operate to promote or restrict the use of non-English languages or bilingualism. Capitalist economies may very well approach bilingualism very differently from socialist economies. Both must be embedded in their historical and political frames in order for the researcher to understand how bilingualism is valued.

Applied linguists have looked at the value of individual bilingualism in international commerce, its role in selling vs. buying, and in international negotiation. In market economies, bilingual groups have also been studied for their market value and for developing the most effective advertising strategies and media. Language policies in the workplace as well as the union hall (especially as these might be officially regulated in the nonpublic or private sectors) have received attention in the legal systems and popular media of different countries, but little attention from applied linguistic researchers. Other issues generated in this area include language training for representatives of international companies and for domestic workers (e.g., bilingual proficiencies for teachers, court interpreters, telephone-service employees) to improve job performance and productivity.

At a level above that of individual bilingualism, the relationship between national multilingualism and various types of economic indicators has been re-examined recently. Addressing an important issue in language planning and policy, researchers have again asked whether national multilingualism hinders or helps national economic development; current answers suggest that there is little direct relationship between the two (Fishman and Solano 1989).

8. APPLIED LINGUISTICS
PERSPECTIVES
ON BILINGUALISM

Applied linguistics is and can be one of the most powerful of the social and behavioral sciences because it trades on the core of intellectual and human exchange: language, but it suffers from an identity crisis. Three steps help set up an applied linguistics structure: (1) selection of a 'real-world' issue, problem, or question; (2) selection of a research or practitioner perspective; and (3) application of linguistic research and research on language done by other disciplines.

Any applied discipline must first, by definition, be empirical in nature—it must deal in worldly goods. This does not make it devoid of theory; rather, theory must explain the real world. What it puts in a secondary place is theory and research that are not empirical, that are abstract.[7] To 'do' applied linguistics, then, one must begin by identifying a question, problem, or situation that involves empirical data and language.

The next step in applied linguistics is to select a research or practitioner perspective. Each perspective involves different procedures and standards. If the basic motivation for the work is to gain knowledge, then one is working from a research perspective that is constrained and guided by the canons and ethics of research work. if one is interested primarily in solving a problem using linguistic knowledge to carry out or improve work, then one is working from a practitioner perspective. In the overwhelming majority of cases, research on language instruction, literacy development, language assessment, language therapy and rehabilitation, and (particularly for this chapter) language maintenance all create issues and raise problems which must be addressed from a practitioner perspective.

The third step is to select the linguistic research and studies that are useful in guiding the research or in 'problem solving.' Research studies will normally generate their own data for analysis, contributing to knowledge building (secondary-data analysis notwithstanding). Practitioner application of linguistic research and language studies, more often than not, are constrained to the particular situation of work and do not usually involve an independent generation of data for analysis, though it is capable of doing so (e.g., writing research and literacy development, language assessment and communicative competence).

9. CONCLUSION

The research field of bilingualism is still at an early stage. The discussion in this chapter should indicate the range of research issues and research questions that have yet to be resolved, though current work is producing some exciting and suggestive results. Given the wide range of individuals who might qualify as bilingual, depending on one's definition, the most productive research will most likely be of a practical nature. Even here, however, there is considerable confusion and looseness in practical attempts to address the bilingual's needs, whether the context is child education, adult-service assistance, legal support, etc. Perhaps the greatest gains in promoting bilingualism will emerge from the educational context, despite less-than-enthusiastic efforts by many educators to understand bilingualism and biculturalism. From a practical, applied linguistics perspective, the point to remember is that all language instruction—whether in a foreign or in a second language, whether employing conventional language or sign language—is at bottom intended to produce some sort of bilingualism. The problem is that those who are involved in language instruction—and in the range of related activities (i.e., syllabus design, materials development, assessment)—are not always terribly precise about what sort of bilingualism is to be produced, for what segment(s) of the population, to serve what ends, and at what cost. It will, therefore, remain an important goal of applied linguistic activity to assist in improving language instruction and in changing the attitudes that surround first- and second-language use and language learning in schools.

NOTES

1. If we define the culture construct as how human beings adapt to their environment and each other, then we can provide an operational definition such as the following: "Culture is a dynamic, creative, and continuous process including behaviors and values learned and shared by people that guides them in their struggle for survival and gives meaning to their lives" (Arvizu et al. 1978). As 'meaning' and 'meaningful' become more important in linguistic work, particularly in sociolinguistics, pragmatics, discourse studies, ethnography of communication, and communication-based instructional methods for second and foreign languages, then better descriptions and analyses of 'culture' and 'multiculturalism' must be developed.

2. The *Journal of Language and Social Psychology* began publishing in 1982.

3. Although taxonomies of code switching have been developed, suffice it to say that the literature makes at least the distinction between intrasentential and intersentential code switching.

4. An important distinction here is between a 'subtractive' bilingualism and an 'additive' bilingualism. The distinction is based on whether or not the native or first language is being maintained while one is acquiring the second language (additive bilingualism), or is not being developed and maintained, or is even being discouraged (subtractive bilingualism).

5. The rationale for much of this delay in second- and foreign-language instruction was rooted in nativist and xenophobic fears. The assumption that "foreign" ideologies were carried by these languages rationalized the delay in instruction. It allowed for "democracy to take hold in the student" before being introduced to possible foreign influences (Leibowitz 1971).

6. I am broadening the term to include not only cultural elites who choose the language(s) of their work strategically for political ends, but also other organized efforts at influencing language policies.

7. As defined by *The Random House Dictionary* (1980:4): "Conceived apart from any concrete realities or specific objects."

SUGGESTIONS FOR FURTHER READING

A general overview of the field can be found in two articles by Kachru (one in Kaplan et al. 1981, the other in Kaplan et al. 1985). Recent research in bilingualism is discussed in Crawford 1989; Genesee 1988; Grosjean 1982; Homel et al. 1987; Hakuta 1986; and Vaid 1986. Recent country-by-country surveys are available in Paulston 1988; Spolsky 1986b; and Wolfson and Manes 1985. Educational issues relating to minorities in the United States may be found in Baker 1988; Crawford 1989; Cummins 1986a, 1989; Edelsky 1986; McKay and Wong 1988; and Trueba 1989. Multilingual Matters Ltd. offers an extensive listing of publications on bilingualism. Journals focusing on bilingualism and bilingual education include *NABE Journal*, *Linguistics and Education*, and *Journal of Multilingual and Multicultural Development*.

QUESTIONS FOR FURTHER DISCUSSION

1. On the basis of Macias' discussion, it is possible to define a 'bilingual'?

2. Wallace Lambert proposes the term "balanced bilingual." Is such an individual possible, or is every individual bent in the direction of one or another of the languages s/he manages? How does a consideration of different language use in different contexts affect how this question might be answered?

3. If an individual manages two or more languages, is that individual able to use his/her language equally well in all registers or in all circumstances?

4. Charles Ferguson has suggested that the term *mother tongue* is not only not very useful, but actually may be misleading. How does Ferguson's view affect on the definition of bilingualism in Macias' article?

5. How does the notion of language loyalty, as developed by Joshua Fishman, influence any discussion of bilingualism?

6. Compare Macias' view of the psychological perspective on bilingualism with the view expressed by McLaughlin and Zemblidge.

7. How do Macias' comments on education compare with those presented in Judd's chapter? What is the relation between discussions of bilingualism and language-in-education planning? What relations are there between Macias' discussion of bilingualism and Kaplan's and Palmer's discussion of literacy?

8. Given the views of Macias, Kaplan, and Judd in this volume, is language diversity in a population a problem or a resource to be developed?

An Introduction to
Language Use and the Professions

In recent years, there has been increasing interest among applied linguists in the uses of language in various professional and occupational contexts. It is clear that the kinds of verbal interactions that were used as the bases for audio-lingual drills do not represent anything like the full range of possibilities in any language. The interest in the language of the classroom is discussed briefly in the article by Morley in this volume, but there are a number of other specialized discourse areas that have received attention. Swales (1987) discusses interactions between scientists, and the following chapter by Maher and Rokosz focuses attention on discourse in legal and medical contexts. Such discussion has important implications for applied linguists because these fields also create environments in which speakers have markedly unequal status, and in which the outcome of interaction may have profound implications for individuals. Tannen (1984) noted the significance for minority women of oral interaction with medical practitioners, and in a series of studies Candlin and his colleagues (1976) looked at the interactions between practitioners and patients in psychiatric treatment. Shuy (1987) has examined the role of language in testimony and has discussed ways in which applied linguistics can facilitate clarity. There are a number of additional important studies that examine other types of unequal exchanges in relation to both law and medicine. One of the more complex problems in this context relates to interactions in which one member of a two-way interchange is not a native speaker, and in which, as a consequence, there may be both linguistic and cultural fracturing.

Judd has noted problems that occur in the context of language in education, particularly when teachers are unaware of the different interactional practices of students from other cultures and ethnic groups. What Maher and Rokosz have to say in regard to medical English and pedagogical applications, and especially what they have to say about the education of medical practitioners has to be seen in the light of Judd's discussion. Maher's and Rokosz's comments concerning English as an international language of medicine, as well as their comments concerning dialect differences between practitioners and patients, should be considered in relation to some of Kaplan's views about language planning. Additionally, the chapter by Macias has implications for their discussion. The area of language use in the professions is clearly of great concern to applied linguists, since the professions (especially the helping professions) represent loci of real-world, language-based problems, in most instances involving potentially serious outcomes. With respect to language in the professions, as Maher and Rokosz suggest, not only linguistic information, but information from a number of related fields and from the professions themselves has to be brought to bear. While language in the professions has been a central concern, there are a number of other special contexts that have not perhaps received the attention they deserve. Strevens talks about the work done on language in maritime navigation (i.e., SEASPEAK), but there are additional important areas for study; e.g., the language of prisoners, language use in religious practice, language in politics, language use in civil-service bureaucracy, language use in office-reception encounters, language use in teacher meetings, language use in youth gangs, and the like.

While Maher and Rokosz focus most of their attention on legal and medical contexts, taking in each case a different perspective—a more theoretical analysis for legal contexts, a more practical and instructional analysis for medical contexts—the methods of analysis employed illustrate a range of investigative issues. The research procedures Maher and Rokosz discuss also have further application in the other fields noted above. Their article opens the area for discussion and highlights a number of ideas that can be investigated, but the chapter should be seen as an illustrative introduction only; much remains to be done.

Language Use and the Professions

John Maher and Denise Rokosz
International Christian University and University of Edinburgh

1. INTRODUCTION

A medical interview, testifying in court as a witness, or negotiating commercial transactions are not speech situations that speakers can normally manage following a routine script. Language users involved in institutionalized encounters exploit different communicative strategies with differing degrees of success in order to participate in these interactions. An institutional setting is a social construct bound by rules and set patterns of socially determined behavior. These patterns of behavior can be maintained as an internal system of organization: role, hierarchy, and group relations give the interaction its (appearance of) coherence and consent. These relations are guided by several concerns: professional competence, bureaucratic efficiency, public satisfaction, and the maintenance of professional identity. The professional is also concerned with the reorienting of some of the conventional rules of language use. For example, in courtroom interaction, professionals are, by and large, the only ones allowed to ask questions—witnesses only answer the questions. Like witness examinations, the doctor-patient interaction exhibits some of the same preconceptions, conflicts of interest, and potential for misunderstanding.

In addition to the legal and medical contexts, professional or institutionalized language use, as described above, may also be observed in business negotiations, office exchanges, public professional gatherings, classroom discourse, bureaucratic/political language use, scientific reporting of research, etc. In all situations of use, there is typically an imbalance in the power relation between interactants; set sequences of language patterns are regularly employed; and the exchange tends to reinforce the professional identity(s) established by the context. Rather than explore the entire range of language use in professional contexts, a field now much too large and expanding to be treated in simple summary coverage, we will examine only two professional contexts in sufficient detail to highlight the issues and research directions which applied linguists pursue: legal language in the courtroom and doctor-patient interviews (cf. Kaplan et al. 1987).

Within the legal and medical professions, effective language use depends, among other things, on professionals' abilities to interview as a way of gaining critical information from participants. Participants interact with strikingly dissimilar knowledge about each other (e.g., the lawyer may have already been 'briefed' on the witness; similarly, the doctor working on referral may have a complete set of notes about a patient prior to the encounter, and interviewing is a way of eliciting information pertinent to the institutionalized concerns of the professional.

Questioning is a salient part of such professional encounters; however, communication depends not only on the professional's ability to use questions, but also on the hearer's or audience's ability to interpret questions, articulate answers, and assess the pragmatic goals of the speaker (Graesser and Black 1985; Shuy 1987a). The pragmatic goals of speakers are not easily definable, but they are frequently based on an institutionalized 'agenda' that the professional follows. Doctors seek to gain a comprehensive patient history to understand fully the symptoms and illnesses, while lawyers are similarly engaged in the procedural concerns of not only ordering the appearance of witnesses, but also influencing the interpretation of testimony as it relates to a claim or charge.

2. LEGAL VOICES IN COURTROOM COMMUNICATION

Legal proceedings, not unlike other institutional encounters, have a number of speakers, and the immediate hearers are not always the intended audience. The intended audience of a lawyer cross-examining a witness is not the witness, but the judge or jury. Lawyers, as well, are not the 'source' of messages conveyed through questioning, but rather are representatives of an 'institutional voice' speaking to an audience through a public identity or role. The institutional voice can be heard in questioning, for example, when the lawyer is concerned with proving the legal relevance of some fact, and questioning serves to establish the legal (as opposed to linguistic) relevance of that fact to the case.

2.1. Institutional Voices

Expanding on the notion of institutional voice, we should note a number of observations about legal discourse. As previously mentioned, in such discourse the typical speaker-hearer interaction is displaced, and lawyers' professional identities are infused with an authoritative knowledge of the law. Lawyers for the two sides deliver opening statements, make pleas for their clients, control testimony, offer summations, and influence the decisions that are rendered. All this happens in a public forum where the verdict is not only seen to be a result of the arguments put forward, but the verdict itself is one that is legally justifiable. Disputes are resolved in an argumentative way, with two lawyers engaging in fact discovery and presentation, while at the same time attempting to influence how much weight is assigned to each fact. This resolution can be viewed from the point of argumentation where speakers are not only involved in a reason-giving (or not reason-giving as the case may be) activity, but are also involved in an activity in which conflicting perspectives about a claim or charge are present—conflicting perspectives that may well erupt into disagreements about the interpretation of past events and intentions.

A key feature of the courtroom as an institutional setting, and one alluded to above, is that speakers are not involved in a reflexively cooperative situation. Gricean maxims for conversation (governing the truthfulness, informativeness, relevance, and manner of information) could be viewed as systematically held in abeyance or continually flouted. The cooperative model of communication is one based on mutual understanding and equal status of speakers, but there is clearly an asymmetry of status underlying courtroom communication. Speakers giving testimony cannot consciously agree to 'cooperate according to the purpose of the interaction' when they do not know exactly what the immediate purposes are. Lawyers, through questioning, strategically arrange the interpretation of information, and, more important, rearrange the previous 'configuration of meanings' introduced in previous portions of the discourse. 'Confession' of a fact directs the audience's attention to the importance of that information to the case. More important, such confessions are intended to reinforce a perspective held about the witness' reliability to give evidence. Lawyers are not engaged in eliciting information because they lack it; rather, questioning is a means to bring the audience into contact with information ordered temporally and thematically to say something about the claims before the court, as well as about the knowledge, beliefs, motives, and personalities of the witnesses and defendants.

Witnesses and defendants testify within a questioning environment that is directed at constructing the 'facts' for an audience to consider. While witnesses may believe that their participation is that of narrating events that they were involved in, the telling of 'the whole story' is not one that the court is interested in hearing; it is only interested in information that fits into legal categories of facts. What counts as a fact, as opposed to an opinion or mere speculation, is precisely the point on which the institutional voice and its deliberative aspects are exercised. A lawyer tries to delimit the potential range of responses and control of the inferences an audience may draw; s/he relies on witnesses' not telling all that may be relevant, and relevance is a legal category that conflicts with the notion of conversational relevance (i.e., in conversations, hearsay is often considered a legitimate source of information). Simultaneously, witnesses must call on a stock of extra- and meta-linguistic knowledge to cope with this sort of discourse sphere, which may look like any other argumentative speech situation but is not. Information about their credibility and truth as witnesses is continually assessed by the way they respond, and 'resistance' is one mode that forces the professionals to state openly the institutionalized concerns (Harris 1989).

2.2. Testifying in Court

Testifying in court has been studied within a number of disciplines, including psychology (Loh 1981), sociology (Carlen 1976; McBarnett 1981; O'Barr 1982), argumentation (Beach 1985; Willard 1983), legal rhetoric (Goodrich 1986), and linguistics (Danet 1984; Harris 1989; Fairclough 1989; Penman 1987; Shuy 1987a, 1988). For example, psycholegalists (Loh 1981) have been studying pretrial influences on a jury, the process of jury selection, the presentation of eyewitness testimony, and, more generally, how memory is involved in the storing and recalling of information relevant to legal proceedings. Loftus (1975) reported on the malleability of an eyewitness's memory of an event when implicative verbs were used in questioning. Questions that signaled a degree of severity often produced correspondingly severe descriptions of events (e.g., What speed were the cars traveling at when they *hit, bumped, smashed,* etc?). Following her research, others have sought to broaden the scope of eyewitness research as it pertains to legally useful methods of incrimination.

Listeners' judgements about the credibility, honesty, etc. of witnesses has been investigated by O'Barr, who brought a sociological perspective to courtroom contexts. He examined four modes of courtroom testimony: powerless vs. powerful speech (identified by hedges and assertiveness features); narrated vs. fragmentary testimony (the use of temporal adjectives and false starts); hypercorrect style (the use of overly technical words that are inappropriate; e.g., *ambulatory* instead of *walking*); and interruptions and overlap style. In the first category (powerless vs. powerful), people who used fewer hedges and intensifiers were rated higher in areas of truthfulness, competence, persuasiveness, and intelligence. Similarly, witnesses who narrated their testimonies, and who did not appear to have much hypercorrection in lexical choices, were also rated higher in these areas. O'Barr (1982) comments that juries may penalize witnesses who hypercorrect, as this makes their testimony appear insincere and less convincing.

Another study, by Wodak (1980), has introduced the relationship between class and testifying styles by investigating 'style switching' among various socioeconomic groups. Wodak found that:

1. Middle-class defendants maintain one linguistic style throughout the whole transaction. They manage conflicts, and ambivalence is not manifest.
2. Working-class defendants do not know the situation. They will react strongly to parameters like fear. They shift styles more often.
3. Lower–middle class defendants are very insecure in such a formal situation, having no stable identity. They try to speak as well as possible, leading to hypercorrection.
4. Previously convicted defendants know the situation. They are self-assured and do not shift. They continue in their dialect.

Both O'Barr and Wodak mention that style shifting of presentation modes may also have to do with the educational level of the speaker, and this is an area that should be explored further. The notion of strategic competence in applied linguistics is also a concept that may prove fundamental to evaluating communication between speakers. The diversity in the educational background (both formal and informal settings), the level of individual ego-impermeability, and previous experiences of new or conflicting speech situations may be decisive features of what listeners seem to be judging in these two studies, rather than judging strictly the socioeconomic status of the witness.

Turning to linguistic aspects of courtroom testimony, the apparent brevity of most responses in questioning makes testifying both similar to and dissimilar from conversational argument situations. For example, Jackson and Jacobs (1981) state that, in conversational arguments, it is easier to offer repairs when too little has been said; but when too much has been said, the speaker becomes disadvantaged as many doors for disagreement are opened. In testifying, as with conversational arguments, partial and short answers are desired. On direct examination, this forestalls introduction of new information that could offer a controversial perspective on the claims being put forward. Yes/no answers are sufficient (and desired) without further explanation, and this contrasts with other situations in which brevity of response may flout the Gricean maxim of quantity.

2.3. Cross-Examination, Leading Questions, and the Presentation of Evidence

Cross-examination is an argumentative speech situation. If a lawyer decides to cross-examine a witness at all, he does so because of a need to "put an acceptable face on uncomfortable facts." Mauet (1980:240) explains the generally accepted purpose of cross-examination as follows:

(a) Elicit favorable testimony. This involves getting the witness to agree with those facts which support the case put by the defence; and (b) conduct a destructive cross (the second purpose). This involves asking the kinds of questions which will discredit the witness or his testimony so that the jury will minimize or disregard them.

Clearly, cross-examination is intended to reveal progressively contradictions and inconsistencies, as well as to introduce doubts such that the audience will reconsider the value of the witness' evidence. In cross-examination, a lawyer tries to recycle information to make it appear favorable to his prospective. He can do this in a number of ways. He can attempt to impeach the convictions, interests, or credibility of evidence previously given by a witness by confronting him with his previous statements. He may attempt to test the accuracy of observation or recollection by using demonstrations. He may restrict the witness from providing explanations by stating facts and asking for agreement (as with tag questions). Perhaps most important, cross-examination allows for leading questions, a primary weapon in courtroom exchanges. These may be loosely defined as questions that indicate the lawyer's attitude toward the content of the testimony, and that initiate a confrontation between the information and the listeners' interpretations of the previous discourse.

Leading questions are a difficult area of research precisely because their pragmatic nature is culled from different discourse 'spheres' that are not easily accessible to the hearers. Leading questions are often thought to be those that have an obvious presupposition of a statement whose truth value is disputable (e.g., What did you do after you left the bar?). But this offers an incomplete picture of exactly what leading questions are designed to accomplish; they invariably require an audience to reassess the inferences generated from the previous discourse. Pragmatic considerations are the core problem complicating adequate descriptions of leading questions; these considerations affect speaker and utterance meaning (not strictly sentence meaning), as leading questions are intended to inform the audience of the expectations, beliefs, and/or attitudes that a lawyer has concerning particular information. For example, a lawyer may try to introduce or highlight the witness's (un)willingness to answer questions with verbs like *admit*, implying that the witness would not have taken responsibility for the information earlier on in the discourse. Determining the pragmatic interpretation of this verb is not simply a matter of word meaning, but also of the particular question asked and its context of utterance.

Linguistically, leading questions may best be described as those that can be multiply marked by pragmatic devices. These pragmatic devices mark a range of what may be called *epistemic attitudes*, introduced into the discourse by intonation, negation, modals, certain verbs, implicating lexical items, etc. Leading questions clearly involve the lawyer's conveying certain beliefs, and, in many examples which follow, many questions have also been multiply marked with cohesion devices and repetition, as well as the various epistemic markers noted above (e.g., So, what you're really saying is . . .).

Not all leading questions are equally damaging or 'coercive,' however, primarily due to the potential ambiguity of the multiple markings. While we can talk about the various structural features associated with leading questions (use of tag questions, factive verbs, if-then constructions etc.), it is only through examining a stretch of discourse that their informational impact can be felt. Rather than insist that all tag questions are 'coercive' (Danet 1980), or that all hedging mechanisms exemplify 'powerless' modes of speaking, the effects of leading questions need to be understood by taking into account their place in the discourse. The two aspects of the 'leadingness' of questions have to do with, first, the pragmatic marking of utterances, and second, the extent to which at least one of those markers, because of its argumentative value for the ongoing discourse, highlights the exchange to signal controversial information.

Numerous pragmatic devices can instantiate the argumentative claims being voiced by the cross-examiner; tag questions provide a good example. Tag questions often appear in cross-examination, and medially placed tags figure prominently; these call for agreement from the witness before s/he has even heard the rest of the proposition. Consider the example below where the medially placed tag question calls for confirmation of a number of controversial propositions. Another leading question then refers to the entire stretch of discourse.

Q: You know, *don't you*, that Mrs. Whitney, in the country, close to her own home has erected three private houses for her three children, in addition to her central home down there where her eight grandchildren are being raised. *Don't you know that?*

(Wellman 1979:261)

2.4. States of Belief and Reported Events

In the courtroom, factuality assessments have a significance that is unparalleled in other speech contexts, as 'facts' constitute proof for deciding the guilt or innocence of an accused. Factive verbs such as *know, realize, make sense, disclose, discover, become aware, bear in mind* (Kartunnen 1973) are all predicates that assume the factuality of the embedded predication. Factive verbs direct the audience's attention to the validity of the information given in the (that) complement clauses (e.g., The witness discovered that she was not at home.) or other constructions (infinitival and nominalized). Questions in which factive verbs preface disputed or incomplete information are leading because the witness has to agree or disagree with whether or not s/he knew of some assumed fact; the fact itself is not open to discussion. Such questions are coercive when the indirect assertions are controversially laden with new or recycled information that differs from the witness's previously stated position. The following example illustrates how factives can act in a manner to underscore the lawyer's commitment to the truth of the embedded proposition.

> Q: *Do you know* that about that time, there is evidence to suggest that actual attacks were being carried out from there on Catholic property?
>
> A: There is.

Rather than insist on the factuality of his/her client's position, the lawyer may, alternatively, choose to concentrate on implying the indefensibility of his/her adversary's. Argumentative verbs are useful for this purpose as they "express a relation between the current truth claim and other claims made by S(peaker) or H(earer)" (Leech 1983:224). Thus, verbs such as *admit, contest, deny, claim, allege,* and *insist* indicate what the speaker believes about the other positions held by the hearer. The lawyer reintroduces what the witness has previously said in a manner which makes a comment about the witness's willingness to be informative or his/her willingness to be truthful. For example, if a witness says 'X,' the statement may later become 'an admission of X.' These reporting verbs signal metalinguistic propositions about the witness such that a witness who is said to admit to X accepts a moral responsibility for not willingly introducing the information sooner—a reflection on his/her genuine lack of truthfulness. In cross-examinations in particular, argumentative verbs highlight the lawyer's belief about the quality and quantity of the witness's evidence. *Did you say* often becomes *Haven't you admitted . . .* , or *You claim that . . .* becomes *So you contest that . . . .* The if-then construction is also a favorite device in cross-examination, and the introduction of hypothetical situations is assumed to be relevant and potentially true. The problem with these constructions is that the conclusions may not be ones that are natural truths (i.e., logically true).

Another method of influencing states of belief includes instances in which the questioner noticeably omits the conditional nature of the witness's response (with an if-then construction) when s/he reformulates previous testimony. This happens in the example below; the questioner recycles the witness's response and drops the condition under which it was initially stated.

> A: But wait a minute. I want to say this. *If* Mrs. Whitney insists upon bringing up her eight grandchildren and my child as well, she can only have a mania for rearing children.
>
> Q: Then your response is this: that as to your mother, you think she is money mad and as to Mrs. Whitney, that she has an obsession to bring up children, is that it?

In reformulating the witness's response, dropping the conditional nature of her prior statement, the lawyer sets up an interpretation of motives for child custody perceived by the witness as distorted or obsessive.

Frequently, witnesses blurt out information that could prove disastrous to the lawyer's case. In order to downplay the significance of this kind of information, the lawyer might say something like: *Yes, we'll come to that shortly,* or: *I'll ask you about that in a minute,* indicating to the audience that what the witness has just said will be dealt with in the near future. Whether or not that happens is another matter, though. If, however, the lawyer wants to show that the witness is being somewhat obstinate in answering questions, even though that may not be the case, s/he can demand responses with phrases like: *I didn't ask you about that. What I asked about . . . ,* or: *Answer the question,* or, even harsher: *Never mind X. What about Y?* The following excerpt illustrates some of the ways in which a lawyer can direct the audience to ignore a witness's testimony.

Q: You went on questioning him after that, didn't you?

A: No sir.

Q: Have a look at your own notes.

A: When he asked to see a solicitor, I said he could and I would go make further inquiries. He then called me a bastard and I said "What do you mean by that?"

Q: *Go on.* You know that later on in the interview you resumed questioning a man who said to you he didn't want to tell you anything until he had seen his solicitor. You asked him how he got the money. You asked him what job it was.

A: I don't think in fact, sir, that I have asked a question until he had made an admission of the offence. The rest in between time were statements I believe.

Q: *But I am not concerned with that.* The fact is that here is a man who says he doesn't want to speak to you until he has got a solicitor and you nevertheless in the same interview go on questioning him. That is right, isn't it?

A: As I say sir I don't believe I put another question to him until . . .

Q: *Never mind about 'until.'*

A: I certainly asked a question after he made an admission of the offence.

(Graham 1983:161)

This example illustrates well the capabilities of lawyers to influence the testimony and the audience's belief states through an array of linguistic devices and construction types.

3. APPLIED LINGUISTICS
AND LANGUAGE USE IN
LEGAL CONTEXTS

The study of how such linguistic devices and procedures influence courtroom outcomes has become increasingly a concern of applied-linguistics research. Over the last ten years, it has become evident that the use of language in the courtroom has a significant influence on the outcome of legal proceedings. There are four areas in particular where legal issues have become part of the applied linguist's purview: English in legal education; language rights of minorities; lawyer-client interaction; and courtroom communication. These topics do not exhaust the areas of interest for applied linguists, but do reflect the sorts of research being pursued. Much of the preceding discussion has centered on courtroom communication; in the following section, the emphasis will be placed on language rights of minorities and English in legal education as two further illustrations.

Defining and defending the rights of linguistic minorities in legal contexts has become an increasingly important issue, not simply for the sake of research, but because of the real-world problems and dilemmas that arise in these contexts and require resolution. Language-minority groups need access to the legal system through their own language, information and advice in their own language when involved in legal disputes, and legal council in their own language when accused or giving testimony. Currently, in the United States and most European countries, language is recognized, along with race and religion, as a basic human right, but what this means is still widely disputed.

In the United States, the bilingual-education movement has gained enormous ground since the early 1970s, but it is now under considerable threat from battles being waged in the courts and in the offices of state governments. The period of the 1980s witnessed the rise of a new linguistic nationalism with potentially harmful politico-legal consequences. Across the United States, states have introduced legislation declaring English the 'official' language. The rise of linguistic nationalism signals a radical departure from tolerance of other cultures within mainstream American life, and this may well be a legitimizing move toward abrogating the responsibilities of institutions to enforce bilingual access to their services and procedures protecting that access. All of these events may have a serious effect on the rights of language-minority groups to legal representation and access to the legal system. Applied linguists studying language use in legal contexts are concerned about these questions and seek to resolve such language-related problems when these situations arise.

Another area in which applied linguists have had an influence on language use in legal contexts is in the training of lawyers and court profession-

sleep; don't leave me. From this univalent description of bodily states, the individual is able to progress to the most complex and subtle expressions of pain or disease. Medical treatment is, in effect, largely determined by the patient's expression of distressing feelings. Signals of disease can be categorized into three types: alterations in the involuntary physiological system; changes in behavior; or verbal explanations/descriptions (as in the response to questioning). This latter mode of communication is limited by the nature and extent of the common language shared by the doctor and patient. It is the patient's right to report abnormalities in physical or medical conditions and it is the doctor's obligation to formulate a language sufficiently sensitive to help the patient define with a high degree of accuracy the magnitude, frequency, intensity, etc., of the symptoms of the distress.

Within this professional domain, however, the role of applied linguistics extends beyond its capacity to analyze semantic structures of disease communication in the consultation event. There are conventional rules of behavior of the medical scientist/health provider and patient in a wide range of contexts, both oral and written as well as paralinguistic. Identifying the speech behavior of the schizophrenic, writing a medical-journal article, presenting medical research orally, testing the linguistic proficiency of health professionals, analyzing communication breakdowns between doctor-nurse-patient, investigating lexico-semantic problems of disease classification and nomenclature, decision-making in a medical school over which is to be the language of instruction, and which foreign language is to be taught, are some of the issues to which applied linguistics has direct relevance in the field of medicine.

4.1. Doctor-Patient Interaction

Generally speaking, doctors are expected to be sensitive to the semiotics of disease communication; gait, posture, the movement of the body, smell, skin color, eyes, the facial expression of emotion, and so on, may constitute important diagnostic signals of certain conditions. However, systematic analysis of verbal behavior by doctors and patients reveals a different and more complex communicative event. Such analysis has important educational implications, in particular, for the improvement of doctors' communication skills in the medical consultation. Moreover, as the doctor-centered model of the consultation (the form still widely propounded in medical schools) is being increasingly challenged by a better educated and questioning lay public, a serious reassessment of the organization of interpersonal behavior in medical consultation is now needed. Certainly there are signs of a growing shift in attitudes toward the values and interpersonal behavior contained within the consultation encounter. A recent illustration of this is the requirement set by the American Board of Internal Medicine that all applicants who seek to take the specialty examination in internal medicine must be certified by the director of the residency program as demonstrating 'humanistic qualities.'

Applied linguists have turned their attention to the above-mentioned issues in a variety of ways. For instance, Shuy (1974, 1975, 1979) identified three problem areas in doctor-patient communication:

1. The problem of jargon;
2. Cross-cultural differences in attitudes to sickness, health, and social distance; and
3. The rigid question-answer format of the traditional medical consultation.

Prince et al. (1982) have described hedging in physician's discourse based on a corpus of data collected from recordings of doctors' morning rounds. And women's language in medical interviews has been studied by Bonnano (1982). Hedges, euphemisms, tag questions, and intensifying expressions were studied, stressing the extent to which the sex variable in linguistic behavior formed a serious communication barrier between physicians and patients.

By analyzing the appropriacy of speech in social situations, it is possible to reject the notion that the consultation is the 'same' social interaction across medical disciplines, but also to identify the communicative features common to all of them. Therefore, what may be a common form of elicitation in an ENT (ear, nose, and throat) examination may be inappropriate or take a different form in a genito-urinary examination, and be much more inappropriate in dental surgery, in which verbal interaction has even more unique characteristics. It is also possible to question whether, given the widespread concern over the use of medical jargon or the alleged depersonalization of the presenting patient, a 'depersonalized' doctor-patient interaction—in a special context—is not the advisable norm. An example of this is the field of obstetrics-gynecology. A matter-of-fact stance is adopted by both patient and staff when examination of the pelvic area is carried out. Medical participants in the examination want to make it clear to the patient and themselves that private concerns, aesthetic interest, and sexual feelings are firmly left behind when they enter the hospital. Medical talk serves to desexualize and depersonalize the encounter in order to sustain the social reality that no one is embarrassed, and that "this is a medical situation." Emerson (1970) has found that medical-dictionary jargon, used instead of ordinary language, assists in reality building. Lexical selection of alternative words helps bypass sexual imagery, while the definite article replaces the pronoun adjective when referring to certain body parts: doctors refer to *the* vagina and not *your* vagina.

Problems of terminology and the neutral interpretation of the language of distress constitutes a further problem for doctor-patient interaction. Consider the differences between doctors' and patients' interpretations of common medical terms. An example is the folk-linguistic understanding of medical/anatomical labels in which hypertension is interpreted as arising from 'stress' or 'tension' in people's daily lives. Patients may diagnose themselves as hypertense as a physical reflection of social and environmental stresses, even in the absence of medical evidence for 'hypertension.' This phenomenon may have important implications. Consider the problems arising from the misunderstanding of the terms *carcinogenic, gallbladder, liver,* and *stomach.* A patient awaiting cholecystectomy is likely to become extremely anxious if, like many people, s/he believes that the gallbladder is concerned with the storage of urine.

Studies have shown that psychiatrists clearly differentiate between 'anxiety,' 'depression,' and 'irritability,' whereas patients see them as overlapping. The misconceptualization of ill-health can lead to mistakes in the identification of symptoms during a medical interview. If somatic symptoms such as shakiness and palpitations are considered to be characteristic of 'depression' and 'anxiety,' then this would affect the responses of patients to such questions as *Do you feel depressed?* or *Do you feel anxious?*

How different sociocultural groups present an illness—utilizing the language of distress—is a fertile area for applied-linguistics study with genuine applications for the communication skills training of linguistically disadvantaged ethnic minorities. As Helman (1984) points out, a physician who is unable to interpret the verbal/nonverbal information presented by the patient is in danger of making the wrong diagnosis. Zborowski (1952), in his study of the responses to pain by Irish, Italian, and Jewish patients in New York, found that the more emotional the 'language of distress,' the more likely the patient was to be labeled 'neurotic' or 'overemotional.' Studies of Italians have shown that they present their illnesses in a more voluble and dramatic way, complaining of many more symptoms than the Irish, and that they tend to be diagnosed as having neurotic or psychological conditions such as 'tension headaches,' ' functional problems,' or 'personality disorders.' The Irish, in turn, were given neutral diagnoses such as 'nothing found in test,' without being labeled 'neurotic.' The problem remains, therefore, that the linguistic/ semiotic encoding of disease, being dependent upon the total sociocultural context of the presenting patient, may not be identified or understood by the physician in consultation. For instance, Irish stoicism could lead to serious disorders being missed in the presentation of illness.

The ability to interpret covert messages in interviews is similarly important for health professionals so that they may identify possible psychological or physical abnormalities. A knowledge of the implications of what linguists term 'voice quality,' or the unique physiological characteristics of a person's voice, may help to guard against stereotyped expectations of patients. For example, we regularly evaluate interlocutors as friendly, slow-witted, overbearing, intelligent, aggressive, etc. on the basis of voice quality. Phonetic and phonological features can signal at least two characteristics relevant for interpersonal communication: social status and a person's affective state. An individual might be perceived as angry, threatening, unemotional, dull, or sarcastic through the variable features of voice pitch. It might, in fact, be valuable to investigate what the precise features of the typically monotonous and emotionless intonation of the medical consultation are. In psychiatric diagnosis, voice quality together with grammatical structure can be a crucial indicator of the person's mental state at a certain moment.

Occupational status (professional, blue-collar, etc.), regional dialect (urban, rural, etc.), and social group (ethnic minority, upper class, gay, etc.) may be identified (sometimes mistakenly so) by the medical interlocutor and trigger a behavior that may be condescending, paternalistic, or overbearing. A contrasting example is that of a Japanese doctor's reaction to a patient's dialect in a consultation (in Japanese). This doctor in a rural university hospital once constantly referred to the nurse for help in interpreting the strongly inflected speech of a patient. The latter obviously was unable, or did not recognize the need to switch from local dialect to standard Japanese. The doctor, it must be remembered, will speak a 'standard dialect,' the social norm for that professional class of persons. However, consider the following example taken from a Scottish doctor. Here there may have been some miscategorization of the social status of the patient or reversal of expectations about how a doctor should talk—hence the nonunderstanding.

D: So . . . how's your water?

P: What? My what?

D: The . . . er . . . your urine.

P: It's okay.

From the above discussion, the doctor-patient relationship may be seen as a communicative event in which both healer/comforter and sufferer are involved in the mutual exchange of complex messages. This exchange is even more complex when doctor and patient are involved in psychotherapy, particularly with the need to recognize and interpret covertly expressed information.

4.2. Language and Psychiatry

Disturbances or disorders in the speech of the mentally ill have long been an object of linguistic attention. Schizophrenia has been a major focus of study, especially since the schizophrenia concept, much criticized, has problems in defining itself. Will (1975) defines it as trouble in maintaining human relations; the *Diagnostic and statistical manual* for the American Psychiatric Association (DSM, 1980) defines schizophrenia more narrowly as involving "at least one of the following: delusions, hallucinations, or certain characteristic types of thought disorder." Despite definitional problems, whether as "trouble in human relations" or "delusions, hallucinations, and thought disorder," close attention to the language/verbal-discourse patterns of the patient remains crucial to the diagnosis. The study of language in schizophrenia offers many linguistic insights into the language structure, language uses, illness diagnoses, and the possibilities of treatment.

Bleuler, the Swiss psychiatrist who assigned the term *schizophrenia* to this group of psychiatric illnesses, observed in severely sick patients a variety of peculiar intonation patterns.

> Speech may be abnormally loud, abnormally soft, too rapid, or too slow. Thus, one patient speaks in a falsetto voice, another mumbles, a third grunts. A catatonic speaks in precisely the same fashion during inspiration as during expiration; another has no intonation at all. (1950:148–49)

This observation was investigated further by phoneticians employing spectographic studies. Otswald (1965), for example, classified the vocal disturbances of one patient into "chant," "screech," and "normal" vocalizations. The patient's voice was shown to be "screechy" almost exclusively while uttering meaningful speech and "normal" when uttering nonsense and stereotyped content. The psychiatric interpretation was that the patient uttered his most meaningful speech when he indicated a most urgent need to be heard by screeching.

Other studies of schizophrenic speech have focused on 'language reduction,' indicated by a patient's half-finished utterances; 'verbigeration,' the repetition of the same world groups continuously without accentuation or intonation; 'pseudodialogue,' the appearance of a conversation with a partner; 'language ecstasy,' the use of a language's actual sound qualities as the medium through which emotion is expressed. Disattention (Cromwell and Dokecky 1973), distractibility (Grant et al. 1975), an inability to comprehend relevance and redundancy (Maher 1972), and a variety of pragmatic features of psychotic conversation have also been noted in linguistic analyses. Analyses of linguistic structure beyond the sentence in the interactional skills of psychotic patients are few (cf. Baltaxe and Simmons 1975). Obviously, the various forms of communicative behavior, styles of interaction, and the social skills that the person learns as a means of expressing social relationships are of particular concern to the psychotherapist who is provided, through either individual or group therapy, with a kind of 'laboratory' for the analysis of many forms of communicative behavior.

"Language," Maclean (1989:296) points out, "much more than non-verbal behavior is the instrument by which the tasks of the consultation are achieved. As well as being used to send and receive messages, language, like non-verbal behavior, can 'give off' information." An obvious example is the powerful influence of the patient's accent on a physician's diagnosis. More than any other area of psychiatry, psychotherapy provides insights into the nature of interpersonal behavior. In particular, the study of 'how we talk' and 'what we say' may be of practical use to many other areas of medicine (e.g., to most forms of medical interviews and consultation).

Psychodynamic therapy is a model whereby specific tools are employed—clarification, interpretation, confrontation, and 'working through'—to facilitate communication, encourage the expression of disease, develop understanding, and foster lasting change. The underlying principle of verbal psychotherapy is precisely that how we talk and organize our thoughts, as well as what we talk about, both influence and disclose mental realities. Labov and Fanshel (1977), in an analysis of therapeutic discourse, described the organization of pragmatic and syntactic information and reasoning processes. Lennard and Bernstein (1960), Matarazzo et al. (1968), and others have revealed the growing similarity of patient-and-therapist behavior with respect to affective and communicative acts: the convergence of word usage, sentence length, utterance length, interpersonal orientation (ratio of *I* to *you* for each speaker), interruption, and response-latency behavior. The discovery of 'tracking' phenomena (converging language use) and the identification of special boundaries and rules of discourse in psychotherapy have revealed the special uses of language in this context. Because therapists use language to enable clients to learn new and precise ways of expression, it should only be expected that therapeutic communication is not like ordinary conversation. Psychiatric/psychotherapeutic interview encounters have established rules of communication that must be learned and adhered to by all participants.

Going beyond conventional descriptions of diadic therapy (done in pairs), the extended field of family therapy, in which group interaction takes place, is fertile ground for linguistic description. The pragmatic feedback of reflection, for instance, is a crucial device in group interaction. It consists of the therapist's conducting of the investigation by means of feedback from the family in response to the information that the therapist solicits from them about their relationship: "So tell me how you see the relationship between your sister and your mother."

Three features of this interaction are of interest to the linguist. It is a pragmatically defined feature of family dysfunction that family members do not communicate effectively, or at all, with one another. By forcing members to, as it were, metacommunicate with each other, common patterns of interaction are dramatically disrupted. In addition, this reflective method (sometimes referred to as *circularity*) establishes triadic patterns or nesting of interaction where before there were only two interactants, or perhaps none. Finally, the Gricean maxim of conversational cooperation or willingness to communicate is, in family therapy, being actively re-established. In such therapy, try as it may, the family cannot avoid communicating.

5. MEDICAL ENGLISH AND PEDAGOGICAL APPLICATIONS

If communicative competence is one goal of therapeutic interaction, it is also, in a related way, the initial goal of doctors who are obliged to work in a foreign language. The field of teaching/learning English for medical purposes belongs to the pedagogical branch of applied linguistics. Consider the problems of the nonnative-English-speaking doctor who has to communicate with patients and colleagues in English. Such doctors may well have studied in English-medium schools or medical faculties. They have mastered a code of academic English and are at home with textbooks and journals in English. However, they often have difficulty in asking a patient about the duration of a headache. Texts seek to develop the English-language skills required by foreign medical personnel for successful communication in their work or study. Courses, such as that by Glendinning and Holmstrom (1987), are based on the linguistic analysis of recorded data of doctor-patient and doctor-doctor communication. In keeping with current models of medical-discourse analysis (Cicourel 1981, 1982; Maher 1981a, 1981b), texts might note, for example, how a native English-speaking doctor instructs, explains, and reassures while conducting an examination. Texts such as that mentioned above employ an ethnographic approach to the channels and styles of communication, and also make use of authentic documents.

The field of English-language teaching/learning is not confined to overseas doctors in Britain or the United States. In medical schools around the world, English is taught as part of the medical-education curriculum (Maher 1985). Medical students are fortunate if language teachers are aware of and respond to that important area of language teaching that (1) focuses on the specific English-language needs of the medical learner; (2) focuses on themes and topics specific to the medical fields; and (3) focuses on a restricted range of skills that may be required by the medical learner; e.g., for writing a medical paper, preparing a talk for a medical meeting, etc. (Maher 1986b). The work of Glendinning and Homstrom (1987) is one instance of the burgeoning field of language-skills preparation in this area. It is important to emphasize also that the language teacher need not be a medical specialist in order to teach students, doctors, or nurses. As in the case of the above-mentioned book, problem-solving activities allow the doctor to use his professional knowledge while exercising English skills. The doctor or student provides the required specialist input, while the teacher concentrates on ensuring that the communication is effective and accurate. This approach, of course, requires that the teacher's orientation be sufficiently learner-centered to allow such new ways of learning.

5.1. Language and Medical Education

The growing importance of English in modern medical communication is indicated to some degree by the widespread teaching of English in medical schools around the world. But what empirical evidence is there to support this view and to justify the continued teaching of English in medical curricula? These questions can be addressed in two ways. First, we can demonstrate the spread of English in some medical-education systems by referring to longitudinal data on languages of instruction supplied by medical schools of individual countries (W.H.O. Directory of Medical Schools 1953, 1957, 1970, 1975/77). Second, we can examine by longitudinal analysis the language of articles listed in *Index Medicus* (Maher 1986b).

The reality of three important sociolinguistic concepts: language spread, language maintenance, and language decline, is well illustrated in the shifting situations of the world's medical schools. English has supplanted Arabic in Egyptian medical education and by 1970 had replaced Turkish, French, and German in Afghanistan (where Dari and Pushtu are other languages of instruction). The Afghan situation since the Soviet occupation in 1979 has, reportedly, moved the instructional language now toward Russian. English now coexists with Burmese in Burma, where before 1970 there was English-medium instruction only. In some countries, such as Sri Lanka, regional languages (Sinhalese and Tamil) have become used for instruction along with English. Colonial languages have declined in some systems: French and Portuguese in India, and Dutch in Indonesia. There is clearly a desire to maintain regional languages as vehicles of medical instruction. A Maltese-language examination is obligatory in the matriculation examination, although English is the official language of instruction at the Faculty of Medicine and Surgery. In Ireland, all Irish-born students are required to have a working knowledge of Irish Gaelic. More significant, however, than official declarations on what language is employed in medical education is the high degree of English-mixing with other languages in the teaching materials used. Maher (1985) has shown this to be the case in Japan, and it is obviously true of other countries also. In the Korean entry of the W.H.O. data (1975/1977), there is a footnote: "English is used in medical textbooks."

5.2. English as an International Language of Medicine

Turning to the field of biomedical communication, a recent study (Maher 1986a, 1989) has described global trends in language preference. A computer-based investigation of *Index Medicus*, showing the language of journal articles over a seventeen-year period, 1966–1983, indicates that the number of articles published in English has increased steadily (by 19 percent) over this period. In 1980 the total (189,616) included 20 percent published in countries other than the United States and the United Kingdom. About 8 percent were published in three countries: Japan, Germany, and France. This increase in the volume of English-language articles was not matched by a similar increase in the number of German-language articles, which had fallen five percentage points during the same period.

In terms of the volume of medical publications by national grouping, while the United States accounts for a substantial 32.2 percent of all articles written in English internationally, the geographical spread of publications in that language is significant. In India, Singapore, and Pakistan, for example, where English is used as a functional first language in the domain of the medical profession, and in commonwealth countries such as Canada and Australia, there is a steady production of English-language writing in medical journals. But if we compare the number of articles in Japanese journals with that of English-speaking Canada, Australia, and New Zealand, we find, surprisingly, that Japan, where English is a foreign language, produced more medical articles in English in 1980 than all of these English-speaking countries combined (cf. Grabe 1988).

A new situation has arisen, therefore, with regard to the expansion as well as the 'ownership' of English. The use of this language as an instrument of international communication and education in medicine is expanding steadily. Also, English cannot be said to be the personal property of any single nation, even the circle of those speaking English. Rather, it is the possession of any individual who, or nation which, chooses to use it. From the data available, English would appear to be used widely in countries where English is not the first language, at least to the extent that domestic, internationally distributed journals of medicine are published in English (cf. Kachru 1985a; Strevens in this volume).

English as a foreign language (EFL) is taught as a compulsory subject in many medical schools around the world, but with possibly less urgency than the sociolinguistic realities of modern international medicine demands. Fluency in reading is the minimum requirement not only for the comprehension of international journals, but also for local in-house publications in countries where English is not the first language. Also, there will be a growing need to write accurately in English, especially for postgraduate students around the world; but recognition of these needs must be made in the early stages of medical education.

These pedagogical issues, combined with the advances now being made in our understanding of doctor-patient interaction, and medical discourse in general, emphasize the importance of applied-linguistics insights into communicative events, not only in medical contexts, but also in numerous other professional contexts.

6. CONCLUSION

From the two domains explored in some detail, it is evident that applied-linguistics research has much to offer to language communication in professional contexts. The possibilities of linguistic miscommunication are too great in professional contexts, and the attendant problems are potentially too serious, to ignore the ways language can be used and misused. In fact, current research in analyses of conversational style leads to much the same conclusions, and its findings are highly compatible with the analyses of communication problems presented in this chapter (cf. Gumperz 1982; Tannen 1984, 1986). Further, it is clear that issues raised in professional contexts have implications for the choice and use of an instructional language in education contexts, for language policy and planning decisions, for research in bilingualism and bilingual-education schemes, and even for language testing, particularly for the development of specialized and preprofessional tests.

Research in language use in professional domains offers a useful tool for understanding how communication difficulties arise and can suggest possible solutions when linguistic miscommunication has serious consequences, whether the solution be short-term recognition of problems and modification of language use or long-term training in language skills. In this regard, the study of language in the professions is an ideal example of applied linguistics as the attempt to understand and solve real-world, language-based problems.

SUGGESTIONS FOR
FURTHER READING

Important overviews of language use in professional contexts may be found in Coleman 1989; DiPietro 1982; Fisher and Todd 1986; Kaplan et al. 1987; Kramerae, Schulz, and O'Barr 1984; and Lauren and Nordman 1989. Language use in medical contexts are specifically addressed in Mishler 1984 and Pettinari 1988; in legal contexts in Danet 1984; O'Barr 1982; and Shuy 1987a; in educational contexts in Bloome 1987, 1989; Boggs 1985; Cazden 1987; Cook-Gumperz 1986; Heath 1983; Schieffelin and Gilmore 1986; Spindler and Spindler 1987; Tannen 1986; in science contexts in Bazerman 1988; Gilbert and Mulkay 1984; van Naerrson and Kaplan 1987; Latour 1987; and Simons 1989; and in business in Johns 1987; Neu 1986; and Odell and Goswami 1985; in media in Davis and Walton 1983; Geis 1982, 1987; Harris 1983; Kress 1983; Kuo 1984; and van Dijk 1985, 1987.

Applications of language use for language teaching (particularly ESP) are discussed in Hutchinson and Waters 1987; Swales 1985; and Trimble 1985, as well as in numerous articles in the journal *English for Special Purposes*.

QUESTIONS FOR
FURTHER DISCUSSION

1. What are some of the research tools employed by Maher and Rokosz that could readily be applied to the analysis of other contexts of language use in applied-linguistics research?

2. Compare Maher's and Rokosz's descriptions of medical and legal language under various conditions with the work on classroom language reported by Morley.

3. In the courtroom, the formal transcript of what is spoken by witnesses, attorneys, and judges becomes the official record. What implications exist for the accuracy of the record because formal transcripts are free of intonation marking of any sort?

4. Is there any way in which the power relationship in medical and legal discourse can be modified to improve outcomes without substantially distorting the existing systems? Should there be a way to modify those relationships?

5. In language-planning terms (cf. Kaplan's discussion of English as the language of science and technology), what are the implications of the emergence of English as the international language of medicine?

6. Compare Maher's and Rokosz's discussion of language in the training of legal and medical professionals with Judd's views of language-in-educational planning.

7. Compare Maher's and Rokosz's discussion of various legal environments with Macias' views of the status of bilingual minorities.

8. Clearly, various polities employ varying legal systems—e.g., Koranic law, Napoleonic law, Soviet law, etc. As international business expands, is it likely that varying legal practices and the varying uses of language in the law will have implications for the practice of business and, perhaps, even for the ethics of business?

9. Maher and Rokosz discuss the notion of institutionalized language. Does institutionalized language, in his sense, occur in multinational corporations (e.g., IBM, Royal Dutch Petroleum, DeBeers, etc.), and, if it does, does that occurrence have any implications for language spread, language contact, and language death? (Consider corporate expansion into Third-World countries where the corporations are obliged to support educational and language policies for its newly hired workers.)

An Introduction to
Applied Linguistics and Computer Applications

The use of computers to address applied-linguistics issues can be traced back to the early machines of the 1950s. Some of the earliest uses of the computer for these purposes are still important today, though current procedures have radically changed the way in which computers are used. Early applications of computers in machine translation and parsing, in statistical analyses of data, in language testing, in stylistic analyses, and in language learning provided the groundwork for later, more sophisticated uses. At present, as computer applications in applied linguistics have become more widespread, most researchers no longer rely on access to centralized mainframe computers; instead, they work from their offices over networked or free-standing microcomputers with almost the same computing power as early mainframes. The decreasing costs of computers and their ever-increasing accessibility in the academic environment are radically changing researchers' attitudes, so that computers are viewed as essential tools in applied linguistics. Computing workstations of the future may also radically change the ways that applied linguists are trained, making mainframe computers obsolete for all but supercomputing tasks. Accompanying the tremendous increase in access and computing power, an enormous array of software has been written that allows the researcher to perform complex computations and create innovative programs for many applied-linguistics purposes.

At the same time, it is important to recognize that the computer is little more than a tool. The notion of the 'intelligent' computer is still far off in the future. As Biber points out, the computer depends on the skills and creativity of the human programmer; the machine itself still does no more than retrieve, count, and match. It is not the intelligence of the computer that allows it to perform extraordinary feats, but the ways humans utilize the computer. Since the power of the computer is constrained by human ability to program and create, the computer is not likely to become the android of science fiction. Its limitations are often as apparent as its abilities.

In order to integrate computers more appropriately into applied-linguistics research, it is important to examine the various current roles of computers in applied-linguistics research and to consider its increasing role in the future. In the chapter that follows, Biber explores these various applications. He traces the development of computer applications in terms of 'practical,' 'theoretical,' and 'applied' approaches. From his discussion, it is clear that the line between theory and application is difficult to define and will likely blur further in the future. As a result, new computer uses in applied linguistics may become quite different from present uses. Since the computer is a tool that has yet to reach its full potential, there are great possibilities for computers to reconceptualize applied-linguistics research. However, it is also apparent that computer applications will not provide answers apart from an understanding of the contexts in which they are used. Computers are tools, and the evidence that they provide must be considered within larger language-variation and language-learning contexts. As language-testing and language-acquisition research have discovered, various social, cultural, and individual contextual factors play a large role in the understanding of language-based problems and issues. The applications of computers in applied-linguistics research must be viewed in much the same light.

Applied Linguistics and Computer Applications

Douglas Biber
Northern Arizona University

1. INTRODUCTION

Until recently, many applied linguists were unaware (or unconcerned) that computers might provide important pedagogical and research tools. In the past, much of the research activity in applied linguistics centered around language teaching and language learning at a level of inquiry that did not have a great need for the computer. As the discipline of applied linguistics has changed and grown, however, the value of computers for a variety of tasks (such as statistical analysis, textual analysis, and computer-assisted language learning [CALL]) has become apparent. The greater accessibility of the computer for academic purposes has also contributed to the increasing demand for computer literacy. Tasks that might have required considerable expense and expertise on a mainframe computer can now be easily accomplished on a microcomputer. The greatly expanded research options offered to applied linguists by this increasing accessibility and affordability have, in turn, made the computer an indispensable companion for practicing applied linguists.

As has been noted elsewhere in this volume, applied linguistics is an emerging discipline incorporating increasingly more domains of skill and knowledge as it develops and matures. The computer must be seen as a major contributor to these changes in the field, particularly so since the mid-1970s. In the 1980s the computer was, and in the 1990s will remain, an indispensable tool for a variety of tasks and applications. The future will undoubtedly find yet more uses for it, and thus the computer will further shape the development of applied linguistics as a discipline. At present, certain skills related to the computer might not have obvious applications. For example, many applied linguists would question the need to know a computer language for programming purposes. It may well be the case, however, that such skills will become important over the next decade. Similar to the evolution of attitudes concerning the use of statistical techniques, which were viewed as nonessential in the 1960s, but are now considered crucial to research, it would not be surprising if computer-programming skills took on important research uses in the 1990s.

In reading the following discussion, it is important to distinguish between computers and computer programs (or hardware and software). Computers are electronic machines that perform three basic tasks: comparing data, moving data, and counting. Computer programs, on the other hand, are the instructions to a computer that combine these basic tasks to perform much more complicated tasks, such as word processing and statistical analysis.

Computational applications in applied linguistics, following the trend set by computer technology generally, are being developed at an extremely rapid rate, so rapid that tasks considered difficult ten years ago are now done with ease. Applications that formerly required consultants are now done by novice computer users. Thus, the following discussion should be seen as an effort to portray a field that is evolving rapidly; in some respects, what is offered here is a 'current history' rather than a 'state-of-the-art' account of computer applications.

2. COMPUTER APPLICATIONS IN LINGUISTICS

One tends to think of computers being used for engineering applications, such as the designing of cars and stereos, or for business applications, such as the processing of insurance claims or booking airline seats. It would surprise most of us to know that linguistic applications were among the earliest uses of computers. Yet this is the case. From the early 1950s on, researchers have been trying to use computers to translate texts from one language to another. Although these early efforts achieved few successes, they helped establish linguistic processing as one of the primary applications of computers.

There have been three major types of projects that use computational tools for language analysis, distinguished by the relationship between the computer resources and linguistic theory. We label the three types as follows:

1. 'Practical'—task-oriented with a working computer program as the goal; making full use of computer resources; linguistic theory subordinate;

2. 'Theoretical'—theory oriented with a working computer model as the goal; certain computational resources excluded as not theoretically motivated; and

3. 'Applied'—computers used as a research tool to investigate linguistic issues.

In 'practical' and 'theoretical' projects, a functioning computer program is one of the primary research goals, whereas computers are used only as research tools in 'applied' studies. 'Practical' and 'theoretical' projects both fall under the general umbrella of computational linguistics within the field of artificial intelligence, which attempts to model cognitive capabilities and investigate how machines can be made to perform 'intelligent' tasks. Computational linguists attempt to model linguistic understanding and production processes, for applications such as machine translation (automatic translation of text from one language to another), information retrieval (searching large corpora of text for specific types of information), and man-machine interaction (conversational interactions between a human and a computer). The term *computational linguistics* has traditionally been reserved for this kind of research even though there are many other applications of computers in linguistics.

The goal of 'practical' projects is to make a computer achieve the highest possible level of linguistic performance, often for specific business or engineering applications. For example, researchers (and science-fiction writers) have long been fascinated by the possibility of humans' interacting with computers using a human language (rather than being forced to use highly restrictive computer commands). A computer that could understand and respond to human language would allow experienced users to compute more efficiently; and it would open the world of computers to a wide range of novice users. Human-machine interaction has thus been a major concern of 'practical' researchers. Other concerns include machine translation, information retrieval, and providing access to expert systems, all of which require automated use of the machines' power; they have no counterpart in any mainline linguistic theory. Researchers taking a 'practical' approach are not atheoretical, however; rather, they claim to be extending linguistic theory by identifying and analyzing feasible (as opposed to theoretically possible) types of linguistic processing (see, e.g., Winograd 1977, 1980, 1983; Schank and Wilensky 1977).

In contrast, the 'theoretical' approach gives priority to linguistic theory and uses computers to model theory. In fact, until recently theoretical linguists have rejected the value of computational research, claiming that because there has been no underlying theory, this research contributes little to our scientific knowledge of language (e.g., Dresher and Hornstein 1976, 1977a, 1977b). In the late 1970s, though, this situation changed, and theoretical linguists began to model specific linguistic theories on computers.

Finally, projects falling under the 'applied' type of research use computers as research tools to investigate linguistic issues. As noted above, the computer program in this case has no independent theoretical interest of its own; rather, it is useful only as a tool to discover and analyze linguistic patterns that would be hard to discern by unaided examination of the data. Specific applications include statistical analyses, language testing, linguistic characterizations of text, dictionary making/lexicography, and computer-assisted language learning.

The present paper concentrates on this third type of research, since it is the area of most concern and interest to applied linguistics. Section 3 discusses a wide range of computational applications in linguistics, including those based on the processing of text corpora and those based on statistical analysis. Section 4 turns to a special 'practical' application that has become important within applied linguistics: software for computer-assisted language learning. Finally, section 5 summarizes research in 'computational linguistics' (including both 'practical' and 'theoretical' types of research).

3. THE COMPUTER AS A RESEARCH TOOL FOR LINGUISTIC ANALYSIS

It is worth emphasizing that there is no intrinsic 'intelligence' in computers; artificial intelligence applications (described in section 5) are possible only because of the efforts of human researchers and programmers. In fact, computers themselves are notably unintelligent—they can perform only three basic tasks: (1) comparing two pieces of data; (2) counting; and (3) moving data. An 'intelligent' application, such as recognizing that an English sentence is grammatical, is based on a complex series of simple data comparisons and movements. A recognition program might proceed as follows: The first word in a sentence is compared with a list of words in a computerized dictionary (the dictionary containing a list of words and the grammatical category of each word). If one of the comparisons is a match, then the program retrieves information about the grammatical category of that word (this retrieval of information being simply a movement of data). That grammatical category is then compared to the grammatical category of the first word position in different possible sentence structures of English. If a match is found, the program progresses to the second word in the sentence to determine if its grammatical category matches that of the second word position in the sentence structure. Through a continuing series of comparisons, a computer can recognize a grammatical sentence of English. In this example, the computer itself performs only two simple, repetitious tasks: comparing two pieces of data and moving data (retrieving grammatical information); but a computer program combines these simple tasks to accomplish an 'intelligent' recognition task.

The strengths of a computer are found in the way that it performs tasks, rather than in the complexity of those tasks. Computers perform tasks accurately and rapidly, and they do not 'get bored'; they can perform a repetitious task indefinitely with no change in accuracy. Computers do not make mistakes, although computer programs frequently do. That is, a computer accurately performs the instructions of a computer program, but the logic of the program can be incorrect. For example, say there is a need to write a program to compute the average of three numbers, found by adding the three numbers together and dividing by 3. In the program, the computer is mistakenly instructed to multiply the three numbers together rather than summing them. The computer would perform these instructions accurately; for example, it would accurately compute the 'average' of 3, 4, and 5 to be equal to 20 ($[3 \times 4 \times 5]/3$); the incorrect result is due to the programmer's mistake rather than to a computer error.

The strengths of computers make them ideal for analyzing large bodies of data. In linguistics, there are two major applications of this type: studies that require analysis of large text samples, and studies that require statistical analysis of a large group of numbers (e.g., test scores, vocabulary counts, sentence lengths). Text-based applications depend primarily on comparisons and the moving of data (although they also frequently use counting tasks), while statistical applications depend primarily on complex sequences of counting tasks. Section 3.1 below deals with text-based studies, and section 3.2 describes the use of computers for statistical analyses.

3.1. Text-Related Research

Computational analyses of text corpora are used for two main purposes in linguistics: (1) for empirical analyses of lexicon and syntax, and (2) for analyses of the stylistic characteristics of different kinds of texts. In the first case, a large computerized collection of texts is used to provide a solid empirical base for lexical or syntactic analyses. In the second case, identification of the linguistic characteristics of the texts in the corpus is the goal of analysis, and the computer is used as a research tool to achieve that goal.

There are a number of computerized text corpora that have been developed for these purposes. The first well-known corpus was developed in the 1960s at Brown University by W. Nelson Francis and Henry Kucera (cf. Francis and Kucera 1982). This corpus, known as the *Brown Corpus*, consists of 500 American English texts, each over 2,000 words long. (The entire corpus is thus over one million words of running text.) The texts, which were published in 1961, are taken from a wide range of written genres, including press reportage, editorials, religious writing, biographies, scientific writing, government documents, and fiction. This corpus thus provides a very good sample of published American English and has been used for a number of stylistic and register studies (see below).

A second corpus of published British English texts has been developed at Lancaster, Oslo, and Bergen and is known as the *LOB Corpus* (cf. Johansson 1982; Johansson and Hofland 1988). The texts in the *LOB Corpus* were chosen to parallel the texts in the *Brown Corpus*, so that the two corpora can be used for comparison of British and American written English. A third well-known corpus is the *London-Lund Corpus*, which comprises 87 spoken-text samples, each approximately 5,000 words long (cf. Svartvik and Quirk 1980; Johansson

1982). The texts in this corpus represent a wide range of speaking situations, including face-to-face conversations, telephone conversations, radio sports and nonsports broadcasts, interviews, panel discussions, and public speeches. All three of these corpora are available, in varying formats, from the International Computer Archive of Modern English (ICAME), an organization which also publishes the *ICAME Journal*, at the Norwegian Computing Center for the Humanities, Bergen, Norway.

Other computerized corpora include: the *Leuven Drama Corpus* (containing approximately one million words of British English drama), the *Birmingham Collection of English Text* (containing more than twenty million words of running text; see Renouf 1984 and the discussion below); and the *Oxford Text Archive*, which contains many texts, including entire novels, from various historical periods and languages. Finally, there are several extremely large private-sector corpora, although it is more difficult to get reliable information about them. For example, Garside et al. (1987:6) report that IBM has several text corpora, one of which contains approximately sixty million words, and that Mead Data Corporation apparently has a text corpus of about five billion words (used for information retrieval).

One of the best examples of a project using computerized corpora for lexical analyses is the Collins Co-Build Project at the University of Birmingham in England. This project is using the Birmingham Collection of Texts (which comprises over twenty million words of running text) to develop dictionaries of English based on actual language use (Sinclair 1987; Sinclair et al. 1987). The goal of the dictionaries is to include only words and uses found in the corpus to represent the range and typicality of actual word use in English. The definitions for each word present the meanings and the syntactic functions of the word in the corpus. This format and philosophy are quite different from that followed in standard dictionaries. which are not based on any particular body of text. Text-based corpora analysis of this type can influence linguistic theory itself, in addition to dictionary making; for example, new information on the use of certain language forms is just being discovered as an outcome of this corpora project (Sinclair 1988).

The *Oxford English Dictionary* (*OED*) is not based on a computerized corpus of texts, but the dictionary itself is now computerized, facilitating lexicographic research projects, as well as more efficient revisions of the dictionary (the last revision required 70 years to complete). The computerized version of the dictionary allows users to search for information in ways that cut across the classification of information in the dictionary (i.e., according to lexical entry). For example, a user could collect together information on a particular part of speech (e.g., nouns), quotations by particular authors, similar sound-sequence patterns, all definitions that use a certain word, lists of adjectives with particular derivational endings (e.g., *-al*), or word lists in a particular subject area or semantic domain (Johansson 1988). Computer access to the OED thus greatly increases the research possibilities provided by this resource.

There have also been recent syntactic analyses that use a computerized corpus as an empirical database. For example, Garside, Leech, and Sampson (1987) advocate a "corpus-based paradigm" within the general field of computational linguistics. This project uses probabilistic techniques for syntactic analysis, and it is based on natural discourse domains (in particular the *LOB Corpus*), rather than invented example sentences. In this approach, there is no a priori distinction made between 'grammatical' and 'ungrammatical' sentences; rather, any sentence that occurs in natural discourse is considered worthy of analysis. Because these researchers see their work as a subfield of computational linguistics, their work will be discussed more fully in section 5. This project is mentioned here, though, because it illustrates a major new way of doing syntactic analysis—one that considers the full range of constructions that actually occur in natural discourse, and uses probabilistic methods for analysis, in contrast to the traditional approach that is based on an absolute distinction between grammatical and ungrammatical sentences, and considers only invented 'grammatical' sentences.

Computational stylistic analyses of text have been carried out by both linguistic and literary scholars. Literary studies have been concerned with the analysis of particular works of literature, of genres, of author styles, and of period styles, while linguistic studies have focused on analysis of registers (i.e., different everyday varieties of language, such as telephone conversations, sports broadcasts, newspaper articles). Surprisingly, many of the studies that have been grouped into this subfield actually make minimal use of computers. For example, many studies are considered computational simply because they use statistical techniques to analyze style (e.g., Birch 1985; Smith 1986, 1987). Many of these studies focus on issues of attribution of authorship, using statistical patterns to determine the author of a written text (e.g., Morton 1986; Smith 1987).

Other studies are computational only in the sense that they use computerized text corpora (e.g., Stenström 1986a). More frequently, researchers use computers to compile word lists or concordances for use in analysis of the vocabulary of a text. A full concordance lists every occurrence of each word in a text in alphabetical order, together with the preceding and following sentential context and a line-number identifier. The sentential context enables the researcher to analyze the use of each occurrence of a word, and the line-number identifier enables the researcher to locate the word in its original context. Some lexical studies focus only on those words that occur once in a text; other focus on determiners, pronouns, and other function words, all of which are among the most frequent words in a text. Literary studies of this type include Burton's (1973) work on Shakespeare and Crosland's (1975) work on Fitzgerald. Linguistic studies of this type, often based on the *Brown, LOB,* and *London-Lund Corpora* (described above), are extremely common; for example, Aijmer's studies of linguistic hedges (1986a), *actually* (1986b), and *oh* (1987); Stenström's studies of *really* (1986b) and *right* as a 'carry-on signal' in conversation (1987); Tottie's analyses of negation (1982, 1985) and adverbials (1986). Issue number 10 of the journal *ICAME News* includes a bibliography of nearly 300 publications based on the *Brown, LOB,* or *London-Lund Corpus.*

Finally, there are relatively few studies that use computers for stylistic analysis based on syntax, because the automatic analysis of syntactic structure is so difficult. In fact, some of these studies have coded syntactic categories manually in texts, using a computer only to count the frequency of various grammatical codes (e.g., Milic 1967). In other studies, automatic parsing programs are used for syntactic analysis (e.g., Oakman 1975). A recent series of studies combines automatic parsing programs and advanced statistical techniques to analyze the underlying parameters of register variation in English (Biber 1988). Computer programs are used to compute the frequency of lexical features (e.g., nominalizations, conjuncts, and time adverbials) and syntactic features (e.g., WH relative clauses, conditional adverbial clauses, *that* complement clauses). Statistical techniques are used to identify the co-occurrence patterns among the linguistic features (cf. section 3.2). Linguistic features co-occur in texts because they work together for shared functional purposes (e.g., for informational integration or elaboration). Each co-occurrence pattern thus represents an underlying parameter of variation, and collectively they can be used to characterize and compare various kinds of text. For example, this research approach has been used to compare spoken and written registers in English (Biber 1986, 1988) and other languages (Besnier 1988; Biber and Hared 1989), the differences between American and British written genres (Biber 1987), the linguistically well-defined text types of English (Grabe 1987, Biber 1989), the stance types of English (i.e., the systematic ways of marking attitude and certainty; Biber and Finegan 1989a), and the evolution of written style in English over the last four centuries (Biber and Finegan 1989b).

Most of the above syntactic analyses required computer programs written specifically for the project in question. There are, however, several computer packages available that do not require programming knowledge for their use. Three of these, the Oxford Concordance Program (OCP), the CLOC Package (developed at the University of Birmingham), and the CHILDES Package are used to generate a variety of word lists and concordances, which can be used for lexical and morphological analysis. Another package, called OXEYE (a revision of the package EYEBALL, undertaken at Oxford University), performs syntactic parsing, although the analyses are not always correct, and the output from this program requires manual editing to correct any errors. Further information about these computer packages, and about the use of computers for textual analyses generally, can be found in Hockey (1980) and Butler (1985a).

3.2. Statistical Analyses in Applied Linguistics

There was a time when statistical analyses were not common in applied-linguistics studies, and those that were carried out were done manually. Since the late 1970s, however, the use of statistics in applied linguistics has increased both in frequency and in sophistication, and computers have been instrumental in both tendencies. In the 1970s and early 1980s, computerized packages for statistical analysis (e.g., SAS, SPSS, and BMDP) were found primarily on mainframe computers of major universities. These computers are relatively difficult to use, requiring at least knowledge of: (1) a log-on procedure (to connect to the computer); (2) how to edit a data set (how to enter data into permanent storage on the computer); (3) how to write a statistical program (knowing the particular commands for the statistical package); and (4) how to submit a job for execution (that is, since many users share a mainframe computer, there are commands to run some particular program and to insure that one gets the results back). In the last few years, statistical programming has become much more accessible with the rise of powerful statistical packages available on personal computers; often these are not much more difficult to use than a sophisticated word-processing program.

Some statistical techniques are not difficult to perform manually; for example, procedures that compare groups with respect to a single variable (e.g., T-test or ANOVA), or that analyze the relationship between two variables (e.g., correlation or the chi-square test) can all be computed using fairly simple formulas that require only basic arithmetic. These formulas, though, require extensive, repetitious (and therefore boring) calculations that quickly become tedious for studies with many observations (e.g., studies that include scores for many different students). In contrast, as noted above, computers perform repetitious tasks quickly and accurately, and they are ideal for statistical applications. It only requires a single computer command to compute one of the above statistical procedures, regardless of how large the study is. Computer packages have made the use of statistics much more accessible to average users. This is even more obvious with respect to the use of multivariate statistical techniques, which describe the relations among several variables in a single analysis (techniques such as multiple regression, path analysis, factor analysis, cluster analysis, and multidimensional scaling). These procedures require complex computations (on matrices rather than individual values), and they are difficult, and extremely tedious and time-consuming, to perform manually. Using computers, though, these procedures can be performed as easily as the single-variable procedures, for both types of procedure require only a single command. This ease of computation has associated dangers, however. The computer will produce results even when a particular statistical technique is not appropriate, and computers simply produce quantitative results with no indication of how the numbers should be interpreted or used. Using a computerized statistical package, a novice user could be computing the results of complex statistical procedures after only a few hours; but it is extremely likely that the resulting analyses would be meaningless. Computerized packages take the pain out of statistical analyses, but they cannot substitute for detailed study of the basis and use of each technique. A good introductory text on the use of statistical techniques in linguistic analyses is Butler (1985b), and Woods et al. (1986) gives a somewhat more advanced treatment.

Computers have also been used to develop new testing procedures. One of the recent trends in testing has been a movement from pencil-and-paper testing to testing on a computer (Dandonoli 1989; Larson 1989; Larson and Madsen 1985). Although there are several complications, computerized techniques enable highly accurate and efficient language testing. Complications include the need, on the part of the testee, to be familiar with a computer keyboard, the cost involved in providing enough computers (or terminals) to each test site, and the large question concerning the validity of discrete-item tests (see Davies in this volume).

4. COMPUTER APPLICATIONS FOR LANGUAGE LEARNING AND TEACHING

Most computer applications relating to language education have been carried out under the umbrella of computer-assisted language learning (CALL; sometimes also referred to as CAI [computer-assisted instruction] or CALI [computer-assisted language instruction]). CALL is now a huge and rapidly expanding field of computer application. This section will survey certain developments in CALL, but not describe in any detail specific CALL programs in use or in development; indeed, entire books are now not adequate to provide such coverage. Instead, the goal here is to provide a sense of the development of CALL and the directions that CALL might take in the future. It should also be noted that CALL is still a language-learning approach of the future rather than of the present. Its effectiveness has yet to be demonstrated on a large scale, and most descriptions are based on learning potential rather than on learning results.

The popularity of CALL is partly due to the desire to incorporate new ideas and techniques into language learning; more important, CALL offers unique advantages in language-learning contexts which, if applied appropriately, should improve learning. Advantages typically asserted to be associated with CALL include:

1. Individualization—students may have learning programs tailored to their individual skill-levels and learning needs;

2. Adaptability—students can choose new activities and exercises as their interests and their skills develop;

3. Objectivity—the computer treats all students alike;

4. Tirelessness—the computer will repeat the exercises in the same manner without fatigue;

5. Motivation—game/adventure activities, extensions of skills, and opportunities for real communication can improve motivation for learning;

6. Ability to do complex operations—more complicated CALL programs can perform operations that could not be done by a teacher (e.g., parsing analysis in Writer's Workbench); and

7. Thorough recordkeeping—the computer can keep track of how students used the computer, for how long, doing what activities, making how many and what types of mistakes, etc.

These, and other advantages, have influenced arguments for the incorporation of computers into language-learning and -teaching contexts.

Even though CALL had been a reality since the 1960s, only in the 1980s has it become a realistic enterprise as well as a feasible one (Ahmad et al. 1985; Higgins and Johns 1984; Underwood 1984). Earlier efforts were severely constrained by the nonaccessibility of equipment, very high costs, limited instructional capabilities, nonintegration with curricula, and unrealistic expectations. It is safe to say that, while many serious problems exist with respect to CALL, many of the early problems have either been solved or are currently receiving attention. These issues and others are addressed in the following discussion of CALL, organized into four sections: research on CALL effectiveness; recent innovations in CALL hardware and software; developments in CALL concerning elementary education and the teaching of reading, writing, ESL, and foreign languages; and ongoing problems in the use of CALL.

4.1. Research on CALL Effectiveness

There is little doubt now that CALL can provide a useful supplement to other language-learning practices, but the sometimes zealous rush to use CALL has preceded careful evaluation of its actual pedagogical worth (Bickes and Scott 1989; Bursten 1989; Flint 1987; Hirvela 1988, 1989; Reinking 1987; Wyatt 1988). Research on the success of CALL lags far behind the development and implementation of CALL materials in the classroom, and exaggerated claims for language learning with CALL, particularly of second languages, have led to some disappointment and confusion. In first-language reading and writing instruction, there has been considerably more research with results that can be described as mixed at best; of the two, reading research shows more positive results than does writing research overall (cf. Blanchard et al. 1987; Hawisher 1989; Hoot and Silvern 1988; Kamil 1987; Reinking 1987). Research on computer-assisted teaching of modern languages holds out much promise, as major investments have been made in large-scale language-learning projects for instruction in French, German, Russian, and Spanish (Flint 1989a). At present, however, the overall results of these efforts have yet to provide clear demonstrations of significant improvement over noncomputerized language instruction. Over the last decade, CALL has, perhaps, shown the least development in ESL/EFL instruction. This is primarily due to the lack of major institutional support for the use of computers in most ESL instruction. ESL and bilingual instruction in public schools receive the support of established educational systems and government grants, though most research in this area draws on reading and writing research done in public schools (e.g., Hawisher and Selfe 1989; Hoot and Silvern 1988; Johnson 1988; Kreeft-Payton and Mackinson-Smith 1988; Sayers 1988).

The most useful applications of CALL are now seen as those efforts intended to integrate uses of the computer into the language-learning curriculum, rather than to add them on or to create stand-alone options. As Pederson notes:

> CALL, in and of itself, does not result in more and better learning; rather, it is the specific way instruction is encoded in CALL software that has the potential of affecting learning positively, for specific learners in specific contexts. (1987:107)

Much current research and development is now moving to satisfy the criterion of appropriate curricular integration; however, this movement toward curricular integration requires much greater time and effort than that involved in the creation of independent materials that may not adapt the computer well to learner needs. It is fair to say, however, that computers may soon offer greater promise for language learning than has been the case to date.

4.2. CALL Innovations

Until recently, most CALL software presented only mechanical drills of language structure (rather similar to the language-laboratory audiotapes of the

1960s), offering little or no possibility of meaningful interaction. The combination of educational dissatisfaction with these simple drill-and-practice approaches and the recent innovations in both hardware and software are rapidly reshaping educational perspectives on computer uses, as is the growing effort on the part of CALL developers to respond to current language-learning approaches and educational needs. A number of recent language-learning programs and projects are incorporating advances in artificial-intelligence research by using human-computer interactive dialogue (e.g., language adventures such as ZORK, MYSTERY HOUSE, SPION), parsing systems (Writer's Workbench, Quill, JUEGOS COMMUNICATIVOS, STATION) and knowledge systems (hypermedia, hypertext). A number of experimental large-scale projects have combined these features as major components of language-learning curricula (e.g., Athena Project, Alexis Project, TALK Project). Discussions of these and many other applications of artificial intelligence are discussed in Flint (1987, 1989b), Balajthy (1987, 1988), Frase (1987a, 1987b), Louie and Rubeck (1989), and Underwood (1987, 1989a, 1989b).

Word processing is becoming a major means for practicing and developing language skills through the use of workstations, networks, and electronic mail. While the educational application of computers for word processing has only recently become widely available, its potential for improving student writing is widely accepted. Word processors reduce the effort required for the mechanical rewriting or retyping of a paper, provide much interaction with the written medium, and allow students to 'publish' clean manuscripts easily. These features, as well as others, have led to much research on the uses of computers in writing instruction, even at very early grade levels (e.g., Quill, Writing to Read).

Speech technology in CALL applications has also added a new and important innovation, particularly to reading instruction. The ability to hear words, syllables, and sounds allows nonreaders to interact with text and learn to relate sound to form and meaning (Olson and Wise 1987; Rosegrant 1988; Strickland et al. 1987). Similar applications in second-language learning have great potential but are less well developed (aside from application in a few major foreign-language instruction projects). Speech production is much more advanced than speech recognition in instructional applications and will remain so for the foreseeable future due to the state of technology and the cost limitations in speech recognition. Both speech synthesizers (computers that create voice sound) and speech digitizers (computers that use prerecorded sound) are being developed; each has its advantages and disadvantages (Blanchard et al. 1987). Prerecorded digitized speech in combination with videodisc and compact disc [CD] technology is likely to be the most useful development of speech applications in CALL.

Video applications in CALL have proven to be a major new direction for research. Stemming from the early use of TV and videotapes for language instruction, the recent combination of video/audio innovations with the computer suggests considerable potential for truly innovative instruction. Interactive video (IAV) applications for CALL, combined with a computer workstation, are already being produced for a number of foreign languages (Blanchard et al. 1987; Bush and Crotty 1989; Flint 1989a; Gale 1989; Rivera-La Scala 1989; Swanson 1988). Originally set up to operate with laser-discs, these programs are now using CDs (CD-ROM; ROM = read-only memory), which provide much greater storage capacity, combine multimedia and sound data, and are considerably cheaper. The interactive applications programs using CD-ROMs (referred to as CD-interactive [CDI] programs) now allow the learner to interact with large amounts of text, video, and audio material. This is clearly a direction for the future, rather than a current reality for CALL.

Other innovations with current application to CALL that may increase in prominence are the use of computer workstations (more powerful than microcomputers), local-area networks (LANs), and electronic mail. Many large CALL projects in foreign-language teaching involve workstation applications (e.g., the Athena project, the Writer's Workbench). Workstations are considerably more powerful than microcomputers and are capable of multiple tasking, sophisticated graphics, and much greater storage and computing power. Of course, the price tag matches the extraordinary capabilities. As workstations become more common and find wider applications outside of science, cost will come down and adjustments to CALL needs will increase (Cavalier and Dexheimer 1989; Lerman 1988; Weisseman 1988). Local-area networks combine computers and workstations to share resources and programs among all the terminals hooked together. On a larger scale, some U.S. universities have developed local networks that extend throughout an entire university campus (e.g., Brown University, Carnegie-Mellon University, the University of Minnesota). In essence, this means that anyone on the system can talk to anyone about anything, and all software resources are equally accessible. On a more limited scale, electronic mail allows individuals to talk to everyone else who has access to the mail system, and this use of the computer is more readily applicable to CALL. Use of electronic mail to promote interactive communication with other groups and cultures has proved to be a successful technique of CALL. Classes talk to other classes across the city, in other states, and in other countries. Letters, research projects, and joint publications all become possible for elementary-school students as well as college students. For example, the mail network described in Sayers (1988), *de Orilla a Orilla*, connects over 500 teachers and students in thirteen states and in Argentina, Israel, Japan, Mexico, Puerto Rico, and Spain (Daiute 1985; Kreeft-Payton and Mackinson-Smyth 1988; Levin et al. 1985; Sayers 1988; Spitzer 1989).

Much of the work on these innovative applications of technology to language learning is still in the experimental stage. The costs for development and implementation are still well beyond most users' resources. They may, however, represent commonplace features of language-learning curricula in the not-too-distant future. As the rapid accessibility of the microcomputer has changed the way people interact with computers on a personal level, so also will it change the shape of language instruction in many contexts. These innovative technologies may become readily accessible and affordable much more quickly than most educators might anticipate.

4.3. Developments in Writing, Reading, Language Arts, and Second-Language Instruction

Of all the areas in which computers have been used to teach language skills, writing has received the most attention and research. Primarily through the use of instructional word-processing programs, writing instruction by means of computers has a well-defined research base, extensive instruction development, and widespread application. There are many obvious advantages to word processing for writing instruction, though there are also equally obvious drawbacks. The more successful uses of computers have involved writing packages that extend beyond grammar practice and editing drills to assistance in the writing process itself (e.g., Writer's Workbench, HBJ Writer, Epistle). Overall, research on computers and writing has had mixed results; the research suggests that students write more, have fewer mechanical errors, and have better attitudes when using computers. However, there appears to be no overall gains in revision and writing quality for computer users over nonusers (Hawisher 1989).

CALL in reading instruction has an equally long history of research and development. In the case of reading, the results are slightly better than for writing. The many reading packages, adventure games, text analyses, vocabulary and grammar exercises, rate and recognition activities together seem to have a positive influence when supported by the curriculum, and when used appropriately. The largest array of software options is available for reading instruction, and this array of options may be the most important factor in reading success with computers (e.g., Blanchard et al. 1987; Reinking 1987; Strickland et al. 1987). The gradual incorporation of hypertext and hypermedia is likely to make reading instruction even more successful, as students will have fingertip access to entire libraries of information for cross-referencing and explanations. Such a vast store of knowledge should also help students improve their ability to write expository and argumentative essays.

Early instruction in the language arts is rapidly becoming a new source of CALL development and implementation. The use of computers for emergent writing and writing using the language experience approach (LEA) has given young students the ability to interact and communicate via the written medium. Early writing programs, such as Quill and Writing to Read, both provide frameworks for early writing instruction, assistance, and practice.

While the problems with computer use by young children are significant, the results of early writing on computers suggest that the effort is worthwhile. The ability to use electronic mail to communicate with other classes and other schools enhances the communicative value of writing for these children, and the opportunity to 'publish' and develop newsletters appears to be highly motivational (Daiute 1985; Hoot and Silvern 1988; Wresch 1987).

The generalized uses of computers in second-language learning have been somewhat less successful. With regard to foreign-language instruction, there are a number of large projects with impressive computer abilities (e.g., Flint 1989b). The research on the effectiveness of these major projects is not yet comprehensive enough to yield arguments for the wide dissemination of similar projects. In much other foreign-language instruction, the use of computers is almost nonexistent. In ESL/EFL instruction, the money and manpower for equivalent large-scale projects does not, at present, exist (Menke 1989). Most ESL computer applications and research are individual efforts, often adapting CALL materials developed for first-language reading and writing instruction. While many dedicated ESL/EFL researchers are working on the often unique issues arising from the interaction of second-language learners with computers, such research is difficult to conduct without major institutional commitments. Many CALL specialists will also readily admit that there is not a lot of research on second-language teaching that argues persuasively for the use of CALL over non-CALL instruction.

4.4. Ongoing Problems with CALL

As many of the early obstacles to the use of CALL have been eliminated, new issues come to the fore. Costs have come down; materials are more accessible and suitable to a variety of curricular contexts; teachers and students are becoming more comfortable with computers in their environment; and research is providing some evidence of CALL's effectiveness, when it is applied appropriately. At the same time, both old and new problems continue to challenge CALL instruction. The bewildering array of software created for CALL, much of which is of inferior quality, leads many teachers and curriculum specialists to be skeptical, especially when there are so many enthusiastic and sweeping testimonials for CALL. Teacher resistance to CALL is common and will probably not diminish until appropriate attention is given to teacher training in CALL, the implementation of CALL in the classroom, and its limits in specific contexts. Costs, hardware maintenance, and software incompatibility are all still serious problems for many teachers interested in CALL. Real individualization of instruction, at present, is still only a dream, because students are able to choose only from what is available in a given program. These issues become yet more confusing as newer, and more expensive, technologies begin to filter into CALL applications in the classroom. In the final analysis, the overriding concerns for successful CALL applications will include the need to train teachers, to develop software which can be integrated into specific teaching curricula, to provide evidence from research for the effectiveness of CALL, and to develop applications of CALL that are adaptable to teacher needs, rather than expecting teachers to adapt themselves to the computer. All of these changes are possible, but are yet to become established principles in CALL.

5. COMPUTATIONAL LINGUISTICS

As noted in the introduction, computational linguistics elevates the computer system to the end-product: a working computer system that models some aspect of language processing is the final goal of this research (Haugeland 1985; Johnson 1988). One of the earliest concerns within computational linguistics was machine translation—using computers to translate texts from one language to another. Work on machine translation began in the early 1950s (conceptual work was begun even earlier). In the earliest research, the major problem was assumed to be one of vocabulary and of devising ways to use large-scale dictionaries to translate individual words from one language into another. Linguistic structure above the word level was largely ignored. Even at this level, the problems were overwhelming, because most words have multiple meanings, and it is very difficult to decide among them without actually understanding the text. For example, Bar-Hillel (1960) discusses the meaning of *pen* in the two sentences *The pen is in the box* and *The box is in the pen*, pointing out that a translation program needs to be able to make inferences based on general knowledge of the world and the particular situational context of interaction, in addition to word-level semantics. Further, Barr and Feigenbaum (1981) point out that the early work in machine translation was done without the aid of modern computational concepts (such as arrays, pushdown stacks, and recursive procedures, which enable repeated processing of linguistic structure) and without the aid of recent work in syntactic theory (e.g., notions such as phrase structure, transformational rules, augmented transition networks). Given these severe limitations, it is not surprising that the early efforts at machine translation ended in frustration. In 1966 the U.S. National Academy of Science concluded that machine translation was not feasible and recommended that all federal funding for this area be eliminated; by 1975 there were no federally funded machine-translation projects in the United States. More recently, though, interest in machine translation has been revived because of advances both in computational techniques and linguistic theory. Currently, several machine-translation systems are being developed by government agencies and industry, with considerably more success than earlier efforts. Barr and Feigenbaum (1981) and Slocum (1985) present good introductions to work on machine translation, and two recent issues of *Computational Linguistics* (volume 11, 1–2, 1985) are devoted to recent advances in this area.

Although the earliest work in computational linguistics was carried out in support of machine-translation projects, by far the largest amount of research in this area has been directed toward the development of human-machine interaction. As noted above, much of this research is not based on any particular linguistic theory. Rather, the goal is to achieve a meaningful interaction as efficiently as possible. One of the best-known programs of this type is named ELIZA (Weizenbaum 1966). This program depends on a set of pre-established patterns to imitate a 'nondirective' therapist interacting with a patient. An interaction with ELIZA might look something like the following:

> Patient: I came today because I'm unhappy.
>
> ELIZA: Do you think coming here will help you not to be unhappy?
>
> Patient: It's just that I'm always depressed.
>
> ELIZA: I'm sorry to hear that you are always depressed.
>
> Patient: I just wish that my father loved me.
>
> ELIZA: Tell me more about your family.
>
> Patient: Sometimes I think that you don't really listen to me.
>
> ELIZA: What makes you think I don't really listen to you?

The program underlying ELIZA is extremely simple. It involves a set of pre-defined patterns and associated transformations for the response. For example, the pattern in the last dialogue turn above is:

> (1 you 3 me)

and the transformation rule is:

> (What makes you think I 3 you?)

By a clever use of patterns and alternating transformations, ELIZA simulates a concerned therapist. The program has essentially no basis in linguistic theory; neither the pattern nor the transformations are motivated by a particular theory. Rather, they were chosen simply because they work; the research goal in this case was to demonstrate that relatively complex and 'meaningful' interaction is possible using very simple computational and linguistic structures.

Later systems for man-machine interaction were considerably more complex. Some of these were developed to facilitate the use of information-retrieval systems (e.g., LUNAR [Woods et al. 1972, described in Barr and Feigenbaum 1981], which was developed to help geologists analyze data from the Apollo-11 mission). Other systems, similar to ELIZA, were developed to test a particular conceptualization of the natural language understanding process, rather than for a specific application. For example, SHRDLU (Winograd 1972) was developed in an effort to integrate syntax, semantics, and knowledge of the world into a single system. Two other well-known systems, SAM (Script Applier Mechanism) and PAM (Plan Applied Mechanism), were developed by Schank and Abelson (1977) in an attempt to understand entire stories rather than only individual sentences. In general, recent research in computational linguistics has given more attention to the analysis of discourse structure and the ways in which individual propositions work together to make the overall point(s) of a story (Britton and Black 1985; Grosz et al. 1989; Meyer 1985).

Another large area of research in computational linguistics concerns speech synthesis and speech recognition. From an acoustic point of view, each speech sound is simply a combination of waves of specific frequencies and amplitudes. It is thus possible artificially to create, or to synthesize, a word, phrase, or sentence, by combining the appropriate waves for all of the sounds into a single speech-like wave.[1] Applications of speech synthesis have become widespread, including educational toys, telephone-operator assistance, announcements in elevators (e.g., "going up"), announcements in automobiles (e.g., "the door is open"), and even talking magazine advertisements. Research on speech recognition, designed to recognize spoken utterances, has not progressed as far as speech synthesis, although probably more effort has been expended on it. Existing programs are able to process a fairly large number of words spoken in isolation by a single speaker——the speaker records the words onto a computer, and the recognition program then matches subsequent spoken words against the acoustic patterns of these prerecorded words. The main problem confronting a generalized speech-recognition program is that each person pronounces a word differently (in fact, a single individual never repeats exactly the same pronunciation). The more demographic differences there are between two speakers (e.g., sex, social dialect, geographic dialect), the greater the differences between their pronunciations of the same word. A speech-recognition program cannot accurately distinguish between the case when a single speaker utters two different words and the case when two different speakers utter the same word—from an acoustic perspective, in both cases there appear to be two different words. Ongoing research is attempting to integrate speech recognition with other aspects of natural-language understanding, using analyses of syntax and semantics to help decode the speech signal.

Most of the above projects can be considered 'practical' because they are directed to achieving specific results rather than testing a theoretical orientation. Recently, though, several 'theory-driven' projects have focused on syntactic analysis (or parsing). Specifically, there have been projects associated with the extended standard theory of transformational grammar (Chomsky

1977a; Marcus 1980; cf. Grabe in this volume), generalized phrase-structure grammar (GPSG; Gazdar et al. 1985), and lexical-functional grammar (LFG; Kaplan and Bresnan 1982). This last example, LFG, illustrates a particularly profitable interaction between theory development and computational implementation, in that the theory is strongly influenced by earlier computational work using augmented transition networks.

Another recent breakthrough in language-related computational research was made by the researchers developing connectionist and parallel-distributed processing models of language processing. This line of research arose out of frustration with the limitations of linear processing models of language, which assumed that the brain executed one task at a time (very rapidly). In contrast, these researchers claim that the brain performs many processing functions at the same time (based on recent studies in neurolinguistics that show the existence of parallel, or multiple simultaneous, brain-excitation patterns), and they have developed computer models to simulate multiple simultaneous processing of language. In these projects, the computer is being used as a fairly direct test of a linguistic theory, in that the language behavior of the computer is directly compared with the language behavior of human beings (e.g., McClelland 1987; Rumelhart et al. 1986; Sampson 1987).

Finally, as mentioned in section 3, Garside, Leech, and Sampson (1987) advocate a new "corpus-based paradigm" for computational linguistics, in contrast to the artificial-intelligence approach adopted by other studies. Most working systems intended to replicate natural-language understanding are extremely limited in their domain of application because a general understanding system would require extensive inferencing based on particular contexts. Recall, for example, the two meanings of *pen* discussed above as an illustration of the difficulties in machine translation; a general-purpose system would need to be able to distinguish among situational domains, and infer that *pen* would most likely refer to a writing instrument in an office domain, but would most likely refer to a small enclosure in a farm or yard domain. Since researchers have not yet successfully developed programs for general inferencing, most practical projects are domain-limited. In contrast, the corpus-based approach uses probabilistic methods so that the analysis is much more robust in different domains; the approach makes no claim to model human intelligence and is based on the assumption that there are no absolute rules of grammar. Thus, any input sentence will be assigned some analysis (whereas more traditional systems would simply reject many sentences as 'ungrammatical'). As work within this paradigm progresses, it should prove particularly useful for applications such as human-machine interaction which do not require absolute accuracy, but do require a flexible system able to analyze varied textual input.

There are many additional areas of ongoing research in computational linguistics, and this chapter has only briefly summarized the few projects specifically mentioned here. Fuller surveys of the field can be found in Barr and Feigenbaum (1981), Grishman (1986), Tennant (1980), and Winograd (1983), and research articles can be found in the journal *Computational Linguistics*.

6. CONCLUSION

This paper has distinguished among 'applied,' 'practical,' and 'theoretical' projects. In closing, it seems necessary to emphasize that these distinctions are useful for this exposition but not at all absolute. For example, practical projects are clearly applied, in that they are developed to meet real-world concerns. Theoretical projects become practical and applied when they develop useful tools (e.g., for text-based research or language learning) or other products (e.g., a successful human-machine interface). Applied projects are theoretical to the extent that they are based on or pursue specific theoretical concerns. This paper has attempted to give an overview of these various subfields, but it has not been possible to describe any of them in detail; rather, the goal has been to provide a foundation, so that interested readers can pursue their particular interests with a sense of how they relate to the whole field.

NOTES

1. The process is actually much more complicated than simply combining a series of sounds, because speech is continuous (with transitions between sounds), rather than being made up of a combination of discrete units. One of the most effective methods of synthesis is linear predictive coding (LPC), which uses a technique similar to multiple-regression analysis to identify the best fitting combination of acoustic waves.

SUGGESTIONS FOR FURTHER READING

Since this chapter covers an extraordinary range of information, a few major sources for each area are noted. In the area of the computer as a research tool in linguistics, see Biber 1988; Butler 1985a; Hockey 1980; Garside et al. 1987; and Sinclair 1987. For readable introductions to statistics in linguistics, see Butler 1985b; Hatch and Farhady 1983; and Woods et al., 1986. Computers and CALL in various contexts are given good treatment in Ahmad et al. 1985; Flint 1987, 1989b; Hawisher and Selfe 1989; Hoot and Silvern 1988; and Reinking 1987. Computational linguistics and language-processing issues are presented in Haugeland 1985; Slocum 1985; and Winograd 1980. Journals include *Academic Computing*, *CALICO*, *Computational Linguistics*, *The ICAME Journal*, *Language Testing*, *Literary and Linguistic Computing*, and *System*.

QUESTIONS FOR FURTHER DISCUSSION

1. Which applications of computers in applied linguistics are most relevant to your interests, and why?

2. What sort of view into the future does Biber's chapter suggest? Will computers become increasingly more important in applied linguistics or not? If so, then in what ways?

3. Biber argues that computer uses in applied linguistics can be understood in terms of 'practical,' 'theoretical,' and 'applied' studies. Do these headings provide a useful division of the topic? What other typology could be used in its place?

4. Why is the computer so useful for research on stylistics and lexicography? How might issues indicate the relevance of computer applications for language-in-the-professions concerns?

5. How important will the use of the computer become in language testing? Compare Biber's brief discussion with the chapter by Davies.

6. Compare Biber's analysis of CALL with the chapters on language teaching and language learning by McLaughlin and Zemblidge, Morley, and Savignon. Which of the three latter chapters is the most compatible with Biber's?

7. How would Biber's chapter best be incorporated within the general overview of applied linguistics given by Strevens? Are the two chapters compatible? If so, then how specifically?

8. Are there any applied-linguistics issues in computer applications that Biber does not discuss? How central are these other issues in applied linguistics? Which topics might he have given more coverage to?

An Introduction to
Becoming an Applied Linguist

Virtually every article in this volume has argued that there is a separate and distinct field called applied linguistics, that the field subsumes a number of other areas, that the field is concerned with the solution of language-based real-world problems, and that those solutions implicate information not only from linguistics but also from a variety of other disciplines, including at least psycho- and sociolinguistics and learning theory. If, indeed, there is such a field, it must of necessity be possible to become educated (or trained) in it.

Both Grabe and Kaplan have had the practical experience of developing academic curricula for the education of applied linguists. One of the inevitable issues that arises in the development of such curricula relates to the amount of linguistics that applied linguists must know. Arguments have raged in academic institutions about the specification of syntactic and semantic knowledge requisite for doing work in applied linguistics. This question is addressed in some detail in the following article. A second matter that has required substantial discussion is the amount of statistical and computer skill necessary to function as an applied linguist. The third area of concern relates to the other kinds of skills that applied linguists need to have. For example, should an applied linguist have extensive knowledge of learning theory, teaching methodology, planning theory, or human-resource–development theory? This list is endlessly expandable.

As the list expands, it raises two important additional questions. The first of these relates to the logical locus for such a degree. Is it by definition interdisciplinary? Can it be housed in a department of linguistics that also (or primarily) teaches general linguistics, or can it be housed in an educational faculty, an English faculty, or a modern languages faculty? The second of the two questions relates to the duration of study. Curricula are tied to time; students rightly expect to finish in something under a lifetime. How much of what kind of education can reasonably be required of a student in the 72–90 postgraduate units that are generally required by a doctoral program (or the 36 units generally required for the first postgraduate degree)? Indeed, is applied linguistics a field that requires the doctorate, or will some other sort of certification serve better? And what sorts of employment are available in the real world for individuals who are trained in this way? To put it in a slightly different way: Is the field vigorous enough to provide employment for graduates of applied-linguistics programs? Finally, because the field is a new one, and there are not yet many people specifically trained in it (i.e., many scholars who profess applied linguistics were trained in other fields), where will the faculty for such programs come from, and who will provide leadership for the field as it matures? Grabe and Kaplan try to address some of these issues, but their primary concern is to define a curricular framework that might produce applied linguists.

Becoming an Applied Linguist

William Grabe and Robert B. Kaplan

Northern Arizona University and University of Southern California

1. INTRODUCTION

In an emerging field of study, there will always be some amount of confusion with respect to its guiding assumptions, methods, and objectives; this problem has been evident in applied linguistics. At issue is the simple question: What is applied-linguistics research, and who is an applied linguist? Until the 1980s, in fact, this confusion generally held sway over the field, a field in search of its own theoretical base and guiding philosophy. While it has never been difficult to define applied linguistics generally (it is the field that seeks to solve language-based problems/issues), there has typically been considerable confusion as to the scope of applied-linguistics concerns and applied-linguistics research.

Through the 1950s, 1960s, and 1970s, applied linguistics was typically seen as concerned with practical aspects of language teaching, language learning, and language testing. With the appearance of Kaplan (1980b), it became clear that many applied linguists viewed the field in much broader terms, taking seriously the notion that applied linguistics deals with a wide range of language-based problems. In addition to language learning and teaching, language assessment is again firmly grounded in applied linguistics (see the chapter by Davies in this volume). Furthermore, research once assigned to sociolinguistics is now being recognized as falling within the domain of applied linguistics, including language use in professional contexts (Maher and Rokosz in this volume), forensic linguistics, document design, literacy (Palmer and Kaplan in this volume), cross-cultural communication, language attitudes and language choice (Macias in this volume), and language policy and planning (Judd and Kaplan in this volume). One clear indication of this shift is the recent volume by Trudgill (1984), *Applied sociolinguistics*. Applied linguistics has also come to include within its scope other language-related concerns such as language handicap and rehabilitation (Crystal 1984), lexicography (Hartmann 1985), information transfer (Grabe 1988; Kaplan 1987; Large 1985), and international Englishes (Kachru 1985b, 1988).

While the various chapters of the current volume make clear the broader scope of applied linguistics, there comes with this growth and maturity of the field a new concern. If applied linguistics, as a discipline, is so far-reaching, how does one become trained to be an applied linguist by means of some coherent program of study. It is clear that an applied linguist should be trained in linguistics first, if the field's name is not to be totally empty. It is not, however, an absolute requirement that applied linguists do their primary research within general linguistics. Second, it is necessary that an applied linguist have expertise in a related field or discipline, be this education, psychology, sociology, anthropology, psychometrics, political science, the information sciences, artificial intelligence, the health professions, professional training, etc. While it may appear equally plausible to specialize in a related field first, and then acquire the necessary linguistic expertise, there is a tendency in related fields toward a less sophisticated view of language than is required for dealing with language-based problems or issues.

Third, the applied linguist must also take an interdisciplinary perspective that may require knowledge of a number of related fields. It is not usually possible for an applied linguist to gain sufficient expertise over such a broad range of disciplines, so s/he must often work with professionals in related disciplines, drawing on their greater knowledge and using this knowledge to create an interdisciplinary response to problems that cross disciplinary boundaries. For example, if we take language planning as the prototypical area of applied-linguistics endeavor, it is clear that a coherent language-planning activity requires the participation of a team including, on the linguistic side, phonologists, lexicographers, grammarians, sociolinguists, psycholinguists, assessment specialists, literacy specialists, and language-education specialists, and, in addition, on the nonlinguistic side, professional planners, anthropologists, economists, specialists in education administration, and so on. Clearly, no one person—certainly no one applied linguist—can possess all these skills. The principle investigator should be an applied linguist, but s/he will need access to all the other specialists in order to get the job done.

In this way, the applied linguist is both a specialist and a generalist. The specializations are, of necessity, in linguistics and in one or two other domains of knowledge. The generalist knowledge is accumulated as concerns/problems are encountered and responses sought. At the heart of the issue remains the question of how applied linguists are to be trained. Specifically, what are the sorts and ranges of knowledge required of someone if s/he is to be successful as an applied linguist.

2. CONSTRAINTS ON THE TRAINING OF APPLIED LINGUISTS

There are a few preliminary comments that are in order before describing the sorts and ranges of knowledge required for preparation to practice applied linguistics. These comments deal with basic constraints on the training of applied linguists. First, it would seem that the training necessary for an applied linguist can probably be accomplished only at a large research-oriented university in which the related disciplines are available to complement the linguistic foundations that an applied linguistics program itself is responsible for. Second, and related to the first point, it should be clear from the above discussion that a program in applied linguistics cannot be seen only as a language teacher-training program. While that surely is one important domain of applied-linguistics inquiry, it cannot be considered to subsume all that applied linguistics encompasses. This is a major reason why applied linguistics sees a linguistic foundation, rather than an educational foundation, as basic. For this reason, it is also more realistic that an applied-linguistics program be housed in a linguistics department or an English department, or be structured as a freestanding department, rather than be placed within a school of education. Third, it should be apparent that the making of an applied linguist is a complex and time-consuming endeavor, one that cannot be relegated to MA-level training. Rather, while the foundations of linguistic knowledge and perhaps also of language teaching and language learning may be inculcated at the MA level, the more specialized knowledge and training will require an education to the Ph.D. level. Not only are the time requirements more suitable to the Ph.D. level of education, but the interdisciplinary requirements of the field demand the many years of study and independent research that is expected of the doctoral student. The complexity of requirements for the making of a productive applied linguist should become evident as the various knowledge domains relevant to the field are explored.

There is also, finally, the question of the centrality of English to the endeavors of applied linguistics. For better or worse, much of the research and many of the issues in applied linguistics have been examined via the medium of English and the research reported in English-language publications. It is true that applied linguistics is not centrally concerned with knowledge of English but with knowledge of language per se. This issue is a complex one and will be addressed in more detail in the concluding section of the chapter. Suffice it to say that, apart from Europe (both Eastern and Western) and the

English-speaking world (Australia, Britain, Canada, India, New Zealand, and the United States), little research in applied linguistics is reported and circulated in other-than-local documents and publications.

The above-mentioned constraints are particularly relevant to applied linguistics because of the strongly interdisciplinary nature of the field. These constraints also reflect the complex knowledge base required of an applied linguist, and it is these knowledge bases that we now address. In order to make sense of the various sorts of knowledge relevant to applied linguistics, it is perhaps best not to consider the knowledge needed in a discipline-specific manner, but to rethink the array of knowledge, to organize it in some manner different from current 'departmental' configurations. We have, therefore, set up a categorization of knowledge relevant to applied linguistics without respecting current academic boundaries. We will, of course, relate these knowledge domains not only to various issues and topics of study, but also to the related disciplines whence much of this knowledge has emerged. There are four knowledge domains, as we presently envisage them:

A. Linguistics
   1. Basic
   2. Formal
   3. Educational
B. Language and mind
C. Language and society
D. Literacies and tools
   1. Basic
   2. Quantitative
   3. Computer

These are not optional domains, but represent the range of knowledge an applied linguist will have to be acquainted with, admittedly to varying degrees. In the rest of the chapter we would like to explore this taxonomy of knowledge as it pertains to the training of applied linguists.

3. LINGUISTICS

One of the reasons why linguists, on the one hand, and language teachers and English teachers, on the other hand, do not seem to be able to discuss language with each other stems from the assumption by professors of formal linguistics that the linguistics student has a sufficient background in pedagogical and descriptive grammar at the onset of his/her linguistics training. A more careful assessment reveals that many linguists are not as familiar with traditional grammar and language usage, usually of English, as formal linguists suppose. Often, linguists and applied linguists learn about these descriptive and prescriptive aspects of the language in the course of some research. However, the basic descriptive and usage information is typically not made available to the linguist or applied linguist until s/he is well into the curriculum of his or her program, leading the student into potential waste of time or duplication of task. A firm grounding in descriptive language knowledge, as well as in certain prescriptive usage information is vital for the practicing applied linguist. It enables the applied linguist to speak to educators and traditional English faculty on a common ground; it provides the awareness necessary to train others in seeing the differences between description and prescription and in seeing the role for each kind of knowledge in the educational enterprise. Perhaps even more important, it allows the applied linguist to bridge the gap between research in formal linguistics and the assumptions about language often held by teachers and university faculty in English, education, and the modern languages.

Such a knowledge of basic linguistics would include a sound description of the student's native language. It would further require an awareness of traditional terminology so that connections can be made between various traditional and descriptive approaches, for clearly there is no one descriptive approach to language. Basic linguistic knowledge includes more than a passing knowledge of prescribed usage; rather, it implies an ability to explain the difference between descriptive grammar and prescriptive rules of usage. This distinction also requires a recognition of the educational importance of each aspect of the language. Basic linguistics also treats the differences between spoken and written language (obviously varying in terms of local constraints, situation by situation). In addition, some knowledge of the development of writing systems as unique media of communication is necessary. Finally, basic linguistics provides some treatment of the historical development of standard usage, grammars, and other language resources commonly used by educators.

With respect to formal linguistics, it is essential that an applied linguist have a solid grounding in the eponymic discipline (Grabe in this volume). Within the domain of formal linguistics, knowledge of phonetics, phonology, morphology, syntax, and semantics would be essential. Beyond this basic foundation, an applied linguist will have specialist knowledge in one or more of these areas; for example, an applied linguist will have specialist knowledge in phonetics and phonology or in syntax and semantics. It is difficult to imagine an applied linguist undertaking appropriate research without such a knowledge base in formal linguistics. While it may not be necessary for an applied linguist to be a primary researcher in formal linguistics (that is, to write articles on syntactic theory, etc.), an applied linguist should be current in his/her chosen field of specialization and be conversant with the most recent research in the field.

The third field within the linguistics domain is educational linguistics, including the theory and practice of language teaching, language learning, and language testing. While educational linguistics (Spolsky 1978b; Stubbs 1988) is most commonly interpreted in applied linguistics as instruction in English as a second language (ESL) or in English as a foreign language, that is too narrow a scope, because educational linguistics deals with foreign-language instruction, language-arts instruction, more advanced writing instruction, and native-language literacy; it also deals with curriculum development and materials preparation, as well as policy issues (which may be very complex in multilingual contexts; cf. Spolsky 1986b; Paulston 1988). Finally, applied linguistics has recently begun to address social and psychological factors in the learning environment; most interesting to the applied linguist are those arising out of a multilingual, multicultural context.

It is beyond dispute that nearly half of all applied-linguistics research relates to language learning and teaching, typically of English to speakers of other languages (Kaplan in this volume). This skewing of educational linguistics is apparent in the large numbers of books and journals worldwide that deal with English as a second language (van Els et al. 1984; Kaplan et al. 1988; Stern 1983). Changes in the last ten years have served to alter this general view. In the 1980s, research on second-language instruction in European languages has been increasingly reported in journals of applied linguistics and related disciplines (Andersen 1984; Kaplan et al. 1989; Perdue 1984; Pfaff 1987). Many studies of students learning a second European language have now appeared. There is also a growing interest in the instruction of children of guest workers in Europe, those children who may speak a non-European language, and who come from economically disadvantaged backgrounds (e.g., Verhoeven 1987). Regardless of the particular context in which a second language is learned, the field of language teaching is an essential component of an applied linguist's background knowledge, not only because language teaching is so central to applied linguistics generally, but also because many other language-related problems have some connection with language instruction in one form or another, as the subsequent discussion indicates.

The 1980s have also witnessed a greater awareness in applied-linguistics research of foreign-language instruction in the United States. While much previous foreign-language instruction in the United States, whether at the tertiary level or in secondary schools, relied on texts written by scholars of literature and organized around a grammar-translation approach, recent trends in foreign-language teaching and text materials have indicated a growing awareness of student needs and a growing sophistication in methods and materials in effective materials (Lantolf and LaBarca 1987; vanPatten and Lee 1990; Savignon 1983; Savignon and Berns 1984, 1987; Swaffer 1988; cf. Savignon in this volume).

Gradually, applied linguists are becoming more involved in language-arts education; that is, early first-language education that stresses school-valued genres of language use (Wong-Fillmore 1986). In the United States, this trend is influenced by the numbers of students entering primary and secondary schools whose first language is not English, or whose first dialect is other than standard English. The impetus for this area of investigation comes from education (in particular from bilingual education), from sociology (Bernstein 1972a, 1972b), and from sociolinguistics (e.g., the various studies by Labov and his colleagues showing that 'disadvantaged' students come to schools with language differences, not language deficits; cf. Edwards 1885; Stubbs 1980; Wells 1986). These avenues of inquiry have led to recent research centered on the classroom; that research has examined teacher-student interaction, cross-cultural interaction, home-school differences in language and literacy uses, and the assumptions guiding school-based literacy instruction (Cazden 1988; Graff 1987; Heath 1983, 1985, 1986a, 1986b; Street 1984; Tannen 1986; Wells 1986). This area of education research also includes examination of social and psychological contexts for learning in educational settings. For applied linguists interested in language-arts education, the related fields of education and sociology, particularly topics concerning disadvantaged students and literacy development, are essential knowledge bases.

An area in educational linguistics taking on greater importance in the 1980s, particularly in the United States, is the teaching of advanced writing skills in late secondary schooling and in first-year college courses. The extent of the language-based problem represented by inadequate advanced writing skills is only now being given consideration. For years, college composition instructors have been dealing with the problems of students unable to write at acceptable university-entrance levels (Rose 1985). An awareness of this problems has resulted in the rise of a substantial history of composition research, often within rhetoric programs. With the increasing recognition that students at secondary schools need to develop their writing ability, English education has combined with research on composition to seek means to achieve more effective writing instruction. Applied linguists have become increasingly interested in this issue, as more second-language and second-dialect students move through the educational system and encounter writing problems. Certainly these problems also occur in geographic areas where English is not a native language (e.g., Hong Kong, Singapore), and in other language settings as well. Thus, recent research on writing in applied linguistics has drawn extensively from composition research and English education to explore solutions to the writing problems of students whose first language is not English (Hudelson 1989b; Johnson and Roen 1988). This concern applies to immigrant and indigenous non-English–speaking populations, as well as to international students coming to the United States for tertiary-level study. In countries other than the United States, where less stress is placed on the advanced writing skills of students, this issue may not yet be as pressing, but awareness is increasing as literacy expands.

Applied linguists have also become much more aware of the need to study aspects of curriculum and materials development, particularly as these apply to the delivery of second-language instruction. Until the 1970s, most discussions of second-language instruction seemed to assume that some methodology would answer all instructional questions. The demise of the audio-lingual method and the increasing sophistication of instruction in a broad range of contexts has led to much greater consideration of school, sponsor, and student needs; the specification of language skills and subject matter; and the effectiveness of materials developed for these various purposes. Much of the impetus for these developments has originated within ESL/EFL contexts (Dubin and Olshtain 1986; Johnson 1989; Nunan 1989; Yalden 1987); however, recent research has explored the contributions that the field of education can make to these areas (Nunan 1988; Pennington 1985; Richards 1984b; Rodgers 1989).

Finally, applied linguists have, for quite some time, been interested in the development of language policies related to education, and in the use of education to implement language policies first formulated outside the educational infrastructure. The specific name for this research is language-in-education policy and planning (cf. Judd in this volume). It has long been assumed by language-planning specialists that educational contexts are a major vehicle for the dissemination of planned language change, and that schools implement policies that have been formulated elsewhere, whether in governmental agencies or in language academies. More recent examination of the influence and formulation of language-in-education policies indicate that such a straightforward and direct transmission of policy may not always be the case. Baldauf (1989), for example, discusses a number of Australian educational contexts and argues that many educational systems create language policy as they go along, with very little outside direction, and, for that matter, very little guidance. The role of language-in-education policy and planning is only now receiving the attention it deserves as a separate area of study, rather than as an appendage of studies of language policy and planning undertaken for more general purposes.

An applied linguist should have some familiarity with all of these areas of educational linguistics, most centrally with the types of second-language instructional contexts. Of other aspects of educational linguistics, no more than background knowledge may be required, depending on the applied linguist's specialization.

4. LANGUAGE AND MIND

The study of the relationship between language and the mind is the province of psycholinguistics. It is also studied extensively in cognitive psychology. From the perspective of applied linguistics, the study of language and mind is most commonly conducted in research on second-language acquisition. This, however, is only one aspect of the language-mind connection, one taking its knowledge base from first-language and child-language acquisition (e.g., Foster 1990; Hyams 1986; MacWhinney 1987; Slobin 1985). In fact, psycholinguists and cognitive psychologists are also very much concerned with how the mind comprehends language—with the nature of the processing systems involved; how they interact; what subprocessing components exist; how they are organized; how memory is organized; how knowledge retrieval works, etc. Psycholinguistics is also concerned with how language is produced—what the components of a production model are; how the components interact; how production models differ from comprehension models, etc. Additionally, psycholinguistics is interested in mind-brain interactions and language pathology—where various sources of language knowledge are located in the brain; how these brain centers interact; how the brain accommodates second-language knowledge; how the brain acts when it is injured or diseased, etc. All of these areas represent important sources of knowledge for the applied linguist (Caplan 1987; Carlson and Tannenhaus 1988; Curtiss 1988; Garnham 1985; Kean 1988; Tannenhaus 1988).

Applied linguists, as noted above, have made the greatest use of acquisition research (Kaplan et al. 1989). This is readily apparent, as applied-linguistics research of a psycholinguistic nature invariably centers on acquisition rather than on processing or pathology (Genesee 1988; Huebner 1989; Scovel 1988; cf. Fletcher 1990). This is true not only in training courses for applied linguists but also in publications in the field. It is in acquisition that applied linguistics has had its greatest influence on learning research. Such research as that in grammar and vocabulary development (Gass 1989; Klein 1986; Krakowian 1989; McLaughlin 1987), discourse development (Carrell 1989; Hudelson 1989a; Larsen-Freeman 1980, 1990; Scarcella 1989; Widdowson 1979, 1984), communicative competence (Beebe 1988; deKeyser 1989; Wolfson 1989; Wolfson and Judd 1983), cognitive variables, and learner variables (Brown 1987; Chamot and O'Malley 1987; Faerch and Kaspar 1983; Kachru 1989; O'Malley et al. 1987; Oxford-Carpenter 1989) all focus on various aspects of the acquisition process.

In contrast to the above advances, one seldom finds studies of language processing from a second language perspective. Those few studies that have been published typically involve bilingual research and are performed by educational psychologists (Hakuta et al. 1987). This imbalance has led to a number of advances in the study of language learning, but has also created a very narrow view of the scope of second-language acquisition. While quite a lot has been learned about the grammatical and discourse development of second-language speakers, and more recently about learner and cognitive strategies, in fact very little is known about the comprehension and production characteristics of second-language learners (cf. McLaughlin in this volume). One indication of this gap lies in the small quantity of research done on reading-comprehension and writing-production processes in comparison to the quantity of research done on the study of utterance structures of second-language learners (cf. Carrell 1989; Hudelson 1989a; Segalowitz 1986; Vaid 1986; Verhoeven 1987). Research on language processing by second-language learners is a vast open territory for future applied-linguistics research (cf. Bereiter and Scardamalia 1987; Koster 1987; Perfetti and McCutchen 1987).

Disciplines related to the study of the language-mind field that complement psycholinguistics include educational psychology and cognitive psychology. An applied linguist must be familiar with the theoretical assumptions and research that characterize these fields, and that influence current second-language research. This is particularly important in the cases in which research in second-language acquisition has led to assertions about and approaches to teaching second languages (e.g., Krashen and Terrell 1983). Any understanding of language teaching today requires some recognition of these assumptions in teaching practices and a critical evaluation of the strengths and weaknesses of these assumptions (Ellis 1985; McLaughlin 1987). Applied linguists should also be exposed to the research on processing done in psycholinguistics, an area that has heretofore been largely ignored in the training of applied linguists (Carlson and Tannenhaus 1988; Garnham 1985; Oakhill and Garnham 1988; Tannenhaus 1988). A number of the current assumptions about language teaching, particularly those about the teaching of reading and writing, are contradicted by current research on language processing, and many teachers and applied linguists are not aware of this contradiction (cf. Perfetti and McCutchen 1987; Stanovich 1986).

5. LANGUAGE AND SOCIETY

Perhaps the domain of knowledge on which the applied linguist has come to rely most heavily is that concerned with the relationship between language and society, with sociolinguistics being the source field for research. Research topics such as discourse analysis, register analysis, language use in professional contexts, language and disadvantage, cross-cultural interaction, communicative competence, societal bilingualism, language spread, language maintenance, language shift, and language policy and planning, are all important aspects of sociolinguistic research. Applied linguists are also engaged in such research, though usually with a specific application in mind. In fact, sociolinguistic research also has concern for real-world applications; thus the appellation *applied* sociolinguistics.

Applied linguists must have more than a passing knowledge of sociolinguistic research and its potential applications. In many cases, such applications represent the very sorts of responses applied linguists need to make with respect to particular language concerns and issues. Most central for applied linguists is a strong foundational knowledge in discourse analysis in its various guises: text analysis, contrastive rhetoric, conversational analysis, ethnomethodology, ethnography of speaking, and conversational style (Connor and Kaplan 1987; Scarcella 1989; Schiffrin 1988). These represent the basic "tools of the trade" for applied linguists. Without discourse analysis much research in sociolinguistics and in applied linguistics would lack the wherewithal to determine viable solutions or responses to language-based problems. Indeed, the notion of communicative competence itself would have little meaning without discourse analysis.

Applied linguistics and sociolinguistics actually come together in the areas typically defined as macrosociolinguistics. Applied linguists are interested in all aspects of bilingualism, including societal bilingualism and the phenomenon of diglossia. While the term *languages in contact* may cover areas beyond even sociolinguistics (such as phonological borrowing or structural development of creole languages), it is more typically concerned with issues such as multilingualism, language status, language attitudes, language choice, language spread, language maintenance, and language shift (Fasold 1984). Each of these areas has direct consequences for applied-linguistics research and must be seen as a basic knowledge domain for the applied linguist. In the area of language policy and language planning, sociolinguistics and applied linguistics actually merge. Language policy and planning has, for some time, been recognized as an activity of applied linguistics, though it is also seen as an aspect of macrosociolinguistics, or, as Fishman (1972) suggests, the sociology of language.

The relationship between language and society is the subject matter of a knowledge domain that is becoming more and more the province of applied linguistics, as well as of sociolinguistics (as indicated in various chapters in this volume). Of all the branches of linguistic research, sociolinguistic research is at the moment the one most closely intertwined with applied linguistics (Grabe in this volume); applied linguists must therefore have a strong background in sociolinguistics if they are to be productive researchers in many of the topics currently central to applied linguistics.

6. LITERACIES AND TOOLS

In addition to knowing technical information deriving from linguistics and from other specific academic disciplines, the applied linguist needs to have command of a number of literacy skills. These constitute the essential tools needed to do the job; they are mentioned here not so much in the sense that they must constitute part of the training curriculum, but because they are really prerequisite to that curriculum.

The most basic of these skills is language literacy. Any individual working in any subfield of linguistics must have some knowledge of other languages, must be able to write with considerable facility in his/her first language, and must be able to read technical material fluently and intelligently.

In addition to knowing well his/her first language, the applied linguist ought to be familiar with a number of other languages. It is, of course, generally desirable that an applied linguist have experience living in another culture and using other languages (discussed below) than his or her native culture and language. The familiarity at issue here, however, consists of having a good understanding of the structure and organization of other languages. To that end, an applied linguist (assuming a native English-speaking background) ought to be able to use (e.g., know the structure of), to some degree at least, one other Indo-European language (e.g., French, German, Italian, Russian, Spanish), one non-Indo-European language (e.g., Arabic, Chinese, Farsi, Japanese, Quechua), and one classical language (Anglo-Saxon, Hebrew, Latin, Old Norse, Sanscrit), each most likely learned in the classroom. This kind of knowledge constitutes a resource for evaluating formal linguistic structures, linguistics research, second-language acquisition research, language-learning experience, communicative competence, and cross-cultural interaction; it provides insights into language processing in more than one language.

Because applied linguists conduct and publish the results of research, they must be able to write competently in order to present their findings to the larger academic community, as well as to groups of nonspecialists who may be making decisions about the applicability or implementability of applied research. Since so much applied-linguistics activity centers around literacy, it is important that applied linguists not only be competent writers themselves, but have an understanding of the writing process so that they can deal intelligently with issues in writing pedagogy and in the relationship between written language and the sociology of knowledge.

Because knowledge is to some extent cumulative in all scientific disciplines, applied linguists, like all other specialists, must be able to access information and to understand how information in this field is organized and stored. Such knowledge certainly implies awareness of the traditional published sources in the field (books and journals, circulating papers, conference proceedings, etc.), but it also implicates the ability to understand electronic information storage and retrieval. In sum, applied linguists must understand how knowledge accumulates and is passed along, how to access on-line data bases, and how to use existing information in their own research (Fuller 1984; Grabe and Kaplan 1986; Kaplan and Grabe in press; Swales 1987).

These skills—the knowledge of other languages, the ability to manipulate the written word with reasonable skillfulness, and the ability to access information in a variety of modalities—are basic requisites of the applied linguist and are prerequisite to any academic program of training.

Since the mid-1970s, the need for quantitative literacy has been apparent in virtually any area of linguistic or applied-linguistics research. Basic mathematical skills are the foundation for understanding numerical data and for presenting it in an understandable way. Language testing, for example, requires such skills even in the most basic conceptualization of teacher training. Teacher trainees must be able to understand the notions of normal distribution, of normed scoring (e.g., as in SAT, GRE, GMAT, TOEFL, etc., or as in intelligence testing). Teacher trainees need to understand percentages and percentiles, as well as various scoring procedures employed in the development of achievement tests.

Additionally, quantitative skills permit the interpretation and organization of descriptive statistical information. Included here are such notions as means, standard deviations, and Z-scores, all central to the understanding and communication of research results. Such fundamental descriptive concepts underlie much work in applied linguistics.

Perhaps most important for applied linguists, however, is some knowledge of inferential statistics. Research results reported in the literature or presented in conference papers now regularly assume a good command of such statistical procedures as T-tests, Chi-Square analyses, basic correlational procedures, ANOVAs, and other similar procedures. Obviously, it remains possible to read the introductions and conclusion of research articles containing such information, but such a strategy requires a willingness to accept uncritically the procedures used and the interpretation of the given data. Given the large quantity of research information available and the fact that findings are often contradictory, it is simply not sufficient to read only the framing parts of technical articles and to ignore questions of research design, statistical methodology, and interpretation of numerical results. It is, further, highly desirable, that students in this area become familiar with the more advanced multivariate concepts such as multiple regression analysis, factor analysis, multidimensional scaling, MANOVA, cannonical correlation, cluster analysis, and discriminant analysis. These procedures appear with increasing frequency in the literature as the means of analyzing complex data sets and research questions.

These skills—basic mathematics, descriptive statistics, and, ideally, multivariate statistics—are central to research and scholarship in applied linguistics, and, like the language skills described above, are both requisite to work in the field and, for the most part, prerequisite to advanced graduate study.

Basic computer literacy has become so widespread among U.S. college students that it is more likely to be assumed even than language literacy skills. Whereas the ability to type with reasonable proficiency was once adequate to graduate study, it is clear that students at present must be possessed of word-processing ability at a relatively high level. However, students from the developing world are not likely to have had the advantage of long-term exposure to computers and to such now-basic abilities as word processing, and the matter may have to be given some attention in the first year of graduate study in this country. Students need, most obviously, word-processing skills in order to become more productive graduate students; it is assumed that this skill will carry over into the professional activities of the applied linguist. This requirement will, however, not be assumed among applied linguists in developing countries and should be addressed as part of a student's training. The cost of having access to a computer may be an impediment in certain contexts, but this skill is, nevertheless, a form of literacy needed by all professional applied linguists.

More specific computer skills applicable to applied linguists include the use of computers to input data and to undertake statistical procedures involving convenient statistical packages (e.g., SAS, SPSS, Systat, etc.). The ready availability of microcomputer programs, along with the rapidly increasing power of the packages available for microcomputer use, allow students to undertake, on their own, procedures that once were available only through mainframe applications. The ability to establish data bases involves not only the mechanical entry of numerical data but also the decisions necessary to the organization of data for subsequent analysis. Such considerations apply not only to numerical data, but to textual data bases as well. Since there are no universally accepted input procedures for text, it seems especially important that students understand both the technical procedures and the intellectual decisions involved.

The issues of creating textual data bases raises the issue of the growing concern with research on language corpora, involving not only statistical manipulation but the use of programs capable of counting various discourse functions (cf. Biber 1985, 1988; Garside et al. 1987; Leech and Candlin 1986; Sinclair 1987). Similarly, in certain kinds of applied research, the use of census data becomes significant, and such data requires the ability to select and isolate relevant information from large data samples so that the information may be used in applied research. The use of sociolinguistic surveys has also increased, and it is helpful for students to know how to design questionnaires so that the data collected through them can be easily entered into a computer, and that once entered, various statistical procedures can be performed to interpret them. Such techniques as those employing semantic differential measures provide useful questionnaire approaches.

Most usefully, computer literacy includes facility with programming languages. In some instances, applied research simply requires the ability to create programs. Not only in discourse analysis, but also in computer-assisted language learning (CALL), research often requires the ability to program. In the last decade, more powerful programming languages (e.g., LISP, PROLOG, SNOBOL, TURBO-PASCAL, etc.) have become available. These languages are not easy to master, but in the area of CALL, at least, authoring systems and authoring languages have also become available. Authoring languages work much the same way that statistical packages work; that is, an authoring language offers the user a wide variety of programming options with which to create language-teaching materials without the necessity of having to learn a complex programming language. Authoring languages simplify the process by providing a user-friendly editing program. Authoring systems are the simplest option of all; they provide programs for creating language lessons with options for adjusting the basic teaching program to individual lesson content inserted by the user (Ahmad et al. 1985; Jones and Fortesque 1987).

These skills—word processing, the application of statistical packages, entering of numerical and textual data into computers, and the ability to program and/or use authoring systems and languages—are also essential training areas. Unlike the previous two literacy-skill areas, however, it cannot be assumed that these can be made prerequisite to graduate study; certainly, it is likely that programming languages and the application of statistical procedures to language information are skills that will have to be taught, or at least made available and encouraged, as part of graduate training programs.

7. THE INTERACTION OF KNOWLEDGE DOMAINS

In reviewing the sorts of knowledge needed by applied linguists to become productive professionals, a number of things become readily apparent. First, no applied linguist can come to know all the sorts of information that is discussed here to the depth of knowledge that is required for specialists in a number of these fields. Second, it is equally clear that an applied linguist who is not aware of the range of fields and domains of knowledge which may come into play in the course of applied-linguistics research is limited in perspective and is less likely to be an effective trainer of future applied linguists. Further, a more narrowly defined applied linguist, say a researcher in second-language acquisition who feels no need to be open to the broader array of applied-linguistics issues, will invariably lack the ability to translate his/her research into the uses and applications demanded of applied linguistics generally. Third, the range of knowledge domains presented in relation to applied linguistics drives home the notion that applied linguistics is truly interdisciplinary in one respect, while still very much a linguistic enterprise in another respect.

Bearing all this in mind, one must come to grips with the process of training new applied linguists in such a way that they recognize the breadth of the discipline while also receiving foundational in-depth training so that they may use the language-based skills and resources productively in research. It would seem, then, that an applied linguist must be trained in a core of knowledge, which would vary somewhat from training center to training center. This core knowledge must be grounded in linguistics (general, socio-, psycho-) and include the ability to employ a number of literacies and skills (linguistic, mathematical, and computer). The student of applied linguistics must also carve out one or more areas of specialization; such specializations may be within linguistics (such as second-language acquisition, literacy, etc.) or in related disciplines (such as cognitive psychology, education, rhetoric, anthropology, etc.). However these knowledge domains are configured in the training of the applied linguist, these sorts of knowledge will still be applied to a finite set of applied-linguistics topics. This perspective on training can be illustrated in figure 1.

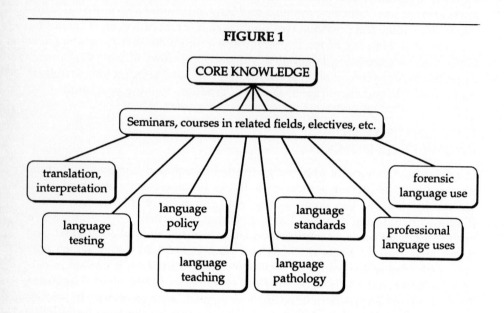

FIGURE 1

From figure 1, the inference may be drawn that applied linguistics is divisible into eight subdisciplines. We are not recommending a set of eight courses that an applied-linguistics program ought to include; indeed, these knowledge domains may be configured in a number of different ways, depending upon existing curricular structure and faculty talent. In fact, we have used the eight sub-areas as illustrative only. It may well be that there are other useful sub-areas of applied linguistics; it is also entirely likely that a discipline such as applied linguistics will necessarily redefine itself and its subdomains differently in the future as new language-based problems and contexts for language use arise. The essential point of figure 1 is that training in applied linguistics will move from a core of knowledge to specialized areas of training. These specializations will then allow the applied linguist to pursue productive research in specific areas of applied-linguistics concerns. Another way to visualize this training would be to view it as a pyramid (see figure 2), with the foundational knowledge being broad; upon that broad base would be built related sets of knowledge from areas of linguistics or from other disciplines; these sets of knowledge provide the specific research tools that would then allow one to specialize in an area of applied linguistics.

FIGURE 2

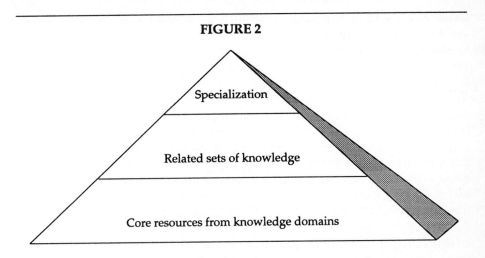

8. CONCLUSION

In one respect, these illustrations offer an appropriate point at which to conclude this discussion of how to become an applied linguist. In other respects, these illustrations are only the beginning point for a number of specific issues in the preparation of applied linguists that do not depend primarily on the academic training itself. These would include the need for field training of some sort. For example, applied linguists who specialize in language-teaching concerns must have direct experience as language teachers, whether the context be in national or public elementary or secondary institutions, or in university settings, or in private institutions of various types.

A second requirement would be practical experience living in another culture and functioning in another language. Such experiences create perspectives on language problems, language training, and language uses that cannot be provided by university training. Furthermore, these experiences provide invaluable cross-cultural training and shape language attitudes in ways that cannot otherwise occur.

A third concern, and one most important to this discussion, indeed the entire book, is the issue of applied linguistics as an English-based discipline. Much of the literature and research in applied linguistics, particularly in the educational issues, has historically been presented in the perspective of English as a second language. Other research areas of applied linguistics in the literature are also primarily documented in English. There has developed a sense of the discipline such that it is widely thought that to be an applied linguist one must be an English speaker. The response to this belief is not a simple one, and there is, in fact, some truth to the notion that applied linguistics is an English-based discipline, though it by no means must necessarily be the case.

Because applied linguistics is a very young discipline (cf. Strevens in this volume) beginning with only the second half of the twentieth century, and because applied linguistics originated almost simultaneously in Britain and the United States, its spread to other areas of the globe has been slow. Since the Association Internationale de Linguistique Appliquée (AILA) originated in Western Europe, there has been a good representation of applied-linguistics interests in the academies of the West European nations, but the spread of the discipline into the rest of the world, especially the Third World, has been slow because the discipline has not quickly become indigenized (e.g., there are few major training centers outside the United States and Britain); because the identification of the discipline with English has created around it an aura of cultural imperialism; and because the economic situations of Third-World countries has not permitted centers to develop or research to be undertaken there. Applied linguistics has suffered from the classic problem of paternalism: organizations like UNESCO, the World Bank, and the Ford Foundation have supported applied-linguistics work in the Third World, but they have sent British and American scholars to do it. Those itinerant scholars were unable to implant the discipline into local educational structures, nor were they able to provide adequate direct training because their missions were always directed at practical (often short-term) solutions.

When one examines the research publications in applied linguistics, it becomes apparent that a well-informed applied linguist needs access to information published in English. This fact should not be surprising, as it is only indicative of a wider trend in the natural and social sciences, in which a large part of the important research is written and published in English (Baldauf and Jernudd 1983; Grabe 1988; Grabe and Kaplan 1986; Kaplan 1987). At the same time, the trends of research on second-language acquisition indicate an increase in research comparing two European languages or one European language and a guest-worker language, such as Turkish. Not only is the research not done in English, but more of this work is being published in languages other than English. There is no particular reason why applied-linguistics research cannot be carried out in any language. In many cases, the lack of research is not due to the 'language' of the language problem, but rather to the lack of applied linguists who are trained to do research and function in these language milieus. There are, obviously, major centers of research around the world; e.g., the Regional English Language Centre (RELC) in Singapore, the Institute of Indian Languages in Mysore, Bourguiba Institute in Tunisia, etc.

It is nevertheless fair to say that if an applied linguist wants his/her ideas to become known, the language of publication must, at some point, be English. This is not to assert the dominance of English as the language of applied linguistics, but to recognize that applied linguistics is only one of many academic disciplines in which ideas are most usefully disseminated in English. This, however, should not be a rationale for ignoring the language-based problems that occur in languages other than English (or other European languages), and pursuing potential solutions with all the resources that a well-trained applied linguist can marshall.

There are further issues that could be addressed, though the three above would appear to be the most significant. In each case, the resolution of these issues lies, at least in part, in adequate training of the applied linguist as a foundation for further exploration. And it has been the goal of this chapter to specify those knowledge domains that must be considered in the training of future applied linguists. The many domains and subdomains of knowledge considered in this chapter clearly extend beyond the range of individual applied linguists in the sense that no applied linguist can be expected to have specialist knowledge in all domains. At the same time, we would assert, a practicing applied linguist should have been exposed at least to a passing acquaintance with the full range of knowledge areas and skills discussed here.

While a discussion of the issue of the applied linguist's training has been a goal of the chapter, a larger goal may also have been achieved. In the course of defining the sorts of knowledge pertinent to that training, we have indirectly contributed to a definition of applied linguistics; we have specified the sorts of knowledge upon which applied linguistics depends, the sorts of knowledge from related fields that contribute to a definition of applied linguistics, and the sorts of skills applied linguists use to address language-based problems and concerns. In applied linguistics, as in all disciplines, the definition of the knowledge requisite for aspiring practitioners must overlap substantially with the definition of the knowledge that proscribes the discipline. As the latter changes, the former must change. When the elements in the equation stop changing, a paradigm change becomes essential. We believe that the discussion of training needs for future applied linguists leads to a useful dialogue on the nature of applied linguistics more generally, and we hope that this chapter will stimulate much further discussion.

SUGGESTIONS FOR FURTHER READING

There is, in fact, not very much written on the training of applied linguists; it is most often assumed that programs in applied linguistics at various universities have already addressed this issue in their curriculum. However, considering the great diversity of programs and the lack of public discussion, it may well be more the case that tradition, habit, and hiring practices dictate any given applied-linguistics curriculum. Discussion of this issue does arise in Kaplan (1980b) and in Tomic and Shuy (1987). The assumptions of an applied-linguistics curriculum is also outlined in Stern (1983). It is, of course, our feeling that the chapters in the present volume also suggest the range of training that should be undertaken in the training of applied linguists.

QUESTIONS FOR FURTHER DISCUSSION

1. The chapter by Strevens and that by Kaplan and Grabe try to define the history and scope of applied linguistics. How do their views correlate with the curricular perspective proposed here?

2. To what extent does the proposed curriculum address the needs articulated in the chapters by Judd and Macias?

3. To what extent is the view of second-language acquisition articulated by McLaughlin and Zembledge accommodated in the proposed curricular perspective?

4. To what extent is language testing (as discussed by Davies) and language teaching (as discussed by Morley and Savignon) represented in the proposed curricular perspective?

5. Are there alternative ways (to that presented in this chapter) to prepare people for careers in applied linguistics? Which aspects of the above plan may be more important, and which may be less important?

6. How extensive should the natural-language skill of an applied linguist be; that is, how many languages, from what language families, and to what level of proficiency should s/he know? How will the desired level of proficiency be certified?

7. Grabe and Kaplan present two figures to show the interrelationship of various kinds of skills and knowledge they believe to be appropriate to the education of applied linguists. How realistic are these representations? Can any normal human being achieve the implied objectives within a reasonable time?

8. Grabe and Kaplan touch on the question of language of publication, and Kaplan has quite a lot to say about it in his chapter on language policy. Is the issue a straightforward one? Is there an issue of cultural imperialism involved in this question? Is it possible for applied linguists to have a linguistically broad publications activity (e.g., publish in five languages)?

9. Grabe and Kaplan argue that applied linguistics covers a broad range of fields such as second-language acquisition, discourse analysis, speech therapy, language testing, etc. (See also Kaplan and Grabe, and Strevens, in this volume). Do you agree with this assessment? Are there other valid interpretations in which applied linguistics assumes a much narrower scope?

Bibliography

Aarts, J. and W. Meijs (eds.). 1984. *Corpus linguistics: Recent development in the use of computer corpora in English language research.* Amsterdam: Rodopi.

Aarts, J. and W. Meijs (eds.). 1986. *Corpus linguistics II.* Amsterdam: Rodopi.

ACTFL. 1986. *ACTFL proficiency guidelines.* Hastings-on-Hudson, NY: Arthor.

Ahmad, K. et al. 1985. *Computers, language learning and language teaching.* New York: Cambridge University Press.

Aijmer, K. 1986a. "Discourse variation and hedging." In J. Aarts and W. Meijs *Corpus linguistics II.* Amsterdam: Rodopi. 1–18.

Aijmer, K. 1986b. "Why is *actually* so popular in spoken English?" In G. Tottie and I. Backlund (eds.), *English in speech and writing: A symposium.* Studia Anglistica Upsaliensia 60. Stockholm: Almqvist and Wiksell. 119–130.

Aijmer, K. 1987. "*Oh* and *ah* in English conversation." In W. Meijs (ed.), *Corpus linguistics and beyond.* Amsterdam: Rodopi. 61–86.

Akmajian, A., D. Demers, and M. Harnish. 1984. *Linguistics.* 2d. ed. Cambridge, MA: MIT Press.

Alderson, C. 1982. Introduction. In C. Alderson and A. Hughes (eds.), *Issues in language testing.* ELT Documents No. 111. London: Pergamon Press. 5–8.

Alderson, C. (ed.). 1985. *Lancaster practical papers in English language education.* Vol. 6: *Evaluation.* London: Pergamon Press.

Alderson, C. and A. Hughes (eds.). 1982. *Issues in language testing.* ELT Documents, no. 111. London: Pergamon Press.

Alderson, C., K. Krahnke, C. Stansfield (eds.). 1987. *Reviews of English language proficiency tests.* Washington, DC: TESOL Publications.

Allen, J.P.B. and S. P. Corder (eds.). 1973–1977. *The Edinburgh course in applied linguistics.* Vol. I, *Readings for applied linguistics,* 1973; Vol. II, *Papers in applied linguistics,* 1975; Vol. III, *Techniques in applied linguistics,* 1974; Vol. IV, *Testing and experimental methods* (J.P.B. Allen and A. Davies, eds.), 1977. Oxford: Oxford University Press.

Allwright, R. 1979. "Language learning through communicative practice." In C. Brumfit and K. Johnson. (eds.), *The communicative approach to language teaching.* Oxford: Oxford University Press. 166–82.

Allwright, R. 1988. *Observation in the language classroom.* New York: Longman.

Allwright, R. and K. Bailey. 1989. *Focus on the learner: An introduction to classroom research for teachers.* New York: Cambridge University Press.

A-LM (Audio-lingual materials). 1961. *French: Level one.* New York: Harcourt Brace and World.

American Psychiatric Association. 1980. *Diagnostic and statistical manual of mental disorders.* 3d ed. Washington, DC: American Psychiatric Association.

Andersen, R. 1978. An implicational model for second language research. *Language Learning* 28.2.221–82.

Andersen, R., ed. 1984. *Second languages: A cross linguistic perspective.* Rowley, MA: Newbury House.

Anderson, H. and N. Rhodes. 1984. "Immersion and other innovations in U.S. elementary schools." In S. Savignon and M. Berns (eds.), *Initiatives in communicative language teaching.* Reading, MA: Addison-Wesley. 167–81.

Anderson, J. 1977. *On case grammar.* London: Croom Helm.

Anderson, S. 1985. *Phonology in the twentieth century.* Chicago, IL: University of Chicago Press.

Anderson, S. 1988. "Morphological theory." In F. Newmeyer (ed.), *Linguistics: The Cambridge survey,* Vol. 1. New York: Cambridge University Press. 146–91.

Andersson, T. 1971. Bilingual education: The American experience. [ED 048581].

Andrews, A. 1988. "Lexical structure." In F. Newmeyer (ed.), *Linguistics: The Cambridge survey,* Vol. 2. New York: Cambridge University Press. 60–88.

Angelis, P. 1987. Applied linguistics: Realities and projections. Paper presented at the 1987 Annual Conference of the American Association for Applied Linguistics, San Francisco, December 1987.

Appel, R. and P. Muyskens. 1987. *Language contact and bilingualism.* London: Edward Arnold.

Appleton, N. 1978. *Multilingualism and the courts.* Los Angeles, CA: Evaluation, Dissemination and Assessment Center, California State University, Los Angeles.

Applewhite, S. 1979. "The legal dialect of bilingual education." In R. Padilla (ed.), *Bilingual education and public policy in the United States.* Ypsilanti, MI: Eastern Michigan University. 3–17.

Ard, J. and J. M. Swales. 1986. English for international teaching assistants: What ESL institutes can offer. *TESOL Newsletter* 20.21–22.

Arnove, R. and H. Graff (eds.). 1987. *National literacy campaigns.* New York: Plenum Press.

Arvisu, S., W. Snyder, and P. Espinoza. 1980. *Demystifying the concept of culture: Theoretical and conceptual tools.* Los Angeles, CA: Evaluation, Dissemination and Assessment Center, California State University, Los Angeles.

Ashworth, M. 1985. *Beyond methodology: Second-language teaching and the community.* New York: Cambridge University Press.

Aspira v. NYC Board of Education (1974). Civ. No. 4002.

Atkinson, J. and P. Drew. 1979. *Order in court.* Atlantic Highlands, NJ: Humanities Press.

Austin, J. L. 1962. *How to do things with words*. Cambridge, MA: Harvard University Press.

Bachman, L. 1988. An investigation into the construct validity and comparability of two tests of English as a foreign language: The Cambridge-TOEFL comparability study. (Report on the pilot phase). Urbana, IL: University of Illinois. Mimeo.

Bachman, L. 1989. "Language testing—SLA research interfaces." In R.B. Kaplan et al. (eds.), *Annual review of applied linguistics (1988)*, Vol. 9. New York; Cambridge University Press. 193–209.

Bachman, L. 1990a. "Assessment and evaluation." In R.B. Kaplan et al. (eds.), *Annual review of applied linguistics (1989)*, Vol. 10. New York: Cambridge University Press. 210–26.

Bachman, L. 1990b. *Fundamental considerations in language testing*. Oxford: Oxford University Press.

Bailey, K., F. Pialorsi and J. Zukowski/Faust (eds.). 1984. *Foreign teaching assistants in U.S. universities*. Washington, DC: NAFSA.

Bailey, N., C. Madden, and S. Krashen. 1974. Is there a "natural sequence" in adult second language learning. *Language Learning* 24.2.235–43.

Baker, K. and A. de Kantor (eds.). 1983. *Bilingual education: A reappraisal of federal policy*. Lexington, MA: Heath.

Baker, C. 1988. Normative testing and bilingual populations. *Journal of Multilingual and Multicultural Development* 9.5.399–409.

Baker, C.L. 1989. *English syntax*. Cambridge, MA: MIT Press.

Baker, M. 1988. *Incorporation*. Chicago, IL: University of Chicago Press.

Balajthy, E. 1987. "Implications of artificial intelligence research for human-computer interaction in reading instruction." In D. Reinking (ed.), *Reading and computers*. New York: Teachers College Press. 40–54.

Balajthy, E. 1988. "Computer-based feedback for editing in the early grades." In J. Hoot and S. Silvern (eds.), *Writing with computers in the early grades*. New York: Teacher's College Press. 160–80.

Baldauf, R. 1989. "Language planning and education." In R. Baldauf and A. Luke (eds.), *Language planning and education in Australasia and the South Pacific*. Clevedon, Avon: Multilingual Matters. 14–24.

Baldauf, R. and B. Jernudd. 1983. Language of publication as a variable in scientific communication. *Australian Review of Applied Linguistics* 6.1.97–108.

Baldauf, R. and A. Luke (eds.). 1989. *Language planning and education in Australasia and the South Pacific*. Clevedon, Avon: Multilingual Matters.

Baltaxe, C. and J. Simmons. 1975. Language in childhood psychosis: A review. *Journal of Speech and Hearing Disorders* 40.439–58.

Barber, C. 1962. "Some measurable characteristics of modern scientific prose." Reprinted in J. Swales (ed.), *Episodes in ESP*, 1985, New York: Pergamon Press. 3–14.

Bar-Hillel, Y. 1960. "The present status of automatic translation of languages." In F.L. Alt (ed.), *Advances in computers*, Vol. 1. New York: Academic Press. 63–91.

Barnwell, D. 1989. Proficiency and the native speaker. *ADFL Bulletin*. 42–46.

Barr, A. and E. Feigenbaum (eds.). 1981. *The handbook of artificial intelligence.* Los Altos, CA: William Kaufmann.

Barwise, J. and J. Perry. 1983. *Situations and attitudes.* Cambridge, MA: MIT Press.

Basbøll, H. 1988. "Phonological theory." In F. Newmeyer (ed.), *Linguistics: The Cambridge survey,* Vol. 1. New York: Cambridge University Press. 192–215.

Bateson, G. 1972. *Steps to an ecology of mind.* New York: Ballantine Books.

Bazerman, C. 1988. *Shaping written knowledge.* Madison, WI: University of Wisconsin Press.

BBC. 1975. *Follow me.* London: British Broadcasting Company.

Beach, W. 1985. Temporal density in courtroom interaction: Constraints on the recovery of past events in legal discourse. *Communication Monographs* 52.1–18.

Beckman, M. 1988. "Phonetic theory." In F. Newmeyer (ed.), *Linguistics: The Cambridge survey,* Vol. 1. New York: Cambridge University Press. 216–38.

Beebe, L. (ed.). 1988. *Issues in second language acquisition.* New York: Newbury House.

Beer, W. and J. Jacobs (eds.). 1985. *Language policy and national unity.* Totowa, NJ: Crane Publishing.

Bennett, W. and M. Feldman, 1981. *Reconstructing reality in the courtroom.* Rutgers, NJ: Rutgers University Press.

Bennett-Kastor, T. 1988. *Analysing children's language.* New York: Basil Blackwell.

Benson, J. and W. Greaves (eds.). 1985a. *Systemic perspectives on discourse.* Vol. 1. *Selected theoretical papers from the 9th international systemic workshop.* Norwood, NJ: Ablex.

Benson, J. and W. Greaves (eds.). 1985b. *Systemic perspectives on discourse.* Vol. 2. *Selected applied papers from the 9th international systemic workshop.* Norwood, NJ: Ablex.

Bereiter, C. and M. Scardamalia. 1987. *The psychology of written composition.* Hillsdale, NJ: Lawrence Erlbaun Associates.

Beretta, A. 1987a. Language program evaluation. Ph.D. diss., University of Edinburgh.

Beretta, A. 1987b. "The Bangalore project: Description and evaluation." In S. Savignon and M. Berns (eds.), *Initiatives in communicative language teaching II.* Reading, MA: Addison-Wesley. 83–106.

Beretta, A. 1989. Attention to form or meaning? Error treatment in the Bangalore project. *TESOL Quarterly* 23.2.283–303.

Bernhardt, E. 1988. Research needs in teacher education. Paper presented at the 22d Annual TESOL Convention, Chicago, IL, March 1988.

Berns, M. 1990a. "'Second' and 'foreign' in second language acquisition/foreign language learning: A sociolinguistic perspective." In B. VanPatten and J. Lee (eds.), *Second language acquisition/foreign language learning.* Clevedon, Avon: Multilingual Matters. 3–11.

Berns, M. 1990b. *Functional approaches and communicative competence: English language teaching in non-native contexts.* New York: Plenum.

Bernstein, B. 1972a. "Social class, language and socialization." In P.P. Giglioli (ed.), *Language in social context.* Baltimore, MD: Penguin. 157–78.

Bernstein, B. 1972b. "A critique of the concept 'Understanding education.'" In C.B. Cazden, V. John, and D. Hymes (eds),. *Functions of language in the classroom*. New York: Teachers College Press. 135–51.

Berry, M. 1975. *An introduction to systemic linguistics*. New York: St. Martin's Press.

Besnier, N. 1988. The linguistic relationships of spoken and written Nukulaelae registers. *Language* 64.707–36.

Betchell, T. 1979. Against bilingual education. *Harper's* 258.1545.30–33.

Biber, D. 1985. Investigating macroscopic textual variation through multi-feature/multi-dimensional analyses. *Linguistics* 23.337–60.

Biber, D. 1986. Spoken and written textual dimensions in English: Resolving the contradictory findings. *Language* 62.384–414.

Biber, D. 1987. A textual comparison of British and American writing. *American Speech* 62.99–119.

Biber, D. 1988. *Variation across speech and writing*. Cambridge, UK: Cambridge University Press.

Biber, D. 1989. A typology of English texts. *Linguistics* 27.3–43.

Biber, D. and E. Finegan. 1989a. Styles of stance in English: Lexical and grammatical marking of evidentiality and affect. *Text* 9.93–124.

Biber, D. and E. Finegan. 1989b. Drift and the evolution of English style: A history of three genres. *Language* 65.487–517.

Biber, D. and M. Hared. 1989. A corpus-based approach to genre variation in Somali. Paper presented at the Fourth International Congress of Somali Studies, Mogadishu, Somalia, July 1989.

Bickes, G. and A. Scott. 1989. On the computer as a medium of language teaching. *CALICO Journal* 6.3.21–32.

Billig, M. et al. 1988. *Ideological dilemmas: A social psychology of everyday thinking*. Newbury Park, CA: Sage Publications.

Biouer, J. D. 1989. "Language program evaluation: A synthesis of exercising possibilities." In R.K. Johnson (ed.), *The second language curriculum*. New York: Cambridge University Press. 222–41.

Birch, D. 1985. The stylistic analysis of large corpora of literary text. *Association for Literary and Linguistic Computing Journal* 6.33–38.

Blair, R. (ed.). 1982. *Innovative approaches to language teaching*. Rowley, MA: Newbury House.

Blanchard, J., G. Mason, and D. Daniel. 1987. *Computer applications in reading*. 3d ed. Newark, DE: International Reading Association.

Blanco, G. 1978. "The implementation of bilingual/bicultural education programs in the United States." In B. Spolsky and R. Cooper (eds.), *Case studies in bilingual education*. Rowley, MA: Newbury House. 454–99.

Bley-Vroman, R. 1988. "The fundamental character of foreign language learning." In W. Rutherford and M. Sharwood Smith (eds.), *Grammar and second language teaching*. New York: Newbury House. 19–30.

Bley-Vroman, R. and C. Chaudron. 1988. Review essay: A critique of Flynn's parameter-setting model of second language acquisition. *University of Hawaii Working Papers in ESL* 7.67–107.

Blueler, E. 1950. *Dementia Praecox or the group of schizophrenias*. Trans. by J. Zinkin. New York: International Universities Press.

Bloom, A. 1987. *The closing of the American mind*. New York: Simon and Schuster.

Bloome, D. (ed.). 1987. *Literacy and schooling*. Norwood, NJ: Ablex.

Bloome, D. (ed.). 1989. *Classrooms and literacy*. Norwood, NJ: Ablex.

Bloomfield, L. 1933. *Language*. New York: Holt, Rinehart and Winston.

Boggs, S. 1985. *Speaking, relating and learning: A study of Hawaiian children at home and at school*. Norwood, NJ: Ablex.

Bolinger, D. 1968. The theorist and the language teacher. *Foreign Language Annals* 2.30–41.

Bonnano, M. 1982. "Women's language in the medical interview." In R. Di Pietro (ed.), *Linguistics and the professions*. Norwood, NJ: Ablex. 27–38.

Bowen, D., H. Madsen, and A. Hilferty. 1985. *TESOL: Techniques and procedures*. Rowley, MA: Newbury House.

Breen, M. 1987. Contemporary paradigms in syllabus design. 2 parts. *Language Teaching* 20.2.81–92, 20.3.157–74.

Breen, M. and C. Candlin. 1980. The essentials of a communicative curriculum in language teaching. *Applied Linguistics* 1.89–112.

Briggs, C. L. 1986. *Learning to ask. A sociolinguistic appraisal of the role of the interview in social science research*. Cambridge, UK: Cambridge University Press.

Bright, B. (ed.). Forthcoming. *Oxford international encyclopedia of linguistics*. New York: Oxford University Press.

Brindley, G. 1986. *The assessment of second language proficiency: Issues and approaches*. Adelaide: National Curriculum Resource Centre, Adult Migrant Education Program.

Brinton, D., M. Snow, and M. Wesche. 1989. *Content-based second language instruction*. New York: Newbury House.

Brisk, M. 1981. Language policies in American education. *Journal of Communication* 163.1.3–15.

Britton, B. and J. Black (eds.). 1985. *Understanding expository text*. Hillsdale, NJ: Lawrence Erlbaum Associates.

Brooks, N. 1960. *Language and language learning: Theory and practice*. New York: Harcourt, Brace and World.

Brown, G. and G. Yule. 1983. *Discourse analysis*. New York: Cambridge University Press.

Brown, H.D. 1973. Affective variables in second language acquisition. *Language Learning* 23.231–44.

Brown, H.D. 1976. "What is applied linguistics?" In R. Wardhaugh and H.D. Brown (eds.), *A survey of applied linguistics*. Ann Arbor: University of Michigan Press. 1–7.

Brown, H.D. 1987. *Principles of language learning and teaching.* 2d. ed. Englewood Cliffs, NJ: Prentice-Hall, Inc.

Brown, H.D., M. Ehrman, and K. Davis. 1988. Myers-Briggs personality types and second language learning strategies. Paper presented at the 22d Annual TESOL Convention, Chicago, IL, March 1988.

Brown, R. 1973. *A first language: The early stages.* Cambridge, MA: Harvard University Press.

Brown, R. and A. Gilman. 1972. "The pronouns of power and solidarity." In J. Fishman (ed.), *Readings in the sociology of language.* The Hague: Mouton Publishers. 252–75.

Browne, S. 1988. High technology for language programs. *Lablife.* Warren, MI: General Motors Research Laboratories 12.1–2.

Bruffee, K. 1986. Social construction, language, and the authority of knowledge: A bibliographic essay. *College English* 48.8.773–90.

Brumfit, C. 1980. From defining to designing: Communicative specifications versus communicative methodology in foreign language teaching. *Studies in Second Language Acquisition* 3.1–9.

Brumfit, C. (ed.). 1983. *Language teaching projects for the third world.* ELT Documents No. 116. London: Pergamon Press.

Brumfit, C. 1984. *Communicative methodology in language teaching.* Cambridge, UK: Cambridge University Press.

Brumfit, C. and K. Johnson (eds.). 1979. *The communicative approach to language teaching.* Oxford: Oxford University Press.

Bursten, J. 1989. Toward better tutorial CALL: A matter of intelligent control. *CALICO* 6.4.75–89.

Burt, M., H. Dulay, and E. Hernandez-Chavez. 1975. *Bilingual syntax measure.* New York: Harcourt Brace Jovanovich.

Burton, D.M. 1973. *Shakespeare's grammatical style.* Austin, TX: University of Texas Press.

Bush, M. and J. Crotty. 1989. "Interactive videodisc in language teaching." In W. Flint (ed.), *Modern technology in foreign language education: Applications and projects.* Lincolnwood, IL: National Textbook Company. 75–95.

Butler, C. 1985a. *Computers in linguistics.* Oxford: Blackwell.

Butler, C. 1985b. *Statistics in linguistics.* Oxford: Blackwell.

Butler, C. 1985c. *Systemic linguistics: Theory and application.* London: Batsford.

Butler, C. 1989. Systemic models: Unity, diversity and change. *Word* 40.1/2.1–35.

Byrd, P., J. Constantinides, and M. Pennington. 1989. *The foreign teaching assistant's manual.* New York: Collier Macmillan.

California Department of Education. 1986. *Beyond language: Social and cultural factors in schooling language minority students.* Los Angeles, CA: Evaluation, Dissemination and Assessment Center, California State University, Los Angeles.

Campbell, R. 1978. "Notional functional syllabuses: 1978. Part 1." In C. Blatchford and J. Schachter (eds.), *ON TESOL 1978.* Washington, DC: TESOL Publications. 15–19.

Canale, M. 1983. "From communicative competence to communicative language teaching." In J. Richards and R. Schmidt (eds.), *Language and communication*. London: Longman. 2–27.

Canale, M. 1988. "The measurement of communicative competence." In R.B. Kaplan et al. (eds.), *Annual review of applied linguistics (1988)*, Vol. 9. New York: Cambridge University Press. 67–84.

Canale, M. and M. Swain. 1980. Theoretical bases of communicative approaches to second language teaching and testing. *Applied Linguistics* 1.1–47.

Candlin, C., C. Burton, and J. Leather. 1976. Doctors in casualty: Specialist course design from a database. *International Review of Applied Linguistics* 14.245–72.

Cantoni, G. 1987. *Content-area language instruction: Approaches and strategies*. Reading, MA: Addison-Wesley.

Caplan, D. 1987. *Neurolinguistics and linguistic aphasiology: An introduction*. New York: Cambridge University Press.

Carlen, P. 1976. *Magistrates' justice*. London: Martin Robinson.

Carlson, G. and M. Tannenhaus (eds.). 1988. *Linguistic structure in language processing*. Boston, MA: Kluwer.

Carrell, P. 1984. The effects of rhetorical organization on ESL readers. *TESOL Quarterly* 18.3.441–69.

Carrell, P. 1989. "Second language acquisition and classroom instruction: Reading." In R.B. Kaplan et al. (eds.), *Annual review of applied linguistics (1988)*, Vol. 9. New York: Cambridge University Press. 223–42.

Carrol, B. 1980. *Testing communicative performance*. Oxford: Pergamon Press.

Carroll, J. 1956. Introduction. In B. Whorf, *Language, thought, and reality: Selected writings of Benjamin Lee Whorf*. Cambridge, MA: MIT Press. 1–34.

Carroll, J. 1966. "The contributions of psychological theory and educational research to the teaching of foreign languages." In A. Valdman (ed.), *Trends in language teaching*. New York: McGraw-Hill. 93–106.

Carroll, J. 1981. "Twenty-five years of research on foreign language aptitude." In K. Diller (ed.), *Individual differences and universals in language learning aptitude*. Rowley, MA: Newbury House. 83–118.

Carroll, J. and S. Sapon. 1959. *Modern language aptitude test* (MLAT). New York: The Psychological Corporation.

Carter, R. 1987. *Vocabulary: Applied linguistic perspectives*. London: Allen and Unwin.

Carter, R. and M. McCarthy (eds.). 1988. *Vocabulary and language teaching*. New York: Longman.

Castro, R. 1981. *The influences of educational policy on language issues*. Forestville, CA: Creative Solutions. [ED 212172]

Cavalier, R. and J. Dexheimer. 1989. ICEC: A collaborative effort to advance education computing, 1983–1989. *Academic Computing* 4.3.16–18, 58–60.

Cazden, C. 1987. "Language in the classroom." In R.B. Kaplan et al. (eds.), *Annual review of applied linguistics (1986)*, Vol. 7. New York: Cambridge University Press. 18–33.

Cazden, C. 1988. *Classroom discourse. The language of teaching and learning*. Portsmouth, NH: Heinemann.

Cazden, C., S. Michaels, and P. Tabors. 1985. "Spontaneous repairs in sharing time narratives: The intersection of metalinguistic awareness, speech event, and narrative style." In S. Freedman (ed.), *The acquisition of written language*. Norwood, NJ: Ablex. 51–64.

Celce-Murcia, M. and D. Larsen-Freeman. 1983. *The grammar book: An ESL/EFL teacher's course*. Rowley, MA: Newbury House.

Chaudron, C. 1988. *Second language classrooms*. Cambridge, UK: Cambridge University Press.

Chafe, W. (ed.). 1980. *The pear stories*. Norwood, NJ: Ablex.

Chafe, W. 1982. "Integration and involvement in speaking, writing, and oral literature." In D. Tannen (ed.), *Spoken and written language: Exploring orality and literacy*. Norwood, NJ: Alex. 35–53.

Chafe, W. 1985. "Linguistic differences produced by differences between speaking and writing." In D. Olson, N. Torrance, and A. Hilyard (eds.), *Literacy, language and learning: The nature and consequences of reading and writing*. Cambridge, UK: Cambridge University Press. 105–23.

Chafe, W. and J. Danielowicz. 1987. Properties of spoken and written language. In R. Horowitz and S. Samuels (eds.), *Comprehending spoken and written language*. San Diego, CA: Academic Press. 83–115.

Chaika, E. 1988. *Language: The social mirror*. 2d ed. New York: Newbury House.

Chamot, A. and M. O'Malley. 1987. The cognitive academic language learning approach: A bridge to the mainstream. *TESOL Quarterly* 21.2.227–49.

Chastain, K. 1975. Affective and ability factors in second-language acquisition. *Language Learning* 25.153–61.

Chastain, K. 1976. *Developing second language skills: From theory to practice*. 2d ed. Chicago, IL: Rand McNally.

Cheng, P. 1985. Restructuring versus automaticity: Alternative accounts of skill acquisition. *Psychological Review* 9.214–23.

Chomsky, N. 1957. *Syntactic structures*. The Hague: Mouton.

Chomsky, N. 1959. Review of: B.F. Skinner, *Verbal behavior*. *Language* 35.1.26–58.

Chomsky, N. 1965. *Aspects of the theory of syntax*. Cambridge, MA: MIT Press.

Chomsky, N. 1966. "Linguistic theory." In R. Mead (ed.), *Northeast conference on the teaching of foreign languages*. Menasha, WI: George Banta. Reprinted in J. Oller and J. Richards (eds.), *Focus on the learner*, 1973. Rowley, MA: Newbury House. 29–35.

Chomsky, N. 1975. *Reflections on language*. New York: Pantheon.

Chomsky, N. 1977a. *Essays on form and interpretation*. Amsterdam: North-Holland.

Chomsky, N. 1977b. "On WH-movement." In P. Culicover, T. Wasow, and A. Akmajian (eds.), *Formal syntax*. New York: Academic Press. 71–132.

Chomsky, N. 1981. *Lectures on government and binding*. Dordrecht: Foris.

Chomsky, N. 1986. *Knowledge of language*. New York: Praeger.

Chomsky, N. 1988. *The Managua lectures*. Cambridge, MA: MIT Press.

Christie, F. 1989. *Language education*. New York: Oxford University Press.

Churchill, S. 1988. *The education of linguistic and cultural minorities in the OECD countries*. San Diego, CA: College-Hill Press.

Cicourel, A. 1981. "Language and medicine." In C. Ferguson and S.B. Heath (eds.), *Language in the USA*. New York: Cambridge University Press. 407–29.

Cicourel, A. 1982. "Language and the structure of belief in medical communication." In *AILA proceedings*. Copenhagen: Studia Linguistics. 71–85.

Clahsen, H. and P. Muyskens. 1989. The UG paradox in L2 acquisition. *Second Language Research* 5.1–29.

Clanchy, M. 1979. *From memory to written record: England 1066–1377*. Cambridge, MA: Harvard University Press.

Clark, J. 1972. *Foreign language testing: Theory and practice*. Philadelphia, PA: Center for Curriculum Development.

Clark, J. 1987. *Curriculum renewal in school foreign language learning*. Oxford: Oxford University Press.

Clarke, M. 1976. Second language acquisition as a clash of consciousness. *Language Learning* 26.2.377–90.

Clarke, M. and J. Handscombe (eds.). 1983. *On TESOL 1982: Pacific perspectives on language learning and teaching*. Washington, DC: TESOL.

Clay, M. 1975. *What did I write?* Auckland, New Zealand: Heinemann.

Cobarrubias, J. and J. Fishman (eds.). 1983. *Progress in language planning*. New York: Mouton.

Coe, R. 1986. "Teaching writing: The process approach, humanism, and the context of 'crisis.'" In S. de Castell, A. Luke, and K. Egan (eds.), *Literacy, society, and schooling: A reader*. New York: Cambridge University Press. 270–312.

Coffin, E. 1988. Using interactive video in language teaching: Lecture-demonstration. The University of Michigan.

Cole, S. 1980. *Attitudes towards bilingual education among Hispanics: A nationwide survey*. New York: Center for Social Sciences, Columbia University. [ED 235295]

Coleman, H. (ed.). 1989. *Working with language*. Berlin: Mouton.

Collier, V. 1987. Age and rate of acquisition of second language for academic purposes. *TESOL Quarterly* 21.4.617–41.

Collier, V. 1989. How long? A synthesis of research on academic achievement in a second language. *TESOL Quarterly* 23.3.509–31.

Comrie, B. 1988. "Linguistic typology." In F. Newmeyer (ed.), *Linguistics: The Cambridge survey*, Vol. 1. New York: Cambridge University Press. 447–61.

Comrie, B. 1989. *Language universals and linguistic typology*. 2d ed. Chicago, IL: University of Chicago Press.

Comrie, B. and E. Keenan. 1979. Noun phrase accessibility revisited. *Language* 55.3. 649–64.

Connor, U. and R.B. Kaplan (eds.). 1987. *Writing across languages: Analysis of L2 text.* Reading, MA: Addison-Wesley.

Cook, V. 1985. Universal grammar and second language learning. *Applied Linguistics* 6.1.2–18.

Cook, V. 1989. *Chomsky's universal grammar.* New York: Basil Blackwell.

Cook, W. 1981. *Case grammar.* Washington, DC: Georgetown University Press.

Cook-Gumperz, J. (ed.). 1986. *The social construction of literacy.* New York: Cambridge University Press.

Cooper, R. (ed.). 1982. *Language spread: Studies in diffusion and social change.* Bloomington, IN: Indiana University Press.

Cooper, R. 1989. Language planning and social change. Cambridge: Cambridge University Press.

Corder, S.P. 1967. The significance of learners' errors. *International Review of Applied Linguistics* 5.161–70.

Corder, S.P. 1971. Idiosyncratic dialects and error analysis. *International Review of Applied Linguistics* 9.147–59.

Corder, S.P. 1976. "The study of interlanguage." In G. Nickel (ed.), *Proceedings of the fourth international congress of applied linguistics.* Stuttgart: Hochschul-Verlag. 2.9–34.

Coste, D. et al. 1976. *Un niveau-seuil.* Strasbourg: Council of Europe.

Court Interpreters Act (1978). United States Federal Legislation.

Couture, B. (ed.). 1986. *Functional approaches to writing: Research perspectives.* Norwood, NJ: Ablex.

Cox, B. et al. 1990. Good and poor elementary readers' use of cohesion in writing. *Reading Research Quarterly* 25.1.47–65.

Crandall, J. (ed.). 1987. *ESL through content-area instruction.* (ERIC/CAL). Englewood Cliffs, NJ: Prentice-Hall Regents.

Crandall, J. and A. Grognet. 1983. "English for special purposes in adult ESL." In M. Clarke and J. Handscombe (eds.), *On TESOL 1982.* Washington, DC: TESOL Publications. 273–84.

Crawford, J. 1989. *Bilingual education: History, politics, theory, and practice.* Trenton, NJ: Crane Publishing.

Cressy, D. 1980. *Literacy and the social order.* Cambridge, UK: Cambridge University Press.

Criper, C. and A. Davies. 1986. *The ELTS validation study.* Unpublished report to the British Council and the University of Cambridge Local Examinations Syndicate, Edinburgh.

Cromer, W. 1970. The difference model: A new explanation for some reading difficulties. *Journal of Educational Psychology* 61.471–83.

Cromwell, R.L. and P.R. Dokecki. 1973. "Schizophrenic language: A disattention interpretation." In S. Rosenberg and J.H. Kaplan (eds.), *Developments in applied psycholinguistic research.* New York: Macmillan. 84–96.

Crookes, G. 1988. Tasks and task-based learning and teaching. Lecture-workshop presented at the University of Michigan, Ann Arbor, MI.

Crosland, A.T. 1975. The concordance and the study of the novel. *Association for Literary and Linguistic Computing Journal* 3.190–96.

Crystal, D. 1981. *Directions in applied linguistics*. London: Academic Press.

Crystal, D. 1984. *Linguistic encounters with language handicap*. New York: Basil Blackwell.

Crystal, D. 1987. *The Cambridge encyclopedia of language*. New York: Cambridge University Press.

Cummins, J. 1979. Cognitive/academic language proficiency, linguistic interdependence, the optimal age question and some other matters. *Working Papers in Bilingualism* 19.197–205.

Cummins, J. 1980. The cross-lingual dimensions of language proficiency: Implications for bilingual education and the optimal age issue. *TESOL Quarterly* 14.2.175–87.

Cummins, J. 1981. "The role of primary language development in promoting educational success for language minority students." In California Office of Bilingual Education, *Schooling and language minority students: A theoretical framework*. Los Angeles, CA: Evaluation, Dissemination, and Assessment Center, California State University, Los Angeles. 3–50.

Cummins. J. 1983. *Language and literacy learning in bilingual instruction*. Austin, TX: Southwest Educational Development Laboratory.

Cummins, J. 1984. *Bilingualism and special education: Issues in assessment and pedagogy*. Clevedon, Avon: Multilingual Matters.

Cummins, J. 1986a. Empowering minority students: A framework for intervention. *Harvard Educational Review* 56.1.18–36.

Cummins, J. 1986b. Cultures in contact: Using classroom microcomputers for cultural interchange and reinforcement. *TESL Canada Journal* 3/2.13–31.

Cummins, J. 1989. Language and literacy acquisition in bilingual contexts. *Journal of Multilingual and Multicultural Development* 10.1.17–31.

Cummins, J. and M. Swain. 1983. Analysis-by-rhetoric: Reading the text or the reader's own prejudices? A reply to Edelsky et al. *Applied Linguistics* 4.1.23–41.

Cummins, J. and M. Swain. 1986. *Bilingualism in education*. London: Longman.

Curran, C. 1972. *Counseling-learning: A whole-person model for education*. New York: Grune and Stratton.

Curran, C. 1976. *Counseling learning in second languages*. Apple River, IL: Apple River Press.

Curtain, H. 1986. Integrating language and content instruction. *ERIC/C11 News Bulletin* 9.1.10–11.

Curtain, H. and C. Pesola. 1987. *Languages and children—making the match*. Reading, MA: Addison-Wesley.

Curtiss, S. 1988. "Abnormal language acquisition and the modularity of language." In F. Newmeyer (ed.), *Linguistics: The Cambridge survey*, Vol. 2. New York: Cambridge University Press. 96–116.

Daiute, C. 1985. "Do writers talk to themselves?" In S. Freedman (ed.), *The acquisition of written language*. Norwood, NJ: Ablex. 133–59.

Danet, B. 1980. Language and the legal process. *Law and Society Review* 14.445–564.

Danet, B. (ed.). 1984. *Text* (special issue on studies in legal discourse). The Hague: Mouton.

Danoff, M. 1978. *Evaluation of the impact of ESEA Title VII Spanish/English bilingual education programs*. Palo Alto, CA: American Research Institute.

Davies, A. 1971. Language aptitude in the first year of the U.K. secondary school. *RELC Journal* 2.1.4–19.

Davies, A. 1990. *Principles of language testing*. Oxford: Basil Blackwell.

Davies, P. 1987. *The cosmic blueprint*. London: Heinemann.

Davis, H. and P. Walton (eds.). 1983. *Language, image, media*. Oxford: Basil Blackwell.

De Avila, E. 1987. "Bilingualism, cognitive function and language minority group membership." In P. Homel et al. (eds.), *Childhood bilingualism: Aspects of linguistic, cognitive and social development*. Hillsdale, NJ: Lawrence Erlbaum Associates. 149–69.

de Beaugrande, R. 1984a. *Text production*. Norwood, NJ: Ablex.

de Beaugrande, R. 1984b. "The linearity of reading: Fact, fiction or frontier." In J. Flood (ed.), *Understanding reading comprehension*. Newark, DE: International Reading Association. 45–74.

de Beaugrande, R. and W. Dressler. 1981. *Introduction to text linguistics*. New York: Longman.

de Castell, S., A. Luke, and K. Egan (eds.). 1986. *Literacy, society, and schooling: A reader*. New York: Cambridge University Press.

de Keyser, R. 1989. "Communicative processes and strategies." In R.B. Kaplan et al. (eds.), *Annual review of applied linguistics (1988)*, Vol. 9. New York: Cambridge University Press. 108–21.

de Saussure, F. 1916/1959. *Course in general linguistics*. Edited by C. Bally and A. Seehehaye, tr. W. Baskin. New York: Philosophical Library.

Diamond, S. 1980. *Historical aspects of bilingualism in the United States*. New York: Center for the Social Sciences, Columbia University. [ED 235293]

Diaz, S., L. Moll, and H. Mehan. 1986. "Sociocultural resources in instruction: A context-specific approach." In California Dept. of Education, *Beyond language: Social and cultural factors in schooling language minority students*. Los Angeles, CA: Evaluation, Dissemination and Assessment Center, California State University, Los Angeles. 187–230.

Dik, S. 1978. *Functional grammar*. Amsterdam: North-Holland.

DiPietro, R. (ed.). 1982. *Language and the professions*. Norwood, NJ: Ablex.

Dittmar, N. 1982. Ich fertig arbeite—nicht mehr spreche Deutsch: Semantische Eigenschaften pidginisierter Lernervarietäten des Deutschen. *Zeitschrift für Literaturwissenschaft und Linguistik* 45.9–34.

Dittmar, N. 1989. "SLA models and issues: Acquisition of semantics." In R.B. Kaplan et al. (eds.), *Annual review of applied linguistics (1988)*, Vol. 9. New York: Cambridge University Press. 54–71.

Dondonoli, P. 1989. "The ACTFL computerized adaptive test of foreign language reading proficiency." In W. Flint (ed.), *Modern technology in foreign language education.* Skokie, IL: National Textbook Co. 291–300.

Dowty, D., R. Wall, and S. Peters. 1981. *Introduction to Montague semantics.* Dordrecht: Reidel.

Drake, G. 1984, "Problems of language planning in the United States." In J. Edwards (ed.), *Linguistic minorities, policies and pluralism.* London: Academic Press. 144–49.

Dresher, B. and N. Hornstein. 1976. On some supposed contributions of artificial intelligence to the scientific study of language. *Cognition* 4.321–93.

Dresher, B. and N. Hornstein. 1977a. Response to Schank and Wilensky. *Cognition* 5.147–50.

Dresher, B. and N. Hornstein. 1977b. Reply to Winograd. *Cognition* 5.377–92.

DSM-III, 1980. *Diagnostic and statistical manual of mental disorders.* 3d ed. Washington, DC: American Psychiatric Association.

Dubin, F. and E. Olshtain, 1986. *Course design.* New York: Cambridge University Press.

Dulay, H. and M. Burt, 1972. Goofing: An indication of children's second language learning strategies. *Language Learning* 22.2.235–52.

Dulay, H. and M. Burt. 1973. Should we teach children syntax? *Language Learning* 23.2.245–58.

Dulay, H. and M. Burt. 1974a. Errors and strategies in child second language acquisition. *TESOL Quarterly* 8.2.129–36.

Dulay, H. and M. Burt. 1974b. Natural sequences in child second language acquisition. *Language Learning* 24.1.37–53.

Duran, R. 1987. "Metacognition in second language behavior." In J. Langer (ed.), *Language, literacy and culture.* Norwood, NJ: Ablex. 49–63.

Duran, R. et al. (eds.). 1985. *The TOEFL from a communicative viewpoint in language proficiency: A working paper.* Research Report No. 18. Princeton, NJ: Educational Testing Service.

Eastman, C. 1983. *Language planning: An introduction.* San Francisco: Chandler and Sharp.

Eckman, F. 1984. "Universals, typologies and interlanguage." In W. Rutherford (ed.), *Language universals and second language acquisition.* Philadelphia, PA: John Benjamin. 79–105.

Edelsky, C. 1986. *Writing in a bilingual program: Habia una Vez.* Norwood, NJ: Ablex.

Edwards, J. (ed.). 1984. *Linguistic minorities, policies and pluralism.* London: Academic Press.

Edwards, J. 1985. *Language, society and identity.* New York: Basil Blackwell.

Edwards J. 1986. "Language and educational disadvantage: The persistence of linguistic deficit theory." In K. Durkin (ed.), *Language development in the school years.* Cambridge, MA: Brookline Books. 139–54.

Ehrman, M. 1986. *Learning styles project. Working Papers.* Arlington, VA: U.S. Foreign Service Institute.

Eisenstein, M. 1985. "On the printing press as an agent of change." In D. Olson, A. Luke, and K. Egan (eds.), *Literacy, language and learning*. New York: Cambridge University Press. 19–33.

Ellis, R. 1985. *Understanding second language acquisition*. New York: Oxford University Press.

ELTB. 1986. Working papers on English language teaching by broadcast project. Washington, DC: U.S. Information Agency.

Emerson, J. 1970. "Behavior in private places: Sustaining definitions of reality in gynecological examination." In H.P. Dreitzal (ed.), *Recent sociology*, no. 2. New York: Collier Macmillan. 73–97.

Enç, M. 1988. "The syntax-semantics interface." In F. Newmeyer (ed.), *Linguistics: The Cambridge survey*, Vol. 1. New York: Cambridge University Press. 239–54.

Engels, L. 1968. Applied linguistics. *ITL Review of Applied Linguistics* 1.2–11.

Enkvist, N. 1987. "Text linguistics for the applier: An orientation." In U. Connor and R.B. Kaplan (eds.), *Writing across languages: Analysis of L2 text*. Reading, MA: Addison-Wesley. 23–43.

Enright, D.S. and M. McCloskey. 1988. *Integrating English*. Reading, MA: Addison-Wesley.

Enwall, B. 1977. "Responding to today's issues." In J. Phillips (ed.), *The language connection: From the classroom to the world*. Skokie, IL: National Textbook Company. 123–49.

Epstein, N. 1977. *Language, ethnicity and the schools: Policy alternatives for bilingual-bicultural education*. Washington, DC: George Washington University Press.

Faerch, C. and G. Kasper (eds.). 1983. *Strategies in interlanguage communication*. New York: Longman.

Fairclough, N. 1989. *Language and power*. London: Longman.

Fasold, R. 1984. *The sociolinguistics of society*. New York: Basil Blackwell.

Fasold, R. 1990. *The sociolinguistics of language*. New York: Basil Blackwell.

Faucett, L. et al. 1936. *Vocabulary selection for the teaching of English as a foreign language*. London: King.

Fawcett, R. and D. Young (eds.). 1988. *New developments in systemic linguistics*, Vol. 2. New York: Pinter.

Felix, S. 1981. The effect of formal instruction on second-language acquisition. *Language Learning* 31.1.81–112.

Felix, S. 1987. *Cognition and language growth*. Dordrecht: Foris.

Ferguson, C. and S. Heath (eds.). 1981. *Language in the United States*. New York: Cambridge University Press.

Fernando, L. 1985. "Comments on H.G. Widdowson, *The teaching, learning and study of literature*." In R. Quirk and H.G. Widdowson (eds.), *English in the world: Teaching and learning the language and literatures*. New York: Cambridge University Press. 197–99.

Fillmore, C. 1968. "The case for case." In E. Bach and R. Harms (eds.), *Universals in linguistic theory*. New York: Holt Rinehart and Winston. 1–90.

Fillmore, C. 1977. "The case for case reopened." In P. Cole and J. Sadock (eds.), *Syntax and semantics,* Vol. 8. New York: Academic Press. 59–82.

Fine, J. (ed.). 1988. *Second language discourse.* Norwood, NJ: Ablex.

Fine, J. and R. Freedle (eds.). 1983. *Developmental issues in discourse.* Norwood, NJ: Ablex.

Finegan, E. and N. Besnier. 1989. *Language: Its structure and use.* San Diego, CA: Harcourt Brace Jovanovich.

Firbas, J. 1986. "On the dynamics of written communication in the light of the theory of functional sentence perspective." In C. Cooper and S. Greenbaum (eds.), *Studying writing: Linguistic approaches.* Beverly Hills, CA: Sage. 40–71.

Firth, J.R. 1957. *Papers in linguistics: 1934–1951.* London: Oxford University Press.

Fisher, S. and A. Todd (eds.). 1986. *Discourse and institutional authority: Medicine, education and law.* Norwood, NJ: Ablex.

Fishman, J. 1965. The status and prospect of bilingualism in the United States. *Modern Language Journal* 49.3.143–55.

Fishman, J. 1972. "The sociology of language." In P.P. Giglioli (ed.), *Language in social context.* Baltimore, MD: Penguin. 45–58.

Fishman, J. (ed.). 1974. *Advances in language planning.* The Hague: Mouton.

Fishman, J. 1978. A gathering of vultures: The "legacy of decency" and bilingual education in the U.S.A. *NABE Journal* 2.2.13–16.

Fishman, J. (ed.). 1978. *Advances in the study of societal multilingualism.* The Hague: Mouton.

Fishman, J. 1980. "Bilingual education in the United States under ethnic community auspices." In J. Alatis (ed.), *Current issues in bilingual education.* Georgetown University Round Table on Languages and Linguistics. Washington, DC: Georgetown University Press. 8–13.

Fishman, J. 1981. "Language policy: Past, present and future." In C. Ferguson and S.B. Heath (eds.), *Language in the U.S.A.* New York: Cambridge University Press. 516–26.

Fishman, J. 1985. *The rise and fall of the ethnic revival.* New York: Mouton.

Fishman, J., C. Ferguson, and J. Das Gupta (eds.). 1968. *Language problems of developing nations.* New York: Wiley.

Fishman, J. et al. (eds.). 1966. *Language loyalty in the U.S.* The Hague: Mouton.

Flaste, R. 1989. The power of concentration. *Good Health Magazine, New York Times.* Oct. 8, 1989.

Fletcher, P. 1990. "Language pathology." In R.B. Kaplan et al. (eds.), *Annual review of applied linguistics (1989),* Vol. 10. New York: Cambridge University Press. 26–36.

Fletcher, P. and M. Garman (eds.). 1986. *Language acquisition.* 2d ed. New York: Cambridge University Press.

Flint, W. (ed.). 1987. *Modern media in foreign language education: Theory and implementation.* Lincolnwood, IL: National Textbook Company.

Flint, W. 1989a. "Modern technology in foreign language education: A synopsis." In

W. Flint (ed.), *Modern technology in foreign language education: Applications and projects.* Lincolnwood, IL: National Textbook Company. 1–10.

Flint, W. (ed.). 1989b. *Modern technology in foreign language education: Applications and projects.* Lincolnwood, IL: National Textbook Company.

Flower, L. and J. Hayes. 1980. "The dynamics of composing: Making plans and juggling constraints." In W. Gregg and E. Steinberg (eds.), *Cognitive processes in writing.* Hillsdale, NJ: Lawrence Erlbaum Associates. 31–50.

Flynn, S. 1983. "Similarities and differences between first and second language acquisition: Setting the parameters of universal grammar." In D. Rogers and J. Sloboda (eds.), *Acquisition of symbolic skills.* New York: Plenum. 485–500.

Flynn, S. 1987. *A parameter-setting model of L2 acquisition: Experimental studies in anaphora.* Dordrecht: Reidel.

Flynn, S. 1988. "Second language acquisition and grammatical theory." In F. Newmeyer (ed.), *Linguistics: The Cambridge survey,* Vol. 2. New York: Cambridge University Press. 53–73.

Fong, K. 1978. Cultural pluralism. *Harvard Civil Rights-Civil Liberties Law Review* 13.1.133–73.

Foster, C. 1982a. Defusing the issues in bilingualism and bilingual education. *Phi Delta Kappan* 63.5.342–44.

Foster, C. 1982b. "American bilingualism: The need for a national language policy." In B. Hartford, A. Valdman, and C. Foster (eds.), *Issues in international bilingual education: The role of the vernacular.* New York: Plenum. 291–98.

Foster, S. 1990. *The acquisition of language.* New York: Longman.

Foster, W. 1976. Bilingual education: An educational and legal survey. *Journal of Law and Education* 5.2.149–71.

Francis, W. N. and H. Kucera. 1982. *Frequency analysis of English usage: Lexicon and grammar.* Boston, MA: Houghton Mifflin.

Frase, L. 1987a. "Technology, reading, and writing." In J. Squire (ed.), *The dynamics of language learning.* Urbana, IL: National Council of Teachers of English. 294–308.

Frase, L. 1987b. "Computer analysis of written materials." In D. Reinking (ed.), *Reading and computers: Issues for theory and practice.* New York: Teacher's College Press. 76–96.

Freed, B. 1984. "Proficiency in context: The Pennsylvania experience." In S. Savignon and M. Berns (eds.), *Initiatives in communicative language teaching.* Reading, MA: Addison-Wesley. 211–40.

Freed, B. (ed.). 1990. *Foreign language acquisition research and the classroom.* Lexington, MA: D.C. Heath.

Fries, C. C. 1945. *Teaching and learning English as a foreign language.* Ann Arbor, MI: The University of Michigan Press.

Fromkin, V. and R. Rodman. 1986. *An introduction to language.* 4th ed. New York: Holt, Rinehart and Winston.

Fuller, S. 1984. *Schema theory in the representation and analysis of text.* Ph.D. diss., University of Southern California.

Gaarder, A. 1964. Conserving our linguistic resources. *PMLA* 80.2.19–23.

Gaarder, A. 1978. "Bilingual education: Central questions and concerns." In H. LaFontaine et al. (eds.), *Bilingual education*. Wayne, NJ: Avery. 33–38.

Gale, L. 1989. "Macario, Montevidisco, and interactive Digame: Developing interactive video for language instruction." In W. Flint (ed.), *Modern technology in foreign language education: Applications and projects*. Lincolnwood, IL: National Textbook Company. 235–48.

Gardner, R. and W. Lambert. 1972. *Attitudes and motivation in second language learning*. Rowley, MA: Newbury House.

Garnham, A. 1985. *Psycholinguistics: Central topics*. Baltimore, MD: Edward Arnold.

Garside, R., G. Leech, and G. Sampson (eds.). 1987. *The computational analysis of English: A corpus-based approach*. New York: Longman.

Gass, S. 1989. "Second language vocabulary acquisition." In R.B. Kaplan et al. (eds.), *Annual review of applied linguistics (1988)*, Vol. 9. New York: Cambridge University Press. 92–106.

Gass, S. and C. Madden (eds.). 1985. *Input in second language acquisition*. Rowley, MA: Newbury House.

Gass, S. and L. Selinker (eds.). 1983. *Language transfer in language learning*. Rowley, MA: Newbury House.

Gass, S. and E. Varonis. 1985. "Task variation and non-native negotiation of meaning." In S. Gass and C. Madden (eds.), *Input in second language acquisition*. Rowley, MA: Newbury House. 149–61.

Gass, S. et al. (eds.). 1989. *Variation in second language acquisition: Psycholinguistic issues*. Clevedon, Avon: Multilingual Matters.

Gattegno, C. 1972. *Teaching foreign languages in schools: The silent way*. New York: Educational Solutions, Inc.

Gault, A. 1980. "Realizing the potential, broadening the base." In J. Phillips (ed.), *The new imperative: Expanding the horizons of foreign language education*. Skokie, IL: National Textbook Company. 117–32.

Gawthorp, R. 1987. "Literacy drives in preindustrial Germany." In R. Arnove and H. Graff (eds.), *National literacy campaigns*. New York: Plenum. 29–48.

Gazdar, G. 1979. *Pragmatics: Implicature, presupposition and logical form*. New York: Academic Press.

Gazdar, G. et al. 1985. *Generalized phrase stucture grammar*. Cambridge, MA: Harvard University Press.

Gee, J. 1986. Orality and literacy: From *the savage mind* to *ways with words*. *TESOL Quarterly* 20.4.717–46.

Geis, M. 1982. *The language of television advertising*. New York: Academic Press.

Geis, M. 1987. "Language and media." In R.B. Kaplan et al. (eds.), *Annual review of applied linguistics (1986)*. Vol. 7. New York: Cambridge University Press. 64–73.

Genesee, F. 1987. *Learning through two languages*. New York: Newbury House.

Genesee, F. 1988. "Neuropsychology and second language acquisition." In L. Beebe (ed.), *Issues in second language acquisition: Multiple perspectives*. New York: Newbury House. 79–112.

George, H. 1972. *Common errors in language learning*. Rowley, MA: Newbury House.

Gibson, E. and H. Levin. 1975. *The psychology of reading*. Cambridge, MA: MIT Press.

Gilbert, G. and M. Mulkay. 1984. *Opening Pandora's box: A sociological analysis of scientists' discourse*. Cambridge: Cambridge University Press.

Givón, T. 1984. "Universals of discourse structure and second language acquisition." In W. Rutherford (ed.), *Language universals and second language acquisition*. Philadelphia, PA: John Benjamin. 109–33.

Givón, T. (ed.). 1979. *Discourse and syntax*. Syntax and semantics 12. New York: Academic Press.

Givón, T. (ed.). 1983. *Topics continuity in discourse: A quantitative cross-language study*. Philadelphia, PA: John Benjamin.

Glazer, S. 1989. "Oral language and literacy development." In D. Strickland and L. Morrow (eds.), *Emerging literacy: Young children learn to read and write*. Newark, DE: International Reading Association, 16–26.

Glendinning, E. and B. Holmstrom. 1987. *English in medicine: A course in communication skills*. Cambridge, UK: Cambridge University Press.

Goldman, S. and H. Trueba (eds.). 1988. *Becoming literate in English as a second language*. Norwood, NJ: Ablex.

Goldsmith, J. 1990. *Autosegmental and metrical phonology*. New York: Basil Blackwell.

Goodman, K. 1986. *What's whole in whole language*. Portsmouth, NH: Heinemann.

Goodman, K. (ed.). 1968. *The psycholinguistic nature of the reading process*. Detroit, MI: Wayne State University Press.

Goodrich, P. 1986. *Reading the law*. London: Basil Blackwell.

Goody, J. 1977. *The domestication of the savage mind*. Cambridge, UK: Cambridge University Press.

Goody, J. 1986. *The logic of writing and the organization of society*. Cambridge, UK: Cambridge University Press.

Goody, J. 1987. *The interface between the written and the oral*. Cambridge, UK: Cambridge University Press.

Goody, J. and I. Watt. 1972. "The consequences of literacy." In P.P. Giglioli (ed.), *Language and social context*. Baltimore, MD: Penguin. 311–57.

Gough, K. 1968. "Implications of literacy in traditional China and India." In J. Goody (ed.), *Literacy in traditional societies*. Cambridge, UK: Cambridge University Press. Reprinted in E. Kintgen, B. Kroll, and M. Rose (eds.), *Perspectives on literacy*. Carbondale, IL: Southern Illinois University Press, 1988. 44–56.

Grabe, W. 1985. "Written discourse analysis." In R.B. Kaplan et al. (eds.), *Annual review of applied linguistics (1984)*, Vol. 5. New York: Cambridge University Press. 101–23.

Grabe, W. 1987. "Contrastive rhetoric and text-type research." In U. Connor and R.B. Kaplan (eds.), *Writing across languages: Analysis of L2 text*. Reading, MA: Addison-Wesley. 115–37.

Grabe, W. 1988. English, information access, and technology transfer: A rationale for English as an international language. *World Englishes* 7.1.63–72.

Grabe, W. and R.B. Kaplan. 1986. Science, technology, language, and information: Implications for language and language-in-education planning. *International Journal of the Sociology of Language* 59.47–71.

Grabe, W. and R.B. Kaplan. 1988. "Writing in a second language: Contrastive rhetoric." In D. Johnson and D. Roen (eds.), *Richness in writing: Empowering ESL students*. New York: Longman. 263–283.

Graesser, A. and J. Black (eds.). 1985. *The psychology of questions*. Hillsdale, NJ: Lawrence Erlbaum Associates.

Graff, H. 1979. *The literacy myth: Literacy and social structure in the nineteenth century city*. New York: Academic Press.

Graff, H. (ed.). 1982. *Literacy and social development in the west*. Cambridge, UK: Cambridge University Press.

Graff, H. 1987. *The legacies of literacy*. Bloomington, IN: Indiana University Press.

Graham, M. 1983. *Tightening the reins of justice in America: A comparative analysis of criminal jury trails in England and the U.S.* Westport, CN: Greenwood.

Grant, J. and R. Goldsmith. 1979. *Bilingual education and federal law: An overview*. Austin, TX: Dissemination and Assessment Center for Bilingual Education.

Grant, S., I. Steingard, and N. Freedman. 1975. Organization of language behaviour and cognitive performance in chronic schizophrenia. *Psychiatry* 84.621–28.

Graves, D. 1983. *Writing: Teachers and children at work*. Portsmouth, NH: Heinemann.

Graves, D. 1984. *A researcher learns to write*. Portsmouth, NH: Heinemann.

Greenbaum, S. (ed.). 1985. *The English language today*. New York: Pergamon Press.

Greenbaum, S. 1988. *Good English and the grammarian*. New York: Longman.

Greenberg, J. 1974. *Language typology: A historical and analytic overview*. The Hague: Mouton.

Greenberg, J. (ed.). 1966. *Universals of language*. 2d ed. Cambridge, MA: MIT Press.

Greene, J. 1972. *Psycholinguistics*. Baltimore, MD: Penguin.

Grice, H. 1967. *Logic and conversation*. University of California, Berkeley. Unpublished manuscript.

Grice, H. 1975. "Logic and conversation." In P. Cole and J. Morgan (eds.), *Speech acts. Syntax and semantics 3*. New York: Academic Press. 41–58.

Grice, H. 1978. "Further notes on logic and conversation." In P. Cole (ed.), *Pragmatics. Syntax and semantics 9*. New York: Academic Press. 113–27.

Grimes, J. 1976. *The thread of discourse*. The Hague: Mouton.

Grishman, R. 1986. *Computational linguistics: An introduction*. Cambridge, UK: Cambridge University Press.

Grittner, F. 1969. *Teaching foreign languages*. New York: Harper and Row.

Grosjean, F. 1982. *Life with two languages: An introduction to bilingualism*. Cambridge, MA: Harvard University Press.

Grosz, B. et al. 1989. "Discourse." In M. Posner (ed.), *Foundations of cognitive science.* Cambridge, MA: MIT Press. 437–68.

Gruber, J. 1976. *Lexical structures in syntax and semantics.* New York: North-Holland.

Guiora, A., R. Brannon, and C. Dull. 1972. Empathy and second language learning. *Language Learning* 22.111–30.

Guiora, A. et al. 1972a. The effects of experimentally induced changes in ego state on pronunciation ability in second language: An exploratory study. *Comprehensive Psychiatry* 13.223–30.

Guiora, A. et al. 1972b. Empathy and second language learning. *Language Learning* 22.111–30.

Gumperz, J. 1982a *Discourse strategies.* Cambridge, UK: Cambridge University Press.

Gumperz, J. 1986. "Interactional sociolinguistics in the study of schooling." In J. Cook-Gumperz (ed.), *The social construction of literacy.* New York: Cambridge University Press. 45–68.

Gumperz, J. (ed.). 1982b. *Language and social identity.* New York: Cambridge University Press.

Gumperz, J. and D. Hymes (eds.). 1964. *The ethnography of communication* (Special issue of *American Anthropologist*) 66.6.part 2.

Gumperz, J. and D. Hymes (eds.). 1972. *Directions in sociolinguistics: The ethnography of communication.* New York: Holt, Rinehart and Winston.

Guthrie, E. 1984. "Intake, communication, and second language teaching." In S. Savignon and M. Berns (eds.), *Initiatives in communicative language teaching.* Reading, MA: Addison-Wesley. 35–54.

Hagege, C. 1983. *Language reform: History and future.* 3 Vols. Hamburg: Buske Verlag.

Hakuta, K. 1976. Becoming bilingual: A case study of a Japanese child learning English. *Language Learning* 26.321–51.

Hakuta, K. 1986. *Mirror of language.* New York: Basic Books.

Hakuta, K. 1988. "Why bilinguals?" In F. Kessel (ed.), *The development of language research and language researchers.* Hillsdale, NJ: Lawrence Erlbaum Associates. 229–318.

Hakuta, K. and H. Cancino. 1977. Trends in second-language acquisition research. *Harvard Educational Review* 47.294–316.

Hakuta, K., B. Ferdman, and R. Diaz. 1987. "Bilingualism and cognitive development: Three perspectives." In S. Rosenberg (ed.), *Advances in applied psycholinguistics.* Vol. 2. *Reading, writing, and language learning.* New York: Cambridge University Press. 284–319.

Hakuta, K. and J. Suben. 1986. "Bilingualism and cognitive development." In R.B. Kaplan et al. (eds.), *Annual review of applied linguistics (1985),* Vol. 6. New York: Cambridge University Press. 35–45.

Haley-James, S. (ed.). 1981. *Perspectives on writing in grades 1–8.* Urbana, IL: National Council of Teachers of English.

Hall, E. 1959. *The silent language.* New York: Doubleday and Company.

Hall, E. 1966. *The hidden dimension.* New York: Doubleday and Company.

Halliday, M.A.K. 1970. "Language structure and language function." In J. Lyons (ed.), *New horizons in linguistics*. Baltimore, MD: Penguin. 140–65.

Halliday, M.A.K. 1973. *Exploration in the functions of language*. London: Edward Arnold.

Halliday, M.A.K. 1975. *Learning how to mean: Explorations in the development of language*. London: Edward Arnold.

Halliday, M.A.K. 1978. *Language as social semiotic*. London: Edward Arnold.

Halliday, M.A.K. 1985. *An introduction to functional grammar*. Boston, MA: Edward Arnold.

Halliday, M.A.K. 1987. "Spoken and written modes of meaning." In R. Horowitz and S. Samuels, *Comprehending oral and written language*. New York: Academic Press. 55–82.

Halliday, M.A.K. 1989. *Spoken and written language*. Oxford: Oxford University Press.

Halliday, M.A.K. and R. Hasan. 1976. *Cohesion in English*. London: Longman.

Halliday, M.A.K. and R. Hasan. 1989. *Language, context, and text: Aspects of language in a social-semiotic perspective*. Oxford: Oxford University Press.

Halliday, M.A.K., A. McIntosh, and P. Strevens. 1964. *The linguistic sciences and language teaching*. London: Longman.

Halliday, M. and R. Fawcett (eds.). 1988. *New developments in systemic linguistics*, Vol. 1. New York: Pinter.

Hammarberg, B. 1989. "Acquisition of phonology." In R.B. Kaplan et al. (eds.), *Annual review of applied linguistics (1988)*, Vol. 9. New York: Cambridge University Press. 23–41.

Harmer, J. 1983. *The practice of English language teaching*. London: Longman.

Harris, D. 1969. *Testing English as a second language*. New York: McGraw-Hill.

Harris, R. (ed.). 1983. *Information processing research in advertising*. Hillsdale, NJ: Lawrence Erlbaum Associates.

Harris, S. 1989. "Defendant resistance to power and control in court." In H. Coleman (ed.), *Working with language*. Berlin: Mouton. 131–64.

Harste, J., V. Woodward, and C. Burke. 1984. *Language stories and literacy lessons*. Portsmouth, NH: Heinemann.

Hartmann, R.R.K. 1985. Lexicography: A contrastive survey. In R.B. Kaplan et al. (eds.), *Annual review of applied linguistics (1984)*, Vol. 5. New York: Cambridge University Press. 125–38.

Hasan, R. 1987. "Directions from structuralism." In N. Fabb et al. (eds.), *The linguistics of writing*. New York: Methuen. 103–22.

Hasan, R. 1989. *Linguistics, language, and verbal art*. New York: Oxford University Press.

Hasan, R. and J. Martin (eds.). 1989. *Language development: Learning language, learning culture*. Norwood, NJ: Ablex.

Hasher, L. and R. Zacks 1979. Automatic and effortful processes in memory. *Journal of Experimental Psychology: General* 108.356–88.

Hatch, E. and H. Farhady. 1982. *Research design and statistics for applied linguistics*. Rowley, MA: Newbury House.

Hatch, E., J. Gough, and S. Peck. 1985. "What case studies reveal about system, sequence, and variation in second language acquisition." In M. Celce-Murcia (ed.), *Beyond basics*. Rowley, MA: Newbury House. 37–59.

Haugeland, J. 1985. *Artificial intelligence: The very idea*. Cambridge, MA: MIT Press.

Haugen, E. 1956. *Bilingualism in the Americas: A bibliography and research guide*. Tuscaloosa, AL: University of Alabama.

Haugen, E. 1978. "Bilingualism, language contact, and immigrant languages in the U.S.: A research report, 1956–1970." In J. Fishman (ed.), *Advances in the study of societal multilingualism*. The Hague: Mouton. 1–112.

Havelock, E. 1976. *Origins of Western literacy*. Toronto: Ontario Institute for Studies in Education Press.

Hawisher, G. 1989. "Research and recommendations for computers and composition." In G. Hawisher and C. Selfe (eds.), *Critical perspectives on computers and composition instruction*. New York: Teacher's College Press. 44–73.

Hawisher, G. and C. Selfe (eds.). 1989. *Critical perspectives on computers and composition instruction*. New York: Teacher's College Press.

Hawkins, J. 1979. Implicational universals as predictors of word order. *Language* 55.3.619–48.

Hawkins, J. 1983. *Word order universals*. New York: Academic Press.

Hawkins, J. (ed.). 1989. *Explaining language universals*. New York: Basil Blackwell.

Hawkins, L. 1972. "Extra school factors that influence language learning." In D. Lange and C. James (eds.), *Foreign language education: A reappraisal*. Skokie, IL: National Textbook Company. 321–40.

Hayden, R. 1979. Toward a national foreign language policy. *Journal of Communication* 29.2.93–101.

Heath, S. 1976. A national language academy? Debate in the new nation. *International Journal of the Sociology of Language* 11.9–13.

Heath, S. 1977. "Our language heritage: A historical perspective." In J. Phillips (ed.), *The language connection: From the classroom to the world*. Skokie, IL: National Textbook Company. 23–51.

Heath, S. 1978a. "Bilingual education and national policy." In J. Alatis (ed.), *International dimensions of bilingual education*. Washington, DC: Georgetown University Press. 53–66.

Heath, S. 1978b. *Teacher talk: Language in the classroom*. Washington, DC: Center for Applied Linguistics, ERIC Clearinghouse for Languages and Linguistics. [Language in Education: Theory and Practice, 4] [ED 158 575]

Heath, S. 1983. *Ways with words*. New York: Cambridge University Press.

Heath, S. 1985. "Literacy or literate skills? Considerations for ESL/EFL learners." In P. Larson, E. Judd, and D. Messerschmidt (eds.), *On TESOL 1984*. Washington DC: TESOL Publications. 15–28.

Heath, S. 1986a. "Critical factors in literacy development." In S. deCastell, A. Luke, and K. Egan (eds.), *Literacy, society and schooling: A reader*. New York: Cambridge University Press. 209–29.

Heath, S. 1986b. "Sociocultural contexts of language development." In California Office of Bilingual Education, *Beyond language: Social and cultural factors in schooling language minority children.* Los Angeles, CA: Evaluation, Dissemination and Assessment Center, California State University, Los Angeles. 143–86.

Heath, S. 1987. "The literate essay: Using ethnography to explode myths." In J. Langer (ed.), *Language, literacy and culture: Issues of society and schooling.* Norwood, NJ: Ablex. 89–107.

Heaton, J. 1975. *Writing English language tests.* London: Longman.

Heidelberger Forschungsprojekt "Pidgin Deutsch." 1976. *Untersuchungen zur Erlernung des Deutschen durch ausländische Arbeiter.* Heidelberg: Germanistisches Seminar der Universität Heidelberg.

Heller, M. 1985. "Sociolinguistics: Theory." In R.B. Kaplan et al. (eds.), *Annual review of applied linguistics (1984),* Vol. 5. New York: Cambridge University Press. 47–58.

Helman, C. 1984. "Disease and pseudo-disease: A case history of pseudo-angina." In R. Hahn and A. Gaines (eds.), *Physicians of Western medicine: Anthropological approaches to theory and practice.* Dordrecht: Reidel. 43–64.

Henning, G. 1987. *A guide to language testing: Development, evaluation, research.* New York: Newbury House.

Herron, C. 1982. Who should study a foreign language: The myth of elitism. *Foreign Language Annals* 15.6.441–49.

Heyde, A. 1977. "The relationship between self-esteem and the oral production of a second language." In H. Brown, C. Yorio, and R. Crymes (eds.), *On TESOL 1977. Teaching and learning English as a second language: Trends in research and practice.* Washington, DC: TESOL. 226–40.

Higgins, J. and T. Johns. 1984. *Computers in language learning.* Reading, MA: Addison-Wesley.

Higgs, T. V. (ed.). 1982. *Curriculum, competence, and the foreign language teacher.* Skokie, IL: National Textbook Company.

Higgs, T. (ed.). 1984. *Teaching for proficiency, the organizing principle.* Skokie, IL: National Textbook Company.

Higgs, T. 1984. "Language teaching and the quest for the holy grail." In T. Higgs (ed.), *Teaching for proficiency, the organizing principle.* Skokie, IL: National Textbook Company. 1–10.

Hillocks, G. 1986. *Research on written composition.* Urbana, IL: National Conference on Research in English.

Hinds, J. 1983a. "Linguistics and written discourse in particular languages: Contrastive studies: English and Japanese." In R.B. Kaplan et al. (eds.), *Annual review of applied linguistics (1982),* Vol. 3. New York: Cambridge University Press. 78–84.

Hinds, J. 1983b. Contrastive rhetoric: Japanese and English. *Text* 3.185–95.

Hinds, J. 1987. "Reader versus writer responsibility: A new typology." In U. Connor and R.B. Kaplan (eds.), *Writing across cultures: Analysis of L2 text.* Reading, MA: Addison-Wesley. 141–52.

Hirsch, E. 1987. *Cultural literacy*. Boston, MA: Houghton Mifflin.

Hirvela, A. 1988. Marshall McLuhan and the case against CAI. *System* 16.3.299–311.

Hirvela, A. 1989. The case against CAI: A reply to John Higgins. *System* 17.1.61–65.

Hockey, S. 1980. *A guide to computer applications in the humanities*. Baltimore, MD: Johns Hopkins University Press.

Hoey, M. 1983. *On the surface of discourse*. London: Allen and Unwin.

Hoey, M. 1986. "Overlapping patterns of discourse organization and their implications for clause relational analysis of problem-solution texts." In C. Cooper and S. Greenbaum (eds.), *Studying writing: Linguistics approaches*. Beverly Hills, CA: Sage Publications. 187–214.

Hofman, J. 1974a. The prediction of success in language planning: The case of chemists in Israel. *International Journal of the Sociology of Language* 1.39–65.

Hofman, J. 1974b. Predicting the use of Hebrew terms among Israeli psychologists. *International Journal of the Sociology of Language* 3.53–65.

Homel, P. et al. (eds.). 1987. *Childhood bilingualism: Aspects of linguistic, cognitive and social development*. Hillsdale, NJ: Lawrence Erlbaum Associates.

Hoot, J. and S. Silvern (eds.). 1988. *Writing with computers in the early grades*. New York: Teacher's College Press.

Hopper, P. (ed.). 1982. *Tense and aspect: Between semantics and pragmatics*. Philadelphia, PA: John Benjamin.

Horn, L. 1988. "Pragmatic theory." In F. Newmeyer (ed.), *Linguistics: The Cambridge survey*, Vol. 1. New York: Cambridge University Press. 113–45.

Hornby, A. 1954. *A guide to patterns and usage in English*. London: Oxford University Press.

Horowitz, R. 1987. "Rhetorical structure in discourse processing." In R. Horowitz and S. Samuels (eds.), *Comprehending spoken and written language*. San Diego, CA: Academic Press. 117–59.

Horrocks, G. 1987. *Generative grammar*. New York: Longman.

Houston, R. 1988. *Literacy in early modern Europe*. New York: Longman.

Howatt, A.P.R. 1984. *A history of English language teaching*. New York: Oxford University Press.

Hudelson, S. 1989a. "Writing in a second language." In R.B. Kaplan et al. (eds.), *Annual review of applied linguistics (1988)*, Vol. 9. New York: Cambridge University Press. 210–22.

Hudelson, S. 1989b. *Write on: ESL children writing*. Englewood Cliffs, NJ: Prentice-Hall.

Huebener, T. 1961. *Why Johnny should learn foreign languages*. Philadelphia, PA: Chilton.

Huebner, T. 1979. Order of acquisition vs. dynamic paradigm: A comparison of method in interlanguage research. *TESOL Quarterly* 13.1.21–28.

Huebner, T. 1989. "SLA: Models and issues." In R.B. Kaplan et al. (eds.), *Annual review of applied linguistics (1988)*, Vol. 9. New York: Cambridge University Press. 5–22.

Hughes, A. 1989. *Testing for language teachers*. New York: Cambridge University Press.

Hughes, A. and D. Porter (eds.). 1983. *Current developments in language testing*. London: Academic Press.

Hulstijn, J. and W. Hulstijn. 1984. Grammatical errors as a function of processing constraints and explicit knowledge. *Language Learning* 34.23–43.

Hutchinson, T. and A. Waters. 1987. *English for speific purposes: A learning-centered approach*. Cambridge: Cambridge University Press.

Hyams, N. 1986. *The acquisition of parameterized grammar*. Dordrecht: Reidel.

Hymes, D. 1972. "On communicative competence." In J. Pride and A. Holmes (eds.), *Sociolinguistics*. Baltimore, MD: Penguin. 269–93.

Hymes, D. 1974. *Foundations of sociolinguistics*. Philadelphia: University of Pennsylvania Press.

Hymes, D. 1989. Postscript. *Applied Linguistics* 10.2.244–50.

Hymes, D. and J. Fought. 1981. *American structuralism*. The Hague: Mouton.

Hymes, D. (ed.). 1971. *Pidginization and creolization of language*. Cambridge, UK: Cambridge University Press.

Ioup, G. and S. Weinberger (eds.). 1987. *Interlanguage phonology: The acquisition of a second language sound system*. Cambridge, MA: Newbury House.

Jackson, H. 1988. *Words and their meaning*. New York: Longman.

Jackson, S. and S. Jacobs. 1981. The collaborative production of proposals in conversational argument and persuasion: A study of disagreement regulation. *Journal of the American Forensic Association* 18.7790.

Jackendoff, R. 1972. *Semantic interpretation in generative grammar*. Cambridge, MA: MIT Press.

Jacobs, R. 1990. *An outline of English syntax*. New York: Oxford University Press.

Jagger, A. and T. Smith-Burke (eds.). 1985. *Observing the language learner*. Newark, DE: International Reading Association.

James, A. and J. Leather (eds.). 1987. *Sound patterns in second language acquisition*. Dordrecht: Foris.

Jenkins, S. and J. Hinds. 1987. Business letter writing: English, French, and Japanese. *TESOL Quarterly* 20.2.327–49.

Johansson, S. (ed.). 1982. *Computer corpora in English language research*. Bergen: Norwegian Computing Center for the Humanities.

Johansson, S. 1988. The *New Oxford English Dictionary* project: A presentation. *ICAME Journal* 12.37–41.

Johansson, S. and K. Hofland. 1988. *Frequency analysis of English vocabulary and grammar based on the LOB corpus*, Vol. 1. Oxford: Clarendon Press.

Johns, A. 1986. Coherence and academic writing: Some definitions and suggestions for teaching. *TESOL Quarterly* 21.2.247–65.

Johns, A. 1987. "The language of business." In R.B. Kaplan et al. (eds.), *Annual review of applied linguistics (1986)*, Vol. 7. New York: Cambridge University Press. 3–17.

Johnson, D. and D. Roen (eds.). 1988. *Richness in writing.* New York: Longman.

Johnson, K. and K. Morrow (eds.). 1981. *Communication in the classroom.* London: Longman.

Johnson, M. 1988. "Word processing in an English as a second language classroom." In J. Hoot and S. Silvern (eds.), *Writing with computers in the early grades.* New York: Teacher's College Press. 107–21.

Johnson, R. (ed.). 1989. *The second language curriculum.* New York: Cambridge University Press.

Jones, C. and S. Fortescue. 1987. *Using computers in the language classroom.* New York: Longman.

Jowett, G. and V. O'Donnell. 1986. *Propaganda and persuasion.* Newbury Park, CA: Sage Publications.

Judd, E. 1984. "TESOL as a political act: A moral question." In J. Handscombe, R. Orem, and B. Taylor (eds.), *On TESOL 83.* Washington, DC: TESOL Publications. 265–73.

Judd, E. 1987. The English language amendment: A case study on language and politics. *TESOL Quarterly* 21.1.113–35.

Jupp, T. and S. Hodlin. 1975. *Industrial English: An example of theory and practice in functional language teaching.* London: Heinemann.

Kachru, B. 1981. "Bilingualism." In R.B. Kaplan et al. (eds.), *Annual review of applied linguistics (1980),* Vol. 1. New York: Cambridge University Press. 2–18.

Kachru, B. (ed.). 1982. *The other tongue: English across cultures.* Urbana, IL: University of Illinois Press.

Kachru, B. 1984. "The alchemy of English: Social and functional power of non-native varieties." In C. Kraemarae, M. Schulz, and W. O'Barr (eds.), *Language and power.* Beverly Hills, CA: Sage Publications. 177–93.

Kachru, B. 1985a. "Institutionalized second-language varieties." In S. Greenbaum (ed.), *The English language today.* New York: Pergamon Press. 211–26.

Kachru, B. 1985b. Current issues in bilingualism: An update of directions in research. In R.B. Kaplan et al. (eds.), *Annual review of applied linguistics (1984),* Vol. 5. New York: Cambridge University Press. 11–34.

Kachru, B. 1986. *The alchemy of English.* New York: Pergamon Press.

Kachru, B. 1988. "The spread of English and sacred linguistic cows." In P. Lowenberg (ed.), *Language spread and language policies: Issues, implications and case studies.* Georgetown University Round Table on Languages and Linguistics. Washington, DC: Georgetown University Press. 207–28.

Kachru, Y. 1989. "Cognitive and cultural styles." In R.B. Kaplan et al. (eds.), *Annual review of applied linguistics (1988),* Vol. 9. New York: Cambridge University Press. 149–63.

Kaestle, C. 1985. The history of literacy and the history of readers. *Review of Research in Education.* 12.1.11–53.

Kamil, M. 1987. "Computers and reading research." In D. Reinking (ed.), *Reading and computers: Issues for theory and practice.* New York: Teacher's College Press. 57–75.

Kaplan, R.B. 1966. Cultural thought patterns in intercultural education. *Language Learning* 16.1.1–20.

Kaplan, R.B. 1980a. "On the scope of linguistics, applied and non-." In R.B. Kaplan (ed.), *On the scope of applied linguistics*. Rowley, MA: Newbury House. 57–66.

Kaplan, R.B. (ed.). 1980b. *On the scope of applied linguistics*. Rowley, MA: Newbury House.

Kaplan, R.B. 1983. "Electronic media, instructional technology, and language instruction in planning the use of English as a language of wider communication in non-English–speaking countries." In K. Ando et al. (eds.), *FLEAT special lectures*. Tokyo: Language Laboratory Association of Japan. 65–74.

Kaplan, R.B. 1987. English in the language policy of the Pacific Rim. *World Englishes* 6.2.137–48.

Kaplan, R.B. 1988. "Contrastive rhetoric and second language learning: Notes toward a theory of contrastive rhetoric." In A. Purves (ed.), *Writing across languages and cultures*. Newbury Park, CA: Sage. 275–304.

Kaplan, R.B. and W. Grabe. In press. "The fiction in science writing." In H. Schroeder (ed.), *Subject-oriented text*. Hamburg: Springer Verlag.

Kaplan, R.B. et al. (eds.), 1980–1990. *Annual review of applied linguistics*, Vols. 1–10. New York: Cambridge University Press.

Kaplan, R.N. and J. Bresnan. 1982. "Lexical-functional grammar: A formal system for grammatical representation." In J. Bresnan (ed.), *The mental representation of grammatical relations*. Cambridge, MA: MIT Press.

Karmiloff-Smith, A. 1986. "Stage/structure versus phase/process in modelling linguistic and cognitive development." In I. Levin (ed.), *Stage and structure: Reopening the debate*. Norwood, NJ: Ablex. 164–90.

Kartunnen, L. 1973. Presupposition in compound sentences. *Linguistic Inquiry* 4.169–93.

Kaye, J. 1989. *Phonology: A cognitive view*. Hillsdale, NJ: Lawrence Erlbaum Associates.

Kean, M.L. 1988. "Brain structures and linguistic capacity." In F. Newmeyer (ed.), *Linguistics: The Cambridge survey*, Vol. 2. New York: Cambridge University Press. 74–95.

Keating, R. 1963. *A study of the effectiveness of language laboratories*. New York: Institute of Administrative Research, Teachers College, Columbia University.

Keenan, E. and B. Comrie. 1977. Noun phrase accessibility and universal grammar. *Linguistics Inquiry* 8.1.63–99.

Keenan, E. and L. Faltz. 1985. *Boolean semantics for natural language*. Dordrecht: Reidel.

Kelly, L. 1969. *25 centuries of language teaching*. Rowley, MA: Newbury House.

Kempson, R. 1988. "Grammar and conversational principles." In F. Newmeyer (ed.), *Linguistics: The Cambridge survey*, Vol. 2. New York: Cambridge University Press. 139–63.

Kennedy, G. 1983. *Language planning and education policy*. Winchester, MA: George Allen and Unwin.

Kinginger, C. 1989. Task variation and classroom learner discourse. Ph.D. diss., University of Illinois.

Kinneavy, J. 1971. *A theory of discourse*. New York: W. Norton.

Kintgen, E., B. Kroll, and M. Rose (eds.). 1988. *Perspectives on literacy*. Carbondale, IL: Southern Illinois University Press.

Kjolseth, R. 1972. "Bilingual education programs in the United States: For assimilation or pluralism?" In B. Spolsky (ed.), *The language education of minority children*. Rowley, MA: Newbury House. 94–121.

Klein, W. 1981. "Some rules of regular ellipsis in German." In W. Klein and W. Levelt (eds.), *Crossing the boundaries in linguistics: Studies presented to Manfred Bierwisch*. Dordrecht: Reidel. 51–78.

Klein, W. 1986. *Second language acquisition*. New York: Cambridge University Press.

Kloss, H. 1977. *The American bilingual tradition*. Rowley, MA: Newbury House.

Koster, C. 1987. *Word recognition in foreign and native language*. Dordrecht: Foris.

Krakowian, B. 1989. "Acquisition of morphology and syntax." In R.B. Kaplan et al. (eds.), *Annual review of applied linguistics (1988)*, Vol. 9. New York: Cambridge University Press. 42–53.

Kramarae, C., M. Schulz, and W. O'Barr (eds.). 1984. *Language and power*. Beverly Hills, CA: Sage Publications.

Kramsch, C. 1986. From language proficiency to interactional competence. *Modern Language Journal* 70.366–72.

Krashen, S. 1976. Formal and informal linguistic environments in language acquisition and language learning. *TESOL Quarterly* 10.2.157–68.

Krashen, S. 1978. "The monitor model for second language acquisition." In P. Gingras (ed.), *Second-language acquisition and foreign language teaching*. Arlington, VA: Center for Applied Linguistics. 1–26.

Krashen, S. 1981. *Second language acquisition and second language learning*. Oxford: Pergamon Press.

Krashen, S. 1982. *Principles and practice in second language acquisition*. Oxford: Pergamon Press.

Krashen, S. 1985. *The input hypothesis: Issues and implications*. New York: Longman.

Krashen, S. and T. Terrell. 1983. *The natural approach: Language acquisition in the classroom*. New York: Pergamon Press.

Kreeft-Payton, J. and J. Mackinson-Smyth. 1988. "Writing and talking about writing: Computer networking with elementary students." In D. Johnson and D. Roen (eds.), *Richness in writing*. New York: Longman. 100–19.

Kress, G. (ed.). 1976. *Halliday: System and function in language*. New York: Oxford University Press.

Kress, G. 1983. Linguistic processes and the mediation of 'reality': The politics of newspaper language. *International Journal of the Sociology of Language* 40.43–57.

Kuno, S. 1978. "Japanese: A characteristic OV language." In W. Lehmann (ed.), *Syntactic typology*. Austin, TX: University of Texas Press. 57–138.

Kuno, S. 1986. *Functional linguistics*. Chicago, IL: University of Chicago Press.

Kuo, E. 1984. Television and language planning in Singapore. *International Journal of the Sociology of Language* 48.49–64.

Laberge, D. and S. Samuels. 1974. Towards a theory of automatic information processing in reading. *Cognitive Psychology* 6.293–323.

Labov, J. 1988. Assessing what a second language learner knows through student-teacher interaction. *Working Papers in Educational Linguistics* 4.2.1–29.

Labov, W. 1966. *The social stratification of English in New York City*. Washington, DC: Center for Applied Linguistics.

Labov, W. 1972a. *Sociolinguistic patterns*. Philadelphia, PA: University of Pennsylvania Press.

Labov, W. 1972b. *Language in the inner city: Studies in the black English vernacular*. Philadelphia, PA: University of Pennsylvania Press.

Labov, W. 1972c. "The logic of non-standard English." In P.P. Giglioli (ed.), *Language and social context*. Baltimore, MD: Penguin. 179–218.

Labov, W. (ed.). 1980. *Locating language in time and space*. New York: Academic Press.

Labov, W. and D. Fanshel. 1977. *Therapeutic discourse: Psychotherapy as conversation*. New York: Academic Press.

Lado, R. 1957. *Linguistics across cultures: Applied linguistics for language teachers*. Ann Arbor, MI: University of Michigan Press.

Lado, R. 1961. *Language testing: The construction and use of foreign language tests*. London: Longman.

Ladusaw, W. 1988. "Semantic theory." In F. Newmeyer (ed.), *Linguistics: The Cambridge survey*, Vol. 1. New York: Cambridge University Press. 89–112.

Lamb, S. 1966. *Outline of stratificational grammar*. Washington, DC: Georgetown University Press.

Lambert, R. 1987. The case for a national foreign language center: An editorial. *Modern Language Journal* 71.2–11.

Lance, D. 1969. *A brief study of Spanish-English bilingualism: Final report*. Research Project Orr-Liberal Arts—15504. College Station, TX: Texas A&M.

Langer, J. (ed.). 1987. *Language, literacy and culture: Issues of society and schooling*. Norwood, NJ: Ablex.

Lantolf, J. and A. Labarca (eds.). 1987. *Research in second language learning: Focus on the classroom*. Norwood, NJ: Ablex.

LaPonce, J. 1987. *Languages and their territories*. Toronto: University of Toronto Press.

Large, J.A. 1983. *The foreign language barrier: Problems in scientific communication*. London: André Deutsch.

Larsen-Freeman, D. 1975. The acquisition of grammatical morphemes by adult ESL students. *TESOL Quarterly* 9.409–14.

Larsen-Freeman, D. 1985. "Considerations in research design in second language acquisition." In M. Celce-Murcia (ed.), *Beyond basics*. Rowley, MA: Newbury House. 125–36.

Larsen-Freeman, D. (ed.). 1980. *Discourse analysis and second language research*. Rowley, MA: Newbury House.

Larsen-Freeman, D. 1990. "Pedagogical descriptions of language: Grammar." In R.B. Kaplan et al. (eds.), *Annual review of applied linguistics (1989)*, Vol. 10. New York: Cambridge University Press. 187–195.

Larson, J. 1989. "S-CAPE: A Spanish computerized adaptive placement exam." In W. Flint (ed.), *Modern technology in foreign language education*. Skokie, IL: National Textbook Co. 277-89.

Larson, J. and H. Madsen. 1985. Computerized-adaptive language testing: Moving beyond computer-assisted instruction. *CALICO Journal* 3.2.32–36, 43.

Latour, B. 1987. *Science in action*. Cambridge, MA: Harvard University Press.

Laurén, C. and M. Nordman (eds.). 1989. *Special language: From humans thinking to thinking machines*. Clevedon, Avon: Multilingual Matters.

Leech, G. 1971. *Meaning and the English verb*. London: Longman.

Leech, G. 1983. *Principles of pragmatics*. London: Longman.

Leech, G. 1986. "Automatic grammatical analysis and its educational implications." In G. Leech and C. Candlin (eds.), *Computers in English language teaching and research*. New York: Longman. 205–14.

Leech, G. and A. Beale. 1985. "The use of computers in English language research." In V. Kinsella (ed.), *Cambridge language teaching surveys 3*. New York: Cambridge University Press. 5–18.

Leech, G. and M. Short. 1981. *Style in fiction*. New York: Longman.

Leech, G. and J. Svartvik. 1975. *A communicative grammar of English*. New York: Longman.

Leech, G. and C. Candlin (eds.). 1986. *Computers in English language teaching and research*. London: Longman.

Lehiste, I. 1988. *Lectures on language contact*. Cambridge, MA: MIT Press.

Leibowitz, A. 1969. English literacy: Legal sanction for discrimination. *Notre Dame Lawyer* 45.1.7–69.

Leibowitz, A. 1971. *Educational policy and political acceptance: The imposition of English as the language of instruction*. Washington, DC: Center for Applied Linguistics. [ED 147321]

Leibowitz, A. 1976. "Language and the law: The exercise of political power through the designation of language." In W. O'Barr and J. O'Barr (eds.), *Language and politics*. The Hague: Mouton. 449–76.

Leibowitz, A. 1980. *The bilingual education act: A legislative analysis*. Rosslyn, VA: National Clearinghouse for Bilingual Education.

Lennard, H. and A. Bernstein. 1960. *The anatomy of psychotherapy*. New York: Columbia University Press.

Lerman, S. 1988. Unix workstations in academia: At the crossroads. *Academic Computing* 3.3.16–18, 51–55.

Levelt, W.J.M. 1978. Skill theory and language teaching. *Studies in Second Language Acquisition* 1.1.53–70.

Levin, B. 1982. *The making (and unmaking) of a civil rights regulation: Language minority children and bilingual education*. Palo Alto, CA: California Institute for Research on Educational Finance and Government, Stanford University.

Levin, B. 1983. An analysis of the federal attempt to regulate bilingual education: Protecting civil rights or controlling curriculum. *Journal of Law and Education* 12.1.39–60.

Levin, B. et al. 1985. "Muktuk meets Jacuzzi: Computer networks and elementary school writers." In S. Freedman (ed.), *The acquisition of written language*. Norwood, NJ: Ablex. 160–71.

Levinson, S. 1983. *Pragmatics*. New York: Cambridge University Press.

Lewis, E.G. 1980. *Bilingualism and bilingual education*. Albuquerque, NM: University of New Mexico Press.

Lightbown, P. 1983. "Exploring relationships between developmental and instructional sequences in L2 acquisition." In H. Seliger and M. Long (eds.), *Classroom-oriented research in second language acquisition*. Rowley, MA: Newbury House. 217–45.

Lightbown, P. and L. White. 1987. The influence of linguistic theories on language acquisition research: Description and explanation. *Language Learning* 37.4.483–510.

Lockridge, K. 1974. *Literacy in colonial New England*. New York: Norton.

Loftus, E. 1975. Leading questions and the eyewitness report. *Cognitive Psychology* 7.560–72.

Loh, W.D. 1981. Psycho-legal research. *Michigan Law Review* 79.659–707.

Long, M. 1981. Input, interaction and second language acquisition. *Annals of the New York Academy of Sciences* 379.259–78.

Long, M. 1983. Does second language instruction make a difference? A review of research. *TESOL Quarterly* 17.3.359–82.

Long, M. 1987. Trends in second language classroom research. Paper presented at the annual meeting of the British Association of Applied Linguistics, Nottingham, England.

Long, M. and P. Porter 1985. Group work interlanguage talk, and second language acquisition. *TESOL Quarterly* 19.207–28.

Longacre, R. 1983. *The grammar of discourse*. New York: Plenum.

Louie, S. and R. Rubeck. 1989. Hypertext publishing and the revitalization of knowledge. *Academic Computing* 3.9.20–23, 30–31.

Lozanov, G. 1979. *Suggestology and outlines of suggestopedy*. New York: Gordon and Breach.

Lyons, J. 1970. *New horizons in linguistics*. Harmondsworth: Penguin.

Macias, R. 1979. "Language choice and human rights in the U.S." In J. Alatis (ed.), *Language in public life*. Georgetown University Round Table on Languages and Linguistics. Washington, DC: Georgetown University Press. 86–101.

Macias, R. 1982a. "Language policy, planning, and politics in the United States concerned with language minority issues." In R.B. Kaplan et al. (eds.), *Annual review of applied linguistics (1981)*, Vol. 2. New York: Cambridge University Press. 86–104.

Macias, R. 1982b. "United States language in education policy: Issues in the schooling of language minorities." In R.B. Kaplan et al. (eds.), *Annual review of applied linguistics (1981)*, Vol. 2. New York: Cambridge University Press. 144–60.

Macias, R. 1985. Language and ideology in the United States. *Social Education* (Journal of the National Council for Social Studies) 49.2.97–100.

Macias, R. (ed.). 1988. *Are English language amendments in the national interest? A policy analysis of proposals to establish English as the official language of the U.S.* Claremont, CA: Thomas Rivera Policy Center.

Macias, R. and M. Spencer, 1984. *Estimating the number of language minority and limited English proficient persons in the U.S.: A comparative analysis of the studies.* Los Alamitos, CA: National Center for Bilingual Research.

Mackey, W. 1965. *Language teaching analysis.* London: Longman.

Mackey, W. 1970. A typology of bilingual education. *Foreign Language Annals* 3. 596–608.

Mackey, W. 1972. "The description of bilingualism." In J. Fishman (ed.), *Readings in the sociology of language.* The Hague: Mouton. 554–84.

Mackie, R. 1981. *Literacy and revolution: The pedagogy of Paulo Friere.* New York: Continuum.

Maclean, Joan. 1989. "Approaches to describing doctor-patient interviews." In H. Coleman (ed.), *Working with language: A multidisciplinary consideration of language use in work contexts.* Berlin: Mouton. 261–96.

MacWhinney, B. (ed.). 1987. *Mechanisms of language acquisition.* Hillsdale, NJ: Lawrence Erlbaum Associates.

Madsen, H. 1983. *Techniques in testing.* New York: Oxford University Press.

Maher, B. 1972. The language of schizophrenia: A review and interpretation. *British Journal of Psychiatry* 120.3–17.

Maher, J. 1981a. The scientific manuscript: Overview and guidelines for the ESP/SL instructor. *Cross Currents* 8.2.65–75.

Maher, J. 1981b. Concepts and scientific usage in English. *Bulletin of Shimani Medical University* 3.38–50.

Maher, J. 1985. The role of English in medicine and medical education in Japan. Ph.D. diss., University of Edinburgh.

Maher, J. 1986a. The role of English as the international language of medicine. *Applied Linguistics* 7.2.206–18.

Maher, J. 1986b. English for medical purposes. *Language Teaching* 19.2.102–14.

Maher, J. 1989. "Language use and preference in Japanese medical communication." In H. Coleman (ed.), *Working with language: A multidisciplinary consideration of language use in work contexts.* Berlin: Mouton. 261–96.

Mann, W. and S. Thompson. 1986. Relational propositions in discourse. *Discourse Processes* 9.1.57–90.

Mann, W. and S. Thompson. 1988. Rhetorical structure theory. *Text* 8.243–81.

Marshall, D. 1986. The question of an official language: Language rights and the official language amendment. *International Journal of the Sociology of Language* 60.7–75.

Martin, J. 1989. *Factual writing*. New York: Oxford University Press.

Maslow, L. 1970. *Motivation and personality*. New York: Harper and Row.

Matarazzo, J. et al. 1968. "Speech and silence behavior in clinical psychotherapy and its laboratory correlates." In J. Schlien (ed.), *Research in psychotherapy*. Washington, DC: American Psychological Association. 347–94.

Matute-Bianchi, M. 1979. "The federal mandate for bilingual education." In R. Padilla (ed.), *Bilingual education and public policy in the United States*. Ypsilanti, MI: Eastern Michigan University. 18–38.

Mauet, T. 1980. *Fundamentals of trial techniques*. Boston, MA: Little and Brown.

May, R. 1985. *Logical form: Its structures and derivation*. Cambridge, MA: MIT Press.

Mazurkewich, I. 1984. "Dative questions and markedness." In F. Eckman, L. Bell, and D. Nelson (eds.), *Universals of second language acquisition*. Rowley, MA: Newbury House. 119–31.

McArthur, T. 1983. *A foundation course for language teachers*. Cambridge, UK: Cambridge University Press.

McBarnett, D. 1981. *Conviction*. London: Macmillan.

McClelland, J. 1987. "The case for interactionism in language processing." In M. Coltheart (ed.), *The psychology of reading. Attention and performance XII*. Hillsdale, NJ: Lawrence Erlbaum Associates. 3–36.

McCloskey, J. 1988. "Syntactic theory." In F. Newmeyer (ed.), *Linguistics: The Cambridge survey*, Vol. 1. New York: Cambridge University Press. 18–59.

McClure, E. 1977. "Aspects of code-switching in the discourse of bilingual Mexican American children." In M. Saville-Troike (ed.), *Linguistics and anthropology*. Georgetown University Round Table on Languages and Linguistics. Washington, DC: Georgetown University Press. 93–116.

McGrath, E. 1952. Language study and world affairs. *Modern Language Journal* 36.5. 205–09.

McKay, S. and S. Wong (eds.). 1988. *Language diversity: Problem or resource?* New York: Newbury House.

McLaughlin, B. 1980. Theory and research in second-language learning: An emerging paradigm. *Language Learning* 30.2.331–50.

McLaughlin, B. 1984. *Second language acquisition in childhood*. Vol. 1, *Preschool children*. Hillsdale, NJ: Lawrence Erlbaum Associates.

McLaughlin, B. 1985. *Second language acquisition in childhood*. Vol. 2, *Elementary school years*. Hillsdale, NJ: Lawrence Erlbaum Associates.

McLaughlin, B. 1987. *Theories of second-language learning*. Baltimore, MD: Edward Arnold.

McLaughlin, B. 1990. Restructuring. *Applied Linguistics* 11.2.113–28.

McLaughlin, B., T. Rossman, and B. McLeod. 1983. Second-language learning: An information-processing perspective. *Language Learning* 33.1.135–58.

McLeod, B. and B. McLaughlin. 1986. Restructuring or automaticity? Reading in a second language. *Language Learning* 36.109–23.

Meijs, W. (ed.). 1987. *Corpus linguistics and beyond: Proceedings of the seventh international conference on English language research on computerized corpora*. Amsterdam: Rodopi.

Meisel, J. 1980. "Linguistic simplification." In S. Felix (ed.), *Second language development: Trends and issues*. Tübingen: Narr Verlag. 13–40.

Meisel, J. et al. 1981. On determining developmental stages in natural second language acquisition. *Studies in Second language Acquisition* 3.109–35.

Menke, G. 1989. The impact of computer-assisted instruction on the teaching of English as a second language: A survey of post-secondary ESL programs in the United States. Ph.D. diss., University of Southern California.

Meyer, B. 1975. *The organization of prose and its effect on memory*. Amsterdam: North-Holland.

Meyer, B. 1985. "Prose analysis: Purposes, procedures, and problems." In B. Britton and J. Black (eds.), *Understanding expository text*. Hillsdale, NJ: Lawrence Erlbaum Associates. 11–64.

Michaels, S. 1986. "Narrative presentations: An oral preparation for literacy with first graders." In J. Cook-Gumperz (ed.), *The social construction of literacy*. New York: Cambridge University Press. 94–116.

Milic, L.T. 1967. *A quantitative approach to the style of Jonathan Swift*. The Hague: Mouton.

Milroy, L. 1980. *Language and social networks*. New York: Basil Blackwell.

Milroy, L. 1987. *Observing and analysing natural language*. New York: Basil Blackwell.

Mishler, E. 1984. *The discourse of medicine*. Norwood, NJ: Ablex.

Mishler, E. 1986. *Research interviewing: Context and narrative*. Cambridge, MA: Harvard University Press.

Mohan, B. 1979. Relating language teaching and content teaching. *TESOL Quarterly* 13.2.171–82.

Mohan, B. 1986. *Language and content*. Reading, MA: Addison-Wesley.

Molholt, Garry. 1988. Computer-assisted instruction in pronunciation for Chinese speakers of American English. *TESOL Quarterly* 22.1.91–112.

Moll, L. and S. Diaz. 1985. "Ethnographic pedagogy: Promoting effective bilingual instruction." In E. Garcia and R. Padilla (eds.), *Advances in bilingual education research*. Tucson, AZ: University of Arizona Press. 127–49.

Montaño-Harmon, M. 1988. Discourse features in the composition of Mexican, English-as-a-second-language, Mexican-American/Chicano, and Anglo high school students: Considerations for the formulation of educational policies. Ph.D. diss., University of Southern California.

Morley, J. 1979. "Materials development: The new frontier, not by chance but by design." In C. Yorio, K. Perkins and J. Schachter (eds.), *On TESOL 1979*. Washington, DC: TESOL Publications. 12–22.

Morley, J. 1985. Listening comprehension: Student controlled modules for self-access self-study. *TESOL Newsletter* 19.6.1/32–33.

Morrow, K. 1977. *Techniques of evaluation for a notional syllabus.* Reading, UK: Center for Applied Linguistics Study.

Morton, A.Q. 1986. Once: A test of authorship based on words which are not repeated in the sample. *Literary and Linguistic Computing* 1.1–8.

Moskowitz, G. 1978. *Caring and sharing in the foreign language classroom: A sourcebook on humanistic techniques.* Rowley, MA: Newbury House.

Munby, J. 1978. *Communicative syllabus design.* Cambridge, UK: Cambridge University Press.

Myers, B. 1963/1975. *Myers-Briggs type indicator: Manual.* Palo Alto, CA: Consulting Psychologists Press.

Naiman, N. et al. 1978. *The good language learner* (Research in education series, 7). Toronto: Ontario Institute for Studies in Education.

Nation, R. and B. McLaughlin. 1986. Experts and novices: An information-processing approach to the "good language learner" problem. *Applied Psycholinguistics* 7.41–56.

Nayak, N. et al. 1989. *Language learning strategies in monolingual and multilingual subjects.* Unpublished manuscript, University of California, Santa Cruz.

Neu, J. 1986. American English business negotiations: Training for non-native speakers. *ESP Journal* 5.1.41–57.

Newkirk, T. (ed.). 1986. *To compose: Teaching writing in the high school.* Portsmouth, NH: Heinemann.

Newmeyer, F. 1983. *Grammatical theory: Its limits and possibilities.* Chicago, IL: University of Chicago Press.

Newmeyer F. 1986. *Linguistic theory in America.* 2d ed. Orlando, FL: Academic Press.

Newmeyer, F. (ed.). 1988. *Linguistics: The Cambridge survey.* 4 Vols. New York: Cambridge University Press.

Nichols, P. 1984. "Networks and hierarchies: Language and social stratification." In C. Kramarae, M. Schulz, and W. O'Barr (eds.), *Language and power.* Beverly Hills, CA: Sage Publications. 23–42.

Noblitt, J. 1988. Writing technology and secondary orality. *Academic Computing* 2.34.56–57, 59.

Nunan, D. 1988. *The learner-centered curriculum: A study in second language teaching.* New York: Cambridge University Press.

Nunan, D. 1989. Toward a collaborative approach to curriculum development: A case study. *TESOL Quarterly* 23.1.9–25.

Oakhill, J. and A. Garnham. 1988. *Becoming a skilled reader.* New York: Basil Blackwell.

Oakman, R.L. 1975. Carlyle and the machine: A quantitative analysis of syntax in prose style. *Association for Literary and Linguistic Computing Bulletin* 3.100–14.

O'Barr, W. 1982. *Linguistic evidence.* New York: Academic Press.

O'Barr, W. 1984. "Asking the right questions about language and power." In C. Kramarae, M. Schulz and W. O'Barr (eds.), *Language and power.* Beverly Hills, CA: Sage Publications. 260–80.

O'Barr, W. and J. O'Barr. 1976. *Language and politics*. The Hague: Mouton.

Ochs, E. 1988. *Culture and language development*. New York: Cambridge University Press.

Odell, L. and D. Goswami (eds.). 1985. *Writing in non-academic settings*. New York: Guilford Press.

Ogbu, J. 1987. "Opportunity structure, cultural boundaries, and literacy." In J. Langer (ed.), *Language, literacy and culture: Issues of society and schooling*. Norwood, NJ: Ablex. 149–77.

O'Grady, W., M. Dobrovolsky, and M. Aronoff. 1989. *Contemporary linguistics*. New York: St. Martin's Press.

Ohannessian, S., C. Ferguson, and E. Polomé (eds.). 1975. *Language surveys in developing nations*. Washington, DC: Center for Applied Linguistics.

Oller, J. 1979. *Language tests at school: A pragmatic approach*. New York: Longman.

Oller, J. 1981. "Language testing research." In R.B. Kaplan et al. (eds.), *Annual review of applied linguistics (1980)*, Vol. 1. New York: Cambridge University Press. 124–41.

Oller, J., A. Hudson, and P. Liu. 1977. Attitudes and attained proficiency in ESL: A sociolinguistic study of Chinese in the United States. *Language Learning* 27.1.1–27.

Oller, J. (ed.). 1983. *Issues in language testing research*. Rowley, MA: Newbury House.

Oller, J. and P. Richard-Amato (eds.). 1985. *Methods that work*. Rowley, MA: Newbury House.

Olson, D. 1977. From utterance to text: The bias of language in speech and writing. *Harvard Educational Review* 47.3.257–82.

Olson, R. and B. Wise. 1987. "Computer speech in reading instruction." In D. Reinking (ed.), *Reading and computers: Issues for theory and practice*. New York: Teacher's College Press. 156–77.

O'Malley, J.M. 1988. The cognitive academic language learning approach (CALLA). *Journal of Multilingual and Multicultural Development* 9.1.2.43–60.

O'Malley, J.M. and A. Chamot. 1989. *Learning strategies in second language acquisition*. New York: Cambridge University Press.

O'Malley, J.M., A. Chamot, and C. Walker. 1987. Some applications of cognitive theory to second language acquisition. *Studies in Second Language Acquisition* 9.3.287–306.

O'Malley, J., R. Russo, and A. Chamot. 1983. *A review of the literature on learning strategies in the acquisition of English as a second language*. Roslyn, VA: InterAmerica Research Associates.

O'Malley, J.M. et al. 1985. Learning strategy applications with students of English as a second language. *TESOL Quarterly* 19.3.557–84.

Ong, W. 1982. *Orality and literacy: Technologizing the word*. London: Methuen.

Orasanu, J., M. Slater, and L. Alder (eds.). 1979. *Language, sex and gender: Does la différence make a difference?* New York: New York Academy of Sciences. [Annals, No. 327]

Ornstein, J. 1962. New frontiers in language learning. *Modern Language Journal* 46.3. 110–15.

Oskarsson, M. 1975. The relationship between foreign language proficiency and various psychological variables. Paper presented at the International Congress of Applied Linguistics, Lund, Sweden.

Otheguy, R. 1982. Thinking about bilingual education: A critical approach. *Harvard Educational Review* 52.3.301–14.

Otswald, P.F. 1965. Acoustic methods in psychiatry. *Scientific American* 212.82–91.

Ovando, C. 1983. Bilingual/bicultural education: Its legacy and its future. *Phi Delta Kappan* 64.8.564–68.

Oxford-Carpenter, R. 1989. *Learning strategies*. New York: Newbury House.

Padilla, R. 1983. "Articulating a positive orientation toward bilingual education." In R. Padilla (ed.), *Theory, technology and public policy in bilingual education*. Roslyn, VA: National Clearinghouse for Bilingual Education. 351–64.

Padilla, R. 1984. *Federal shifts in bilingual education: Consequences for local implementation and national evaluation*. Los Alamitos, CA: National Center for Bilingual Research.

Palmer, F. 1981. *Semantics*. 2d ed. Cambridge, UK: Cambridge University Press.

Palmer. F. 1986. *Mood and modality*. New York: Cambridge University Press.

Palmer, F. 1987. *The English verb*. 2d ed. New York: Longman.

Palmer, H. 1921. *The principles of language study*. New York: New World Book Company.

Palmer, H. and F. Blandford. 1939. *A grammar of spoken English*. Cambridge, UK: W. Heffer and Sons.

Pappas, C. 1985. "The cohesive harmony and cohesive density of children's oral and written stories." In J. Benson and W. Greaves (eds.), *Systemic perspectives on discourse*. Vol. 2, *Selected applied papers from the 9th international systemic workshop*. 169–86.

Parker, W. 1961. *The national interest and foreign languages*. Washington, DC: U.S. Government Printing Office.

Partee, B. (ed.). 1976. *Montague grammar*. New York: Academic Press.

Pattison, J. 1982. *On literacy*. New York: Oxford University Press.

Paulston, C. 1971. The sequencing of structural pattern drills. *TESOL Quarterly* 5.2. 197–208.

Paulston, C. 1974. Linguistic and communicative competence. *TESOL Quarterly* 8.3.347–62.

Paulston, C. (ed.). 1988. *International handbook of bilingualism and bilingual education*. New York: Greenwood Press.

Pederson, K. 1987. "Research on CALL." In W. Flint (ed.), *Modern media in foreign language education: Theory and implementation*. Lincolnwood, IL: National Textbook Company. 99–132.

Penman, R. 1987. Discourse in courts: Cooperation, coercion, and coherence. *Discourse Processes* 10.3.201–18.

Pennington, M. 1985. "Effective administration of an ESL program." In P. Larsen, E. Judd, and D. Messerschmidt (eds.), *On TESOL '84*. Washington, DC: TESOL Publications. 301–16.

Perdue, C. (ed.). 1984. *Second language acquisition by adult immigrants: A field manual.* Rowley, MA: Newbury House.

Perera, K. 1984. *Children's writing and reading: Analysing classroom language.* New York: Basil Blackwell.

Perfetti, C. and D. McCutchen. 1987. "Schooled language competence: Linguistic abilities in reading and writing." In S. Rosenberg (ed.), *Advances in applied psycholinguistics.* Vol. 2, *Reading, writing, and language learning.* New York: Cambridge University Press. 105–41.

Pettinari, C. 1988. *Task, talk and text in the operating room: A study in medical discourse.* Norwood, NJ: Ablex.

Pfaff, C. (ed.). 1987. *First and second language acquisition processes.* New York: Newbury House.

Phelps, L. 1985. Dialectics of coherence: Toward an integrative theory. *College English* 47.1.12–29.

Philips, S. 1983. *The invisible culture: Communication in classroom and community on the Warm Springs Indian reservation.* New York: Longman.

Piaget, J. 1926. *The language and thought of the child.* New York: Harcourt and Brace.

Pica, T. et al. 1989. Comprehensible output as an outcome of linguistic demands on the learner. *Studies in Second Language Acquisition* 11.1.63–90.

Pienemann, M. and M. Johnston. 1984. Toward an explanatory model of language acquisition. Paper presented at the 9th ALAA conference, Alice Springs, Australia, Aug.–Sept. 1984.

Pienemann, M. and M. Johnston. 1987a. *A predictive framework of SLA.* Unpublished manuscript. University of Sydney.

Pienemann, M. and M. Johnston. 1987b. "Factors influencing the development of language proficiency." In D. Nunan (ed.), *Applying second language acquistion research.* Adelaide: National Curriculum Resource Centre. 45–141.

Pifer, A. 1978. *Bilingual education and the Hispanic challenge.* New York: Carnegie Corporation. [ED 190336]

Pike, K. 1982. *Linguistics concepts: An introduction to tagmemics.* Lincoln, NE: University of Nebraska Press.

Pike, K. and E. Pike. 1982. *Grammatical analysis.* Arlington, TX: Summer Institute of Linguistics.

Pimsleur, P. 1966. *Language aptitude battery.* New York: Harcourt Brace Jovanovich.

Pincas, J. 1980. Rand meets the president's commission: The life cycle of a non-event. *Annals of the American Academy of Political and Social Science* 449.80–90.

Pinker, S. 1989. *Learnability and cognition.* Cambridge, MA: MIT Press.

Politti, J. 1985. "Comments on H.G. Widdowson, *The teaching, learning and study of literature.*" In R. Quirk and H.G. Widdowson (eds.), *English in the world: Teaching and learning the language and literatures.* New York: Cambridge University Press. 195–96.

Politzer, R. 1960. *Teaching French: An introduction to applied linguistics.* Waltham, MA: Ginn and Company.

Politzer, R. and C. Staubach. 1961. *Teaching Spanish: A linguistic orientation.* Waltham, MA: Ginn and Company.

Posner, M. and C. Snyder. 1975. "Attention and cognitive control." In R. Solso (ed.), *Information processing and cognition: The Loyola symposium.* Hillsdale, NJ: Lawrence Erlbaum Associates. 55–86.

Pouncey, S. 1981. *The federal law of bilingual education.* New York: Center for Social Sciences, Columbia University. [ED 235294]

Prabhu, N. 1987. *Second language pedagogy.* Oxford: Oxford University Press.

Prator, C. 1968. "The British heresy in TEFL." In J. Fishman, C. Ferguson, and J. Das Gupta (eds.), *Language problems of developing nations.* New York: Wiley. 459–76.

President's Commission on Foreign Languages and International Studies. 1979. *Strength through wisdom: A critique of U.S. capability.* Washington, DC: U.S. Government Printing Office.

Preston, D. 1989. *Sociolinguistics and second language acquisition.* New York: Basil Blackwell.

Prince, E. 1988. "Discourse analysis: A part of the study of linguistic competence." In F. Newmeyer (ed.), *Linguistics: The Cambridge survey,* Vol. 2. New York: Cambridge University Press. 164–82.

Prince, E., J. Frader, and C. Bosk. 1982. "On hedging in physician-physician discourse." In R. Di Pietro (ed.), *Linguistics and the professions.* Norwood, NJ: Ablex. 83–97.

Pugh, A. and J. Ulijn (eds.). 1984. *Reading for professional purposes.* London: Heinemann.

Purves, A. 1988. *Writing across languages and cultures.* Newbury Park: Sage Publications.

Putnam, C. 1981. Assessing the assessment: A review of the president's commission report. *Foreign Language Annals* 14.1.11–15.

Quinn, T. 1985. "Functional approaches in language pedagogy." In R.B. Kaplan et al. (eds.), *Annual review of applied linguistics (1984),* Vol. 5. New York: Cambridge University Press. 60–80.

Quirk, R. and S. Greenbaum. 1975. *A concise grammar of contemporary English.* New York: Holt, Rinehart and Winston.

Quirk R. and H. Widdowson (eds.). 1985. *English in the world: Teaching and learning the language and literatures.* New York: Cambridge University Press.

Quirk R. et al. 1972. *A contemporary grammar of English.* New York: Longman.

Quirk, R. et al. 1985. *A comprehensive grammar of English.* New York: Longman.

Radford, A. 1980. *Transformational syntax.* New York: Cambridge University Press.

Radford, A. 1988. *Transformational grammar.* New York: Cambridge University Press.

Rafoth, B. and D. Rubin (eds.). 1988. *The social construction of written communication.* Norwood, NJ: Ablex.

Reimsdyk, H. and E. Williams. 1986. *Introduction to the theory of grammar.* Cambridge, MA: MIT Press.

Reinhart, H. 1981. Caveat emptor: The report of the president's commission. *Modern Language Journal* 65.3.248–53.

Reinking, D. (ed.). 1987. *Reading and computers: Issues for theory and practice.* New York: Teacher's College Press.

Renouf, A. 1984. "Corpus development at Birmingham University." In J. Aarts and W. Meijs (eds.), *Corpus linguistics: Recent developments in the use of computer corpora in English language research.* Amsterdam: Rodopi. 3–39.

Resnick, D. and L. Resnick. 1977. The nature of literacy: An historical exploration. *Harvard Educational Review* 47.3.370–85.

Rice, F. (ed.). 1962. *Study of the role of second languages in Asia, Africa, and Latin America.* Washington, DC: Center for Applied Linguistics.

Richard-Amato, P. 1987. *Making it happen.* New York: Newbury House.

Richards, I.A. 1931 (with series revisions through 1939). *Basic English.* London: Kegan Paul.

Richards, J. 1984a. The secret life of methods. *TESOL Quarterly* 18.1.7–24.

Richards, J. 1984b. Language curriculum development. *RELC Journal* 15.1.1–29.

Richards, J. 1985. *The context of language teaching.* Cambridge, UK: Cambridge University Press.

Richards, J. and T. Rodgers. 1986. *Approaches and methods in language teaching: A description and analysis.* New York: Cambridge University Press.

Richards, J. and R. Schmidt (eds.). 1983. *Language and communication.* New York: Longman.

Rigg, P. and N.S. Enright (eds.). 1986. *Children and ESL: Integrating perspectives.* Washington, DC: TESOL Publication.

Rivera, C. (ed.). 1984a. *Language proficiency and academic achievement.* Clevedon, Avon: Multilingual Matters.

Rivera, C. (ed.). 1984b. *Measurement of communicative proficiency: Models and applications.* Clevedon, Avon: Multilingual Matters.

Rivera, C. (ed.). 1984c. *An ethnographic/sociolinguistic approach to language proficiency assessment.* Clevedon, Avon: Multilingual Matters.

Rivera, C. (ed.). 1984d. *Placement procedures in bilingual education: Education and policy issues.* Clevedon, Avon: Multilingual Matters.

Rivera-La Scala, G. 1989. "The Annapolis interactive video project." In W. Flint (ed.), *Modern technology in foreign language education: Applications and projects.* Lincolnwood, IL: National Textbook Company. 257–61.

Rivers, W. 1964. *The psychologist and the foreign language teacher.* Chicago, IL: University of Chicago Press.

Rivers, W. 1972. Talking off the tops of their heads. *TESOL Quarterly* 6.1.71–81.

Rivers, W. 1981. *Teaching foreign language skills.* 2d ed. Chicago, IL: University of Chicago Press.

Robins, R.H. 1979. *A short history of linguistics.* 2d ed. New York: Longman.

Robins, R.H. 1989. *General linguistics.* 4th ed. New York: Longman.

Robinson, P. 1980. *ESP (English for special purposes).* New York: Pergamon Press.

Rodgers, T. 1989. "Syllabus design, curriculum development and policy determination." In R.K. Johnson (ed.), *The second language curriculum*. New York: Cambridge University Press. 24–34.

Roeming, R. 1962. Foreign language as weapons for defense. *Modern Language Journal* 46.7.299–303.

Roeper, T. 1988. "Grammatical principles of first language acquisition: Theory and evidence." In F. Newmeyer (ed.), *Linguistics: The Cambridge survey*, Vol. 2. New York: Cambridge University Press. 35–52.

Rogers, C. 1951. *Client centered therapy*. Boston, MA: Houghton Mifflin Company.

Ronoff, S. 1988. The language laboratory: Or—it's not just for sleeping anymore. *The Michigan Alumnus* 94.5.30–34.

Rosansky, E. 1976. Methods and morphemes in second language acquisition research. *Language Learning* 26.2.409–25.

Rose, M. (ed.). 1985. *When a writer can't write: Studies in writer's block and other composing problems*. New York: Guilford.

Rosegrant, T. 1988. "Talking word processors for the early grades." In J. Hoot and S. Silvern (eds.), *Writing with computers in the early grades*. New York: Teacher's College Press. 143–59.

Rosenberg, S. (ed.). 1987. *Advances in applied psycholinguistics*. Vol. 2, *Reading, writing and language learning*. New York: Cambridge University Press.

Rotberg, I. 1982. Some legal and research considerations in establishing federal policy in bilingual education. *Harvard Educational Review* 52.2.149–68.

Royal Society of Arts. n.d. *Test in the communicative use of English as a foreign language*. London: Royal Society of Arts.

Rubin, J. 1975. What the good language learner can teach us. *TESOL Quarterly* 9.1. 45–51.

Rubin, J. and B. Jernudd (eds.). 1971. *Can languages be planned?* Honolulu, HI: University of Hawaii Press.

Rubin, J. et al. (eds.). 1977. *Language planning processes*. The Hague: Mouton.

Ruiz, H. 1987. "The impregnability of textbooks: The example of American foreign language education." In S. Savignon and M. Berns (eds.), *Initiatives in communicative language teaching II*. Reading, MA: Addison-Wesley. 33–53.

Rumelhart, D. et al. 1986. *Parallel distributed processing*, 2 Vols. Cambridge, MA: MIT Press.

Rutherford, W. 1968. 1st ed. 1975, 1977. 2d ed. *Modern English*. New York: Harcourt Brace Jovanovich.

Rutherford, W. and M. Sharwood Smith (eds.). 1988. *Grammar and second language teaching*. New York: Newbury House.

Sacks, H., E. Schegloff, and G. Jefferson. 1974. A simplest systematics for the organization of turn-taking for conversation. *Language* 50.4.696–735.

Sajavaara, K. 1978. "The monitor model and monitoring in foreign language acquisition research." In P. Gingras (ed.), *Second language acquisition and foreign language teaching*. Washington, DC: Center for Applied Linguistics. 51–67.

Sampson, G. 1980. *Schools of linguistics.* Stanford, CA: Stanford University Press.

Sampson, G. 1987. "Rumelhart, McClelland, et al.: Parallel distributed processing." *Language* 63.4.871–86.

Santiago, I. 1982. "Third world vernacular/bi-multicultural curricula issues." In B. Hartford, A. Valdman, and C. Foster (eds.), *Issues in international bilingual education: The role of the vernacular.* New York: Plenum. 113–38.

Sapir, E. 1921. *Language.* New York: Harcourt, Brace and World.

Saunders, G. 1988. *Bilingual children: From birth to teens.* Clevedon, Avon: Multilingual Matters.

Savage, L. and J. Dresner. 1986. Vocational ESL: Language tuition leading to employment. *EFL Gazette* 79.10.

Savignon, S. 1972. *Communicative competence: An experiment in foreign language teaching.* Philadelphia, PA: Center for Curriculum Development.

Savignon, S. 1974. "Talking with my son: An example of communicative competence." In F. Grittner (ed.), *Careers, communication, and culture.* Skokie, IL: National Textbook Co.

Savignon, S. 1983. *Communicative competence: Theory and classroom practices.* Reading, MA: Addison-Wesley.

Savignon, S. 1985. Evaluation of communicative competence: The ACTFL provisional proficiency guidelines. *Modern Language Journal* 69.129–34.

Savignon, S. and M. Berns (eds.). 1984. *Initiatives in communicative language teaching.* Reading, MA: Addison-Wesley.

Savignon, S. and M. Berns (eds.). 1987. *Initiatives in communicative language teaching II.* Reading, MA: Addison-Wesley.

Saville-Troike, M. 1989. *The ethnography of communication.* 2d ed. New York: Basil Blackwell.

Sayers, D. 1988. "Bilingual sister classes in computer writing networks." In D. Johnson and D. Roen (eds.), *Richness in writing.* New York: Longman. 120–33.

Scarcella, R. 1989. "Conversational analysis in L2 acquisition and teaching." In R.B. Kaplan et al. (eds.), *Annual review of applied linguistics (1988),* Vol. 9. New York: Cambridge University Press. 72–91.

Schachter, J. 1974. An error in error analysis. *Language Learning* 24.2.205–14.

Schachter, J. 1983. "A new account of language transfer." In S. Gass and L. Selinker (eds.), *Language transfer in language learning.* Rowley, MA: Newbury House. 98–111.

Schachter, J. 1989. Second language acquisition and its relationship to universal grammar. *Applied Linguistics* 9.219–35.

Schachter, J. and M. Celce-Murcia. 1977. Some reservations concerning error analysis. *TESOL Quarterly* 11.3.441–51.

Schank, R. and R. Abelson. 1977. *Scripts, plans, goals and understanding.* Hillsdale, NJ: Lawrence Erlbaum Associates.

Schank, R. and R. Wilensky. 1977. Response to Dresher and Hornstein. *Cognition* 5. 133–46.

Schegloff, E. 1972. "Sequencing in conversational openings." In J. Gumperz and D. Hymes (eds.), *Directions in sociolinguistics*. New York: Holt, Rinehart and Winston. 346–80.

Scherer, G. and M. Wertheimer. 1964. *A psycholinguistic experiment in foreign language teaching*. New York: McGraw Hill.

Schieffelin, B. and P. Gilmore (eds.). 1986. *The acquisition of literacy*. Norwood, NJ: Ablex.

Schiffrin, D. 1987. *Discourse markers*. New York: Cambridge University Press.

Schiffrin, D. 1988. "Conversational analysis." In F. Newmeyer (ed.), *Linguistics: The Cambridge survey*, Vol. 4. New York: Cambridge University Press. 251–276.

Schneider, W. and R. Shiffrin. 1977. Controlled and automatic processing, I: Detection, search, and attention. *Psychological Review* 84.1–64.

Schumann, J. 1975. Affective factors and the problem of age in second language acquisition. *Language Learning* 25.2.209–25.

Schumann, J. 1976. Social distance as a factor in second language acquisition. *Language Learning* 26.1.135–44.

Schumann, J. 1978a. *The pidginization process: A model for second language acquisition*. Rowley, MA: Newbury House.

Schumann, J. 1978b. "Social and psychological factors in second language acquisition." In J. Richards (ed.), *Understanding second and foreign language learning: Issues and approaches*. Rowley, MA: Newbury House. 163–78.

Schumann, J. 1978c. "The acculturation model for second language acquisition." In P. Gingras (ed.), *Second-language acquisition and foreign-language teaching*. Washington, DC: Center for Applied Linguistics. 27–50.

Schumann, J. 1986. Research on the acculturation model for second language acquistion. *Journal of Multilingual and Multicultural Development* 7.5.379–392.

Scollon, R. and S. Scollon. 1981. *Narrative, literacy, and face in interethnic communication*. Norwood, NJ: Ablex.

Scovel, T. 1978. The effect of affect on foreign language learning: A review of the anxiety research. *Language Learning* 28.1.129–42.

Scovel, T. 1983. "Emphasizing language: A reply to humanism, neoaudiolingualism, and notional-functionalism." In M. Clarke and J. Handscombe (eds.), *On TESOL '82: Pacific perspectives on language learning and teaching*. Washington, DC: TESOL Publications. 85–96.

Scovel, T. 1988a. "Multiple perspectives make singular teaching." In L. Beebe (ed.), *Issues in second language acquisition*. New York: Newbury House. 169–90.

Scovel, T. 1988b. *A time to speak*. New York: Newbury House.

Scribner, S. 1987. Introduction. In D. Wagner (ed.), *The future of literacy in a changing world*. New York: Pergamon Press. 19–24.

Scribner, S. and M. Cole. 1981. *The psychology of literacy*. Cambridge, MA: Harvard University Press.

Searle, J. 1969. *Speech acts: An essay in the philosophy of language*. Cambridge, UK: Cambridge University Press.

Searle, J. 1979. *Expression and meaning.* Cambridge, UK: Cambridge University Press.

Segalowitz, N. 1986. "Skilled reading in the second language." In J. Vaid (ed.), *Language processing in bilingual psycholinguistic and neuropsychological perspectives.* Hillsdale, NJ: Lawrence Erlbaum Associates. 3–19.

Selinker, L. 1969. Language transfer. *General Linguistics* 9.2.67–92.

Selinker, L. 1972. Interlanguage. *International Review of Applied Linguistics* 10.3.201–31.

Sells, P. 1985. *Lectures on contemporary syntactic theories.* Chicago, IL: University of Chicago Press.

Shiffrin, R. and W. Schneider. 1977. Controlled and automatic human information processing, II: Perceptual learning, automatic attending, and general theory. *Psychological Review* 84.127–90.

Shih, M. 1986. Content-based approaches to teaching academic writing. *TESOL Quarterly* 20.4.617–48.

Shuy, R. 1974. "Problems of communication in the cross-cultural medical interview." In *Working papers in sociolinguistics,* Vol. 19. Austin, TX: Southwestern Educational Development Laboratory.

Shuy, R. 1975. The medical interview: Problems in communication. *Primary Care* 3. 365–86.

Shuy, R. 1977. The patient's right to clear communications in health and mental health delivery service. *ITL—Review of Applied Linguistics* 35.1–26.

Shuy, R. 1979. "Language policy in medicine: Some emerging issues in the medical interview." In J. Alatis and G. R. Tucker (eds.), *Language in public life.* Georgetown University Round Table on Languages and Linguistics. Washington, DC: Georgetown University Press. 126–36.

Shuy, R. 1984. The decade ahead for applied sociolinguistics. *International Journal of the Sociology of Language* 45.101–11.

Shuy, R. 1987a. "Language and the law." In R.B. Kaplan et al. (eds.), *Annual review of applied linguistics (1986),* Vol. 7. New York: Cambridge University Press. 50–63.

Shuy, R. 1987b. "Linguistic analysis of real estate commission agreements in a civil law suit." In R. Steele and T. Threadgold (eds.), *Language topics: Essays in honor of Michael Halliday,* Vol. 2. Philadelphia, PA: John Benjamin. 333–58.

Shuy, R. 1988. "Changing language policy in a bureaucracy." In P. Lowenberg (ed.), *Language spread and language policy: Issues, implications and case studies.* Georgetown University Round Table on Languages and Linguistics. Washington, DC: Georgetown University Press. 152–74.

Shuy, R., W. Wolfram, and W. Riley. 1968. *Field techniques in an urban language study.* Washington, DC: Center for Applied Linguistics.

Simon, P. 1980. *The tongue-tied American: Confronting the language crisis.* New York: Continuum.

Simons, H.W. (ed.). 1989. *Rhetoric in the human sciences.* Newbury Park, CA: Sage.

Sinclair, J. (ed.). 1987. *Looking up: An account of the COBUILD project.* London: Collins ELT.

Sinclair, J. 1988. The uses of *of*. Forum paper presented at the 1988 TESOL Summer Institute. July, 1988, Flagstaff, AZ.

Sinclair, J. et al. (eds.). 1987. *Collins COBUILD English language dictionary*. London: Collins ELT.

Skehan, P. 1982. *Language aptitude*. Ph.D. diss., University of London.

Skinner, B. 1957. *Verbal behavior*. New York: Appleton-Century-Crofts.

Skutnabb-Kangas, T. 1984. "Children of guest workers and immigrants: Linguistic and educational issues." In J. Edwards (ed.), *Language minorities, policies and pluralism*. London: Academic Press. 17–48.

Slagter, P. 1979. *Un nivel umbral*. Strasbourg: Council of Europe.

Slobin, D. (ed.). 1985. *The crosslinguistic study of language acquisition*. 2 Vols. Hillsdale, NJ: Lawrence Erlbaum Associates.

Slocum, J. 1985. A survey of machine translation: Its history, current status, and future prospects. *Computational Linguistics* 11.1–17.

Smith, F. 1971. *Understanding reading*. 1st ed. New York: Holt, Rinehart and Winston.

Smith, F. 1989. *Understanding reading*. 4th ed. Hillsdale, NJ: Lawrence Erlbaum Associates.

Smith, M.W.A. 1986. A critical review of word-links as a method for investigating Shakespearean chronology and authorship. *Literary and Linguistic Computing* 1.202–6.

Smith, M.W.A. 1987. Hapax legomena in prescribed positions: An investigation of recent proposals to resolve problems of authorship. *Literary and Linguistic Computing* 2.145–52.

Smith, P. 1970. *A comparison of the cognitive and audiolingual approaches to foreign language instruction: The Pennsylvania foreign language project*. Philadelphia, PA: Center for Curriculum Development.

Sperber, D. and D. Wilson. 1986. *Relevance: Foundations of pragmatic theory*. Cambridge, MA: Harvard University Press.

Spindler, G. and L. Spindler (eds.). 1987. *Interpretive ethnography of schooling: At home and abroad*. Hillsdale, NJ: Lawrence Erlbaum Associates.

Spitzer, M. 1989. "Computer conferencing: An emerging technology." In. G. Hawisher and C. Selfe (eds.), *Critical perspectives on computers and composition instruction*. New York: Teacher's College Press. 187–200.

Spolsky, B. 1978a. "Bilingual education in the United States." In J. Alatis (ed.), *International dimensions of bilingual education*. Georgetown University Round Table on Languages and Linguistics. Washington, DC: Georgetown University Press. 268–84.

Spolsky, B. 1978b. *Educational linguistics*. Rowley, MA: Newbury House.

Spolsky, B. 1986a. Teaching Hebrew in the Diaspora: Rationales and goals. *Jewish Education* 54.3.11–19.

Spolsky, B. (ed.). 1986b. *Language and education in multilingual settings*. Clevedon, Avon: Multilingual Matters.

Spolsky, B. 1989a. Communicative competence, language proficiency, and beyond. *Applied Linguistics* 10.2.138–56.

Spolsky, B. 1989b. *Conditions for second language learning: Introduction to a general theory.* New York: Oxford University Press.

Spolsky, B. and R. Cooper (eds.). 1977. *Frontiers of bilingual education.* Rowley, MA: Newbury House.

Spolsky, B. and R. Cooper (eds.). 1978. *Case studies in bilingual education.* Rowley, MA: Newbury House.

Stanovich, K. 1986. Matthew effects in reading: Some consequences of individual differences in the acquisition of literacy. *Reading Research Quarterly* 21.4.360–406.

Stansfield, C. (ed.). 1986. *Toward communicative competence testing: Proceedings of the second TOEFL invitational conference.* ETS/TOEFL research reports, no. 21. Princeton, NJ: Educational Testing Service.

St. Clair, R. and W. Leap (eds.). 1982. *Language renewal among American Indian tribes.* Roslyn, VA: National Clearinghouse on Bilingual Education.

Stedman, L. and C. Kaestle. 1987. Literacy and reading performance in the United States from 1880 to the present. *Reading Research Quarterly* 22.1.8–45.

Steele, R. and T. Threadgold (eds.). 1987. *Topics in language: Essays in honor of Michael Halliday.* 2 Vols. Philadelphia, PA: John Benjamin.

Steinberg, D. 1985. "Psycholinguistics: Application—the writing system as a native language for the deaf." In R.B. Kaplan et al. (eds.), *Annual review of applied linguistics (1984),* Vol. 5. New York: Cambridge University Press. 36–45.

Stenström, 1986a. "A study of pauses as demarcators in discourse and syntax." In J. Aarts and W. Meijs (eds.), *Corpus linguistics: Recent developments in the use of computer corpora in English language research.* Amsterdam: Rodopi, 203–18.

Stenström, 1986b. "What does *really* really do?" In G. Tottie and I. Backlund (eds.), *English in speech and writing: A symposium.* Studia Anglistica Upsaliensia 60. Stockholm: Almquist and Wiksell. 149–64.

Stenström, 1987. "Carry-on signals in English conversation." In W. Meijs (ed.), *Corpus linguistics and beyond.* Amsterdam: Rodopi. 87–120.

Stern, H.H. 1975. What can we learn from the good language learner? *Canadian Modern Language Journal* 31.4.304–18.

Stern, H.H. 1983. *Fundamental concepts of language teaching.* New York: Oxford University Press.

Stern, H.H. 1984. A quiet language revolution: Second language teaching in Canadian contexts—Achievements and new directions. *The Canadian Modern Language Review* 4.4.506–23.

Stevens, E. 1987. "The anatomy of mass literacy in nineteenth-century United States." In R. Arnove and H. Graff (eds.), *National literacy campaigns.* New York: Plenum. 66–122.

Stevick, E. 1976. *Memory, meaning and method.* Rowley, MA: Newbury House.

Stevick, E. 1980. *Teaching languages: A way and ways.* Rowley, MA: Newbury House.

Street, B. 1984. *Literacy in theory and practice.* New York: Cambridge University Press.

Street, B. 1987. "Literacy and social change: The significance of social context in the development of literacy programmes." In D. Wagner (ed.), *The future of literacy in a changing world.* New York: Pergamon Press. 49–64.

Strevens, P. 1977a. Special-purpose language learning: A perspective. *Language Teaching and Linguistics Abstracts* 10.3.145–63.

Strevens, P.D. 1977b. *New orientations in the teaching of English.* New York: Oxford University Press.

Strevens, P.D. 1986. The "EFL" in IATEFL: A distinctive identity. *TESOL Newsletter* 20.4.1/18–19.

Strevens, P.D. 1988a. "Language learning and language teaching: Towards an integrated model." In D. Tannen (ed.), *Linguistics in context: Connecting observation and understanding. Lectures from the 1985 LSA/TESOL and NEH Institutes.* Norwood, NJ: Ablex. 261–74.

Strevens, P.D. 1988b. "Language teaching contributes to and is influenced by the spread of languages." In P. Lowenberg (ed.), *Language spread and language policy: Issues, implications and case studies.* Georgetown University Round Table on Languages and Linguistics. Washington, DC: Georgetown University Press. 320–30.

Strevens, P.D. and F. Weeks. 1985. The creation of a regularized subset of English for mandatory use in maritime communications: SEASPEAK. *Language Planning Newsletter* 11.2.1–6.

Strickland, D., J. Feeley, and S. Wepner. 1987. *Using computers in the teaching of reading.* New York: Teacher's College Press.

Strickland, D. and L. Morrow (eds.). 1989. *Emerging literacy: Young children learn to read and write.* Newark, DE: International Reading Association.

Stubbs, M. 1980. *Language and literacy: The sociolinguistics of reading and writing.* Boston, MA: Routledge and Kegan Paul.

Stubbs, M. 1983. *Discourse analysis.* New York: Basil Blackwell.

Stubbs, M. 1988. *Educational linguistics.* New York: Basil Blackwell.

Svartvik, J. and R. Quirk (eds.). 1980. *A corpus of English conversation.* Lund: C.W.K. Gleerup.

Swaffer, J. 1988. Readers, texts and second Languages: The intercultural processes. *Modern Language Journal* 72.2.123–49.

Swain, M. 1984. "A review of immersion education in Canada: Research and evaluation studies." In *Studies on immersion: A collection for United States educators.* Sacramento, CA: California State Department of Education.

Swain, M. and S. Lapkin. 1984. *Evaluating bilingual education: A Canadian case study.* Clevedon, Avon: Multilingual Matters.

Swales, J. 1984. ESP comes of age? 21 years after "some measurable characteristics of modern science prose." *ASLED-LSP Newsletter* 7.2.9–20.

Swales, J. 1985a. "ESP—the heart of the matter or the end of the affair." In R. Quirk and H. Widdowson (eds.), *English in the world: Teaching and learning the language and literatures.* New York: Cambridge University Press. 212–23.

Swales, J. (ed.) 1985b. *Episodes in ESP.* Oxford: Pergamon.

Swales, J. 1986. Citation analysis and discourse analysis. *Applied Linguistics* 7.1.39–56.

Swales, J. 1987. "Current development and future prospects." In R.B. Kaplan et al. (eds.), *Annual review of applied linguistics (1986)*, Vol. 7. New York: Cambridge University Press. 121–30.

Swales, J. 1988. "Communicative language teaching in ESP contexts." In R.B. Kaplan et al. (eds.), *Annual review of applied linguistics (1987)*, Vol. 8. New York: Cambridge University Press. 48–57.

Swales, J. 1989. Planning an LSP program: Lecture-demonstration. The University of Michigan, Ann Arbor, MI.

Swan, M. and B. Smith. 1987. *Learner English.* New York: Cambridge University Press.

Swanson, C. 1989. Deutsch in Deutschland: Repurposing a foreign language videodisc. *Academic Computing* 4.1.26–27, 49–51.

Tannen, D. 1984. *Conversational style: Analysing talk among friends.* Norwood, NJ: Ablex.

Tannen, D. (ed.). 1986. *Discourse in cross-cultural communication.* (Special issue of *Text* 6.2.)

Tannenhaus, M. 1988. "Psycholinguistics: An overview." In F. Newmeyer (ed.), *Linguistics: The Cambridge survey*, Vol. 3. New York: Cambridge University Press. 1–37.

Taylor, D. 1988. The meaning and the use of the term "competence" in linguistics and applied linguistics. *Applied Linguistics* 9.2.148–68.

Tennant, H. 1980. *Natural language processing.* Princeton, NJ: Petrocelli.

Teitelbaum, H. and R. Hiller. 1977. Bilingual education: The legal mandate. *Harvard Educational Review* 47.2.138–70.

Terrell, T. 1977. A natural approach to the acquisition and learning of a language. *Modern Language Journal* 61.325–36.

Terrell, T. 1985. "The natural approach to language teaching: An update." In J. Oller and P. Richard-Amato (eds.), *Methods that work.* Rowley, MA: Newbury House. 267–83.

Thernstrom, A. 1980. E pluribus plura—Congress and bilingual education. *Public Interest* 60.3–22.

Thompson, S. 1985. Grammar and written discourse: Initial and final purpose clauses in English. *Text* 5.1/2.55–84.

Tomic, O. and R. Shuy (eds.). 1987. *The relation of theoretical and applied linguistics.* New York: Plenum.

Tottie, G. 1982. Where do negative sentences come from? *Studia Linguistica* 36.88–105.

Tottie, G. 1985. The negation of epistemic necessity in British and American English. *English Worldwide* 6.87–116.

Tottie, G. 1986. "The importance of being adverbial." In G. Tottie and I. Backlund (eds.), *English in speech and writing: A symposium.* Studia Anglistica Upsaleinsia 60. Stockholm: Almquist and Wiksell. 93–118.

Tottie, G. and I. Backlund (eds.). 1986. *English in speech and writing: A symposium.* Studia Anglistica Upsaleinsia 60. Stockholm: Almquist and Wiksell.

Trim, J. 1978. *Developing a unit/credit scheme of adult language learning.* Oxford: Pergamon Press.

Trimble, L. 1985. *English for science and technology: A discourse approach.* Cambridge: Cambridge University Press.

Troike, R. 1978. *Research evidence for the effectiveness of bilingual education.* Los Angeles: Evaluation, Dissemination and Assessment Center, California State University, Los Angeles.

Troike, R. and M. Saville-Troike. 1982. "Teacher training for bilingual education: An international perspective." In B. Hartford, A. Valdman, and C. Foster (eds.), *Issues in international bilingual education.* New York: Plenum. 199–219.

Trudgill, P. 1974. *The social differentiation of English in Norwich.* Cambridge, UK: Cambridge University Press.

Trudgill, P. 1983. *On dialect.* Oxford: Basil Blackwell.

Trudgill, P. 1986. *Dialects in contact.* New York: Basil Blackwell.

Trudgill, P. (ed.). 1984. *Applied sociolinguistics.* Orlando, FL: Academic Press.

Trueba, H. 1979. "Research, journalism and politics." In H. Trueba and C. Bernett-Mizrachi (eds.), *Bilingual multicultural education and the professions: From theory to practice.* Rowley, MA: Newbury House. 430–44.

Trueba, H. 1989. *Raising silent voices: Educating the linguistic minorities for the 21st century.* New York: Newbury House.

Trueba, H. (ed.). 1987. *Success or failure? Learning and the language minority student.* New York: Newbury House.

Tucker, G.R., E. Hamayan, and F. Genesee. 1976. Affective, cognitive and social factors in second language acquisition. *Canadian Modern Language Review* 18.111–24.

Tucker, G.R. 1987. Plenary address. Paper presented at the AILA Congress, Sydney, Australia, August 1987.

Tzeng, O. and D. Hung. 1981. "Linguistic determinism: A written language perspective." In O. Tzeng and H. Singer (eds.), *Perception of print.* Hillsdale, NJ: Lawrence Erlbaum Associates. 237–55.

Underwood, J. 1984. *Linguistics, computers and the language teacher.* Rowley, MA: Newbury House.

Underwood, J. 1987. "Artificial intelligence and CALL." In W. Flint (ed.), *Modern media in foreign language education: Theory and implementation.* Lincolnwood, IL: National Textbook Company. 197–225.

Underwood, J. 1989a. Hypercard and interactive video. *CALICO Journal* 6.3.7–20.

Underwood, J. 1989b. Hypermedia: Where we are and where we aren't. *CALICO Journal* 6.4.23–26.

Vaid, J. (ed.). 1986. *Language processing in bilinguals: Psycholinguistic and neuropsychological perspectives.* Hillsdale, NJ: Lawrence Erlbaum Associates.

Valdez, A. 1979. "The role of the mass media in public debate over bilingual education in the United States." In R. Padilla (ed.), *Bilingual education and public policy in the United States.* Ypsilanti, MI: Eastern Michigan University. 175–88.

Valdez, J. (ed.). 1986. *Culture bound: Bridging the cultural gap in language teaching.* Cambridge, UK: Cambridge University Press.

Valdman, A. 1961. *Applied linguistics: French. A guide for teachers.* Boston, MA: D.C. Heath.

Valdman, A. (ed.). 1987. *Proceedings from the Indiana University symposium on the evaluation of foreign language proficiency.* Bloomington, IN: Indiana University, CREDLI.

Valdman, A. 1988. Introduction (to a special issue on the assessment of foreign-language oral proficiency). *Studies in Second Language Acquisition* 10.121–28.

Valette, R. 1978. *Modern language testing: A handbook.* 2d ed. New York: Harcourt, Brace and World.

Vande Kopple, W. 1986. "Given and new information and some aspects of the structures, semantics, and pragmatics of written texts." In. C. Cooper and S. Greenbaum (eds.), *Studying writing.* Beverly Hills, CA: Sage Publications. 72–111.

van Dijk, T. (ed.). 1985. *Discourse and communication: New approaches to the analyses of mass media discourse and communication.* Berlin: deGruyter.

van Dijk, T. 1987. *News as discourse.* Hillsdale, NJ: Lawrence Erlbaum Associates.

Van Ek, J. (ed.). 1975. *Systems development in adult language learning: The threshold level in a European unit credit system for modern language learning by adults.* Strasbourg: Council of Europe. Republished 1980 as *Threshold level English.* Oxford: Pergamon Press.

Van Ek, J. and L. G. Alexander. 1980. *Threshold level English.* Oxford: Pergamon Press.

Van Els, T. et al. 1984. *Applied linguistics and the learning and teaching of foreign languages.* Baltimore, MD: Edward Arnold.

Van Lier, L. 1988. *The classroom and the language learner.* New York: Longman.

Vann, R. 1978. Bilingual education today: The unresolved issues. *Language Arts* 55.2.150–53.

van Naerssen, M. and R.B. Kaplan. 1987. "Language and science." In R.B. Kaplan et al. (eds.), *Annual review of applied linguistics (1986),* Vol. 7. New York: Cambridge University Press. 86–104.

VanPatten, B. 1990. "Theory and research in second language acquisition and foreign language learning: On producers and consumers." In B. VanPatten and J. Lee (eds.), *Second language acquisition/foreign language learning.* Clevedon, Avon: Multilingual Matters. 17–26.

VanPatten, B., T. Dvorak, and J. Lee (eds.). 1987. *Foreign language learning: A research perspective.* New York: Newbury House.

VanPatten, B. and J. Lee (eds.). 1990. *Second languages acquisition/foreign language learning.* Clevedon, Avon: Multilingual Matters.

Vasquez, J. 1978. "Federal, state and local policies as they affect pragmatic activities: A closer look at comprehensive planning." In J. Alatis (ed.), *International dimensions of bilingual education.* Georgetown University Round Table on Languages and Linguistics. Washington, DC: Georgetown University Press. 67–75.

Veltman, C. 1983. *Language shift in the United States.* Berlin: Mouton.

Verhoeven, L. 1987. *Ethnic minority children acquiring literacy.* Dordrecht: Foris.

Vygotsky, L. 1934/1986. *Thought and language.* Trans. and edited by Alex Kozulin. Cambridge, MA: MIT Press.

Wagner, D. (ed.). 1987. *The future of literacy in a changing world.* New York: Pergamon Press.

Wagonner, D. 1988. "Language minorities in the United States in the 1980's: The evidence from the 1980 census." In S. McKay and S. Wong (eds.), *Language diversity: Problem or resource?* New York: Newbury House. 69–108.

Wainman, H. and W. Wilkinson. 1981. Legal English: A functional approach. *Recherches et Echanges.* Paris, Tome 6, No. 2.

Wallerstein, N. 1982. *Language and culture in conflict.* Reading, MA: Addison-Wesley.

Walshe, R. 1981. *Every child can write.* Rozelle, NSW: Primary English Teaching Association.

Wardhaugh, R. 1972. TESOL: Our common cause. *TESOL Quarterly* 6.291–305.

Wardhaugh, R. 1985. *How conversation works.* New York: Basil Blackwell.

Wardhaugh, R. 1986. *An introduction to sociolinguistics.* New York: Basil Blackwell.

Wardhaugh, R. 1987. *Languages in competition.* New York; Basil Blackwell.

Weeks, F., A. Glover, P. Strevens, and E. Johnson. 1984. *SEASPEAK training manual.* Oxford: Pergamon Press.

Weinreich, U. 1953. *Languages in contact.* New York: Linguistic Circle of New York.

Weinstein, B. 1983. *The civic tongue: Political consequences of language choices.* New York: Longman.

Weinstein, B. 1984. "Francophonie: Language planning and national interests." In C. Kramarae, M. Schulz, and W. O'Barr (eds.), *Language and power.* Beverly Hills, CA: Sage Publications. 227–42.

Weisseman, R. 1988. From the personal computer to the scholar's workstation. *Academic Computing* 3.3.10–14, 30–41.

Weizenbaum, J. 1966. ELIZA—a computer program for the study of natural language communication between man and machine. *Communications of the Association for Computing Machinery* 9.36–45.

Wellman, F.L. 1979. *The art of cross-examination.* 4th ed. New York: Collier Macmillan.

Wells, G. 1986. *The meaning makers.* Portsmouth, NH: Heinemann.

Wenden, A. 1987. Metacognition: An expanded view on the cognitive abilities in L2 learners. *Language Learning* 37.4.573–98.

Wenden, A. and J. Rubin (eds.). 1987. *Learner strategies in language learning.* Englewood Cliffs, NJ: Prentice-Hall Regents.

Wertsch, J. 1985a. *Vygotsky and the social formation of mind.* Cambridge, MA: Harvard University Press.

Wertsch, J. (ed.). 1985b. *Culture, communication and cognition: Vygotskian perspectives.* New York: Cambridge University Press.

West, M. 1953. *A general service list of English words.* Longman: London.

White, L. 1988. "Island effects in SLA." In S. Flynn and W. O'Neil (eds.), *Linguistic theory in L2 acquisition.* Dordrecht: Reidel.

White, L. 1989. *Universal grammar and second language acquisition.* Philadelphia, PA: John Benjamin.

Widdowson, H. 1978. *Teaching language as communication.* New York: Oxford University Press.

Widdowson, H. 1979. *Explorations in applied linguistics.* New York: Oxford University Press.

Widdowson, H. 1983. *Learning purpose and language use.* Oxford: Oxford University Press.

Widdowson, H. 1984. *Explorations in applied linguistics II.* New York: Oxford University Press.

Widdowson, H. 1989. Knowledge of language and ability for use. *Applied Linguistics* 10.2.128–37.

Widdowson, H. and C. Brumfit. 1981. "Issues in second language syllabus design." In J. Alatis, R. Altman, and P. Alatis (eds.), *The second language classroom: Directions for the 1980's.* Washington, DC: Georgetown University Press. 197–210.

Wilkins, D. 1976. *Notional syllabuses.* Oxford: Oxford University Press.

Will, O.A. 1975. "Schizophrenia: Psychological treatment." In A.M. Freedman, H. I. Kaplan, and B.J. Sadock (eds.), *Comprehensive textbook of psychiatry/II*, Vol. 1. Baltimore, MD.: Williams and Wilkins. 939–54.

Willard, C. 1983. *Argumentation and the social grounds of knowledge.* Tuscaloosa, AL: University of Alabama Press.

Willig, A. 1985. A meta-analysis of selected studies on the effectiveness of bilingual education. *Review of Educational Research* 55.3.269–318.

Winograd, T. 1972. *Understanding natural language.* New York: Academic Press.

Winograd, T. 1977. On some contested suppositions of generative linguistics about the scientific study of language. *Cognition* 5.151–79.

Winograd, T. 1980. What does it mean to understand language? *Cognitive Science* 4.209–41.

Winograd, T. 1983. *Language as a cognitive process: Syntax.* Reading, MA: Addison-Wesley.

Witte, S. 1983. Topical structure and revision: An exploratory study. *College Composition and Communication* 34.313–41.

Wodak, R. 1980. Discourse analysis and courtroom interaction. *Discourse Processes* 3.369–80.

Wolfson, N. 1989. *Perspectives on sociolinguistics.* New York: Newbury House.

Wolfson, N. and E. Judd (eds.). 1983. *Sociolinguistics and second language acquisition.* Rowley, MA: Newbury House.

Wolfson, N. and J. Manes (eds.). 1985. *Language of inequality.* Berlin: Mouton.

Wong-Fillmore, L. 1986. "Teaching bilingual learners." In M. Wittrock (ed.), *Handbook of research on teaching.* New York: Macmillan. 648–86.

Woods, A. and R. Baker. 1985. Item response theory. *Language Testing* 2.2.117–40.

Woods, A., P. Pletcher, and A. Hughes. 1986. *Statistics in language studies.* Cambridge, UK: Cambridge University Press.

Wresch, W. 1987. *A practical guide to computer uses in the English/language arts classroom.* Englewood Cliffs, NJ: Prentice-Hall.

Wyatt, D. 1988. What can research tell us about CALL? *System* 16.2.221–23.

Yalden, J. 1983. *The communicative language syllabus.* Oxford: Pergamon Press.

Yalden, J. 1987. *Principles of course design for language teaching.* New York: Cambridge University Press.

Yorio, C., K. Perkins, and J. Schachter (eds.). 1979. *On TESOL 1979: The learner in focus.* Washington, DC: TESOL Publications.

Young, R., A. Becker, and K. Pike. 1970. *Rhetoric: Discovery and change.* New York: Harcourt, Brace and World.

Zappert, L. and R. Cruz. 1977. *Bilingual education: An appraisal of empirical research.* Berkeley, CA: Bay Area Bilingual Education League.

Zborowski, M. 1952. Cultural components in responses to pain. *Journal of Social Issues* 8.16–30.

Zobl, H. 1983. Markedness and the projection problem. *Language Learning* 33.293–313.

Zobl, H. 1984. "Cross-language generalizations and the contrastive dimension of the interlanguage hypothesis." In A. Davies, C. Criper, and A. Howatt (eds.), *Interlanguage.* Edinburgh: Edinburgh University Press. 79–97.

Zobl, H. 1989. Modularity in adult L2 acquisition. *Language Learning* 39.1.49–79.